HANDBOOK OF STRESS AND BURNOUT IN HEALTH CARE

HANDBOOK OF STRESS AND BURNOUT IN HEALTH CARE

Jonathon R. B. Halbesleben
EDITOR

Nova Science Publishers, Inc.
New York

For permission to use material from this book please contact us:
Telephone 631-231-7269; Fax 631-231-8175
Web Site: http://www.novapublishers.com

NOTICE TO THE READER

The Publisher has taken reasonable care in the preparation of this book, but makes no expressed or implied warranty of any kind and assumes no responsibility for any errors or omissions. No liability is assumed for incidental or consequential damages in connection with or arising out of information contained in this book. The Publisher shall not be liable for any special, consequential, or exemplary damages resulting, in whole or in part, from the readers' use of, or reliance upon, this material.

Independent verification should be sought for any data, advice or recommendations contained in this book. In addition, no responsibility is assumed by the publisher for any injury and/or damage to persons or property arising from any methods, products, instructions, ideas or otherwise contained in this publication.

This publication is designed to provide accurate and authoritative information with regard to the subject matter covered herein. It is sold with the clear understanding that the Publisher is not engaged in rendering legal or any other professional services. If legal or any other expert assistance is required, the services of a competent person should be sought. FROM A DECLARATION OF PARTICIPANTS JOINTLY ADOPTED BY A COMMITTEE OF THE AMERICAN BAR ASSOCIATION AND A COMMITTEE OF PUBLISHERS.

LIBRARY OF CONGRESS CATALOGING-IN-PUBLICATION DATA

Handbook of stress and burnout in health care / Jonathon R.B. Halbesleben (editor).
    p. cm.
ISBN 978-1-60456-500-3 (hardcover)
    1.   Medical personnel—Job stress. 2. Burn out(psychology) I. Halbesleben, Jonathon R.B.
    RC451.4.M44H36 2008
    616.9'8—dc22
                                      2008005558

Published by Nova Science Publishers, Inc. ✦ New York

CONTENTS

PREFACE

The purpose of this book is to summarize the state of the science in the study of stress and burnout among health care professionals. Moreover, this books seeks to set the agenda for future research in the areas of stress and burnout. Despite the popularity of these topics as subjects for empirical study, particularly among health professionals, there has been no attempt to build a compreshensive summary of the literature concerning stress and burnout in health care. This book fills the void by bringing together leaders in the academic study of stress and burnout and by summarizing the research on the measurement of stress and burnout, the unique causes of this condition for health care professionals as well as the consquences of stress and burnout and the patients they serve. It covers evidence-based mechanisms for the prevention and reduction of stress and burnout. Each chapter provides a synthesis of the critical stress and burnout literature as well as ideas for what research is needed to fill current voids in the literature. The final chapter of the book provides a research agenda to promote research concerning this phenomenon in health professions.

Chapter 1 - Stress and burnout have been the subjects of literally thousands of journal articles and hundreds of books, both academic and in the popular press. Yet it remains a critical workforce issue and one that has a very real cost – estimated to be as much as $145 billion annually (National Institute for Occupational Safety and Health, 2000). While organizations may be more tuned in to the impact of stress on their workforce, it seems highly unlikely (if not impossible) that stress will ever "go away" as an issue for employees.

Health care professionals are cited as among the most studied occupational groups in the study of stress and burnout. Hundreds of studies have been published exploring the causes and impact of stress and burnout specific to health care professionals. Yet, there has been little to no attempt to bring the research concerning stress and burnout in health care contexts together in a comprehensive manner. Moreover, as the literature on this topic has been so extensive, there is a need to not only assess where we are today, but what directions we need to consider for future research.

Chapter 2 - Several theoretical approaches have been used to describe, explain, and predict burnout. In a review of twenty-five years of burnout research, Schaufeli and Buunk (2003) described fourteen theories regarding the individual, organizational and community levels. These theories have led to many relevant insights: however, these insights have typically been scattered, which calls for the need to better integrate and distill current knowledge into more central overarching frameworks. In the early 1990s, scholars adapted Conservation of Resources (COR) theory to understand the process of burnout and stress in organizational settings (e.g. Hobfoll and Freedy, 1993; Hobfoll and Shirom, 2001; Lee and Ashforth, 1996; Wright and Cropanzano, 1998). Since then, COR theory has developed as one of the leading theories in burnout (Halbesleben, 2006; Westman, Hobfoll, Chen, Davidson and Laski, 2005) and the one that meta-analysis of extant studies suggests best fits the data (Lee and Ashforth, 1996). The value of COR theory was further reinforced when research interest shifted towards work engagement and vigor as the positive counterparts of burnout and away from deficit and pathology models. Building on positive psychology (e.g. Seligman and Csikszentmihalyi, 2000), scholars started investigating the positive, sustaining, and protective power of peoples' resources and positive work experiences.

The basic tenet of COR theory (Hobfoll, 1998; 2001) is that people have an innate as well as a learned drive to create, foster, conserve, and protect the quality and quantity of their resources. Many things could be conceived as resources, but COR theory relates to those resources that are key to survival and well-being (e.g., shelter, attachment to significant others, self-esteem), or that are linked to the process of creating and maintaining key resources (e.g., money, credit). According to COR theory, stress occurs under three conditions: (1) when individuals' key resources are threatened with loss, (2) when resources are lost, or (3) when individuals fail to gain resources following significant resource investment. Burnout is one such stress outcome and typically follows from a process of slow bleed out of resources without counterbalancing resource gain or replenishment.

This chapter aims at providing a comprehensive framework of burnout and work engagement from a COR-theoretical perspective.The authors illusrate how research on burnout and work engagement can be advanced by taking fundamental COR-theoretical principles into account. In addition, they show COR theory's implications for the fostering of engagement and the prevention of burnout at work.

Chapter 3 - The massive restructuring initiatives in hospitals in the 1990s resulted in nursing work environments characterized by increased stress and heavy workloads as fewer nurses were available to care for patients with higher acuity and shortened length of stay (Institute of Medicine, 2004). These conditions were stressful for nurses who were frustrated by their inability to provide the quality of care consistent with professional standards. Numerous studies documented increased stress and burnout among nurses and high levels of job dissatisfaction and turnover (Aiken, Clarke, Sloane, Sochalski, Busse, and Clarke, 2001; Aiken, Clarke, Sloane, Sochalski, and Silber, 2002; Cho; Laschinger, and Wong, 2006; Greco, Laschinger, and Wong, 2006). A decade later, hospital administration is struggling to retain nurses currently in the profession and to attract newcomers to the profession. Furthermore, several studies have linked poor working conditions of nurses to negative patient outcomes, most dramatically, patient mortality and increased occurrence of adverse events (Aiken, Smith, and Lake, 1994; Kazanjian, Green, Wong, and Reid, 2005; McGillis Hall, Doran, Baker, Pink, Sidani, O'Brien-Pallas, and Donner, 2003; Tourangeau, Giovanetti, Tu, and Wood, 2002).

Current recruitment and retention efforts focus on creating healthy work environments for nurses aimed at increasing the quality of worklife for nurses and increased quality of patient care. Studies have shown that the quality of worklife of nurses and high quality patient care are closely linked (Leiter, Harvie, and Frizzell, 1998; Vahey, Aiken, Sloane, Clarke, and Vargas, 2004). Research on 'Magnet Hospitals', that is, hospitals that are able to attract and retain nurses because of work environments that support professional nursing practice standards, has identified several elements of the work environment, such as professional autonomy and nurse decisional involvement, that make a difference to nurses' worklife and patient care (Aiken, Smith, and Lake, 1994; Lake, 2002). More recently, Leiter and Laschinger (2006) and Laschinger and Leiter (2006) articulated relationships among five aspects of professional practice environments derived from this research that offer a model for designing effective nursing work environments. In this chapter, the authors describe a model of worklife that links these work environment characteristics to the burnout/engagement process and, subsequently, nurse and patient outcomes. They suggest that this Nursing Worklife Model (Leiter and Laschinger, 2005; Laschinger and Leiter, 2006) can be used to guide management in creating healthy and positive nursing work environments that will both retain nurses currently in the system and attract newcomers to the profession.

Chapter 4 - Results from a recent consumer survey on hospitalization and health care in five countries, including the United States, uncovered considerable public dissatisfaction with the quality and availability of health care. Conducted in response to widespread dissatisfaction with the health system and its impact on hospital care, the study found that 18% of United States and United Kingdom health care recipients and 28% of Canadian patients described their most recent hospitalization experience as fair or poor (Aiken, Clarke, and Sloane, 2002).

Research on the general nature of health care offers considerable insight into the highly stressful nature of this type of work, implicating psychologically demanding working conditions as a major source of the public's dissatisfaction with the current health care system. As evidenced by consumer reports and increasingly negative media coverage, creating organizational environments that allow health care professionals to deliver high quality care should be a top priority. Our job as researchers is to further uncover and understand the critical aspects of these work environments that must be altered and/or developed in order to improve the overall quality of and satisfaction with the health care industry.

Many scholars believe that the strong interpersonal nature of most jobs in the health care industry is a key contributor to the experience of a specific result of workplace stress known as burnout. Furthermore, the effects of burnout on health care workers may be a critical factor contributing to widespread consumer dissatisfaction with the health care system.

In this following chapter, the authors offer a detailed explanation of the burnout phenomenon and its precursors and consequences. They then concentrate on burnout as experienced by those in the health care industry and offer specific recommendations for improving the quality of health care through a reduction of burnout in these demanding work environments.

Chapter 5 - Nurses are the most numerous health professionals in most countries of the world. In the U.S. alone, almost 1.7 million full-time equivalent nurses work in hospitals, and the entire U.S. professional nurse workforce numbers almost 3 million (Steiger, Bausch, Johnson, and Peterson, 2006). A variety of health care providers may have occasional contact with hospitalized patients, but the bedside nurse provides continuous care. Research suggests that burnout among nurses in the U.S. and other industrialized countries is high. Aiken and colleagues observed high levels of burnout among 10,319 nurses working in 303 hospitals in Pennsylvania, Ontario, British Columbia, England, and Scotland (Aiken, Clarke, and Sloane, 2002). In this study, the percentage of nurses with burnout scores above Maslach's norms (Maslach, Jackson, and Leiter, 1996) for medical personnel varied from 54% of nurse respondents in Pennsylvania to 34% of nurse respondents in Scotland. Lower levels of burnout were observed among nurses working in German hospitals, where the length of stay of hospitalized patients is exceptionally long (Aiken, Clarke, Sloane et al., 2001).

Chapter 6 - Burnout is a psychological syndrome that may emerge when employees are exposed to a stressful working environment, with high job demands and low resources (Bakker and Demerouti, 2007; Maslach, Schaufeli and Leiter, 2001). Although most scholars agree that burned-out employees are characterized by high levels of exhaustion and negative attitudes towards their work, there are different views on how the syndrome should be operationalized. The central aim of this chapter is to discuss the theoretical background of the recently introduced Oldenburg Burnout Inventory (OLBI; Demerouti, Bakker, Vardakou and Kantas, 2003), and to test the factor structure of the OLBI among Dutch employees working in one of two occupational sectors: health care and white collar work. The authors' central claim is that the OLBI is a reliable and valid measure for the assessment of burnout (and work engagement) that can be used as an alternative to the widely used Maslach Burnout Inventory (Maslach, Jackson, and Leiter, 1996).

Chapter 7 - The study of occupational stress across cultures is rare; most typical are one-culture studies or comparisons of two cultures, which is insufficient for understanding cultural differences (Hofstede, 2001). The mere fact that in Chinese the word "stress" is translated with two characters that represent the words 'crisis' and 'opportunity' (Hashim and Zhiliang, 2003) and that in Hebrew the word stress is translated into either "pressure" or "tension" (Glazer, 2002) demonstrates the elusiveness of the concept. In this chapter, the author uses the word 'stress' to define an area of study. It is a process in which stressors relate to strains. Stressors are environmental demands or constraints that may yield negative responses. Strains are negative responses that arise when one is unable to cope successfully with stressors. The relationship between stressors and strains is at the core of "stress." Across cultures, reported perceptions of stressors and strains differ and implications of the same stressors on strains differ, as do types of stressors influencing the same strains (Glazer and Beehr, 2005). Thus, culture is the greater context in which stress occurs and implications of culture on stress need to be better understood. This chapter presents a framework for conducting stress research across cultures substantiated with a comprehensive review of literature from different countries and cross-cultural studies.

Crompton and Lyonette (2006) highlight the importance of cultural context in their comparative study of work-life balance in Finland, Norway, Britain, France, and Portugal. Employment of women, state support for mothers' employment, and child-caring responsibilities differ among these countries and influence work-life balance. For example, in Finland and Norway women and men are given cash for care and up to a year of work leave with pay for having children. In these countries there is little work-life conflict. In contrast, in France, incongruence between (a) a liberal policy for women's employment and (b) traditional division of household labor might be a cultural attribute influencing French workers' work-role conflict.

In this chapter, the author makes a case for studying stress across cultures, explains why nurses are the focal group for this chapter, defines culture, and then elaborates on the stress framework.

Chapter 8 - Concerns regarding the mental and physical well-being of student nurses are reported across the world. High levels of sickness, absence and attrition during the educational program mean that this topic is of interest to both the health care systems in which the student will practice and the higher education institute in which the entrant pursues his or her studies. This chapter will examine student nurse stress, distress and coping from a range of theoretical frameworks, including transactional and other relevant interactive models of stress. It will detail the broad categories of situational stress reported by student nurses, high levels of distress they report and examine how students cope.

The literature on stress management in student nurses will be critically evaluated both at the individual student level using cognitive behavioral approaches, the interface between student and organization involving managerial support from clinical and academic sources; and at the organizational level, for example, in terms of curriculum change. Where relevant, comparisons will be made with other types of health care student or those in higher education.

Chapter 9 - There is a growing interest in the psychosocial work environment of health care professionals (e.g., physicians, nurses) since they are at high risk for burnout. Take, for example the work of intensive care nurses. Traditionally, they have heavy workloads and extensive responsibilities, they must care for unstable patients, do accurate routines, and react to extremely urgent matters (Erlen and Sereika, 1997), although their decision latitude is often insufficient to cope effectively with these demands (Sawatzky, 1996). Such working conditions form the breeding ground for job stress. According to the demand-control model (DCM; Karasek, 1979), jobs that combine high job demands with low job control evoke psychological and physical distress ('high strain' jobs). These working conditions eventually deplete nurses' emotional resources and may initiate the burnout syndrome (e.g., Bourbonnais, Comeau and Vézina, 1999; DeRijk, LeBlanc, Schaufeli and DeJonge, 1998).

While job stress perspectives like the DCM try to explain how strain and burnout originate in the work environment, the present chapter takes a different perspective by looking at the social nature of work. Specifically, the authors will discuss research showing that burnout and other work-related states may *transfer* among individuals at the workplace. The notion that burnout may cross over from one employee to another is not new. Several authors have used anecdotal evidence to argue that job-induced strain and burnout may transfer between colleagues (e.g., Cherniss, 1980; Edelwich and Brodsky, 1980; Schwartz and Will, 1953).The authors describe recent, more systematic studies that have provided empirical evidence for this phenomenon.

Chapter 10 - Adverse work schedules are common for health care workers (HCWs). By necessity, they provide around-the-clock coverage, thus shiftwork is often an unavoidable component of the work schedule. In addition to shift work, extended work shifts, quick returns or a break of only 8 hours when changing from one shift to another, mandatory overtime, on-call, and working without breaks are common to maintain staffing levels among registered nurses (RNs). Physicians also have severely extended workdays during their training years. The effect of these schedules is often physical and mental fatigue, which has both short- and long-term effects on the health and safety of HCWs, as well as consequences for patient safety. This chapter will describe the relationship between work schedules and adverse outcomes in HCWs, including the role of both person and system factors in moderating the scheduling effects, and will describe the role of sleep as the critical mechanism for reducing the impact of adverse work schedules on outcomes.

Chapter 11 - Burnout is an affective state, comprised of the feelings of emotional exhaustion, physical fatigue and cognitive weariness, which denotes the depletion of energetic resources resulting from cumulative exposure to chronic work and life stresses (cf. Melamed, Shirom, Toker, Berliner, and Shapira, 2006). Accumulating evidence indicates that burnout is associated with negative health consequences, primarily increased risk of cardiovascular disease (Melamed et al., 2006). Physicians have reported that depletion in their energetic resources tended to lead to the provision of less than optimal patient care (e.g., Firth-Cozens and Greenhalgh, 1997). Additionally, physicians' level of burnout was found to be positively related to the likelihood of their making medical errors (West et al., 2006). Previous research consistently found that one's level of burnout may affect one's co-workers, including within teams of physicians (Bakker, Schaufeli, Sixma, and Bosveld, 2001). Recent studies have documented a growing prevalence of physicians' burnout in many countries (Kushnir, Levhar, and Cohen, 2004; Visser, Smets, Oort, and De Haes, 2003). Despite the rising prevalence rates of burnout among physicians, its objective and subjective antecedents have yet to be systematically investigated, with very few exceptions (e.g., Panagopoulou, Montgomery, and Benos, 2006). Following this rationale, the authors' study focuses on burnout and its objective and subjective antecedents among physicians.

Chapter 12 - This chapter is about the relatively deserted issue of burnout consequences, with a specific, yet characteristic, focus on health professions. Data collected in the two main bibliographical searches available to date (Boudreau and Nakashima, 2002[1]; Kleiber and Enzmann, 1989) indicate that out of a cumulated 4,434 references listed between 1968 and 2002, less than 50 empirical studies have sought to evaluate the link between burnout and occupational performance. The overwhelming majority of investigations still concentrate on burnout etiology, determining factors and correlates, thus leaving scant attention to the "right end"/output stage of the process model.

The chapter addresses a double challenge. First, the authors seek to integrate burnout outcomes within a functional perspective. The authors' purpose is to help reconcile consequences to the disphoric symptom through the prism of quality management. In the context of health professions, staff burnout may thus substantiate a "service-performance gap" (Zeithaml, Parasuraman, and Berry, 1990), where burnout-induced behaviors would affect quality care to the patients (Mawji et al., 2002). Second, their aim is to assess a problematic issue to pave the way for further empirical developments. Specifically, they are interested in staff burnout as a source of patients' maltreatment[2]. Burnout is thus viewed as a dysfunctional factor to patients' well-being.

Chapter 13 - In the late 1990s, consulting firms promoted 'restructuring' of care modalities to reduce the costs of patient care. Since then, work of health care personnel has changed dramatically. Downsizing and especially staff reduction (i.e. registered nurses) provoked studies that related nurse staffing (the nurse-to-patient-ratio) to patient outcomes. It was the work of Linda Aiken and colleagues that reliably showed nurse staffing to be related to both well-being and injuries of nurses and patient outcomes (e.g., Aiken, Clarke, Sloane, Sochalski, and Silber, 2002; Clarke, Rockett, Sloane, and Aiken, 2002; Curtin, 2003; Joint Commission on Accreditation of Health Care Organizations, 2001; Lang, Hodge, Olson, Romano, and Kravitz, 2004; Hickam et al., 2003; Mark, Harless, McCue, and Xu, 2004; National Audit Office, 2005; Needleman, Buerhaus, Mattke, Stewart, and Zelevinsky, 2002; Rafferty et al., 2007; Stewart, and Zelevinsky, 2002; Unruh, 2003; Whitman, Kim, Davidson, Wolf, and Wang, 2002). Numerous studies found strong evidence for non-fatal adverse

---

[1] This work provides a detailed yet non-exhaustive list of burnout citations for the period under review. Additional references are included in the present chapter.

[2] Maltreatment is first defined by three criteria: intent, a cognitive process, and a resulting harm (Rippon, 2000). Yet, in the context of professional care, unintentional harmful behavior or attitude should also be considered, as caregivers may fail to provide assistance without any intention to hurt (NCEA & Westat, 1998).

outcomes such as newly acquired infections (e.g., Needleman et al., 2002). Evidence for the relation between staffing and patient mortality is mixed. Some studies do find a relation (e.g., Aiken et al., 2002), while others do not (e.g. Needleman et al., 2002). There is also evidence that education of personnel is associated with patient safety. In surgical patients, a negative association between the degree of nurse education and patient mortality was found (Callahan, 2004). Moreover, a study by Unruh (2003) confirmed that *registered nurse hours of care* impact the level of adverse events patients suffer from.

Working conditions that are associated with nurse staffing that include overtime, frequent work interruptions, distractions, and conflicting task requirements have been found to be the risk factors most likely to decrease patient safety (Hickam et al., 2003). These work characteristics were also reliably linked to stress and burnout among health care personnel (Schaufeli and Enzmann, 1998). However, the link between nurses' stress and patient safety so far is inconclusive (Hickam et al., 2003) because models or theories are lacking that could help us to understand that link. Hence, this chapter discusses evidence concerning the association of stress and patient safety. Moreover, evidence is explained using action regulation theory (e.g., Frese and Zapf, 1994).

Chapter 14 - There is little doubt in the health care industry that nurses experience high levels of occupational (Jenkins and Elliot, 2004) and job-related stress (Weyers, Peter, Boggild, Jeppesen, and Siegrist, 2006), and this stress often leads to increased levels of burnout and turnover among nursing professionals (Gelsema, Van Der Doef, Maes, Janssen, Akerboom, and Verhoeven, 2006). The cycle of stress, burnout, and turnover is especially problematic in the nursing profession because there is currently a worldwide shortage of qualified nurses that borders on pandemic (Lucero and Sousa, 2006). Furthermore, the value added by nurses to health care organizations and their patients cannot be underestimated, as nurse staffing levels often strongly predict adverse patient health outcomes (Janiszewski Goodin, 2003; Seago and Ash, 2004). Given that turnover costs range between 70% - 200% of a turned-over employee's salary (Kaye and Jordan-Evans, 2001), turnover among nurses strongly predicts the financial survivability of health care organizations (Brown, Sturman, and Simmering, 2003). Traditionally, human resource management (HRM) professionals commence retention programs aimed at reducing turnover and increasing financial performance; thus HRM scholars and practitioners should devote considerable effort in reducing a key cause of nursing turnover: stress-induced burnout.

Chapter 15 - Over the past decades, the level of job stress and burnout has risen alarmingly worldwide. In the 2000 European Working Conditions Survey (EWCS), job stress was found to be the second most common job-related problem (28%) across the EU Member States (Houtman, 2005). Burnout, a form of chronic job stress, is significantly related to negative outcomes for the individual worker, e.g., depression and psychosomatic distress (Schaufeli and Enzmann, 1998), and for the organization, including absenteeism, turnover, and lowered productivity (Cordes and Dougherty, 1993; Lee and Ashforth, 1996; Schaufeli and Buunk, 2003). The associated costs are high. For example, stress and burnout account for 300 million lost working days and cost American businesses an estimated $300 billion per year (American Institute of Stress, 2002, in Halbesleben, Osburn and Mumford, 2006). So, from the individual, the organizational and the social point of view, efforts to combat (chronic) job stress are urgently needed.

A sector in which workers are most at risk of experiencing job stress and burnout are the so-called human services - such as health care, social services, and education - in which contact with other people plays a central role (Houtman, 2005). Next to stressors that are common to workers in other sectors (e.g., high workload, lack of autonomy), human service providers are confronted with (emotional) stressors that are inherent to the direct interaction with individual patients, clients or pupils. Examples of this type of stressor are patients' pain and suffering, or pupils' aggressive behaviours (Dollard et al., 2003). As the number of workers that are employed in the human services is rapidly growing, studies that yield more insight into ways to prevent or alleviate chronic forms of job stress such as burnout seem especially relevant to this sector. In this chapter, the current research on burnout interventions is summarized, followed by an illustration of a burnout intervention program that was implemented in Dutch hospitals among oncology care providers.

Chapter 16 - This book had two primary objectives: to provide a summary of the state of stress and burnout research in health care and to suggest directions for future research. Each of the authors has presented some ideas for future research in their respective chapters. My goal in this chapter is to integrate and elaborate upon those ideas to set an agenda for future research concerning stress and burnout in health care contexts.

Interestingly, but perhaps not surprisingly, the main areas of need in the stress and burnout literature more broadly are highly consistent with the needs within the health care literature (Cordes and Dougherty, 1993; Halbesleben and Buckley, 2004; Maslach, Schaufeli, and Leiter, 2001; Shirom, 2003). Consistent themes emerge, including more development and testing of theory, more development of measurement tools, expansion of international and multidisciplinary research, and an increase in intervention research. A further theme is the need for more research on the conceptualization, measurement, and impact of engagement. While research on this topic has grown dramatically (cf., Schaufeli and Salanova, in press), so has interest from a practical side within health care in part due to an emphasis on workforce engagement as part of the Malcolm Baldridge National Quality Program in the United States. The convergence of interests from health care practitioners and researchers could lead to significant advances in the understanding of the role that engagement plays relative to burnout.

In: Handbook of Stress and Burnout in Health Care   ISBN 978-1-60456-500-3
Editor: Jonathon R. B. Halbesleben   © 2008 Nova Science Publishers, Inc.

Chapter 1

INTRODUCTION:
STRESS, BURNOUT, AND HEALTH CARE

Jonathon R. B. Halbesleben
University of Wisconsin-Eau Claire

Stress and burnout have been the subjects of literally thousands of journal articles and hundreds of books, both academic and in the popular press. Yet it remains a critical workforce issue and one that has a very real cost – estimated to be as much as $145 billion annually (National Institute for Occupational Safety and Health, 2000). While organizations may be more tuned in to the impact of stress on their workforce, it seems highly unlikely (if not impossible) that stress will ever "go away" as an issue for employees.

Health care professionals are cited as among the most studied occupational groups in the study of stress and burnout. Hundreds of studies have been published exploring the causes and impact of stress and burnout specific to health care professionals. Yet, there has been little to no attempt to bring the research concerning stress and burnout in health care contexts together in a comprehensive manner. Moreover, as the literature on this topic has been so extensive, there is a need to not only assess where we are at today, but what directions we need to consider for future research.

WHAT IS STRESS? WHAT IS BURNOUT?
HOW WILL THIS BOOK ADDRESS THEM?

The nature and definition of stress has been subject to intense debate through the literature. One reason for this debate has been difficulty in translating definitions across disciplines; the difficulty is exacerbated by the recognized need by stress researchers to examine stress through a multi-disciplinary lens (Cooper and Dewe, 2004). As an example, early biological studies of stress focused on tests of the body's defense systems to environmental stressors (e.g., Selye, 1950). Historically, psychological studies have focused more globally on issues like one's demands relative to one's ability to respond to those demands (McGrath, 1970), mismatches between the environment and one's expected roles (e.g., Kahn, Wolfe, Quinn, Snoek, and Rosenthal; see also Beehr and Glazer, 2005 for a review) or as reactions to extreme events in one's life (e.g., Caplan, 1964). In light of the variability in conceptualizations of stress, Lazarus (1966; see also Lazarus and Folkman, 1984) has suggested that researchers consider stress a broad term that represents an area of study rather than a specific variable.

In a similar vein as stress, burnout has seen varied definitions and conceptualizations through the literature. The study of burnout grew from Freudenberger's (1974) research where he observed a pattern of emotional depletion among volunteer workers. In her seminal book on this topic, Maslach (1982) defined burnout as "a syndrome of emotional exhaustion, depersonalization, and reduced personal accomplishment that can occur among individuals who do 'people work' of some kind" (p. 3).

More recently, debate has emerged regarding the proper conceptualization of burnout. For example, Shirom and colleagues (cf., Melamed, Shirom, Toker, Berliner, and Shapira, 2006; Shirom, Nirel, Vinokur, present volume) have focused more on the exhaustion element of burnout, but have expanded it to emphasize the emotional, physical, and cognitive aspects of exhaustion. Other researchers (cf., Peeters and LeBlanc, 2001) have retained the emotional exhaustion and depersonalization aspects of burnout, but have dropped the personal accomplishment component. Initially, this was done for methodological reasons (cf., Bouman, te Brake, and Hoogstraten, 2002) but increasingly, authors are arguing that personal accomplishment should not be seen as a component of burnout, but as a correlate or outcome of exhaustion and depersonalization. That said, there remains a great deal of debate concerning the proper conceptualization of burnout, as demonstrated by the proliferation of new measuring burnout, such as the Oldenburg Burnout Inventory (Demerouti, Bakker, Vardakou, andKantas, 2002) and the Shirom-Melamed Burnout Measure (cf., Shirom and Melamed, 2006), that are based on alternative conceptualizations of burnout.

In the present book, we acknowledge the diversity of perspectives regarding stress and burnout. As such, the authors were free to define stress and/or burnout in the manner most consistent with their perspective. While potentially confusing, this approach recognizes the current state of the literature as well as the multi-disciplinary nature of the book's contributors.

AN OVERVIEW OF THE CHAPTERS

The chapters in this volume provide an essential overview of the current and needed research concerning stress and burnout among health care professionals. When I set out to put the book together, I set three goals. First, I wanted to provide an extensive overview of all aspects of stress and burnout as they apply to health care. To that end, I specifically solicited chapters from leading theorists, measurement specialists, and researchers who have contributed to our understanding of what causes stress and burnout, their consequences, and mechanisms for their prevention and amelioration.

Second, I sought to create multi-disciplinary effort, reaching out to researchers in health services, psychology, human resource management, organizational behavior, nursing, and other fields. Many have studied stress and burnout for many years and among the full spectrum of health professionals. I felt that such wide-ranging perspective was needed to truly understand the nature of stress and burnout in health professionals. Perhaps more than any other topic, the study of stress and burnout has been characterized by attention from many disciplines. However, as with many research topics, the integration across disciplines has not always been as seamless as desired. This book is an attempt to address that gap by providing a forum by which multi-disciplinary research can be presented in a unified front.

Finally, I sought to reflect the international nature of stress research in health services. To that end, researchers from seven different countries on three continents have contributed their work. Given the diversity of health systems across the world, yet the seemingly constant concerns with stress and burnout worldwide, it seemed necessary to capture that diversity through the book's contents.

We open the book with summaries of two of the major theories driving research on stress and burnout in health care. Gorgievski and Hobfoll provide a summary of the Conservation of Resources model, a widely-studied model driving research into the causes and consequences of stress, burnout, and engagement. Their theory is intended to apply to a wide variety of settings; as such, we complement their treatment with a model that is health care context-based. Laschinger and Leiter, with their Nursing Worklife Model, provide an integrated model of causes and consequences of burnout and a test of that model with a large sample of Canadian nurses. We then turn to two works that provide overviews of the state of burnout research in health care (Breaux, Meurs, Zellars, and Perrewé) and nursing more specifically (Cimiotti, Aiken, Poghosyan). These chapters set the stage for subsequent chapters that will "drill down" into many of the topics they touch upon. Continuing with a theme of more general chapters that touch on a variety of research issues, Demerouti and Bakker discuss measurement options for burnout and engagement, with a particular focus on a recent tool that is gaining momentum as a viable option for research and practice. We conclude the first section with a summary of cross-cultural issues in stress and burnout among health care professionals by Glazer which highlights the need for greater attention to cross-cultural research in both the stress and burnout literatures as well as the health care literature more broadly.

We then turn our attention to more specific causes of stress among health care professionals. Jones and Pryjmachuk provide a comprehensive summary of research concerning stress among new entrants to the health care professions. Given the significant concerns with retention of such professionals, their work holds critical insights into these issues. Westman and Bakker address important mechanisms for understanding the proliferation of burnout between health care professionals (as well as between health care professionals and their family): crossover and emotional contagion.

Geiger-Brown, Rogers, Trinkoff, and Selby discuss work schedules, a commonly voiced concern among health care professionals, and their relationships with stress. They highlight the issue of sleep in relation to schedules and stress. Shirom, Nirel, and Vinokur examine the role that perceived workload and autonomy play in physician burnout through a study of nearly 900 specialists. They find perceived workload and autonomy may be better predictors of burnout than objective work hours and number of patients seen, suggesting a need to reconsider policies regarding work hours.

The next section addresses two important consequences of stress and burnout in health care. Neveu provides a comprehensive summary of the literature linking burnout with maltreatment of patients. His work provides a startling look at the dark side of burnout.

Elfering and Grebner discuss the relationship between stress and patient safety, developing theory-based strategies for improving patient safety by addressing stress.

Given the startling consequences of stress and burnout in health care, we provide two chapters focused on prevention and reduction of stress. Wheeler focuses on prevention, drawing on the strategic human resource management literature to provide suggestions for positioning health care organizations so that stress is less likely. LeBlanc and Schaufeli summarize the work on burnout intervention, using their own work with oncology care providers as an example program for burnout reduction.

Finally, I conclude the book with an integration of future research directions across the chapters. My goal with the concluding chapter is to provide the reader with those critical "next steps" for stress and burnout research in health care contexts. As noted at the onset, while summarizing the state of the stress and burnout literature in health care is of great value, my true hope is that this book can inspire new lines of research in health care contexts.

As the literature suggests, health care professionals work in jobs that stressful and susceptible to burnout. Most researchers understand that our individual research represents a meager attempt to address the problems of stress and burnout among health care professionals. That said, one must start somewhere. It is my hope that by bringing together the leading researchers in the area in one forum, the resulting synergy may lead to new insights that make a larger contribution toward addressing the problems of stress and burnout within health care contexts.

REFERENCES

Beehr, T. A., and Glazer, S. (2005). Organizational role stress. In J. Barling, E. K. Kelloway, and M. R. Frone (Eds). *Handbook of work stress* (pp. 7-34). Thousand Oaks, CA: Sage.

Bouman, A. H., te Brake, H., and Hoogstraten, J. (2002). Significant effects due to rephrasing of the Maslach Burnout Inventory's personal accomplishment items. *Psychological Reports, 91,* 825-826.

Caplan, G. (1964). *Principles of preventative psychiatry.* New York: Basic Books.

Cooper, C. L., and Dewe, P. (2004). *Stress: A brief history.* Oxford: Blackwell.

Demerouti, E., Bakker, A.B., Vardakou, I., andKantas, A. (2002). The convergent validity of two burnout instruments: A multitrait-multimethod analysis. *European Journal of Psychological Assessment, 18,* 296-307.

Freudenberger, H. J. (1974). Staff burnout. *Journal of Social Issues, 30,* 159-165.

Kahn, R. L., Wolfe, D. M., Quinn, R. P., Snoek, J. D., and Rosenthal, R. A. (1964). *Organizational stress: Studies in role conflict and ambiguity.* New York: John Wiley and Sons.

Lazarus, R. S. (1966). *Psychological stress and the coping process.* New York: McGraw-Hill.

Lazarus, R. S., and Folkman, S. (1984). *Stress, appraisal, and coping.* New York: Springer.

Maslach, C. (1982). *Burnout: The cost of caring.* Englewood Cliffs, NJ: Prentice Hall.

McGrath, J. E. (1970). *Social and psychological factors in stress.* New York: Holt, Rinehart, and Winston.

Melamed, S., Shirom, A., Toker, S., Berliner, S., and Shapira, I. (2006). Burnout and risk of cardiovascular disease: Evidence, possible causal paths, and promising research directions. *Psychological Bulletin, 132*, 327-353.

National Institute for Occupational Safety and Health (2000). National occupational research agenda: 21 priorities for the 21st century. Retrieved November 2, 2007 from www.cdc.gov/niosh/00-143g.

Peeters, M. C. W., and LeBlanc, P. M. (2001). Towards a match between job demands and sources of social support: A study of oncology care providers. *European Journal of Work and Organizational Psychology, 10,* 53-72.

Selye, H. (1950). *The physiology and pathology of exposure to stress.* Montreal: Acta.

Shirom, A., and Melamed, S. (2006). A Comparison of the Construct Validity of Two Burnout Measures in Two Groups of Professionals. *International Journal of Stress Management, 13*(2), 176-200.

In: Handbook of Stress and Burnout in Health Care
Editor: Jonathon R. B. Halbesleben

ISBN 978-1-60456-500-3
© 2008 Nova Science Publishers, Inc.

Chapter 2

WORK CAN BURN US OUT OR FIRE US UP: CONSERVATION OF RESOURCES IN BURNOUT AND ENGAGEMENT

*Marjan J. Gorgievski[*a] and Stevan E. Hobfoll[b]*
[a]Erasmus University of Rotterdam, Institute of Psychology,
Rotterdam, the Netherlands
[b]Kent State University, Department of Psychology, Kent, OH and
Summa Health System, Department of Psychiatry, Akron, OH, USA

Several theoretical approaches have been used to describe, explain, and predict burnout. In a review of twenty-five years of burnout research, Schaufeli and Buunk (2003) described fourteen theories regarding the individual, organizational and community levels. These theories have led to many relevant insights, however, these insights have typically been scattered, which calls for the need to better integrate and distill current knowledge into more central overarching frameworks. In the early 1990's, scholars adapted Conservation of Resources (COR) theory to understand the process of burnout and stress in organizational settings (e.g. Hobfoll and Freedy, 1993; Hobfoll and Shirom, 2001; Lee and Ashforth, 1996; Wright and Cropanzano, 1998). Since then, COR theory has developed as one of the leading theories in burnout (Halbesleben, 2006; Westman, Hobfoll, Chen, Davidson and Laski, 2005) and the one that meta-analysis of extant studies suggests best fits the data (Lee and Ashforth, 1996). The value of COR theory was further reinforced when research interest shifted towards work engagement and vigor as the positive counterparts of burnout and away from deficit and pathology models. Building on positive psychology (e.g. Seligman and Csikszentmihalyi, 2000), scholars started investigating the positive, sustaining, and protective power of peoples' resources and positive work experiences.

---

[*] Correspondence concerning this chapter may be addressed to Marjan Gorgievski-Duijvesteijn, Ph.D., Erasmus University Rotterdam, Dept. of Industrial and Organisational Psychology T13-24, P.O.Box 1738, NL-3000 DR Rotterdam, The Netherlands. Tel.: +31 10 40888799. Fax:+31 10 4089009. Email: Gorgievski@fsw.eur.nl.

The basic tenet of COR theory (Hobfoll, 1998; 2001) is that people have an innate as well as a learned drive to create, foster, conserve, and protect the quality and quantity of their resources. Many things could be conceived as resources, but COR theory relates to those resources that are key to survival and well-being (e.g., shelter, attachment to significant others, self-esteem), or that are linked to the process of creating and maintaining key resources (e.g., money, credit). According to COR theory, stress occurs under three conditions: (1) when individuals' key resources are threatened with loss, (2) when resources are lost, or (3) when individuals fail to gain resources following significant resource investment. Burnout is one such stress outcome and typically follows from a process of slow bleed out of resources without counterbalancing resource gain or replenishment.

This chapter aims at providing a comprehensive framework of burnout and work engagement from a COR-theoretical perspective. We will illustrate how research on burnout and work engagement can be advanced by taking fundamental COR-theoretical principles into account. In addition, we will show COR theory's implications for the fostering of engagement and the prevention of burnout at work.

DEFINING BURNOUT AND WORK ENGAGEMENT

Freudenberger (1974) first conceptualized burnout as a process by which excessive involvement at work leads to excessive depletion of energetic and social resources. This often manifested itself by physical signs, such as exhaustion, fatigue and somatization; behavioral signs such as an inability to hold in emotions and social withdrawal; cognitive signs, such as cognitive tunneling and reluctance to change that is being communicated to other team members and clients in a cynical way; and diminished competence, expressed in working excessively long hours, doing less and less in more and more time. Maslach (1982) later provided a more specific state definition of burnout as a "multi-dimensional construct comprised of emotional exhaustion, depersonalization and diminished personal competence that occurs among those who do "people work" of some kind" (p. 3).

Twenty-five years after the launch of Maslach's ideas and the companion instrument, the Maslach Burnout Inventory (MBI), the prevailing viewpoint is that burnout occurs across all kinds of work settings. Furthermore, exhaustion is generally accepted as the major component of burnout, with less agreement about the other elements of burnout (e.g., Evans and Fisher, 1993; Lee and Ashford, 1996; Shirom, 1989). Some authors argue that developing a detached relationship with the recipients of services may be an occupation-specific response that mainly occurs among human service populations (e.g., Evans and Fisher, 1993). Others, however, have shown that the more general "disengagement from work" is a second core construct characterizing burnout, in addition to exhaustion (Demerouti, Bakker, Nachreiner and Schaufeli, 2001).

In the 1990's, the positive psychology revival has led to interest in work engagement as the positive antipode of burnout (Schaufeli, Salanova, Gonzáles-Romá and Bakker, 2001). In line with Antonovsky's wellness-illness continuum (Antonovsky, 1987), scholars aimed at predicting burnout versus work engagement, rather than focusing research attempts at predicting burnout versus "not being burned out." *Work engagement* can be defined as a persistent, pervasive and positive affective-motivational state of fulfilment in employees

(Schaufeli et al., 2001). It was originally composed of three dimensions (vigor, dedication, and absorption) that were thought to counterbalance the three burnout dimensions. Recent empirical research suggests that vigor and dedication constitute the core dimensions that are direct opposites of the burnout dimensions exhaustion and disengagement (Llorens, Schaufeli, Bakker, and Salanova, 2007). Vigor refers to high levels of energy and mental resilience while working, the willingness to invest effort in work, and persistence in the face of difficulties. Dedication refers to a strong involvement in work, accompanied by feelings of enthusiasm and significance, and by a sense of pride and inspiration.

We propose to use definitions of burnout and engagement that both build on previous empirical findings and have a strong theoretical foundation. Remember that a basic principle of COR theory is that stress ensues when people experience or anticipate resource loss, or fail to gain resources after significant resource investment. Following this principle, we see the process of resource loss, gain, and protection as primary in explaining burnout and work engagement (cf. Buchwald and Hobfoll, 2004). We propose that burnout and engagement are multifaceted phenomena, comprising affective, cognitive and behavioral components that are close co-travellers of one another. The central element of burnout and work engagement is the affective component that results from processes that center on peoples' *intrinsic energetic resources*, more specifically emotional robustness, cognitive agility and physical vigor (Hobfoll and Shirom, 2001; Shirom, 2004). Seen this way, burnout is the end state of a long-term process of resource loss that gradually develops over time depleting energetic resources (Hobfoll and Freedy, 1993), whereas engagement is the resultant of the inverted process of real or anticipated resource gain *enhancing* energetic resources.

Yet, we do not see burnout and work engagement as exactly two opposite poles of the same continuum (cf. Langelaan, Bakker, Van Doornen and Schaufeli, 2006; Shirom, 2004). First, two dimensions can be distinguished in the affective component of burnout and engagement, namely a certain level of arousal versus sleepiness and a positive versus negative affective loading (pleasure versus displeasure). Burnout and engagement can be placed on opposite poles of the arousal versus sleepiness dimension, where burnout is characterized by low arousal and engagement by high arousal. However, empirical evidence shows that pleasure versus displeasure might actually be better represented by two separate, oblique dimensions (Payne, 2001). This means that burnout is thought to be characterized by feelings of medium to high displeasure and little pleasure, and engagement is generally characterized by moderate feelings of pleasure and little displeasure (Shirom, 2004). Moreover, over a relatively short period of time, both positive and negative affective states can be experienced.

Second, the cognitions and behavioral inclinations that are closely interrelated with the changes in energetic resources relate to autonomously operating biobehavioral sytems (Shirom, 2004). Most important of these are the withdrawal oriented behavioral inhibition system that may produce the withdrawal responses that are witnessed in many people who experience burnout, and the approach oriented behavior facilitation system that produces persistence and resilience characterizing engagement. Evidence shows that these two biobehavioral systems, too, operate quite independently from one another (Shirom, 2004), which is another reason why burnout and engagement should not be regarded two opposite sides of the same process.

Third, both the energetic responses of burnout and engagement and co-travelling cognitive and behavioral inclinations are part of a more complex dynamic system of (anticipated) resource gains and losses. These processes are also not each other's mirror images. For example, resource loss is something people will try to prevent at high costs, taking relatively major risks (cf. Tversky and Kahneman, 1974). In contrast, resource gain is something that people will actively seek. However, in the process of gaining resources they will take smaller risks. They will typically try to minimize the costs and need to have an indication that there is a high chance to success. We will outline this dynamic system in more detail below.

PRINCIPLES OF COR THEORY

In order to gain a better understanding of the processes leading to burnout versus work-engagement, we need to explain briefly the principles of COR-theory. COR theory is a motivational theory that rests firstly on the basic tenet that individuals strive to obtain, retain, foster, and protect resources. Resources are entities that have intrinsic or instrumental value, including objects (e.g. car, house, but also luxurious objects) conditions (parental role, being embedded in supportive social networks), personal resources (personal characteristics and skills), and energy resources. There is something quite central and primitive biologically in the acquisition and maintenance of resources. Clearly, resources of health, family, and those resources related to survival are most central, with psychological resources such as self-esteem, self-efficacy, and optimism being key to overall resource management and maintenance. Such primary resources people may seek instinctively (Westman et al., 2005).

In addition, secondary resources aid in gaining or protecting peoples' primary resources. What secondary resources have most value can best be determined on a specific level, within the context of a particular process. The value of most of our potential resources is culturally defined and depends on the social environment that surrounds us. Throughout life we are part of groups and exist in settings that provide us with important resources and place multiple resource demands upon us. These groups set rules, norms and standards for valuing certain assets and behaviors over others that they use for dividing resources among its members. For most adults, work is an important life domain that acts to provide resources directly related to our primary resources. These include not only extrinsic energy resources in the form of an income, but for many people it relates directly to deeper psychosocial resources, such as a sense of coherent and effective self (personal identity, social attachment). Underlying these ideas is a profound difference from the emphasis of much of psychology today. If resources valuation is culturally nested, then appraisal will generally be common for resources within a culture and individual differences are of more minor importance.

The motivation to secure, protect, and gain resources is difficult to extinguish and an ongoing process. According to COR theory this process is governed by several key principles and corollaries. By delineating these principles we may further our understanding of burnout versus engagement. For the purposes of this chapter, we will for the first time place increased emphasis on the relevance of COR theory for engagement.

Principle 1: The Primacy of Resource Loss

According to this principle, resource loss is disproportionately more salient than resource gain, which means that real or anticipated resource loss has stronger motivational power than expected resource gain. However, resource loss is typically accompanied by negative emotions, impaired psychological well-being, and ultimately impaired mental and physical health. Especially when primary resources get threatened, individuals may be inclined to focus on their losses and weaknesses rather than their strengths. In addition, loss experiences are likely to evoke avoidance and loss prevention strategies, rather than an active search for new opportunities for resource gain. The relevant interpretation of the first COR principle for an understanding of engagement is therefore that actual or anticipated loss of significant resources will have major inhibitory impact on the process of engagement that is characterized by positive affect, resilience, and an approach orientation. For fostering engagement, prevention of significant losses is therefore critical. In addition, when individuals are faced with significant threats and losses, the environment may actively need to emphasize individuals' strengths, and encourage striving for gain.

Principle 2: Resource Investment

The second principle of COR theory is that people must invest resources in order to protect against resource loss, recover from losses, and gain resources. Because of this principle, the strategies people employ to offset resource loss may lead to other, secondary losses. If the situation becomes chronic, the resources people employ may get depleted, and they need to shift their strategies towards other, usually less favorable ones at higher costs (e.g., resources need to be invested that are less easy to replenish) and with a smaller chance of success. The attendant principle for the engagement side of the continuum is that people must have the personal and environmental capacity to invest resources to ensure and enhance engaging resource gain processes. This suggests the need for a strong armamentarium of social and personal resources, and these must be vigilantly managed. People and systems are naturally motivated to conserve resources in case of unfavourable circumstances, meaning that they will try to set a minimum at stake, and there will always be a resource reserve that they are less willing to invest.

A related corollary of principle 2 (*Corollary 1*) is that *those with greater resources are less vulnerable to resource loss and more capable of orchestrating resource gain. Conversely, those with fewer resources are more vulnerable to resource loss and less capable of resource gain.* Translated to an emphasis on engagement, people who are personally resource rich in terms of quantity and variety enabling flexible management, or who come from resource rich social groups, settings, and societies will be more capable of sustaining work engagement than those who lack resources themselves or who come from resource poor environments.

Principle 3

COR theory envisions the process of motivation and stress as films, not snapshots. This results in an emphasis on loss and gain cycles. Hence, because people have fewer resources as they lose resources, they are decreasingly capable of withstanding further threats to resource loss. These loss cycles are more momentous and move more quickly than gain cycles. Nevertheless, for work engagement, it is important to highlight that COR theory suggests that gain cycles also build on themselves and as people make some resource gains they experience more positive health and well-being and are more capable of further investing resources to sustain, enhance, and increase the speed of the engagement process. As their resource reservoir strengthens they will be more likely to take increasing resource investment risks that are critical in many high demand work environments where just "staying the course" is tantamount to work failure.

STABILITY AND CHANGE IN RESOURCES

According to COR theory, changes in resource levels, rather than stable or chronic situations, influence peoples' health and well-being (Hobfoll, 2001). People adapt to their circumstances, even to such an extent that they seem to be functioning on a characteristic baseline level or a "dynamic equilibrium." First, research has shown that levels of life event exposure may be quite stable across individuals (Heady and Wearing, 1989; Ormel and Wohlfahrt, 1991; Suh, Diener, and Fujita, 1996). Additionally it was shown that negative as well as positive life events only have a temporary impact on subjective well-being (Cummins, 2000; Heady and Wearing, 1989; Suh et al., 1996), mild psychiatric disorders (Duncan-Jones, Fergusson, Ormel, and Horwood, 1990), burnout scores in non-clinical populations (Schaufeli and Enzmann, 1998) and job engagement (Llorens, et al., 2007). After some time, people generally recover and their well-being tends to revert to a particular set point.

We acknowledge that stability in both life event exposure and health and well-being may be caused by stable personal attributes, such as personality (Cummins and Nistico, 2002; Ormel and Wohlfahrt, 1991; Taylor and Brown, 1994). However, building on COR theory we adopt a broader, more dynamic view concerning homeostasis (Gorgievski-Duijvesteijn, Bakker, Schaufeli and Van de Heijden, 2005; Hobfoll, 2002). Homeostasis is maintained and restored because people develop resource caravans, linkages of resources that build up across the lifespan that are rather stable. Disruptions in resource levels are restored, because complex dynamic systems at different levels interact. They may include mechanisms involving biological processes that restore health resources, or cognitive processes that restore personal resources, such as positive cognitive bias (Cummins and Nistico, 2002) or self-enhancing cognitions (Taylor and Brown, 1994). They also include behavioral and social-relational processes, the wide array of strategies people use to restore and build up their entire resource reservoirs. In addition, people are part of larger systems, including their social environments, such as family, groups and societies, and their natural environments, each having their own dynamics that interact with the dynamics on the individual level. Next we will illustrate this process for burnout and work engagement.

MOBILIZATION AND DEPLETION OF INTRINSIC ENERGETIC RESOURCES

Previously, we have argued that burnout and engagement are processes centered on individuals´ intrinsic energetic resources. A core component of these resources is the energetic state. Energetic states are key to human functioning. Throughout life, the energetic state of the body needs to be in line with the activities people are undertaking in order to process information effectively and display an efficient overt response to the demands they are facing (Gaillard and Wientjes, 1994). Within the individual there is a constant taxing of the energetic state, the processing capacity, as well as the amount of effort needed to react to threats and opportunities. Within boundaries, this cognitive-energetic computational process of taxing demands and adjusting energetic state is mostly autonomous and beyond consciousness, for example prompted by planning and executing a task. Based on the work of Csikszentmihalyi (1997), we expect that this is an inherently pleasant process, which under optimal conditions will result in the peak experience of flow, where people are fully wrapped up in their activity as in a smooth, gracious, steady and easy motion with unbroken continuity.

Often, when people's energetic state is substantively altered from its optimal level it catches peoples' attention, either directly or through increase in resultant negative symptoms (e.g., agitation, depression, headaches, alcohol abuse). People's excitement, boredom or depression may impinge on concentration, performance, and sense of well-being. One of the most common warning signs in such circumstances is fatigue, and as such fatigue has received the greatest attention in the literature.

Fatigue is an adaptive response of the organism, causing attention to shift from the external environment towards internal cues, with the purpose of resource conservation (Desmond and Hancock, 2001). When people experience fatigue; they need to use more conscious processes to restore the balance between energetic state and demands. Generally speaking, people have two options (Gaillard and Wientjes, 1994). One is to take a rest or do tasks that reduce effort in order to replenish energetic resources. For example, in the evening after spending a day at the office, someone may decide to go out for a walk rather than catch up on her e-mails from work. However, depending on what is at stake, people may also maintain levels of performance by putting in extra compensatory effort. This last strategy should not be employed too long, or too frequently, because the physiological and psychological costs of prolonged compensatory effort are high. Compensatory effort is typically accompanied by altered emotional states, such as anxiety, hostility or irritability, and cognitive changes, such as cognitive tunneling, indecisiveness, and lack of creativity (Wickens, Lee, Liu and Becker, 2004). These may lead to secondary costs that further aggravate the situation such as social conflicts. In addition, short-term physical complaints might be related to the acute responses of the autonomic nervous system or endocrine changes, such as palpitations, flushing, trembling, or stomach complaints. Furthermore, susceptible individuals might develop illnesses with a short onset, like migraine attacks (Lovallo, 1997).

In the long term, chronic or recurring episodes of compensatory effort may take its toll in other domains, if it comes without significant resource payoff. The inability to replenish energy resources that were lost in an attempt to cope with demands may lead to long-term fatigue that impairs normal functioning on many aspects in daily life. When energetic states are altered repeatedly or chronically for a prolonged period of time, the biochemical condition of the organism changes. This condition is referred to as "allostatic loa." Allostatic load can be defined as "the cost of chronic exposure to fluctuating or heightened neural or neurendocrine response from repeated or chronic environmental challenge that an individual reacts to as being particularly stressful" (McEwen and Stellar, 1993, p. 2093). The tricky part is that the body still seems to be in balance. However, what people fail to notice is their becoming less flexible in responding to further demands. As a result, the body becomes more vulnerable to signs of distress and disease, such as burnout, asthma, diabetes, and myocardial infarctions. In order to become or stay healthy, vigorous and engaged, reducing allostatic load is crucial.

RESOURCES AT WORK

Why would people repeatedly or chronically put in extra compensatory effort? In part, such extra effort occurs because environments demand it for survival, to achieve significant awards, and because fear of resource loss and its consequences place people on a "must strive to stay even" treadmill. Moreover, of all the different types of resources, energy resources are typically the ones people invest and even deplete, with the expectation based on prior experience that they will get replenished without much effort.

To most people, the working environment is a central life context that, on the one hand, provides resources and opportunities for further growth and resource gain, but, on the other hand, is also accompanied by demands and restraints that contribute to resource depletion. Occupational health research has focused on the role of job demands and resources in predicting burnout and engagement. Empirical results show that burnout is generally predicted by high work demands and lack of job-resources (Schaufeli and Bakker, 2004), which set into motion an energy depletion and motivation depletion process respectively (Demerouti et al., 2001). In contrast, the strongest predictor of job-engagement is having job-resources (Schaufeli and Bakker, 2004). It is our contention that the opportunities and expectations of *further* growth and resource gains that relate to having a rich resource pool lies underneath these findings. This would also explain the perhaps counterintuitive finding that job-demands, too, can predict engagement, especially in case a job is resource rich (e.g., Bakker, Hakanen, Demerouti and Xanthopoulou, 2007). The current engagement literature emphasizes successful job performance and the accompanying boost of efficacy as the central process.

Organizations can provide essential conditions for fostering employee engagement. These conditions include meaningful goals; sufficient resources to enable teams and individuals to overcome obstacles and reach their goals; and positive feedback about accomplishments (Csikszentmihalyi, 1997; Sonnentag, 2002). Job demands can be expected to predict engagement, if meeting those demands has positive attributes for the individual, meaning that it accumulates to significant gains. If there is friction between the goals set by the organization and someone's self-interest, stress is expected to ensue irrespective of goal attainment (Sonnentag, 2002). We will illustrate this with an example from the health-care setting, where significant gains for most individuals can be expected to relate to the core business of providing care. Rewards for care-professionals would typically stem from their work orientation towards improving other peoples' lives (Skovholt, Grier, Hanson, 2001), which is an important aspect of their professional identity, or "*être de raison.*" In this context, having to invest resources in other duties that do not come with rewarding returns, such as reimbursement paperwork and insurance eligibility issues, will typically not be invigorating, and may even be stressful if it is associated with cutting investments on the expense of the quality of care (Keidel, 2002). In contrast, an administrative worker might find it quite rewarding to set up a good administration system and solving legal issues.

Concerning the allocation of sufficient adequate resources, organizations can aim at compensating lack or loss of team and individual resources with strengths and gains on other levels of the organization (Hobfoll, 2001). A positive interaction between the individual, the team and the organization can also come in the form of synergy, a gain spiral whereby individual strengths and gains are linked to strengths and gains on team or organizational level. Some empirical evidence shows that job-resources, such as autonomy, social support, supervisory coaching and opportunities for professional development, are beneficial for workers' engagement because they enhance individuals' resiliency beliefs (self-efficacy, self-esteem and optimism; Xanthopoulou, Bakker, Demerouti and Schaufeli, 2007).

Organizations not always influence individuals' resource reservoirs overtly. Just like individuals, groups and organizations seem to be having a spirit of their own that is being maintained by mechanisms that work in more covert ways, such as shared values (Agle and Caldwell, 1999). Groups can influence the actual instrumentality of resources, by rewarding certain behavior for its merits or punishing it for its setbacks. Creative people can, for example, receive positive feedback and specific resources they need to come up with innovative ideas, such as freedom to collaborate with people from outside their discipline. On the other hand, organizations can punish this same behavior by emphasising that it leads to less voluminous output according to traditional standards, and withdraw resources for that reason. Another example of how organizations can influence the instrumentality of resources is by invalidating certain resources for minority groups. This means that minority groups can be "punished" for using or even possessing certain resources that would actually be important for achieving success, such as ambition (Hobfoll and Shirom, 2001).

Carefully managing an organization's resources is crucial for its survival. In case individuals need to invest resources in goals that further the interest of the organization, it is important that workers experience this as personally relevant. This does *not* mean that there always needs to be a direct personal pay-off. Remember that one of peoples' primary resources is having meaningful relationships and belonging to resourceful social groups. In order to build and protect this vital resource, people have developed a set of social norms that regulate social interactions, and protect collective resources from egoistic individual actions (Biel and Thøgersen, 2006). Such norms guide habitual behavior, and may include rules of exchange between individuals and groups, and benevolent behavior benefiting others directly. Different norms can be activated by other peoples' behaviors and communications that provide clues as to the extent other people, too, are contributing to the group's resources, and perceived fairness of how a groups' resources are again distributed among its members (Biel and Thøgersen, 2006).

Finally, organizations can support their members by defining their own set of outcome standards. Positive feedback is a crucial element in the motivational process (Csikszentmihalyi, 1997; Sonnentag, 2002). In health care, measures of success may sometimes be ambiguous, or not broadly shared by society, such as a comfortable and peaceful death of a terminal patient (Keidel, 2002). In such cases, recognition of supervisors and peers who share the same ideas may gain relevance, which can shift the focus towards the gains rather than losses (e.g. Skovholt, et al., 2001).

BUILDING ENGAGEMENT AT WORK

What follows is an application of the general principles of COR theory to the fostering of engagement and the avoidance of burnout. We emphasize the positive psychology ideas of gaining engagement, rather than the heretofore emphasis in the literature of avoiding burnout. Optimal conditions for job-engagement include person and situation factors, the latter being largely the consequence of management strategy. In general, building an engaged workforce calls for the need to nurture and create ecologies that foster resource development, resource growth, and resource protection of individuals and teams. To illustrate our points, we will "think somewhat outside of the box," and list some resources that may be crucial in the process of fostering engagement, but have not been the focus of engagement research do date, namely flexibility, balance, diversity, interdependence, and tolerance for failure. These resources relate to creativity and innovativeness of teams and individuals. We might call this alternative approach striving for dynamic stability and tolerance for failure. This extends the current focus of much job-engagement literature today on general in-role and organizational citizenship behavior, and outcome aspects of performance, such as customer satisfaction and quality of care, rather than more specific measures of task performance.

Flexibility. Much of what we have written to this point implies that flexibility of the individual and flexibility as a trait of environments are critical for engagement. Individuals' flexibility is critical for addressing stressful challenges (Cheng, and Cheung, 2005). Businesses must be flexible, in other words, innovative, in order to effectively respond to quickly altering market demands (Shimizu and Hitt, 2004). Flexibility on the individual level includes both cognitive and emotional aspects (Cheng and Cheung, 2005). Cognitively, flexibility means being able to "think outside of the box," considering what has not previously been considered and mixing ideas, concepts, and plans in novel ways. Emotional flexibility means being able to tolerate a broad range of emotions and to adapt to changing emotional circumstances (Giardini, and Frese, 2006). People who are emotionally flexible can work well under pressure, tolerate feelings of temporary failure, and keep humor available. Corporations usually do not tolerate a broad range of emotional expressions but rather create social norms to inhibit certain emotions and behaviors as being "wrong." This can include feelings of uncertainty, but also excitement and eccentricity that may accompany creativity and engagement, or expressions that go against the status quo and challenge corporate structures.

Balance. Being out of balance is an important threat to flexibility. Flexibility is typically affected when resources are taxed to the point of breaking or depletion, which can be referred to as allostatic load (cf. McEwen and Stellar, 1993). Allostatic load needs to be prevented both on the individual and the environmental level. Engagement processes require balance and the fostering of fun, love, and close attachments (Csikszentmihalyi, 1994). People need to take time on the personal level and to have time on the environmental level to refuel their resource reservoirs in order to be engaged in an ongoing fashion. It is possible for individuals to have prolonged periods that lack life balance and for business to foster endless work hours and travel, but if organizations keep undermining workers' private life, the result will be a less resilient work force, and workaholism, burnout and health impairment may more likely be the long-term outcomes rather than engagement (cf. Demerouti et al., 2001).

On the job, people also need time to actually meet, to allow ideas to develop, and to immerse themselves in activities. "Time to think" must be actively managed. This demands multi-hour blocks of time, not "New York minute" time frames. Email, cell phones and wireless connectivity are essential tools that enhance flexibility, but expectations of immediate availability through email and cell-phone can be obstructive to engagement, if it means that employees have little opportunities to think, strategize, and plan without interruption.

Diversity. Team diversity, rather than the more typical homogeneity, promotes minority viewpoints, alternative thinking, and more flexible and successful problem solving (Peterson and Nemeth, 1996). Diverse teams with a mix of complimentary skills and people who think differently are the more creative teams (Kurtzberg, 2005). To be skillful is an individual resource. The encouragement of skillfulness in a work environment is tactical and must be managed strategically. It means hiring people with strong skills, but also continuing to encourage their skill development. With the rapid advances of technology and the multiple perturbances in the marketplace this will likely result in less redundancy of skills on a team (Eldridge and Nisar, 2006).

Creating diverse teams also means getting together people who do not normally interact and who have not absorbed the flattening influence of a corporate culture. When the famous psychiatrist Henry Stack Sullivan wanted to create a new kind of psychiatric ward, he found that he could not hire experienced staff, but needed novices. The experienced staff had already learned to be expert at precisely what he did not want them to do (Sullivan, 1953). The downside of creating diverse work teams may be that it takes time for them to learn to fit together and they must learn to manage conflict (Kurtzberg, 2005). Ten white males from similarly backgrounds do not have that challenge, but in spite of their self-congratulatory style, are less likely to generate the diverse solutions required for problem solving (Rodriquez, 1998).

Interdependence, loyalty and tolerance for risk and failure. In order to create and maintain a flexible, diverse and balanced work environment, teams must be managed in ways that keep encouraging change and innovation (Janssen, 2003). Managing diverse work teams demands shared control, which is a dialectical managerial principle that grants employees autonomy, but meanwhile emphasizes that they depend on each other and need to contribute to group goals (Eldridge and Nisar, 2006; Khazanchi, Lewis, and Boyer, 2007). This is called interdependence. People are encouraged to be the dissonant note in a chord, not a false tone. Two key resources that enable workers to do so are self-efficacy "I can do it" and collective efficacy "we need each other to do it," (Bandura, 1997) both of which must be nurtured.

When managing diverse teams, it is strategic to emphasize the positive synergy between people who are experts in different areas, rather than to frame such differences as "compensating for each others' weaknesses". On the other hand, compensating for peoples' disappointments and showing support and loyalty towards teams and individuals who have failed is key to stimulating risk taking that is necessary for innovation. Failure in health care may be a sensitive issue, as errors may have considerable consequences. Yet, empirical research has revealed that higher performing teams in a medical setting also reported more mistakes, and failures relate positively to firm performance (Van Dyck, Frese, Baer, and Sonnentag, 2005). Error management culture characterized by open communications about failure and quick correction of errors was found to be pivotal. Such an environment is supportive and encourages looking for the success that is in the failure, helps analyze what went wrong without punishment or imputing failures as being characterological, thus unchangeable. This way people learn to expect gains in spite of the setbacks. It is quite the opposite of the recent trends in corporate environments where there is little loyalty toward employees and "what did you do for me since lunch?" is the watchword. COR theory emphasizes that inability to generate resource gains after considerable investments is potentially devastating. Failure is never easy; it undermines strength and self-esteem, and decrease individuals' sense of control (Hobfoll, 1998). It is good to be competitive, but if it leads to fear of failure, emphasis will shift to risk aversive approaches to problems, such as laying blame on others.

The larger an organization, the more conscious efforts may be needed to keep a system stable and balanced. To explain, in a small business, entrepreneurs cannot fire themselves and they may find it quite risky to fire any key employee. As such, they might be more likely to stabilize the team environment. They have no other option than to tolerate some degree of failure, learn from their mistakes, rethink where they went wrong, retool, and get back in the fray. Larger corporations are wise to actively replicate this process. Organizations that consider human resources to be peripheral energies rather than key resources, and treat employees as cookie cutter replicates of each other can fire and replace at will. However, such processes undermine teams that are diverse in skill level and problem-solving approach. In addition, fear of layoffs typically weakens individual risk taking essential for innovative engagement and increases cautious strategies (Scott, 2004).

Conclusion

We have outlined a comprehensive framework of burnout and job-engagement based on COR theory, for the first time placing emphasis on job-engagement. We defined burnout and job-engagement as multifaceted phenomena revolving around intrinsic energy resources, or vigor. Cognitive and behavioral inclinations, such as behavioral inhibition versus approach orientation, are considered to be close co-travelers. Burnout results from a slow, stressful process of resource bleed out that is not counterbalanced by resource gains, thus accumulating to significant losses. We proposed that job-engagement is the resultant of the inverted process of real or anticipated resource gains. Gains become significant if they feed into peoples' primary resources, which are essential for survival or relate to basic needs, but they must also support peoples' psychological resources of sense of efficacy, self-esteem, and sense of success.

COR theory emphasizes that changes in resource levels are the principle axis by which burnout and job-engagement process are activated and sustained, or inhibited and curtailed. This means that, no matter how excellent ones' performance, just staying the course without generating further gains is not expected to be very engaging. In such cases, people need to take investment risks in order to initiate further positive changes. Based in this idea we have proposed a new framework for boosting engagement at work based on general principles of COR theory, called striving for dynamic stability and tolerance for failure. The starting point for this framework is creativity and innovativeness as key to job-engagement. The building blocks are flexibility, balance, diversity, interdependence, loyalty, trust and tolerance for failure. We emphasize that these building blocks are important resources on both individual and environmental level, that need to fit together in order to activate and sustain engagement processes. Synergy between individuals, teams and the organization needs to be emphasized where possible, which keeps the focus on strengths and resource gain. Hopefully our framework provides an impetus for extending current job-engagement research towards original dynamic multi-level investigations.

REFERENCES

Agle, B. R., and Caldwell, C. B. (1999). Understanding research on values in business: a level of analysis framework. *Business and Society, 38*, 326-387.

Antonovski, A. (1987). *Unraveling the mystery of health: How people manage stress and stay well.* San Francisco: Jossey Bass.

Bakker, A. B., Hakanen, J. J., Demerouti, E., and Xanthopoulou, D. (2007). Job resources boost work engagement, particularly when job demands are high. *Journal of Educational Psychology, 99*, 274 - 284.

Bandura, A. (1997). *Self-efficacy: The exercise of control.* New York: W. H. Freeman and Company.

Biel, A. and Thøgersen, J. (2006). Activation of social norms in social dilemmas: a review of the evidence and reflections on the applications for environmental behavior. *Journal of Economic Psychology, 28*, 93 - 112.

Buchwald, P., and Hobfoll, S. E. (2004). Burnout in the Conservation of Resources Theory. *Psychologie in Erziehung Und Unterricht, 51*, 247-257.

Cheng, C., and Cheung, M. W. L. (2005). Cognitive processes underlying coping flexibility: differentiation and integration. *Journal of Personality, 73*, 859 - 886.

Csikszentmihalyi, M. (1994). The domain of creativity. In D. H. Feldman, M. Csikszentmihalyi, M. and H.Gardner (Eds.). *Changing the world: A framework for the study of creativity.* Wesport, C. T.: Praeger.

Csikszentmihalyi, M. (1997). *Finding flow, the psychology of engagement with everyday life.* New York, N.Y.: Basic Books.

Cummins, R. A. (2000). Personal income and subjective wellbeing: A review. *Journal of Happiness Studies, 1,* 133-158.

Cummins, R. A., and Nistico, H. (2002). Maintaining life satisfaction: The role of positive cognitive bias. *Journal of Happiness Studies, 3,* 37-69.

Demerouti, E., Bakker, A. B., Nachreiner, F., and Schaufeli, W. B. (2001). The job demands-resources model of burnout. *Journal of Applied Psychology, 86*, 499-512.

Desmond, P. A., and Hancock, P. A. (2001). Active and passive fatigue states. In P. A. Desmond and P. A. Hancock (Eds.), *Stress, workload and fatigue: factors in transporting* (pp. 455-465). New York, N.Y.: Lawrence Erlbaum Associates.

Duncan-Jones, P., Fergusson, D. M., Ormel, J. O., and Horwood, L. J. (1990). A model of stability and change in minor psychiatric symptoms: Results from three longitudinal studies. *Psychological Medicine, monograph suppl. 18*, iii-28.

Eldridge, D., and Nisar, T. M. (2006). The significance of employee skill in flexible work organizations. *International Journal of Human Resource Management, 17*, 918-937.

Evans, B. K., and Fischer, D. G. (1993). The nature of burnout: A study of the three-factor model of burnout in human service and non-human service samples. *Journal of Occupational and Organizational Psychology, 66*, 29 - 38.

Freudenberger, H. J. (1974). Staff burn-out. *Journal of Social Issues, 30*, 159-164.

Gaillard, A. W. K., and Wientjes, C. J. E. (1994). Mental load and work stress as two types of energy mobilization. *Work and Stress, 8*, 141-152.

Giardini, A., and Frese, M. (2006). Reducing the negative effects of emotion work in service occupations: Emotional competence as a psychological resource. *Journal of Occupational Health Psychology, 11*, 63-75.

Gorgievski-Duijvesteijn, M. J., Bakker, A. B., Schaufeli, W. B., and Van der Heijden, P. G. M. (2005). Finances and well-being, a dynamic equilibrium model of resources. *Journal of Occupational Health Psychology, 10*, 210-224.

Halbesleben, J. R. B. (2006). Sources of social support and burnout: A meta-analytic test of the conservation of resources model. *Journal of Applied Psychology, 91*, 1134-1145.

Heady, B. and Wearing, A. (1989). Personality, life events, and subjective well-being: Towards a dynamic equilibrium model. *Journal of Personality and Social Psychology, 57*, 731-739.

Hobfoll, S. E. (1998). *Stress, Culture and Community. The psychology and philosophy of stress.* New York: Plenum.

Hobfoll, S. E. (2001). The influence of culture, community and the nested-self in the stress process: Advancing Conservation of Resources theory. *Journal of Applied Psychology, 50*, 337-396.

Hobfoll, S. E. (2002). Social and psychological resources and adaptation. *Review of General Psychology, 6*, 307-324.

Hobfoll, S. E., and Freedy, J. (1993). Conservation of resources: A general stress theory applied to burnout. In W. B. Schaufeli, C. Maslach and T. Marek (Eds.), *Professional burnout: Recent developments in theory and practice* (pp. 115-133). Washington, D.C.: Taylor and Francis.

Hobfoll, S. E., and Shirom, A. (2001). Conservation of Resources Theory. In R. Golembiewski (Ed.), *Handbook of Organizational Behavior* (pp. 57-80). New York, NY: Dekker.

Janssen, O. (2003). Innovative behaviour and job involvement at the price of conflict and less satisfactory relations with co-workers. *Journal of Occupational and Organizational Psychology ,76*, 347-364.

Keidel, G. C. (2002). Burnout and compassion fatigue among hospice caregivers. *American Journal of Hospice and Palliative Care, 19*, 200 - 205.

Khazanchi, S., Lewis, M. W., Boyer, and K. K. (2007). Innovation-supportive culture: The impact of organizational values on process innovation. *Journal of Operations Management, 25*, 871-884.

Kurtzberg, T. R. (2005). Feeling creative, being creative: An empirical study of diversity and creativity in teams. *Creativity Research Journal, 17*, 51-65.

Langelaan, S., Bakker, A. B., Van Doornen, L. J. P., and Schaufeli, W. B. (2006). Burnout and work engagement: Do individual differences make a difference? *Personality and Individual Differences, 40*, 521-532.

Lee, R. T., and Ashforth, B. E. (1996). A meta-analytic examination of the correlates of the three dimensions of job burnout. *Journal of Applied Psychology, 81*, 123-133.

Llorens, S., Schaufeli, W., Bakker, A., and Salanova, M. (2007). Does a positive gain spiral of resources, efficacy beliefs and engagement exist? *Computers in Human Behavior, 23*, 825-841.

Lovallo, W. R. (1997). *Stress and health: biological and psychological interactions.* London: Sage.

Maslach, C. (1982). *Burnout: the cost of caring.* Englewood Cliffs, N.J.: Prentice Hall.

McEwen, B. S., and Stellar, E. (1993). Stress and the Individual. *Archives of Internal Medicine, 153*, 2093 - 2101.

Ormel, J. O., and Wohlfahrt, T. (1991). How neuroticism, long-term difficulties, and life situation change influence psychological distress: A longitudinal model. *Journal of Personality and Social Psychology, 60*, 744-755.

Payne, R. L. (2001). Measuring emotions at work. In R. L. Payne and C. L. Cooper (Eds.), *Emotions at work* (pp. 107-133). Chichester, U.K.: Wiley and Sons.

Peterson, R. S., and Nemeth, C. J. (1996). Focus versus flexibility: Majority and minority influence can both improve performance. *Personality and Social Psychology Bulletin, 22*, 14-23.

Rodriquez, R. A. (1998). Challenging demographic reductionism: A pilot study investigating diversity in group composition. *Small Group Research, 29*, 744-759.

Schaufeli, W. B., and Bakker, A. B. (2004). Job demands, job resources, and their relationship with burnout and engagement: a multi-sample study. *Journal of Organizational Behavior, 25*, 293-315.

Schaufeli, W. B., and Buunk, B. P. (2003). Burnout: an overview of 25 years of research and theorizing. In M. J. Schabracq, J. A. M. Winnubst and C. L. Cooper (Eds.), The handbook of Work and health psychology. Hoboken: John Wiley and Sons.

Schaufeli, W. B., and Enzmann, D. (1998). *The burnout companion to study and practice: a critical analysis.* London, U.K.: Taylor and Francis.

Schaufeli, W. B., Salanova, M., Gonzalez-Roma, V., and Bakker, A. B. (2002). The measurement of burnout and engagement: a confirmatory factor analytic approach. *Journal of Happiness Studies, 3*, 71-92.

Scott, H. K. (2004). Reconceptualizing the nature and health consequences of work-related insecurity for the new economy: The decline of workers' power in the flexibility regime. *International Journal of Health Services, 34*, 143-153.

Seligman, M. E. P., and Csikszentmihalyi, M. (2000). Positive psychology. *American Psychologist, 55*, 5-14.

Shimizu, K., and Hitt, M. A. (2004). Strategic flexibility: Organizational preparedness to reverse ineffective strategic decisions. *Academy of Management Executive, 18*, 44-59.

Shirom, A. (1989). Burnout in work organizations. In C. L. Cooper and I. Robertson (Eds.), *International Review of Industrial and Organizational Psychology* (pp. 25-48). New York, N.Y.: Whiley.

Shirom, A. (2004). Feeling vigorous at work? The construct of vigor and the study of positive affect in organizations. In P. L. Perrewe and D. Ganster (Eds.), *Research in organizational stress and well-being.* (Vol. 3, pp. 135-165). Greenwich, CN: JAI Press.

Skovholt, T. M., Grier, T. L., and Hanson, M. R. (2001). Career counselling for longevity: Self-care and burnout prevention strategies for counsellor resilience. *Journal of Career Development, 27,* 167-176.

Sonnentag, S. (2002). Performance, well-being and self-regulation. In S. Sonnentag (Ed.), *Psychological management of individual performance* (pp. 405-423). New York: John Wiley and Sons, Ltd.

Suh, E. M., Diener, E., and Fujita, F. (1996). Events and subjective well-being: Only recent events matter. *Journal of Personality and Social Psychology, 70,* 1091-1102.

Sullivan, H. S. (1953). *The interpersonal theory of psychiatry.* New York, N. Y.: Norton.

Taylor, S. E., and Brown, J. D. (1994). Positive illusions and well-being revisited: Separating fact from fiction. *Psychological Bulletin, 116,* 21-27.

Tversky, A., and Kahneman, D. (1974). Judgement under uncertainty. *Science, 185,* 1124 - 1131.

Van Dyck, C., Frese, M., Baer, M., Sonnentag, S. (2005). Organizational error management culture and its impact on performance: a two study replication. *Journal of Applied Psychology, 90,* 1228-1240.

Westman, M., Hobfoll, S. E., Chen, S., Davidson, O. B., and Laski, S. (2005). Organizational stress through the lens of conservation of resources theory. In P. L. Perrewe and D. Ganster (Eds.), *Research in organizational stress and well-being.* (Vol. 4, pp. 167-220). Greenwich, CN: JAI Press.

Wickens, C. D., Lee, J. D., Liu, Y., and Gordon Becker, S. E. (2004). *An introduction to human factors engineering.* Upper Saddle River, NJ: Pearson Education.

Wright, T. A., and Cropanzano, R. (1998). Emotional exhaustion as a predictor of job performance and voluntary turnover. *Journal of Applied Psychology, 83,* 486-493.

Xanthopoulou, D., Bakker, A. B., Demerouti, E., and Schaufeli, W. B. (2007). The role of personal resources in the job demands-resources model. *International Journal of Stress Management, 14,* 121 - 141.

In: Handbook of Stress and Burnout in Health Care   ISBN 978-1-60456-500-3
Editor: Jonathon R. B. Halbesleben   © 2008 Nova Science Publishers, Inc.

Chapter 3

THE NURSING WORKLIFE MODEL: THE ROLE OF BURNOUT IN MEDIATING WORK ENVIRONMENT'S RELATIONSHIP WITH JOB SATISFACTION

Heather K. Spence Laschinger[1] and Michael P. Leiter[2]
[1]Distinguished University Professor and Associate Director Research
School of Nursing, University of Western Ontario,
1151 Richmond Street, London, Ontario N6A 5C1
[2]Canada Research Chair in Occupational Health and Wellness
Centre for Organizational Research and Development
Acadia University, Wolfville, NS, Canada B4P 2R6

The massive restructuring initiatives in hospitals in the 1990s resulted in nursing work environments characterized by increased stress and heavy workloads as fewer nurses were available to care for patients with higher acuity and shortened length of stay (Institute of Medicine, 2004). These conditions were stressful for nurses who were frustrated by their inability to provide the quality of care consistent with professional standards. Numerous studies documented increased stress and burnout among nurses and high levels of job dissatisfaction and turnover (Aiken, Clarke, Sloane, Sochalski, Busse, and Clarke, 2001; Aiken, Clarke, Sloane, Sochalski, and Silber, 2002; Cho; Laschinger, and Wong, 2006; Greco, Laschinger, and Wong, 2006). A decade later, hospital administration is struggling to retain nurses currently in the profession and to attract newcomers to the profession. Furthermore, several studies have linked poor working conditions of nurses to negative patient outcomes, most dramatically, patient mortality and increased occurrence of adverse events (Aiken, Smith, and Lake, 1994; Kazanjian, Green, Wong, and Reid, 2005; McGillis Hall, Doran, Baker, Pink, Sidani, O'Brien-Pallas, and Donner, 2003; Tourangeau, Giovanetti, Tu, and Wood, 2002).

Current recruitment and retention efforts focus on creating healthy work environments for nurses aimed at increasing the quality of worklife for nurses and increased quality of patient care. Studies have shown that the quality of worklife of nurses and high quality patient care are closely linked (Leiter, Harvie, and Frizzell, 1998; Vahey, Aiken, Sloane, Clarke, and Vargas, 2004). Research on 'Magnet Hospitals', that is, hospitals that are able to attract and retain nurses because of work environments that support professional nursing practice standards, has identified several elements of the work environment, such as professional autonomy and nurse decisional involvement, that make a difference to nurses' worklife and patient care (Aiken, Smith, and Lake, 1994; Lake, 2002). More recently, Leiter and Laschinger (2006) and Laschinger and Leiter (2006) articulated relationships among five aspects of professional practice environments derived from this research that offer a model for designing effective nursing work environments. In this chapter, we describe a model of worklife that links these work environment characteristics to the burnout/engagement process and subsequently, nurse and patient outcomes. We suggest that this Nursing Worklife Model (Leiter and Laschinger, 2005; Laschinger and Leiter, 2006) can be used to guide management in creating healthy and positive nursing work environments that will both retain nurses currently in the system and attract newcomers to the profession.

NURSING WORKLIFE MODEL

The model describes relationships among five worklife variables identified by Lake (2002) in her analysis of data using a measure of professional nursing practice environments, Aiken and Patrician's (2000) Nursing Work Index-Revised (NWI-R). The Nursing Worklife Model suggests that these worklife factors interact among themselves to predict the extent of burnout/engagement experienced by nurses, which, in turn, has an impact on nurse and patient outcomes. The model is illustrated in Figure 1.

The five work life factors identified by Lake (2002) as characteristics of professional nursing practice environments include: effective nursing leadership, staff nurse decisional involvement, adequate staffing, collaborative nurse-physician relationships, and use of a nursing model of care (vs. a medical model). Lake argued that the data collected using the NWI-R captured salient characteristics of a supportive professional practice environment in nursing since the items of the measure were derived from interviews with nurses in designated magnet hospitals. She further argued that these characteristics reflect a professional model of work organization, maintaining that this model is more suitable than a traditional bureaucratic model given the complexity and uncertainty of nursing work environments (Alexander, 1982). She contends that in uncertain environments, such as nursing, a professional model facilitates timely decision making when clinical problems arise, in contrast to a hierarchical bureaucratic model that requires many layers of approval in the decision making process. Thus, a professional organizational model decreases the likelihood of delayed identification and treatment of patient problems. These factors were identified in Lake's (2002) analysis of data in two samples: one of survey data from 2,334 nurses in 16 designated US Magnet hospitals, and the other in a 1998 survey of over 11,000 nurses in Pennsylvania.

An exploratory factor analysis of the first sample revealed five factors, which were then validated in the second sample in a confirmatory factor analysis.

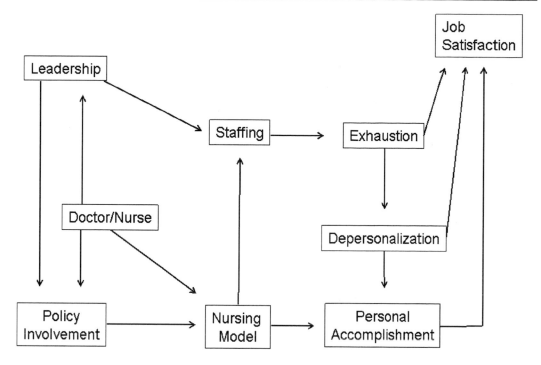

Figure 1. Hypothesized Mediation Model.

Lake intended the new measure, the Practice Environment Scale (PES), to be a composite measure of hospital level professional nursing practice environments. Hospitals that scored highly on this measure would be expected to be supportive of high quality professional nursing practice through a professional model of work organization. Lake, however, did not specify any particular pattern of relationships among the five factors in her study. Specifying those interrelationships is an important step towards articulating an integrated model of nursing worklife. Further, developing the model requires theory to describe the relationships of this structured model of worklife with nurses' worklife crises, such as job burnout.

Burnout

Maslach and Leiter (1997) define burnout as "the index of the dislocation between what people are and what they have to do. It represents erosion in values, dignity, spirit and will-- an erosion of the human soul. It is a malady that spreads gradually and continuously over time, putting people into a downward spiral from which it is hard to recover" (p.17). Burnout comprises chronic emotional exhaustion, cynicism and detachment from work, and feelings of ineffectiveness on the job. A major source of burnout is an overloaded work schedule, that is, having too little time and too few resources to accomplish the job. Lack of control (e.g., a situation in which reducing costs becomes more important than meeting client or employee needs prevails), performing tasks that conflict with employee values and beliefs, and a breakdown in social work factors are also factors that lead to burnout. Performance suffers when work is so fast paced that workers lose a sense of community. Halbesleben and Bowler (2007) found that employee motivation plays an important mediating role between burnout and performance. Finally, unfair management practices may destroy trust and increase disillusionment among employees, leading to symptoms of burnout.

Burnout has been studied extensively in nursing and healthcare. Several studies by Aiken and her colleagues linked lower levels of burnout to work environments that provided job autonomy, control over the practice environment, and good nurse/physician relationships (Aiken et al., 2002; Clarke, Laschinger, Giovannetti, Shamian, Thomson and Tourangeau, 2001). Emotional exhaustion has been related to work pressure (Robinson, Roth, Keim, Levenson, Flentje, and Basher, 1991) and a lack of workplace support (Sims, 1997). Bakker, Killmer, Siegrist and Schaufeli (2000) found that nurses who felt their job demands exceeded associated rewards reported higher levels of emotional exhaustion than those who did not experience such an imbalance. This relationship was particularly strong for nurses with strong needs for personal control. These findings clearly suggest that burnout is a serious problem that is costly for both people and organizations and that every effort must be made to prevent it.

Nursing Worklife Model

Leiter and Laschinger (2006) argued that specifying relationships among Lake's five components of professional practice environments would identify mechanisms by which they influence each other to produce outcomes, and provide targets for worklife interventions. In the Leiter/Laschinger model, leadership is conceptualized as the driving force of the work environment variables, in that it strongly influences other aspects of the professional practice environment. Leadership has a direct effect on staff nurses' involvement in unit decision making, adequate staffing, and nurse/physician collaboration. Leadership also has an indirect influence on use of a nursing model as basis for care on the unit (versus a medical model) through these variables. The quality of nurse/physician collaboration mediates the relationship between leadership and use of a nursing model for care and between leadership and nurses' decisional involvement.

Leadership also has an impact on burnout (emotional exhaustion and performance accomplishment) through staffing adequacy and use of a nursing model of care. When staffing is insufficient to provide high quality care, nurses are more likely to be exhausted. Use of a nursing model of care also directly affects staffing adequacy and nurses' sense of personal accomplishment. This implies that a nursing based model of care would ensure adequate nurse staffing levels to meet the nursing needs of clients and allow nurses to provide high quality professional nursing care. This, in turn, would result in greater feelings of accomplishment by the nurses and should translate into better nurse and patient outcomes. Exhaustion mediates the relationship of the work environment characteristics with depersonalization, which mediates exhaustion's relationship with personal accomplishment (Leiter, 1993).

A central theoretical construct in the model is the role of burnout as a mediator between workplace experiences and a variety of outcomes, including performance, attitudes, and health of employees (Leiter and Maslach, 2004). The MBI operationalization of burnout assesses subjective experiences of energy, involvement, and efficacy that define employees' initial reaction to qualities of the work environment. These experiences in turn influence employees' motivation—or even their capacity—to perform or to maintain their health in the context of ongoing work demands. The central mediating role for burnout leads to a research question regarding the demonstration of mediation and—when mediation is present—considering whether that mediation is partial or complete (Leiter, 2005; Leiter and Shaughnessy, 2006).

Empirical Support for the Nursing Worklife Model

Leiter and Laschinger's (2006) analysis of data from over 8000 Canadian nurses found support for the proposition that the quality of nursing leadership was fundamental to the model. The model proposed that leadership has direct and indirect effects on the other four professional practice worklife factors, which in turn, affects the three dimensions of burnout. More positive ratings of nursing leadership have strong direct relationships with nurses' involvement in unit decisions, nurse-physician collaborative relationships, and staffing adequacy. Nurses' decisional involvement and collaborative relationships with physicians are positively related to a nursing model of patient care (vs. a medical model), which is directly related to the adequacy of staffing. Staffing adequacy, in turn, has a direct relationship emotional exhaustion. As expected in burnout theory, emotional exhaustion has a direct relationship with nurses' cynicism or depersonalization, which in turn, has direct implications for professional efficacy. In a further analysis, Laschinger and Leiter (2006) linked these conditions to patient safety outcomes. In this analysis, the burnout process partially mediated the impact of professional practice characteristics on nurses' reports of adverse events on their units.

The pattern of relationships among the five professional practice factors was replicated in a study of Michigan hospital nurses that linked these factors to nurse job satisfaction (Manojlovich and Laschinger, 2007). In this study, structural empowerment was modeled as a prior condition of the professional practice environment characteristics. The results supported the hypothesized model in that the professional practice domains mediated the relationship between structurally empowering work conditions and nurses' reported work satisfaction. This study, however, did not examine the mediating role of burnout/engagement in the professional practice environment/job satisfaction relationship. In this chapter, we address this gap by investigating the role of the burnout/engagement process in linking worklife factors to nurses' satisfaction with their work (See Figure 1).

METHOD

Participants

The sample used for this analysis was a subset from a larger study: the *International Survey of Hospital Staffing and Organization of Patient Outcomes* (Aiken, Clarke, Sloane, Sochalski, Busse, Clarke et al., 2001) conducted in five countries (Canada, USA, England, Scotland, and Germany). That study explored relationships between hospital work environment characteristics, nurse staffing, and nurse and patient outcomes. In Canada, surveys were sent to nurses working in 292 acute care hospitals in three provinces. In Ontario and BC, stratified random samples of nurses were randomly selected from the registry lists of the provincial licensing bodies. In Alberta, the entire population of acute care nurses was surveyed. Fifty-nine per cent of the nurses returned useable questionnaires (n=17,965).

The results reported in this chapter relate to a subset of the Ontario and Alberta data (n=4,606 and n=3,991, respectively) who provided valid responses on all variables in the analysis (N=8,597). Consistent with the demographic profile of nurses in Canada, nurses averaged 44.1 years of age with 19.2 years of experience in nursing. Eighty three percent of the nurses were diploma prepared. Participants worked full time (59.4%) or part time (39.6%), were predominantly female (97.5%). Most had permanent positions (84.5%), while others had temporary positions (2.8%) or casual positions (12.7%). Of those in casual positions, some preferred a casual position (61.3%) while others preferred a permanent position (38.7%). They had worked in their current hospital for 12.12 years (SD = 7.6). Participants' highest educational credentials included diploma (48.2%), baccalaureate (27.6%), and masters (2.1%). Primary specialty areas included medical/surgical units (64.2%), ICU (12.2%), obstetrics (9.8%), OR/PARR (5.8%), pediatrics (3.9%), and psychiatry (4.1%).

Procedures

Nurses received questionnaires through regular mail in the fall of 1998. Participation was anonymous with instructions to clarify informed consent. The Dillman (2000) technique was used to maximize return rates.

INSTRUMENTS

NWI-PES

In this analysis, we used items on the survey questionnaire included in Lake's (2002) modification of the NWI-R, the NWI-PES. Items capturing each of Lake's five subscales were summed and averaged to create scores for these worklife components. Respondents rated positively worded statements as Strongly Disagree (1), Disagree (2), Agree (3), and Strongly Agree (4). The Canadian survey did not include three items included in Lake's (2002) analysis of USA data: the nurse participation in hospital affairs subscale (Participation) consisted of nine items; the nursing foundations for quality of care subscale (Nursing Model), eight items; nurse manager ability/support of nurses subscale (Leadership), four items; the staff and resource adequacy subscale (Staffing), four items; and the collegial nurse-physician relationships subscale (Nurse/physician Relationship), three items. Lake (2002) established evidence for the construct validity and internal consistency reliability for the NWI-PES.

MBI-HSS

The Maslach Burnout Inventory—Human Service Scale (MBI—HSS) is the original version of this measure, which is the most widely used measure of job burnout (Maslach, Jackson, and Leiter, 1996). The 22-item measure comprises three subscales: emotional exhaustion (9 items), depersonalization (5 items), and personal accomplishment (8 items). The items are framed as statements of job-related feelings (e.g. "I feel burned out from my work", "I feel confident that I am effective at getting things done"), and are rated on a 7-point frequency scale (ranging from "never" to "daily"). Burnout is reflected in higher scores on emotional exhaustion and depersonalization, and lower scores on personal accomplishment. A factor analysis of the data in this study for the MBI-General Survey items replicated the established MBI-General Survey factor structure. A considerable body of research has confirmed the validity and reliability of this measure (Maslach, Schaufeli, and Leiter, 2001; Schaufeli and Enzmann, 1998).

Job Satisfaction

Job satisfaction was measured by two items used in previous research by Aiken and her colleagues. Nurses were asked to rate their current job satisfaction on a 4-point scale ranging from "very dissatisfied" (1) to "very satisfied" (4), and their satisfaction with nursing as a profession, using the identical scale. Responses on the two items were highly correlated ($r = .44$, $p < .001$). Nurses were significantly more satisfied with their profession ($M = 3.09$) than with their jobs ($M = 2.79$), $t_{(8572)} = 30.62, p < .001$).

RESULTS

Table 1 displays the means, standard deviations, Cronbach alpha reliability estimates, and correlations for the variables in the study. The scores on the MBI subscales are close to the usual level for health service professionals (Maslach, Jackson, and Leiter, 1996). Satisfaction was in the positive range of the 1 to 4 scale ($M = 2.94$, $SD = 0.75$). Professional practice environment scores were somewhat positive, ranging from 2.32 to 2.82 on a 4-point scale. Emotional exhaustion and depersonalization are highly correlated ($r = .71$) and both are moderately correlated with personal accomplishment ($r = -.39$ and $r = -.35$, respectively). The strongest correlation with job satisfaction was emotional exhaustion ($r = -.52$). Satisfaction is related fairly consistently with other aspects of the model, with the correlations ranging from .28 to .38. All alpha levels are in the acceptable range above .70.

Table 1. Means, Standard Deviations, Alpha, and Correlations for Latent Variables

	Mean	S. D.	α	1	2	3	4	5	6	7	8
1. Staffing	2.32	0.69	.78								
2. Nurse/Physician	2.82	0.65	.83	.37							
3. Leadership	2.46	0.78	.84	.67	.48						
4. Policy Involvement	2.38	0.54	.79	.64	.47	.89					
5. Nursing Model	2.71	0.49	.72	.63	.51	.73	.82				
6. Emotional Exhaustion	22.34	11.20	.91	-.61	-.22	-.41	-.39	-.39			
7. Personal Acc.	37.38	7.14	.80	.24	.13	.21	.22	.25	-.28		
8. Depersonalization	6.30	5.67	.78	-.43	-.16	-.29	-.28	-.27	.71	-.35	
9. Job Satisfaction	2.94	0.75	.44[a]	.34	.28	.34	.30	.30	-.52	.33	-.37

Note: N=8,560; All correlations significant p<.01.
[a]Correlation of two items.

Data Analysis

The structural equation modeling (SEM) analysis built upon those of Leiter and Laschinger (2006) that confirmed Lake's (2002) factor structure and a structural model of the interrelationships among these five factors. Further, the SEM analysis extends the Laschinger and Leiter's (2006) application of this structural model to explaining nurses' evaluations of patient safety concerns. The analysis reported here substitutes job satisfaction for patient adverse events as the outcome variable in the model. The analysis considers specifically the extent to which the three aspects of burnout mediate the relationship of the NWI-PES factors with job satisfaction as proposed in the Hypothesized Mediation Model (HMM).

These two analyses supported Lake's five-factor solution for the NWI items in conjunction with the three-factor MBI-HSS, with one cross loading of MBI-12 (I feel energetic) on exhaustion as well as its defined loading on personal accomplishment (Leiter and Laschinger, 2005). The analysis identified 10 correlated errors between pairs of items within the MBI-HSS factors and seven correlated errors between pairs of items within the NWI-Lake factors.

Model Testing

The hypothesized model was tested with EQS (Bentler and Chou, 1987). The analysis investigated the factor structure of the 28 items from the Nursing Work Index according to the five factors identified by Lake (2002). The 22 MBI-HSS items were assigned to their respective factors of emotional exhaustion, depersonalization, and personal accomplishment. The CFA confirmed the single factor structures of the two job satisfaction items.

Whereas some items showed a moderate kurtosis, the analysis used the robust analysis option of EQS which corrects for multivariate kurtosis (Byrne, 1994). The following section reports the robust statistics for Chi Square (Satorra-Bentler Scaled Statistics, Satorra and Bentler, 1988), the Bentler-Bonett Non-normed Fit Index (BBNNFI) (1980), Comparative Fit Index (CFI), and Root Mean-Square Error of Approximation (RMSEA).

The SEM analysis is presented in Figure 2. The Hypothesized Mediation Model made a significant improvement over the Independence Model that specified no factor loadings ($\chi^2_{1326\ df}$ = 166,946.22, p < .001). Including the pathways through burnout as specified in the HMM improved the fit significantly ($Dif\chi^2_{83\ df}$ = 150,168.93, p < .001) to the criterion level of CFI >= .900 ($\chi^2_{1243\ df}$ =16,777.29, CFI=.906, IFI=.906, RMSEA=.038). In Hypothesized Mediation Model all coefficients were significant (See Figure 2).

The standardized direct and indirect effects information from the SEM indicates the extent to which burnout mediates the relationships of worklife indicators with job satisfaction. As evident in Table 1, all five NWI factors are significantly correlated with job satisfaction ranging from .28 to .34. The HMM predicts that burnout mediates these relationships.

To examine mediation, we examined a Direct Effects Model (DEM) that supplemented the Hypothesized Mediation Model (HMM) with five paths: one from each NWI factor to job satisfaction.

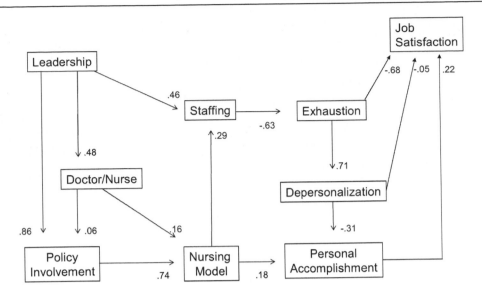

Figure 2. Final Model with SEM Parameter Estimates.

Adding these five paths had little impact on the explained variance for job satisfaction: the Direct Effects Model (DEM) explained 57% of the variance in job satisfaction in contrast with the Hypothesized Mediation Model (HMM) that explained 56% of the variance. As indicated in Table 2, the only predictor for which there is a major increase in total effects is leadership for which total effects increase from .33 (HMM) to .52 (DEM). The total effects for nurse/physician relationship increased from .03 to .10 in the DEM. This pattern suggests that the influence of nurse/physician relationship with job satisfaction is independent of its shared relationship with burnout. Overall, the DEM ($\chi^2_{1238\ df}$ =16,356.92, CFI=.909, IFI=.909, RMSEA=.038) improved the fit significantly over the HMM (Difference $\chi^2_{1238\ df.}$ =420.37, p < .001). The change in chi square is large relative to the modest increase in the explained variance in job satisfaction. This may reflect the power inherent in the very large sample size in this analysis. The chi square statistic is very sensitive to large sample sizes (Kline, 1998).

Table 2. Tests of Mediation by Burnout

	Correlation with Job Satisfaction	HMM Total Effects	DEM Total Effects	DEM Indirect Effects
Staffing	.34	.44	.39	.34
Nurse/Physician Relationship	.28	.03	.10	.02
Leadership	.34	.33	.52	.13
Policy Involvement	.30	.12	.11	.12
Nursing Model	.30	.17	.16	.14

Limitations

The findings of this study must be viewed with caution given the cross-sectional nature of the design, which precludes strong statements on causality. Longitudinal analyses would allow us to examine the dynamic nature of work by measuring changes in perceptions of working conditions over time and the impact of these conditions on nurse and patient outcomes. Replication of the study in other samples of staff nurses is needed to validate the current findings.

DISCUSSION

The analysis presented here extends the Nursing Worklife Model to encompass nurses' satisfaction with their jobs and their profession. The Nursing Worklife Model includes specific elements that are central to nurses' experience of their worklife; it structures these elements in a way that conveys an integrated perspective on worklife. Nurses do not experience various elements of worklife as independent experiences, but make sense of their professional practice environment through a coherent framework with clear relationships among these elements. The analysis confirms as well routes through which worklife experiences connect with job burnout and ultimately to job satisfaction. The model has implications for health care management as well as for future research.

Confirmation of burnout's mediating role is consistent with its central role in translating worklife experiences into performance and well-being. This quality is critical in that it describes a process through which qualities of worklife may influence performance. This process has implications for developing theory by emphasizing the importance of assessing and examining subjective experience at work. It has practical implications by emphasizing the importance of employees' personal evaluation of workplace initiatives. It is not sufficient for management to change problematic areas of worklife, but to do so in a way that assures the awareness, active involvement, and support of employees. The analysis demonstrated a substantial mediating relationship for two of the NWI factors: policy involvement, and nursing model of care. The contrast between the direct and indirect effects model supported a mediating relationship for leadership. The strongest evidence for mediation was for staffing, a measure that could serve as a proxy for workload. Other research has demonstrated that exhaustion mediates the relationship of worklife with outcome variables (Leiter, 2005; Leiter and Maslach, 2004; Leiter and Shaughnessy, 2006). Apparently, staffing encompasses this quality of nurses' evaluation of their work environment.

This latter point reflects the complex quality of the burnout construct. Although it does encompass aspects of job stress, such as chronic exhaustion, the three-part operationalization in the MBI reflects qualities of motivation, values, and meaningfulness as well. For example, nurses' evaluation of staffing does not reflect simply the demands of additional workload resulting for inadequate personnel, but their evaluation of their employers' commitment to quality of services, patient safety, and employee health. These evaluations have potential implications for job satisfaction beyond the impact of additional workload on nurses' energy levels. However, it suggests that the Nursing Worklife Model could be enhanced by a direct measure of experienced workload.

The Nursing Worklife Model provides a perspective on hospital-based nursing that is consistent with that provided by the Areas of Worklife model (Leiter and Maslach, 2004; Maslach and Leiter, 1997). This model includes workload; as well as five other qualities: control, reward, community, fairness, and values. The magnet hospital factors provide a specific focus on a nursing model of care, a core value concern for nurses and staffing levels provide an index of hospitals' realization of these values in action. Nurse/physician relationships are an essential aspect of hospital-based nurses' social environment at work. Policy involvement reflects control at both the unit and the broad institutional levels. Nursing leadership, Lake's fifth factor, encompasses another aspect of nurses' social environment or sense of community in their work setting. The NWI-PES provides a focused perspective on issues pertaining to hospital-based nursing while the AWS pertains to a broad range of work settings with additional consideration of organizational justice and workload.

Implications for Health Care Administrators

The model draws attention to the importance of nursing leadership in creating supportive professional practice work environments in nursing and the need to develop effective nurse leaders to ensure that nurses feel confident and satisfied with their work and that patients receive the quality of care they deserve. Nursing leadership plays an important role in providing the direction and infrastructure to empower nurses to practice professionally and thus deliver high quality care (Clifford, 1998). Reductions in management staff because of restructuring initiatives over the past decade, however, have hindered nurse leaders' ability to lead, given significantly expanded spans of control that have reduced their visibility to staff and availability for mentoring and support (Canadian Nursing Advisory Committee, 2002; Norrish and Rundall, 2001; Walston, Burns, and Kimberly, 2000). Our results so far suggest that this situation must change to prevent nurse burnout and job dissatisfaction and reduce the patient care quality.

Hospital restructuring in the 1990's that brought a significant reduction of the nursing workforce has had a major impact on nurses' work. Although nurses have responded positively to these conditions by increasing their efforts to maintain high quality patient care with fewer resources, their coping resources have been severely compromised. Burnout is the result of accumulated exposure to stressful working conditions and recent research studies have revealed high levels of nurse burnout suggesting that a decade of restructuring may be taking its toll. According to Maslach and Leiter's norms, nurses in two recent studies were experiencing high levels of burnout (Cho et al., 2006; Greco et al., 2006). In Cho et al.'s (2006) study of new graduate nurses, 64% of the sample reported severe levels of burnout, a particularly disturbing result given the current severe nursing shortage. In the Greco et al. (2006) study, 58% of a more general sample of hospital nurses also reported severe levels of burnout. In both studies, nurse burnout was strongly related to the degree of fit between personal expectations and the six areas of worklife described by Leiter and Maslach (2004) as precursors to burnout/engagement. Advanced burnout have been linked to poor physical (Hallman, Thomson, Burell, Lisspers, and Setterlind, 2003; Shirom, 2003) and mental health among employees (Lee and Ashforth, 1996; Schaufeli, Bakker, Hoogduin, Schaap, and Klader, 2001). Nurses whose health is threatened are less likely to provide high quality of care. Early research testing the Leiter and Laschinger (2006) Nursing Worklife Model linking nursing professional practice environment conditions to adverse patient events through the mediating mechanisms of burnout support this contention.

In conclusion, early results of studies testing the Nursing Worklife Model suggest that characteristics of professional nursing work environments described in the magnet hospital research play an important role in the quality of nurses' worklife and are related to nurses' job satisfaction. Furthermore, these conditions are also related to patient outcomes such as frequency of adverse events and nurses perceptions of quality, and burnout appears to be a key mediating process through which work environments affect these outcomes. Our results suggest that nurse administrators may find the Nursing Worklife Model useful in designing strategies to create work environments that allow nurses to practice according to professional standards, thereby increasing work satisfaction, preventing burnout, and ensuring that patients are provided with effective high quality care.

REFERENCES

Aiken, L. H., Clarke, S. P., Sloane, D. M., Sochalski, J. A., Busse, R., Clarke, H. et al. (2001). Nurses' reports on hospital care in five countries: The ways in which nurses' work is structured have left nurses among the least satisfied nurses, and the problem is getting worse. *Health Affairs, 20*, 43-53.

Aiken, L.H., Clarke, S.P., Sloane, D.M., Sochalski, J., and Silber, J. H. (2002). Hospital nurse staffing and patient mortality, nurse burnout, and job dissatisfaction. *Journal of the American Medical Association, 288,* 1987-1993.

Aiken, L. H., and Patrician, P. A. (2000). Measuring organizational traits of hospitals: The revised nursing work index. *Nursing Research, 49(3),* 146-153.

Aiken, L. H., Smith, H. L., and Lake, E. T. (1994). Lower medicare mortality among a set of hospitals known for good nursing care. *Medical Care, 32,* 771-787.

Alexander, J. A. (1982). *Nursing unit organization: Its effects on staff professionalism.* Ann Arbor, MI: UMI Research Press.

Bakker, A. B., Killmer, C. H., Siegrist, J., Schaufeli, W. B. (2000). Effort-reward imbalance and burnout among nurses. *Journal of Advanced Nursing, 31,* 884-891.

Bentler, P.M., and Bonnet D.G. (1980). Significance tests and goodness of fit in the analysis of covariance structures. *Psychological Bulletin, 88,* 588-606.

Bentler, P. M., and Chou, C. P. (1987). Practical issues in structural modeling. *Sociological Methods and Research, 16(1),* 78-117.

Byrne, B. M. (1994). *Structural equation modeling with EQS and EQS/windows: Basic concepts, applications, and programs.* Thousand Oaks, CA: Sage Publications.

Canadian Nursing Advisory Committee. (2002). *Our health, our future: Creating Quality workplaces for Canadian Nurses.* Ottawa, ON: Advisory Committee on Health Human Resources.

Cho, J., Laschinger, H. K., and Wong, C. (2006). Workplace empowerment, work engagement, and organizational commitment of new graduate nurses. *Nursing Leadership, 19(3),* 43-60.

Clifford, J. C. (1998). *Restructuring: The impact of hospital organization on nursing leadership.* San Francisco, CA: Jossey-Bass.

Clarke, H., Laschinger, H. K. S., Giovanetti, P., Shamian, J., Thomson, D., and Tourangeau, A. (2001). Nursing shortages: Workplace environments are essential to the solution. *Hospital Quarterly, 4*(4), 50-57.

Dillman, D. A. (2000). *Mail and internet surveys: The tailored design method (2nd ed.).* New York: John Wiley and Sons.

Greco, P., Laschinger, H. K., and Wong, C. (2006). Leader empowering behaviours, staff nurse empowerment, and work engagement/burnout. *Nursing Leadership, 19(4),* 41-56.

Halbesleben, J. R. B., and Bowler, W. M. (2007). Emotional exhaustion and job performance: The mediating role of motivation. *Journal of Applied Psychology, 92,* 93-106.

Hallman, T., Thomson, H., Burell, G., Lisspers, J., and Setterlind, S. (2003). Stress, burnout and coping: Differences between women with coronary heart disease and healthy matched women. *Journal of Health Psychology, 8,* 433-445.

Institute of Medicine. (2004). *Keeping patients safe: Transforming the work environment of nurses.* Washington, DC: Author.

Kazanjian, A., Green, C., Wong, J., Reid, R. (2005). Effect of the hospital nursing environment on patient mortality: a systematic review. *Journal of Health Services Research Policy, 10*(2), 111–117.

Kline, R. B. (1998). *Principles and practice of structural equation modeling.* New York: Guilford Press.

Lake, E. T., (2002). Development of the practice environment scale of the nursing work index. *Research in Nursing and Health, 25,* 176-188.

Laschinger, H. K., and Leiter, M. P. (2006). The impact of nursing work environments on patient safety outcomes: The mediating role of burnout engagement. *Journal of Nursing Administration, 36,* 259-267.

Lee, R. T., and Ashforth, B. E. (1996). A meta-analytic examination of the correlates of the three dimensions of job burnout. *Journal of Applied Psychology, 81,* 123-133.

Leiter, M. P. (1993). Burnout as a developmental process: Consideration of models. In W. B. Schaufeli, C. Maslach, and T. Marek (Eds), *Professional burnout: Recent developments in theory and research* (pp. 237-250). Washington: Taylor and Francis.

Leiter, M. P. (2005). Perception of risk: An organizational model of burnout, stress symptoms, and occupational risk. *Anxiety, Stress, and Coping, 18,* 131-144.

Leiter, M. P., Harvie, P., and Frizzell, C. (1998). The correspondence of patient satisfaction and nurse burnout. *Social Science and Medicine, 47,* 1611-1617.

Leiter, M. P., and Laschinger, H. K. S. (2005, June). *Demands and values: Implications for nurses' occupational health.* Presentation at the First Canadian Conference for Research on Mental Health in the Workplace. Montreal, Quebec.

Leiter, M. P., and Laschinger, H. K. S. (2006). Relationships of work and practice environment to professional burnout: Testing a causal model. *Nursing Research, 55,* 137-146.

Leiter, M. P., and Maslach, C. (2004). Areas of worklife: A structured approach to organizational predictors of job burnout. In C. Cooper (Ed.), *Handbook of stress medicine and health (2nd ed.)* (pp. 173-192). London: CRC Press.

Leiter, M. P., and Shaughnessy, K. (2006). The areas of worklife model of burnout: Tests of mediation relationships. *Ergonomia: An International Journal, 28,* 327-341.

Manojlovich, M., and Laschinger, H. K. (2007). The nursing worklife model: Extending and refining a new theory. *Journal of Nursing Management, 15,* 256-253.

Maslach, C., and Leiter, M. P. (1997). *The truth about burnout.* (3rd ed.). San Francisco, CA: Jossey-Bass.

Maslach, C., Jackson, S. E., and Leiter, M. P. (1996). *The Maslach Burnout Inventory.* (3rd ed.). Palo Alto, CA: Consulting Psychologists Press.

Maslach, C., Schaufeli, W. B., and Leiter, M. P. (2001). Job burnout. *Annual Review of Psychology, 52,* 397-422.

McGillis Hall, L., Doran, D., Baker, G., Pink, G. H., Sidani, S., O'Brien-Pallas, L., and Donner, G. (2003). Nurse staffing models as predictors of patient outcomes. *Medical Care, 41,* 1069-1109.

Norrish, B. R, and Rundall, T. G. (2001). Hospital restructuring and the work of registered nurses. *The Millbank Quarterly, 79*(1), 55-79.

Robinson, S. E., Roth, S. L., Keim, J., Levenson, M., Flentje, J. R., and Basher, K. (1991). Nurse burnout: Work related and demographic factors as culprits. *Research in Nursing and Health, 14,* 223-228.

Satorra, A., and Bentler, P. M. (1988). Scaling corrections for chi-square statistics in covariance structure analysis. *American Statistical Association 1988 Proceedings of the Business and Economics Sections* (pp. 308-313). Alexandria, VA: American Statistical Association.

Schaufeli, W. B., Bakker, A. B., Hoogduin, K., Schaap, C., and Klader, A. (2001). On the clinical validity of the Maslach Burnout Inventory and the Burnout Measure. *Psychology and Health, 16,* 565-582.

Schaufeli, W. B., and Enzmann, D. (1998). *The burnout companion to study and practice: A critical analysis.* London: Taylor and Francis.

Shirom, A. (2003). The effects of work-related stress on health. In M. J. Schabracq, J. A. M. Winnbust, and C. L. Cooper (Eds.), *Handbook of work and health psychology* (2nd ed., pp. 63-83). New York: Wiley.

Sims, J. (1997). Focus on the future. *Journal of Nursing Management, 4(4),* 20-21.

Tourangeau, A. E., Giovanetti, P., Tu, J. V., and Wood, M. (2002). Nursing-related determinants of 30-day mortality for hospitalized patients. *Canadian Journal of Nursing Research 33(4),* 71-88.

Vahey, D. C., Aiken, L.H., Sloane, D. M., Clarke, S. P., and Vargas, D. (2004). Nurse burnout and patient satisfaction. *Medical Care, 42*(2), 11-66.

Walston, S. L., Burns, L. R., and Kimberley, J. R. (2000). Does reengineering really work? An examination of the context and outcomes of reengineering initiatives. *Health Services Research, 34,* 1363-1368.

In: Handbook of Stress and Burnout in Health Care
Editor: Jonathon R. B. Halbesleben
ISBN 978-1-60456-500-3
© 2008 Nova Science Publishers, Inc.

Chapter 4

BURNOUT IN HEALTH CARE: WHEN HELPING HURTS

*Denise M. Breaux[*1], James A. Meurs[2], Kelly L. Zellars[2] and Pamela L. Perrewé[3]*

[1]Florida State University
[2]University of North Carolina, Charlotte
[3]Florida State University

Results from a recent consumer survey on hospitalization and health care in five countries, including the United States, uncovered considerable public dissatisfaction with the quality and availability of health care. Conducted in response to widespread dissatisfaction with the health system and its impact on hospital care, the study found that 18% of United States and United Kingdom health care recipients and 28% of Canadian patients described their most recent hospitalization experience as fair or poor (Aiken, Clarke, and Sloane, 2002).

Research on the general nature of health care offers considerable insight into the highly stressful nature of this type of work, implicating psychologically demanding working conditions as a major source of the public's dissatisfaction with the current health care system. As evidenced by consumer reports and increasingly negative media coverage, creating organizational environments that allow health care professionals to deliver high quality care should be a top priority. Our job as researchers is to further uncover and understand the critical aspects of these work environments that must be altered and/or developed in order to improve the overall quality of and satisfaction with the health care industry.

Many scholars believe that the strong interpersonal nature of most jobs in the health care industry is a key contributor to the experience of a specific result of workplace stress known as burnout. Furthermore, the effects of burnout on health care workers may be a critical factor contributing to widespread consumer dissatisfaction with the health care system.

---

[*] Correspondence should be addressed to: Denise M. Breaux, The College of Business Florida State University, Tallahassee, FL 32306-1110, dmb06f@fsu.edu. Phone: 850-644-5505. Fax: 850-644-7843

In the following chapter, we offer a detailed explanation of the burnout phenomenon and its precursors and consequences. We then concentrate on burnout as experienced by those in the health care industry and offer specific recommendations for improving the quality of health care through a reduction of burnout in these demanding work environments.

EXAMINING THE BURNOUT CONSTRUCT

Herbert Freudenberger coined the term *burnout* in 1974 while observing fellow volunteers in an alternative care setting (Janssen, Schaufeli, and Houkes, 1999). He described these workers as displaying increased emotional depletion, motivation loss, and lack of commitment to the task. His observations sparked an interest in a stress phenomenon that continues to fascinate many scholars to this day. Subsequent research has labeled burnout as a chronic affective pattern of responses to stressful workplace conditions that involve significant amounts of interpersonal contact (Cordes and Dougherty, 1993). In other words, burnout represents a type of strain experienced most intensely by individuals involved in "people work." The most popular definition of burnout is Maslach and Jackson's (1981) three-part approach. The three components of this description of burnout are emotional exhaustion, depersonalization, and diminished personal accomplishment, and they represent the characteristic reactions to long-term stressful or demanding work environments.

Emotional exhaustion is characterized by energy loss and the feeling that your emotional resources have been depleted. Employees experiencing emotional exhaustion may become increasingly frustrated as they feel less able to care for patients or clients. These fatigued workers generally believe that their emotional resources have been completely depleted. Depersonalization is marked by objectification, emotional detachment, and cynicism toward patients, clients, and others in the organization. Extensive use of jargon, derogatory language, and withdrawal through extended breaks are all symptoms of depersonalization. The final component of burnout, diminished personal accomplishment, is characterized by an increase in negative self-evaluations. Employees may begin to feel less competent at work regarding their achievements and interpersonal relations, viewing their own skills and abilities as insufficient for successfully performing their jobs. These three components of burnout (i.e., emotional exhaustion, depersonalization, and diminished personal accomplishment) comprise the Maslach Burnout Inventory (MBI), the instrument used to develop the majority of our current burnout knowledge.

Antecedents of Burnout

The factors that contribute to burnout range from issues concerning the organizational context to personal characteristics. The antecedents of burnout can be placed into four general categories including organizational/departmental characteristics, job/role characteristics, interpersonal relationships, and personal characteristics.

Organizational and departmental characteristics. Cordes and Dougherty (1993) argued that various aspects of the organization and/or specific department in which the employee works can contribute to the experience of burnout. For example, contingency and non-contingency of organizational outcomes, or the extent to which the organization links rewards and punishments to specific performance objectives, may affect the likelihood of experiencing burnout. Therefore, employees who perceive no viable link between their performance and subsequent instances of reward or penalty may experience increased levels of burnout in response to the ambiguity.

The organizational context, characterized by factors such as the work shift and psychological environment, also has been linked to the burnout phenomenon (Cordes and Dougherty, 1993). Mansfield, Yu, McCool, Vicary, and Packard (1989) developed an index of three dimensions of nursing work including general pressure/uncertainty, routinization of tasks, and coworker interdependence. These researchers suggested that educators and administrators use the index to help match students to areas of expertise that provide the best match between the individual and the specific job context, because a mismatch between person and context may result in increased levels of burnout.

Job and role characteristics. The job-related roles of employees also can enhance feelings of stress. Research as early as the 1960s and 1970s demonstrated that the stressors of role conflict, role ambiguity, and role overload (e.g., Kahn, 1978; Kahn et al., 1964) can all contribute to the burnout experience. Role conflict occurs when employees' expectations are incongruent with those expressed by the persons who prescribe their role. Communication by those in authority of work expectations that are largely incompatible with those understood and internalized by employees may increase the likelihood of burnout. Role ambiguity is related to the amount of predictability in the work environment, thus, burnout is thought to be more prevalent in situations where employees are uncertain about their work goals and the means available for accomplishing them. Role overload, both qualitative and quantitative, can contribute to feelings of burnout. Workers may experience qualitative overload if they feel deficient in the basic skills necessary for effective task completion. Quantitative overload is characterized by the belief that one's work cannot be completed in the time allotted. Employees may experience burnout if they believe that they cannot successfully complete their work due to lack of skill, lack of time, or both.

Interpersonal relationships. Employees require specific job resources in order to successfully navigate stressful work environments while maintaining their psychological well-being. Consequently, the absence of such resources can contribute to the experience of burnout in the workplace. To date, social support has attracted the most extensive amount of investigation in the interpersonal domain of burnout literature, and findings consistently support the idea that a lack of support from coworkers and supervisors is highly associated with increases in burnout (Maslach, Schaufeli, and Leiter, 2001). Work environments that fail to support emotional exchange and active assistance may exacerbate burnout symptoms by isolating employees from each other and discouraging socially supportive relationships. Workplaces characterized by conflict, frustration, and hostility may have the same effect.

Personal characteristics. Although various aspects of the external environment play a critical role in the experience of burnout, specific personal characteristics make some individuals more likely to exhibit burnout symptoms than others in the same environment. For example, younger employees consistently report higher levels of burnout (Anderson and Iwanicki, 1984; Maslach and Jackson, 1981). Some researchers suggest that older employees experience lower levels of burnout because their experience has provided the insight to shift the unmet job expectations they had in the past to more closely fit their present situation (Cordes and Dougherty, 1993). These findings suggest that older, more experienced employees are better able to handle the demands of stressful work environments. Alternatively, they may handle stressful environments by altering their perceptions and reducing their expectations of what is possible in terms of career accomplishment or satisfaction. Moreover, not achieving high expectations can encourage increased levels of burnout (Cordes and Dougherty, 1993). Younger employees tend to be more idealistic and thus may react more intensely when their overly optimistic career expectations are shattered.

Many researchers have investigated the personality correlates of burnout. The results of studies by both Costa and McCrae (1999) and Mills and Huebner (1998) indicated that neuroticism was related to all three MBI facets of burnout. Conscientiousness and agreeableness were also found to be negatively associated with particular components of burnout, and extraversion was demonstrated to be both positively and negatively related to burnout, depending on the particular facet. Other groups of researchers demonstrated that neuroticism, extraversion, and agreeableness each predicted different components of burnout (Zellars, Perrewé, and Hochwarter, 2000), and that mood explained the relationships that extraversion and neuroticism had with some components of burnout (Zellars, Hochwarter, Perrewé, Hoffman, and Ford, 2004). In a 3 year longitudinal study, Burisch (2002) found that *concurrent* personality characteristics predicted burnout, but that changes over time in a person's level of burnout were not associated with personality.

More recently, Cano-García, Padilla-Muñoz, and Carrasco-Ortiz (2005) examined the impact of both personality and contextual characteristics on burnout. They found that both personality and certain contexts were important variables in prediction of burnout, but that personality was more strongly related to burnout for 2 of its 3 components than context. Langelaan, Bakker, van Doornen, Schaufeli (2006) demonstrated that neuroticism was the core personality characteristic of burnout, explaining that these emotionally unstable persons could either be more vulnerable to burnout or that their neuroticism may exacerbate the effects of burnout. Lastly, Bakker, Van Der Zee, Lewig, and Dollard (2006) found that personality moderated relationships between the number of negative experiences and burnout. These results support the contention that personality characteristics, rather than constituting an innate tendency to become burned out, act to exacerbate or protect individuals by making some persons better able to adapt to and recover from stressful situations.

A variety of other personal characteristics also can explain why some individuals are more susceptible to burnout. Studies suggest that married people and those with children are less likely to experience burnout (Maslach and Jackson, 1985), possibly due to therapeutic social support received through family members. Employees' own expectations about their chosen professions and organizations may contribute to the burnout experience (Jackson and Schuler, 1983). Career progress is another personal characteristic that has been linked to the experience of burnout. Specifically, those who experience more upward career mobility may be less likely to experience burnout (Cordes and Dougherty, 1993). Several explanations for reduced burnout are also associated with upward career movement, including reduced contact with clients, feelings of positive contribution, and perceptions of procedural justice regarding promotion systems.

Consequences of Burnout

The characteristic symptoms of burnout include lost creativity, reduced commitment to work, estrangement from various job aspects, physical and emotional ailments, improper attitudes toward the self and clients, and a general feeling of being worn out (Cordes and Dougherty, 1993). As employees experience increasing amounts of the burnout components, they may unknowingly enact harm on themselves, coworkers, clients, and/or the organization. For example, researchers have found that workers experiencing burnout are more likely to be absent from work, to display reduced productivity, or to leave the organization entirely (Leiter and Maslach, 1988; Jackson and Maslach, 1982). Decreased organizational commitment (Leiter and Maslach, 1988) and lower overall quality and quantity of job performance (Maslach and Jackson, 1985) also have been associated with employee burnout.

Burnout has further been connected to various mental and physical health problems including emotional liability, cognitive rigidity, interpersonal cynicism (Piedmont, 1993), increased irritability, depression, anxiety, fatigue, and insomnia, decreased self-esteem, and deteriorating social and family interrelations (Zellars et al., 1999; Burke and Deszca, 1986).

Recent work on the consequences of burnout suggests that emotional exhaustion may decrease job performance through its effects on employee motivation (Halbesleben and Bowler, 2007). Specifically, employees experiencing emotional exhaustion seem less motivated by achievement and status, instead choosing to invest their resources in social relationships. In these situations, behaviors aimed at satisfying job performance goals decline.

BURNOUT IN THE HEALTH CARE INDUSTRY

A great deal of burnout research has focused on workers in the health care profession. Health care workers are believed to be more likely to experience burnout because their jobs are characterized by frequent and direct interpersonal interactions with clients. Furthermore, employees with tremendous responsibility for those with disabilities and/or illnesses seem to be particularly susceptible to burnout. Maslach (1978) suggested that these workers spend a great deal of time concerned with other people's problems and therefore may internalize responsibility for their clients' future health. Because health care workers are particularly prone to the harmful effects of job burnout, we will devote the next few pages to exploring some of the occupations, referred to as "helping professions," that are most likely to have burnout-provoking conditions.

Helping Professions

According to recent research, there is a growing concern within the medical community regarding health care professionals' increased risk for burnout and its effects on the sustainability of the current health care system (Spickard, Gabbe, and Christensen, 2002). Individuals involved in these "helping professions" include physicians, nurses, dentists, those caring for the terminally ill, emergency services personnel, and other health care professionals (Felton, 1998).

Physicians. The Hippocratic Oath traditionally taken by physicians includes a promise to help the sick and to avoid causing unnecessary harm. Physicians spend their lives in pursuit of helping people who are sick and in pain, often in the face of extensive demands on their own time, energy, and mental health. Their jobs are characterized by heavy workloads, life and death decisions, on-call duty, and little time without the possibility of interruptions at work and in the home. Also contributing to their stressful experience is the constant threat of malpractice suits and the exorbitant costs associated with necessary protective insurance—factors that may seem even more frightening when considering that symptoms of burnout have been found to increase physician error (Spickard et al., 2002).

Many physicians have expressed that they would choose another career if they were able to start over and would encourage their children to make different career choices (Felton, 1998). This may be due in large part to the constant onslaught of burnout symptoms commonly experienced by these professionals. Maslach and Leiter (1997) described the excessive demands of caring for the sick combined with inadequate organizational resources (e.g., a shortage of nurses) confronted by physicians as "an erosion of the soul" (p.17). Furthermore, burnout symptoms such as cognitive rigidity, fatigue, and reduced productivity can cause physician errors that may result in deadly human costs.

The tremendous emotional, financial, and human investments associated with physicians' work environments, coupled with the constant contact with ailing patients make it easy to understand why physicians are particularly susceptible to job burnout. However, physicians are not the only workers who experience high levels of burnout in health care settings, because other employees, such as nurses, may spend as much or more time dealing with the sick.

Nurses. Nursing jobs are characterized by constant exposure to sickness and death. Nurses also must assume substantial amounts of responsibility in dispensing potentially life-saving/life-threatening medications to the correct patients at proper times and in precise doses. Additionally, the increasing popularity of shorter work-weeks with extended shift hours means that many nurses are tending to several patients simultaneously for 12 or more hours at a time. Such long shifts coupled with the excessive patient loads faced by many nurses make this profession a breeding ground for the symptoms of burnout.

In a job concerned so centrally with helping others, many nurses are overwhelmed when they discover just how thankless their profession can be. Demanding patients are often heavily medicated or are for some other reason unable to communicate feelings of gratitude to their caretakers. Moreover, the terminal nature of many patients' ailments may promote feelings of helplessness in the nurses providing care. Finally, the current global nursing shortage may provide an additional source of stress for those left to take up the slack.

Dentists. Although not normally exposed to pervasive life and death situations, dentists spend countless hours performing intricate work in uncomfortable positions on patients who are typically unhappy with the situation. Indeed, Felton (1998) found that unsatisfactory interactions with patients, poor posture, and problems with the physical environment all made burnout a significant threat to receiving satisfactory dental care, and Freese (1987) suggested that dentistry was among the most stressful of all occupations.

Health care providers for the terminally ill. Caring for terminally ill patients introduces another layer of stressors into the work environments of many health care professionals. Patients with illnesses such as AIDS and terminal cancer are often depressed due to their grim prognoses and it is understandable that they may not express gratitude to their caretakers.

Furthermore, many of these patients require constant medical attention, and have little expectation of improvement or full recovery. Felton (1998) found that those caring for AIDS patients experienced intense feelings of futility, fatigue, anxiety, and withdrawal. Consequently, caring for the terminally ill involves sizeable investments of time and physical and emotional energy with little possibility for reward in the form of hope or gratitude.

Emergency services personnel. Health care professionals confronting emergency services are continuously exposed to intensely emotional, high-risk, life-threatening situations, which they must respond to with great speed and accuracy. In addition, these workers are at increased risk for infectious diseases due to the time constraints and less than desirable conditions often characteristic of their job. A study of over 100 emergency medical technician union members found that these individuals often exhibit depersonalization, one of the three components of burnout, through the use of inappropriate and morbid humor relating to the barrage of trauma, death, and illness they encounter on a daily basis (Felton, 1998).

Mental health professionals. Aside from those listed above, numerous other individuals in health care settings are prone to experiencing burnout. Mental health workers, for example, must worry about the possibility of violent patient attacks. Nursing home workers are susceptible to burnout due to the high rate of resident deaths. Others affected are physical rehabilitation workers, occupational therapists, and those working with sick infants and children.

Coping Mechanisms

Various coping mechanisms have been suggested to provide relief from the experience of burnout that plagues health care professionals. Among these are social support, some forms of control, and political skill.

Social support. Employees in health care settings may rely on socially supportive colleagues to ease the negative effects of their stressful work environments. Indeed, researchers have found a direct effect between increases in felt social support from coworkers or supervisors and decreased levels of burnout in hospital environments (Constable and Russell, 1986). Also, support can act as a buffer between stressors in the work environment and their potentially harmful effects by helping individuals to *perceive* their situations as less threatening (Cohen and Wills, 1985). A recent study on burnout and its effects on job performance suggest that employees experiencing emotional exhaustion invest most of their motivational resources in socially supportive relationships rather than work performance to ensure continued support in future stressful situations (Halbesleben and Bowler, 2007).

Zellars and Perrewé (2001) defined emotional social support to include activities such as talking, listening, expressing concern, and empathizing with distressed individuals. The researchers stressed the importance of the content of emotionally supportive conversations, suggesting that supportive exchanges with either a positive or empathetic focus may ward off the experience of burnout. Workers engaging in "gripe sessions," however, typically experience greater levels of burnout.

Control. Decades of research have produced general agreement that a sense of control is an important predictor of physical and psychological health (Brim, 1974; Bandura, 1989; Fiske and Taylor, 1991). Individuals in demanding situations who perceive high amounts of control exhibit proactive behaviors such as planning, strategizing, information seeking, and direct action; conversely, those perceiving low amounts of control become confused, escapist, passive, and pessimistic (Skinner and Wellborn, 1994).

In order for health care workers to internalize deep commitment to and responsibility for important outcomes, they must feel that they have sufficient capacity to produce results. Those who perceive inadequate control or authority over the resources necessary to perform their jobs may experience a sense of crisis that eventually manifests as burnout. Researchers have suggested that a sustainable workload, sense of choice, appropriate recognition and reward systems, supportive community, fairness and justice, and meaningful work all contribute to a reduction in burnout (Maslach, Shaufeli, and Leiter, 2001).

Political skill. Political skill refers to "an interpersonal style construct that combines social astuteness with the ability to relate well, and otherwise demonstrate situationally appropriate behavior in a disarmingly charming and engaging manner that inspires confidence, trust, sincerity, and genuineness" (Ferris, Perrewé, Anthony, and Gilmore, 2000, p. 30). Ferris and colleagues (1999; Ferris, Perrewé, Brouer, Lux, Treadway, and Douglas, 2007) suggested that politically skilled individuals perceive a strong sense of control over and understanding of others at work and possess the tactics necessary to produce the results they desire. Also, those with political skill have a network of carefully-developed relationships with individuals used to enhance reputation, inspire trust and confidence in their coworkers, and effectively leverage social connections (Ferris et al., 2007; Perrewé et al., 2000). These increased feelings of confidence, control, and social power explain why those with political skill experience less anxiety and stress in the workplace (Perrewé et al., 2000; Perrewé, Zellars, Rossi, Ferris, Kacmar, Liu, Zinko, and Hochwarter, 2005; Zellars, Perrewé, Rossi, Tepper, and Ferris, in press). Therefore, health care workers with well-developed political skill may be able to attenuate the harmful effects of their stress-inducing work environments.

Implications for the Health Profession

The harmful and deleterious effects associated with the experience of burnout in the health care profession highlight the need for both mechanisms to prevent burnout and those to ease the effects of burnout once it has been experienced. Suggested mechanisms include reducing demands and increasing resources for workers, interventions, feedback, enhanced quality of social relations, and knowledge distribution.

Health care organizations seeking to prevent or decrease the occurrence of employee burnout may find it beneficial to assess the particular demands faced by employees and the specific resources available to them. Because unrealistic job expectations can increase the likelihood of experiencing burnout, this knowledge may be used to develop realistic job previews that would enhance knowledge of and adjustment to the demanding health care work environment (Wanous, 1992). Although health care professionals can expect to experience demanding situations, excessive demands can be quite harmful. Recent research suggests that managers carefully assess the strengths and weaknesses of their departments and use this information to reduce job demands and increase important job resources to diminish the risk for burnout (Bakker, Demerouti, and Verbeke, 2004).

If the experience of employee burnout has become pervasive and institutionalized, health care organizations may seek outside help from intervention agents such as burnout researchers. One intervention approach, referred to as action research, has organization members carefully reflect on their specific concerns before collaborating with intervention agents to develop and test potential solutions to their problems (McNiff, 2000; Reason and Bradbury, 2001). This approach found success in a recent effort to reduce burnout symptoms of the members of a federal fire department, where a follow-up assessment conducted one year after the intervention showed decreased burnout levels and increased positive changes in the department (Halbesleben, Osburn, and Mumford, 2006).The benefits realized from interventions may arise more from their collaborative, tailored nature than from any specific solutions that result (Halbesleben and Buckley, 2004). Because the interventions are interactive and personalized, managers learn to facilitate their own action research in the future as new problems arise (Halbesleben et al., 2006).

The use of enhanced organizational feedback mechanisms may provide another means for reducing the negative effects of a burnout-inducing health care environment. Periodic meetings where supervisors provide positive feedback to employees may be particularly important in health care occupations, as the fast-paced nature of daily activities often precludes the opportunity to focus on anything but the negative outcomes of employee actions. Zellars and colleagues (1999) suggested that, in situations where especially negative outcomes (such as death) are unavoidable, supervisors should provide regular feedback clarifying the employees' roles and emphasize that patient outcomes are largely beyond employee control.

The quality of social relations is an important factor in the functioning of any organization. However, a supportive social environment may be particularly important in health care situations where the psychological well-being of employees is frequently tested. Researchers have suggested that, in general, increases in social support from colleagues and supervisors can reduce and prevent the experience of burnout (Janssen, de Jonge, and Bakker, 1999; Deelstra et al., 2003). Furthermore, patients who received care from units characterized by good administrative support for nurses and positive relations between nurses and doctors reported higher satisfaction with their care than other patients, and their nurses reported significantly lower levels of burnout (Vahey, Aiken, Sloane, Clarke, and Vargas, 2004). The formation of support groups for affected workers may be an important and simple mechanism organizations can introduce to protect their employees from the negative effects of burnout.

Finally, knowledge can be an important weapon in the battle against excessive burnout, and information promoting an awareness of the causes and consequences of burnout may help employees cope more effectively with their situations. Training seminars conducted to distribute burnout-related knowledge are fundamental components of policies that aim to improve the overall quality of health services (Quattrin et al., 2006).

CONCLUSION

The highly stressful and decidedly interpersonal nature of the health care profession makes employees exceptionally vulnerable to the experience of job-related burnout and its harmful physical, psychological, and organizational effects. Characteristics of the organization, job, individual, and interpersonal relationships may contribute to or detract from the levels of burnout employees ultimately experience. Furthermore, social support, feelings of control, and political skill are several ways of coping that may lessen the effects of burnout in health care workers. Additional international research and the development and refinement of new and existing burnout measures will enable a more complete understanding of this phenomenon and will allow the health care industry to better prepare for and cope with burnout's effects on patients, employees, and organizations.

REFERENCES

Aiken, L. H., Clarke, S. P., and Sloane, D. M. (2002). Hospital staffing, organization, and quality of care: Cross-national findings. *Nursing Outlook, September/October*, 187-194.

Anderson, M. B. G., and Iwanicki, E. F. (1984). Teacher motivation and its relationship to burnout. *Educational Administration Quarterly, 20*, 109-132.

Bakker, A. B., Demerouti, E., DeBoer, E., and Schaufeli, W.B. (2003). Job demands and job resources as predictors of absence duration and frequency. *Journal of Vocational Behavior, 62*, 341-356.

Bakker, A. B., Demerouti, E., and Verbeke, W. (2004). Using the job demands-resources model to predict burnout and performance. *Human Resource Management Journal, 43*, 83-104.

Bakker, A.B., Van Der Zee, K.I., Lewig, K.A., and Dollard, M.F. (2006). The relationship between the Big Five personality factors and burnout: A study among volunteer counselors. *The Journal of Social Psychology, 146*, 31-50.

Bandura, A. (1989). Human agency in social cognitive theory. *American Psychologist, 44*, 1175-1184.

Brim, O. G. (1974). *The sense of personal control over one's life*. Invited address presented at the 82nd Annual Convention of the American Psychological Association, New Orleans, LA.

Burisch, M. (2002). A longitudinal study of burnout: The relative importance of dispositions and experiences. *Work and Stress, 16*,1-17.

Burke, R. J., and Deszca, E. (1986). Correlates of psychological burnout phases among police officers. *Human Relations, 39*, 487-502.

Cano-García, F.J., Padilla-Muñoz, E.M., and Carrasco-Ortiz, M.Á. (2005). Personality and contextual variables in teacher burnout. *Personality and Individual Differences, 38*, 929-940.

Cohen, S., and Wills, T. A. (1985). Stress, social support, and the buffering hypothesis. *Psychological Bulletin, 98*, 310-357.

Constable, J. F., and Russell, D. W. (1986). The effect of social support and the work environment upon burnout among nurses. *Journal of Human Stress, Spring*, 20-26.

Cordes, C. L., and Dougherty, T. W. (1993). A review and integration of research on job burnout. *Academy of Management Review, 18*, 621-656.

Costa, P.T., and McCrae, R.R., (1999). Inventario NEO reducido de cinco factores (NEO-FFI). Manual Profesional. Madrid. TEA Ediciones.

Deelstra, J. T., Peeters, M. C. W., Schaufeli, W. B., Stroebe, W., Zijlstra, F. R. H., and van Doornen, L. P. (2003). Receiving instrumental support at work: When help is not welcome. *Journal of Applied Psychology, 88*, 324-331.

Felton, J. S. (1998). Burnout as a clinical entity: Its importance in health care workers. *Occupational Medicine, 48*, 237-250.

Ferris, G. R., Berkson, H. M., Kaplan, D. M., Gilmore, D. C., Buckley, M. R., Hochwarter, W. A., and Witt, L. A. (1999). Development and initial validation of the political skill inventory. Paper presented at the 59th Annual National Meeting of the Academy of Management, Chicago.

Ferris, G. R., Perrewé, P. L., Anthony, W. P., and Gilmore, D. C. (2000). Political skill at work. *Organizational Dynamics, 28*, 25-37.

Ferris, G.R., Perrewé, P.L., Brouer, R.L., Lux, S., Treadway, D.C., and Douglas, C. (2007). Political skill in organizations. *Journal of Management, 33*, 290-320.

Fiske, S. T., and Taylor, S. E. (1991). *Social cognition*. New York: McGraw-Hill.

Freese, A. S. (1987). Dental stress: It can be overcome. *TIC, 46*, 1-3.

Halbesleben, J. R. B., and Bowler, W.M. (2007). Emotional exhaustion and job performance: The mediating role of motivation. *Journal of Applied Psychology, 92*, 93-106.

Halbesleben, J. R. B., and Buckley, M. R. (2004). Burnout in organizational life. *Journal of Management, 30*, 859-879.

Halbesleben, J. R. B., Osburn, H. K., and Mumford, M. D. (2006). Action research as a burnout intervention: Reducing burnout in the federal fire service. *Journal of Applied Behavioral Science, 42*, 244-266.

Jackson, S. E., and Maslach, C. (1982). After-effects of job-related stress: Families as victims. *Journal of Occupational Behaviour, 3*, 63-77.

Jackson, S. E., and Schuler, R. S. (1983). Preventing employee burnout. *Personnel, 60*(2), 58-68.

Janssen, P. P. M., de Jonge, J., and Bakker, A. B. (1999). Specific determinants of intrinsic work motivation, burnout and turnover intentions: A study among nurses. *Journal of Advanced Nursing, 29*, 1360-1369.

Janssen, P. P. M., Schaufeli, W. B., and Houkes, L. (1999). Work-related and individual determinants of the three burnout dimensions. *Work and Stress, 13*, 74-86.

Kahn, R. (1978). Job burnout: Prevention and remedies. *Public Welfare, 36*, 61-63.

Kahn, R., Wolfe, D. M., Quinn, R. P., Snoek, J. D., and Rosenthal, R. A. (1964). *Organizational stress: Studies in role conflict and ambiguity*. New York: Wiley.

Langelaan, S., Bakker, A.B., van Doornen, L.J.P., and Schaufeli, W.B. (2006). Burnout and work engagement: Do individual differences make a difference?. *Personality and Individual Differences, 40*, 521-532.

Leiter, M. P., and Maslach, C. (1988). The impact of interpersonal environment on burnout and organizational commitment. *Journal of Organizational Behavior, 9*, 297-308.

Mansfield, P.K., Yu, L.C., McCool, W., Vicary, J.R., and Packard, J.S. (1989). The job context index: A guide for improving the 'fit' between nurses and their work environment. *Journal of Advanced Nursing, 14*, 501-508.

Maslach, C. (1978). The client role in staff burnout. *Journal of Social Issues, 34*, 111-124.

Maslach, C., and Jackson, S. E. (1981). The measurement of experienced burnout. *Journal of Occupational Behaviour, 2*, 99-113.

Maslach, C., and Jackson, S. E. (1985). The role of sex and family variables in burnout. *Sex Roles, 12*, 837-851.

Maslach, C., and Leiter, M. P. (1997). *The truth about burnout*. San Francisco: Jossey-Bass.

Maslach, C., Schaufeli, W. B., and Leiter, M. P. (2001). Job burnout. *Annual review of Psychology, 52*, 397-422.

McNiff, J. (2000). *Action research in organizations*. London: Routledge.

Mills, L.B., and Huebner, E.S. (1998). A prospective study of personality characteristics, occupational stressors, and burnout among school psychology practitioners. *Journal of School Psychology, 36*, 103-120.

Perrewé, P. L., Ferris, G. R., Frink, D. D., and Anthony, W. P. (2000). Political skill: An antidote for workplace stressors. *Academy of Management Executive, 14*, 115-123.

Perrewé, P.L., Zellars, K.L., Rossi, A.M., Ferris, G.R., Kacmar, C.J., Liu, Y., Zinko, R., and Hochwarter. (2005). Political skill: An antidote in the role overload-strain relationship. *Journal of Occupational Health Psychology, 10*, 239-250.

Piedmont, R. L. (1993). A longitudinal analysis of burnout in the health care setting: The role of personal dispositions. *Journal of Personality Assessment, 67*, 457-473.

Quattrin, R., Zanini, A., Nascig, E., Annunziata, M., Calligaris, L., and Brusaferro, S. (2006). Level of burnout among nurses working in oncology in an Italian region. *Oncology Nursing Forum, 33*, 815-820.

Reason, P., and Bradbury, H. (2001). *The handbook of action research*. London: Sage.

Skinner, E. A., and Wellborn, J. G. (1994). Coping during childhood and adolescence: A motivational perspective. In D. Featherman, R. Lerner and M. Perlmutter (Eds.), *Life-span development and behavior* (pp. 91-133). Hillsdale, NJ: Erlbaum.

Spickard, A., Gabbe, S. G., and Christensen, J. F. (2002). Mid-career burnout in generalist and specialist physicians. *Journal of the American Medical Association, 288*.

Vahey, D. C., Aiken, L. H., Sloane, D. M., Clarke, S. P, and Vargas, D. (2004). Nurse burnout and patient satisfaction. *Medical Care, 24*, 57-66.

Wanous, J. P. (1992). *Organizational Entry*. Reading, MA: Addison-Wesley.

Zellars, K.L., Hochwarter, W.A., Perrewé, P.L., Hoffman, N., and Ford, E.W. (2004). Experiencing job burnout: The roles of positive and negative traits and states. *Journal of Applied Psychology, 34*, 887-911.

Zellars, K. L., and Perrewé, P. L. (2001). Affective personality and the content of emotional social support: Coping in organizations. *Journal of Applied Psychology, 86*, 459-467.

Zellars, K. L., Perrewé, P. L. and Hochwarter, W. A. (1999). Mitigating burnout among high-NA employees in health care: What can organizations do? *Journal of Applied Social Psychology, 29*, 2250-2271.

Zellars, K. L., Perrewé, P. L. and Hochwarter, W. A. (2000). Burnout in health care: The role of the five factors of personality. *Journal of Applied Social Psychology, 30*, 1570-1598.

Zellars, K.L., Perrewé, P.L., Rossi, A.M., Tepper, B.T., and Ferris, G.R. (in press). Moderating effects of political skill, perceived control, and job-related self efficacy on the relationship between negative affectivity and physiological strain. *Journal of Organizational Behavior*.

In: Handbook of Stress and Burnout in Health Care
Editor: Jonathon R. B. Halbesleben

ISBN 978-1-60456-500-3
© 2008 Nova Science Publishers, Inc.

Chapter 5

BURNOUT SYNDROME IN REGISTERED NURSES

Jeannie P. Cimiotti, Linda H. Aiken* and Lusine Poghosyan
Center for Health Outcomes and Policy Research
University of Pennsylvania

Nurses are the most numerous health professionals in most countries of the world. In the U.S. alone, almost 1.7 million full-time equivalent nurses work in hospitals, and the entire U.S. professional nurse workforce numbers almost 3 million (Steiger, Bausch, Johnson, and Peterson, 2006). A variety of health care providers may have occasional contact with hospitalized patients, but the bedside nurse provides continuous care. Research suggests that burnout among nurses in the U.S. and other industrialized countries is high. Aiken and colleagues observed high levels of burnout among 10,319 nurses working in 303 hospitals in Pennsylvania, Ontario, British Columbia, England, and Scotland (Aiken, Clarke, and Sloane, 2002). In this study the percentage of nurses with burnout scores above Maslach's norms (Maslach, Jackson, and Leiter, 1996) for medical personnel varied from 54% of nurse respondents in Pennsylvania to 34% of nurse respondents in Scotland. Lower levels of burnout were observed among nurses working in German hospitals, where the length of stay of hospitalized patients is exceptionally long (Aiken, Clarke, Sloane et al., 2001).

NURSING ROLES

Nursing care has been defined as a difficult art that requires the nurse to supply what the patient needs in knowledge and strength to carry out activities of daily living, and to administer medical treatments prescribed by physicians (Henderson, 2007). The nurse is responsible for constant surveillance of the patient and the safety of the surrounding patient care environment (Clarke and Aiken, 2003). Typically, the nurse is responsible for physiologic and psychologic assessments, medication and treatment administration, ensuring aseptic practices to prevent infection, monitoring all processes related to feeding and

* This research was supported by grants R01-NR04513 and P30-NR05043 (LH Aiken, PI) from the National Institute of Nursing Research, National Institutes of Health.

elimination, provision of comfort and pain control, and teaching patients to manage their health needs at home. The registered nurse works collaboratively with doctors and is often the doctor's eyes and ears, especially in U.S. hospitals where there are relatively few full time inpatient doctors. The nurse is legally responsible for his/her own actions as well as those of caregivers with less formal training, such as licensed practical nurses, and nursing assistants.

The work of nurses involves helping in very intimate circumstances people who are anxious, may be in pain, and sometimes are dying. Nurses are often called upon to make decisions that determine life and death. Some patients are "difficult" because of behaviors that are an obstacle to the provision of good nursing care (Manos and Braun, 2006). Difficult patients often include, but are not limited to those patients with states of altered mentation, substance abusers, those with psychiatric disorders, those who are regularly admitted for uncontrolled chronic conditions, and the dying. Almost one half of the elderly patients admitted to hospitals will develop dementia during their hospitalization (Balas et al., 2007). Nurses providing dementia care report high levels of time pressure, and greater emotional and conflicting demands (Josefsson, Sonde, Winblad, and Robins Wahlin, 2007). Severe burnout has been associated with the quality of working conditions, mainly interpersonal relationships (Poncet et al., 2007). In this study of 2,497 critical care nurses, the likelihood of severe burnout was almost twice as likely to occur when there were conflicts with patients and 39% more likely to occur when caring for dying patients. It has been observed in critical care nurses that providing futile care results in moral distress that is associated with emotional exhaustion (Meltzer and Huckabay, 2004).

It is logical to assume that the high rate of burnout among hospital nurses is explained by stressors inherent in nurses' roles in patient care, and there is some literature suggesting that "hardy" personalities be recruited to nursing or that stress reduction programs be introduced to facilitate coping (van Servellen, Topf, and Leake, 1994). However, there is a much larger and growing literature suggesting that burnout is primarily the result of system level organizational impediments to safe and effective nursing care that are beyond the control of individual caregivers. In this chapter we explore that hypothesis by reviewing recent research on nurse burnout and its consequences and potential solutions.

Organizational Context of Nurse Burnout

Flood and Scott (1987) describe hospitals as having dual bureaucratic and professional structures that represent opposing approaches to managing the performance of complex tasks. Conventional bureaucratic solutions subdivide work among many participants and control their activities through externally-imposed rules and hierarchies. Organizations with professional structures support the efforts of self-regulating individual practitioners who exercise considerable discretion in carrying out their work (Freidson, 1970). Hospital nurses are agents of a bureaucracy but hold professional values and seek peer relations with other professionals and professional modes of organizing their work. Bureaucratic solutions preferred by hospital management to problems such as nurse shortages and financial constraints are often counter to those preferred by nurses who espouse professional models of decision-making (Brannon, 1994). As a result, the complexity of the authority structure in hospitals as it pertains to nurses' autonomy and control over the resources required for safe and effective care has a powerful mediating influence on nurse satisfaction and burnout

(Aiken and Sloane, 1997). Moreover, there is a body of research on stress and coping suggesting that professionals are more likely to develop effective coping strategies to the inherent stressors in work such as in the case of nurses dealing with pain management and dying than to organizational or bureaucratic barriers to job performance over which the individual worker has little control (Pearlin and Schooler, 1978).

There is no better illustration of the impact of organizational factors on nurse burnout than the widespread hospital restructuring of the 1990s that produced dramatic changes to the patient care environment in hospitals in both North America and Europe (Sochalski, Aiken, and Fagin, 1997). Organizational restructuring of hospitals, sometimes referred to as process reengineering, was motivated by cost containment and resulted in nurse workforce downsizing, and hospital mergers, and closures (Norrish and Rundall, 2001). Hospital restructuring resulted in 90% of U.S. hospitals reducing their personnel (Aiken, Clarke, and Sloane, 2001). In addition to a reduction in the number of personnel, CEOs reported cross-training of personnel (physical therapists serving as plebotomists in their spare time), nursing skill mix reduction (decreasing the number and proportion of registered nurses), and reassigning of responsibility for ancillary support services to nurses. Many procedures that once required a hospital admission were shifted to the out-patient setting resulting in significantly increased intensity of nursing care and severity of illness of the remaining inpatients. Thus, as patients' requirements for care in hospitals increased, nursing staff representation in relation to intensity adjusted inpatient hospital days dropped significantly. Furthermore, when compared to nurse reports in 1986, nurses in 1998 consistently rated a decline in the quality of the nurse work environment that included diminished staffing adequacy, nurse manager ability, and hospital managers' regard for nursing.

In Canada, hospital restructuring resulted in higher levels of burnout in hospital nurses (Greenglass and Burke, 2002). Greenglass and Burke observed that nurse reports of job insecurity and the impact of restructuring were positively associated with emotional exhaustion. Similar findings were observed in a sample of hospital-based nurses and those nurses who left hospitals to work in another setting (Burke, 2003). A comparative analysis of these two groups suggested that hospital-based nurses experienced more job dissatisfaction and burnout than nurses working in other sectors.

Health care payment changes at the system level have generally had a significant impact on the work of nurses. In the U.S., the Medicare Prospective Payment System of 1983 and the Balanced Budget Act of 1997 were two legislative events that resulted in a perilous situation for registered nurses (Aiken and Hadley, 1988). As hospital employment grew between 1981 and 1993, it was observed that some categories of hospital personnel such as non-nursing administrators and other professional staff increased to 47% and 50%, respectively (Aiken, Sochalski, and Anderson, 1996). However, during this same time period hospital nursing personnel declined by 7% nationally, with significantly higher rates noted in Massachusetts (27%), New York (25%), and California (20%). Evidence suggests that the Balanced Budget Act alone increased the workload of a registered nurse by 6% (Lindrooth, Bazzoli, Needleman, and Hasnain-Wynia, 2006). Nurses found themselves short staffed, faced with patients who were more acutely ill with more comorbid illnesses than in the past, and shortened lengths of hospital stay where there was less time to provide needed care. Cost containment led to similar changes in hospital staffing in other industrialized countries. Two-thirds of hospital bedside care nurses in five countries reported in 1999 that there were not enough registered nurses available to provide high quality care (Aiken, Clarke, Sloane et al.,

2001). Having an unrealistic workload as a result of nurse staffing deficiencies is an organizational factor beyond the capacity of the individual nurses to change, and is thus a major factor contributing to job dissatisfaction and burnout. Even high burnout associated with the care of the dying can be interpreted in organizational terms to the extent that nurses must provide painful, intrusive care to patients with little chance of benefiting. End of life research documents that doctors and administrators are often unwilling to adhere to Living Wills creating organizationally induced stress for nurses.

Work Characteristics

Interpersonal relationships, role conflict, and work overload are job characteristics that have been linked to burnout. Both role conflict and unpleasant contact with supervisors have been linked to emotional exhaustion in nurses (Leiter and Maslach, 1988). Aiken and colleagues observed that in acute-care hospitals with high patient-to-nurse ratios, nurses were more likely to experience high levels of emotional exhaustion (Aiken, Clarke, Sloane et al., 2002). In a survey of 10,148 registered nurses working in 168 hospitals in Pennsylvania, 43% of the nurse respondents reported high levels of emotional burnout; furthermore, each additional patient per nurse was associated with a 23% increase in the odds of burnout. Burnout was also observed in a sample of nurses working in 30 English trust hospitals (Rafferty et al., 2007), where it was observed that in hospitals with the heaviest workloads nurses were 71% to 91% more likely to report high levels of emotional exhaustion and job dissatisfaction. Similar finding were observed in a sample of registered nurses working in Canadian hospitals (Leiter and Spence Laschinger, 2006). In this study of 8,597 Canadian nurses working in 292 acute care hospitals, it was observed that of all of the work characteristics associated with burnout, the strongest correlation was between nurse staffing and emotional exhaustion. Burnout is inevitable when professionals provide care for too many people (Maslach, 1979). As the ratio increases the result is higher and higher emotional overload until the worker burns out and emotionally disconnects.

In addition to the patient-to-nurse ratio, recent evidence suggests that the number of hours worked by registered nurses is associated with burnout. Park and Lake (Park and Lake, 2005) observed in a sample of 4,320 nurses working in 19 hospitals in New Zealand that the average hours worked by nurses per week was positively associated with the amount of nurses' burnout. Similar findings were observed in study of nurses working in New York City hospitals (Stone, Du et al., 2006). In this comparison of nurses working 8-hour and 12-hour shifts, it was observed that nurses working 12-hour shifts reported higher levels of job satisfaction and lower levels of emotional exhaustion. Though this might appear counterintuitive, nurses working a 12-hour shift work a longer work day, yet they typically work only three days per week.

Organizational Characteristics

Nurses' work generally takes place within complex organizations that include resources, operating rules, and hierarchies (Maslach, Schaufeli, and Leiter, 2001). Aiken's team has focused on methods and measures to empirically quantify features of the nurse work environment using the Revised Nursing Work Index (NWI-R) (Aiken and Patrician, 2000). The 56-item NWI-R has been conceptualized into subscales that measure organizational characteristics of hospital environments that have been demonstrated to be associated with nurse outcomes such as burnout as well as patient outcomes.

Resource adequacy (a scale largely measuring staffing adequacy), administrative support, and nurse-physician relationships are organizational characteristics constructed with the NWI-R are associated with burnout in hospital bedside-nurses (Aiken and Sloane, 1997). In this study of 955 registered nurses working in 40 units of 20 hospitals, it was observed that nurses working in units with high levels of organizational support had lower levels of burnout. Similar findings were observed in a sample of nurses who had migrated to the U.S. (Flynn and Aiken, 2002). The 820 nurses who participated in this study represented 34 different countries of origin. It was observed that the absence of a professional practice environment was a significant predictor of emotional exhaustion in both the U.S. and international nurses. In a sample of 10,319 nurses working in 303 hospitals in North America and Europe, organizational support had a pronounced effect on job satisfaction and burnout (Aiken et al., 2002).

Nurse Characteristics

Relatively few studies have focused on the demographic characteristics of the nurse experiencing burnout. Age, gender, level of educational preparation, and several personality traits have been linked to burnout in registered nurses. In a survey of 9,718 hospital nurses in the UK (Sheward, Hunt, Hagen, Macleod, and Ball, 2005), it was observed that nurse burnout was associated with nurse gender and level of educational preparation. Female nurses were 28% less likely to report emotional exhaustion and degree prepared nurses were 30% more likely to report emotional exhaustion. Similarly, high levels of burnout were observed among nurses with a higher level of educational preparation, longer job tenure (Schulz, Greenley, and Brown, 1995), and younger age (Poncet et al., 2007); low levels of emotional exhaustion were observed in nurses with high levels of personal hardiness (van Servellen et al., 1994). Women comprise 96% of the U.S. nurse workforce (Steiger et al., 2006) and this trend of nursing being primarily a female occupation appears globally as well. Therefore, when gender is examined as a risk factor for burnout in registered nurses the findings must be interpreted with a certain degree of caution.

ADVERSE OUTCOMES ASSOCIATED WITH NURSE BURNOUT

Patient Outcomes

Maslach theorized burnout to be associated with poor health care and developed a measurement tool comprised of three separate components that if present could conceivably provide an explanation for poor health care outcomes (Maslach et al., 1996). The most widely studied component of burnout is emotional exhaustion, a condition likely to impair nurses' concentration and vigilance. A second component in Maslach's conceptualization of burnout was depersonalization of clients which calls forth images of failure to listen and take seriously patient and family complaints that could be early signs of impending complications. The third component was loss of feelings of personal accomplishment which could erode attention to detail and dedication to high quality care.

A substantial body of research has appeared in the literature to suggest an association between the nurse practice environment and adverse outcomes in hospitalized patients. Nurse workload has been linked with medication errors and falls (Blegen and Vaughn, 1998), the spread of pneumonia and urinary tract infections (Kovner and Gergen, 1998; Kovner, Jones, Zhan, Gergen, and Basu, 2002; Needleman, Buerhaus, Mattke, Stewart, and Zelevinsky, 2002), increased mortality (Aiken, Clarke, Sloane et al., 2002), and death from complications of care (failure-to-rescue) (Aiken, Clarke, Sloane et al., 2002; Needleman et al., 2002). Aiken and colleagues observed that nurse staffing and organizational support were associated with nurse burnout and nurse reported quality of care (Aiken, Clarke, and Sloane, 2002). In this study of acute care nurses in North America and Europe, it was observed that in both the best and worst staffed hospitals, those that provided the least organizational support for nursing care were more likely to be rated by nurses as providing low quality care. Nurses in hospitals with the lowest levels of organizational support for nursing care were twice as likely to rate the care on their units as fair or poor. In the U.S. and Canada, where the largest proportion of nurses report high levels of emotional burnout, over one-third of these nurses reported that nosocomial infections were not an infrequent occurrence on their units and one-quarter reported patient falls with injury (Aiken, Clarke, Sloane et al., 2001). More importantly, however, is the observation that in Pennsylvania hospitals poor nurse staffing was associated with high levels of emotional exhaustion, and patient mortality and failure to rescue (Aiken, Clarke, Sloane et al., 2002).

Vahey and colleagues observed that patient satisfaction was associated with burnout in registered nurses (Vahey, Aiken, Sloane, Clarke, and Vargas, 2004). In this study of 820 nurses and 621 patients from 40 units in 20 hospitals, it was observed that on units with adequate staff, good administrative support for nurses, and good nurse-physician relations that patients were more than twice as likely to report high satisfaction with their care, and their nurses reported significantly lower levels of burnout. In addition, the overall level of nurse burnout was associated with patient satisfaction. Patients on units where nurses reported higher than average levels of emotional exhaustion were only half as likely to be satisfied with their care; whereas patient on units where nurses reported higher than average levels of personal accomplishment were more than twice as like to be satisfied with their care. Similar findings were observed in a large hospital in central Canada (Leiter, Harvie, and Frizzell, 1998). In this study on hospital units where nurses reported more emotional exhaustion, patients reported to be less satisfied with their care.

Nurse Outcomes

Adverse nurse outcomes have typically been defined as physical injury, psychological injury such as depression, and intention to leave the profession that occurs directly as a result of patient care. Physical injury to nurses adds to the expense of the organization in the form of additional compensation and paid days off. In the case of exposure to bloodborne pathogens there is the added expense of periodic testing, medication regimens and the emotional trauma associated with the potential acquisition of infectious disease. Recent evidence suggests an association between high levels of burnout and occupational injury in nurses.

Hospital nurses' occupational exposure to bloodborne pathogens through needlestick injuries in the U.S. has been documented (Aiken, Sloane, and Klocinski, 1997). Occupational exposures have also been reported by nurses working in Canada, the UK and Germany (Clarke, Schubert, and Korner, 2007). In the U.S. alone an estimated 600,000 needlestick injuries occur annually; the majority of these injuries occurring among nursing staff (Panlilio et al., 2004). Due to the consequences associated with exposure to bloodborne pathogens such as hepatitis B and human immunodeficiency virus needlestick injuries are an overwhelming concern to the health care industry as a whole. Clarke and colleagues have observed that nurse workload and organizational climate, known determinants of burnout, are associated with needlestick injuries in hospital nurses (Clarke, Rockett, Sloane, and Aiken, 2002; Clarke, Sloane, and Aiken, 2002). In a study of 2,287 nurses representing 22 hospitals across the U.S. it was observed that poor organizational climate and high workload were associated with a 50% to 2-fold increases in the likelihood of needlestick injuries or near misses (Clarke, Rockett et al., 2002). In another study of 1,692 nurses working in 20 U.S. hospitals in was observed that in units where there was low nurse staffing and poor organization climate that nurses were twice as likely to report needlestick injuries and near misses (Clarke, Sloane et al., 2002).

In New York City hospitals it was observed that characteristics of the nurse practice environment and burnout were associated with occupational injuries (Stone, Du, and Gershon, 2007). Stone and colleagues observed that in hospitals where nurses reported a poor practice environment, the likelihood of an occupational injury increased by 44%. A similar finding was observed among a sample of U.S. critical care nurses, where organizational characteristics and magnet hospital accreditation (hospitals noted for good nursing care) were associated with a decrease in the mean number of any type of occupational related injury, musculoskeletal injury, and exposure to blood or body fluids (Stone, Larson et al., 2006).

In addition to occupational physical injuries reported by nurses, a number of reports have surfaced on the psychological injury resulting from nurse burnout. In a sample of New York nurses it was observed that a perceived lack of job control was significantly related to burnout and depression (Glass, McKnight, and Valdimarsdottir, 1993). Suicidal ideation has also been observed in nurses who report a negative work environment and subsequently high levels of emotional exhaustion and depression (Samuelsson, Gustavsson, Petterson, Arnetz, and Asberg, 1997). Samuelsson and colleagues observed that workload and emotional exhaustion were significantly associated with the report of "life was not worth living". Similarly, in a sample of California nurses it was observed that emotional exhaustion was significantly associated with anxiety, depression, and somatization (van Servellen et al., 1994).

Maslach theorized that changing jobs, moving on to an administrative position, or leaving the profession entirely would be common responses to burnout (Maslach, 1978). Aiken and colleagues observed that among Pennsylvania nurses, 43% of those reporting high burnout levels and job dissatisfaction reported the intention to leave their current job within 12 months (Aiken, Clarke, Sloane et al., 2002). Similar findings of burnout associated with intention to leave were found across five countries (Aiken, Clarke, Sloane et al., 2001). In this study nurses planning to leave their jobs within the next year ranged from 23% in the U.S. to 39%

in England. Nurses under the age of 30 years who planned on leaving their present job within the next year ranged from 27% in Germany to 54% in England.

RESOLVING THE ISSUE OF BURNOUT IN REGISTERED NURSES

The expectation of reducing nurse burnout through the modification of nurse and patient characteristics is unrealistic; however, evidence does exist to suggest that improvements can be made to the nurse practice environment thereby potentially eliminating high levels of burnout among registered nurses. In 1999 legislation (AB 394) was enacted in California directing the California Department of Health Services to establish minimum, specific, and numerical nurse-to-patient ratios that would be hospital unit specific. Enforcement of AB 394 began in January 2004 and at the present time a nurse working on a medical-surgical unit in a California hospital can not care for more than five patients at any given time. Since the passage of AB 394 several other states have proposed similar legislation. Preliminary results from Aiken and colleagues evaluation of the California Nurse Staffing Mandates shows that nurse burnout is lower in California hospitals compared to other states (LH Aiken, personal communication, 2007).

IMPROVING THE PRACTICE ENVIRONMENT OF NURSES

During the 1980s, at the time when hospitals reported a shortage of registered nurses, a task force was appointed by the American Academy of Nursing to identify a national sample of hospitals that would be referred to as "magnet" hospitals due to their ability to recruit and retain professional nurses (McClure, Poulin, Sovie, and Wandelt, 1983). The task force of nurse leaders identified 41 "magnet" hospitals and found pronounced similarities among the hospitals regardless of institutional characteristics, such as bed size or locale. The magnet qualities of those hospitals were collapsed into three broad categories: administration, professional practice, and professional development. Kramer and Schmanlenberg extended the original research on magnet hospitals and compared magnet hospitals to the best run corporations in America (Kramer, 1990; Kramer and Schmalenberg, 1988a, 1988b). Using a subset of 16 magnet hospitals, it was observed that magnet hospitals possessed many of the same qualities found in the best performing corporations; a set of shared values that allowed individuals and the organization to strive for excellence. Kramer and Schmalenberg (Kramer and Schmalenberg, 1991a, 1991b) continued their research on magnet hospitals into the 1990s eventually identifying what would be know as the essentials of magnetism: working with nurses who are clinically competent, good nurse-physician relationships, nurse autonomy, supportive nurse manager, control over nursing practice, support for education, and adequate nurse staffing.

Aiken led the first team of researchers in an effort to examine the outcomes of patient care in magnet hospitals (Aiken, Smith, and Lake, 1994). In this landmark study, 39 magnet hospitals were matched on hospital characteristics to 195 non-magnet control hospitals that had at least 100 Medicare discharges. After adjusting for differences in predicted mortality, magnet hospitals had a 5% lower mortality rate; evidence to suggest that the same factors that led hospitals to be identified as effective in the organization of nursing care were also associated with lower mortality in Medicare patients. Similar findings were observed in a study of AIDS patients' 30-day mortality and satisfaction with nursing care (Aiken, Sloane, Lake, Sochalski, and Weber, 1999). In this study of 1,205 patients it was observed that patients in magnet hospitals were 60% less likely to die 30 days from their date of admission. Similar findings were observed in a study of nurses working on dedicated AIDS and scattered-bed units (Aiken and Sloane, 1997). In this study of 820 nurses working in 20 hospitals it was observed that nurses working in scattered-bed units within magnet hospital had lower levels of emotional exhaustion and higher levels of organizational support, when compared scattered-bed units within non-magnet hospitals.

The magnet hospital concept has been operationalized into a program of voluntary accreditation directed by the American Nurses Credentialing Center.[3] Hospitals must demonstrate that they embody the organizational characteristics that have been linked to low burnout such as staffing adequacy, decentralized decision-making, nurse autonomy, good relations between doctors and nurses, and administrative support for nurses (Aiken, 2002). The success of magnet hospitals in achieving significantly lower rates of burnout than non-magnet hospitals suggests that the stressors inherent in the work of nurses can be managed effectively through organizational reforms.

CONCLUSION

Burnout in registered nurses is a complex phenomenon that represents a burden to the health care system. Empirical evidence from the U.S. and abroad suggests that burnout is linked to organizational features of the practice environment of nurses. Nurse staffing levels, support from administrators, and good nurse-physician relationships are the strongest predictors of nurse burnout. Research and experience suggest that improvements can be made to the practice environment of nurses with accompanying decreases in nurse burnout. Magnet accreditation of health care facilities is a means to improve the practice environment of nurses; thereby reducing burnout and its adverse consequences and ultimately improving the quality of patient care.

REFERENCES

Aiken, L. H. (2002). Superior outcomes for magnet hospitals: The evidence base. In M. McClure and A. S. Hinshaw (Eds.), *Magnet Hospitals Revisited: Attraction and Retention of Professional Nurses* (pp. 61-81). Kansas City, MO: American Nurses Association.

Aiken, L. H., Clarke, S. P., and Sloane, D. M. (2001). Hospital restructuring: does it adversely affect care and outcomes? *Journal of Health and Human Services Administration, 23*(4), 416-442.

---

[3] In mid 2007, 256 hospitals have received the coveted magnet award for nursing excellence representing 45 states and Australia, and New Zealand (American Nurses Credentialing Center, 2007).

Aiken, L. H., Clarke, S. P., and Sloane, D. M. (2002). Hospital staffing, organization, and quality of care: Cross-national findings. *Nursing Outlook, 50*(5), 187-194.

Aiken, L. H., Clarke, S. P., Sloane, D. M., Sochalski, J., and Silber, J. H. (2002). Hospital nurse staffing and patient mortality, nurse burnout, and job dissatisfaction. *Journal of the American Medical Association, 288*(16), 1987-1993.

Aiken, L. H., Clarke, S. P., Sloane, D. M., Sochalski, J. A., Busse, R., Clarke, H., et al. (2001). Nurses' reports on hospital care in five countries. *Health Affairs, 20*(3), 43-53.

Aiken, L. H., and Hadley, J. (1988). *Factors affecting the hospital employment of registered nurses. The Secretary's Commission on Nursing Final Report, Vol 2*. Washington, DC: US Department of Health and Human Services.

Aiken, L. H., and Patrician, P. A. (2000). Measuring organizational traits of hospitals: the Revised Nursing Work Index. *Nursing Research, 49*(3), 146-153.

Aiken, L. H., and Sloane, D. M. (1997). Effects of organizational innovations in AIDS care on burnout among urban hospital nurses. *Work and Occupations, 24*(4), 453-477.

Aiken, L. H., and Sloane, D. M. (1997). Effects of specialization and client differentiation on the status of nurses: the case of AIDS. *Journal of Health and Social Behavior, 38*(3), 203-222.

Aiken, L. H., Sloane, D. M., and Klocinski, J. L. (1997). Hospital nurses' occupational exposure to blood: prospective, retrospective, and institutional reports. *American Journal of Public Health, 87*(1), 103-107.

Aiken, L. H., Sloane, D. M., Lake, E. T., Sochalski, J., and Weber, A. L. (1999). Organization and outcomes of inpatient AIDS care. *Medical Care, 37*(8), 760-772.

Aiken, L. H., Smith, H. L., and Lake, E. T. (1994). Lower Medicare mortality among a set of hospitals known for good nursing care. *Medical Care, 32*(8), 771-787.

Aiken, L. H., Sochalski, J., and Anderson, G. F. (1996). Downsizing the hospital nursing workforce. *Health Affairs, 15*(4), 88-92.

American Nurses Credentialing Center. (2007). Magnet-Designated Facility Information. Retrieved   July   1,   2007,   from http://www.nursecredentialing.org/magnet/searchmagnet.cfm

Balas, M. C., Deutschman, C. S., Sullivan-Marx, E. M., Strumpf, N. E., Alston, R. P., and Richmond, T. S. (2007). Delirium in older patients in surgical intensive care units. *Journal of Nursing Scholarship, 39*(2), 147-154.

Blegen, M. A., and Vaughn, T. (1998). A multisite study of nurse staffing and patient occurrences. *Nursing Economics, 16*(4), 196-203.

Brannon, R. L. (1994). *Intensifying care: the hospital industry, professionalization and the reorganization of the nursing labor process*. Amityville: Baywood.

Burke, R. J. (2003). Survivors and victims of hospital restructuring and downsizing: who are the real victims? *International Journal of Nursing Studies, 40*(8), 903-909.

Clarke, S. P., and Aiken, L. H. (2003). Failure to rescue. *American Journal of Nursing, 103*(1), 42-47.

Clarke, S. P., Rockett, J. L., Sloane, D. M., and Aiken, L. H. (2002). Organizational climate, staffing, and safety equipment as predictors of needlestick injuries and near-misses in hospital nurses. *American Journal of Infection Control, 30*(4), 207-216.

Clarke, S. P., Schubert, M., and Korner, T. (2007). Sharp-device injuries to hospital staff nurses in 4 countries. *Infection Control and Hospital Epidemiology, 28*(4), 473-478.

Clarke, S. P., Sloane, D. M., and Aiken, L. H. (2002). Effects of hospital staffing and organizational climate on needlestick injuries to nurses. *American Journal of Public Health, 92*(7), 1115-1119.

Flood, A. B., and Scott, W. R. (1987). *Hospital Structure and Performance.* Baltimore: The Johns Hopkins University Press.

Flynn, L., and Aiken, L. H. (2002). Does international nurse recruitment influence practice values in U.S. hospitals? *Journal of Nursing Scholarship, 34*(1), 67-73.

Freidson, E. (1970). *Profession of medicine.* New York: Dodd, Mead.

Glass, D. C., McKnight, J. D., and Valdimarsdottir, H. (1993). Depression, burnout, and perceptions of control in hospital nurses. *Journal of Consulting and Clinical Psychology, 61*(1), 147-155.

Greenglass, E. R., and Burke, R. J. (2002). Hospital restructuring and burnout. *Journal of Health and Human Services Administration, 25*(1), 89-114.

Henderson, V. A. (2007). The development of a personal concept. In P. D'Antonio, E. D. Baer, S. D. Rinker and J. E. Lynaugh (Eds.), *Nurses' work: issues across time and place.* New York: Springer Publishing Company.

Josefsson, K., Sonde, L., Winblad, B., and Robins Wahlin, T. B. (2007). Work situation of registered nurses in municipal elderly care in Sweden: a questionnaire survey. *International Journal of Nursing Studies, 44*(1), 71-82.

Kovner, C., and Gergen, P. J. (1998). Nurse staffing levels and adverse events following surgery in U.S. hospitals. *Image - the Journal of Nursing Scholarship, 30*(4), 315-321.

Kovner, C., Jones, C., Zhan, C., Gergen, P. J., and Basu, J. (2002). Nurse staffing and postsurgical adverse events: an analysis of administrative data from a sample of U.S. hospitals, 1990-1996. *Health Services Research, 37*(3), 611-629.

Kramer, M. (1990). The magnet hospitals. Excellence revisited. *Journal of Nursing Administration, 20*(9), 35-44.

Kramer, M., and Schmalenberg, C. (1988a). Magnet hospitals: Part I. Institutions of excellence. *Journal of Nursing Administration, 18*(1), 13-24.

Kramer, M., and Schmalenberg, C. (1988b). Magnet hospitals: Part II. Institutions of excellence. *Journal of Nursing Administration, 18*(2), 11-19.

Kramer, M., and Schmalenberg, C. (1991a). Job satisfaction and retention. Insights for the '90s. Part 1. *Nursing, 21*(3), 50-55.

Kramer, M., and Schmalenberg, C. (1991b). Job satisfaction and retention. Insights for the '90s. Part 2. *Nursing, 21*(4), 51-55.

Lake, E. T. (2002). Development of the practice environment scale of the Nursing Work Index. *Research in Nursing and Health, 25*(3), 176-188.

Leiter, M. P., Harvie, P., and Frizzell, C. (1998). The correspondence of patient satisfaction and nurse burnout. *Social Science and Medicine, 47*(10), 1611-1617.

Leiter, M. P., and Maslach, C. (1988). The Impact Of Interpersonal Environment On Burnout And Organizational Commitment. *Journal of Organizational Behavior, 9*(4), 297-308.

Leiter, M. P., and Spence Laschinger, H. K. (2006). Relationships of work and practice environment to professional burnout: testing a causal model. *Nursing Research, 55*(2), 137-146.

Lindrooth, R. C., Bazzoli, G. J., Needleman, J., and Hasnain-Wynia, R. (2006). The effect of changes in hospital reimbursement on nurse staffing decisions at safety net and nonsafety net hospitals. *Health Services Research, 41*(3 Pt 1), 701-720.

Manos, P. J., and Braun, J. (2006). *Care of the Difficult Patient*. New York: Routledge.

Maslach, C. (1978). Client Role In Staff Burn-Out. *Journal of Social Issues, 34*(4), 111-124.

Maslach, C. (1979). Burned-out. *Canadian Journal of Psychiatric Nursing, 20*(6), 5-9.

Maslach, C., Jackson, S. E., and Leiter, M. P. (1996). *Maslach Burnout Inventory Manual, 3rd Ed*. Mountain View: CPP.

Maslach, C., Schaufeli, W. B., and Leiter, M. P. (2001). Job burnout. *Annual Review of Psychology, 52*, 397-422.

McClure, M., Poulin, M., Sovie, M., and Wandelt, M. A. (1983). *Magnet Hospitals: Attraction and Retention of Professional Nurses*. Kansas City: American Nurses Association.

Meltzer, L. S., and Huckabay, L. M. (2004). Critical care nurses' perceptions of futile care and its effect on burnout. *American Journal of Critical Care, 13*(3), 202-208.

Mitchell, P. H., Ferketich, S., and Jennings, B. M. (1998). Quality health outcomes model. American Academy of Nursing Expert Panel on Quality Health Care. *Image - the Journal of Nursing Scholarship, 30*(1), 43-46.

Needleman, J., Buerhaus, P., Mattke, S., Stewart, M., and Zelevinsky, K. (2002). Nurse-staffing levels and the quality of care in hospitals. *New England Journal of Medicine, 346*(22), 1715-1722.

Norrish, B. R., and Rundall, T. G. (2001). Hospital restructuring and the work of registered nurses. *Milbank Quarterly, 79*(1), 55-79.

Panlilio, A. L., Orelien, J. G., Srivastava, P. U., Jagger, J., Cohn, R. D., Cardo, D. M., et al. (2004). Estimate of the annual number of percutaneous injuries among hospital-based healthcare workers in the United States, 1997-1998. *Infection Control and Hospital Epidemiology, 25*(7), 556-562.

Park, S., and Lake, E. T. (2005). Multilevel modeling of a clustered continuous outcome: nurses' work hours and burnout. *Nursing Research, 54*(6), 406-413.

Pearlin, L. I., and Schooler, C. (1978). The structure of coping. *Journal of Health and Social Behavior, 19*(1), 2-21.

Poncet, M. C., Toullic, P., Papazian, L., Kentish-Barnes, N., Timsit, J. F., Pochard, F., et al. (2007). Burnout syndrome in critical care nursing staff. *American Journal of Respiratory and Critical Care Medicine, 175*(7), 698-704.

Rafferty, A. M., Clarke, S. P., Coles, J., Ball, J., James, P., McKee, M., et al. (2007). Outcomes of variation in hospital nurse staffing in English hospitals: cross-sectional analysis of survey data and discharge records. *International Journal of Nursing Studies, 44*(2), 175-182.

Samuelsson, M., Gustavsson, J. P., Petterson, I. L., Arnetz, B., and Asberg, M. (1997). Suicidal feelings and work environment in psychiatric nursing personnel. *Social Psychiatry and Psychiatric Epidemiology, 32*(7), 391-397.

Schulz, R., Greenley, J. R., and Brown, R. (1995). Organization, management, and client effects on staff burnout. *Journal of Health and Social Behavior, 36*(4), 333-345.

Sheward, L., Hunt, J., Hagen, S., Macleod, M., and Ball, J. (2005). The relationship between UK hospital nurse staffing and emotional exhaustion and job dissatisfaction. *Journal of Nursing Management, 13*(1), 51-60.

Sochalski, J., Aiken, L. H., and Fagin, C. M. (1997). Hospital restructuring in the United States, Canada, and Western Europe: an outcomes research agenda. *Medical Care, 35*(10 Suppl), OS13-25.

Steiger, D. M., Bausch, S., Johnson, B., and Peterson, A. (2006). *The Registered Nurse Population: Findings from the March 2004 National Sample Survey of Registered Nurses*. Rockville, MD: U.S. Department of Health and Human Services

Stone, P. W., Du, Y., Cowell, R., Amsterdam, N., Helfrich, T. A., Linn, R. W., et al. (2006). Comparison of nurse, system and quality patient care outcomes in 8-hour and 12-hour shifts. *Medical Care, 44*(12), 1099-1106.

Stone, P. W., Du, Y., and Gershon, R. R. (2007). Organizational climate and occupational health outcomes in hospital nurses. *Journal of Occupational and Environmental Medicine, 49*(1), 50-58.

Stone, P. W., Larson, E. L., Mooney-Kane, C., Smolowitz, J., Lin, S. X., and Dick, A. W. (2006). Organizational climate and intensive care unit nurses' intention to leave. *Critical Care Medicine, 34*(7), 1907-1912.

Vahey, D. C., Aiken, L. H., Sloane, D. M., Clarke, S. P., and Vargas, D. (2004). Nurse burnout and patient satisfaction. *Medical Care, 42*(2 Suppl), II57-66.

van Servellen, G., Topf, M., and Leake, B. (1994). Personality hardiness, work-related stress, and health in hospital nurses. *Hospital Topics, 72*(2), 34-39.

In: Handbook of Stress and Burnout in Health Care
Editor: Jonathon R. B. Halbesleben
ISBN 978-1-60456-500-3
© 2008 Nova Science Publishers, Inc.

Chapter 6

THE OLDENBURG BURNOUT INVENTORY: A GOOD ALTERNATIVE TO MEASURE BURNOUT (AND ENGAGEMENT)

Evangelia Demerouti[*1] *and Arnold B. Bakker*[2]
[1]Utrecht University, Department of Social and Organizational Psychology,
Utrecht, the Netherlands
[2]Erasmus University Rotterdam, Department of Work and
Organizational Psychology, Rotterdam, the Netherlands

Burnout is a psychological syndrome that may emerge when employees are exposed to a stressful working environment, with high job demands and low resources (Bakker and Demerouti, 2007; Maslach, Schaufeli and Leiter, 2001). Although most scholars agree that burned-out employees are characterized by high levels of exhaustion and negative attitudes towards their work, there are different views on how the syndrome should be operationalized. The central aim of this chapter is to discuss the theoretical background of the recently introduced Oldenburg Burnout Inventory (OLBI; Demerouti, Bakker, Vardakou and Kantas, 2003), and to test the factor structure of the OLBI among Dutch employees working in one of two occupational sectors: health care and white collar work. Our central claim is that the OLBI is a reliable and valid measure for the assessment of burnout (and work engagement) that can be used as an alternative to the widely used Maslach Burnout Inventory (Maslach, Jackson, and Leiter, 1996).

---

[*] Correspondence: Evangelia Demerouti, PhD, Utrecht University, Dept. of Social & Organizational Psychology, P.O. Box 80.140, 3508 TC Utrecht, the Netherlands. E-mail: E.Demerouti@uu.nl

THE MASLACH BURNOUT INVENTORY

The most commonly used instrument for the measurement of burnout is the Maslach Burnout Inventory (MBI; Maslach and Jackson, 1981, 1986; Maslach et al., 1996). The original MBI was based on the following definition of burnout (Maslach and Jackson, 1986, p.1): "Burnout is a syndrome of emotional exhaustion, depersonalization and reduced personal accomplishment that can occur among individuals who do 'people work' of some kind". The MBI-Human Services Survey (MBI-HSS) is based on this three-dimensional conceptualization of burnout including the scales of emotional exhaustion, depersonalization and (reduced) personal accomplishment. The three-factor structure of the MBI-HSS has been shown to be invariant across occupations and national contexts (Lee and Ashforth, 1996; Schaufeli and Enzmann, 1998). However, this version of the MBI has been developed exclusively for use in human services professions. Accordingly, the three sub-scales of the MBI-HSS are only applicable to employees who work with people. Hence, when studying burnout outside the human services, either the MBI should be adapted or an entirely new instrument needs to be developed.

In response to this call, Schaufeli, Leiter, Maslach and Jackson (1996) developed the Maslach Burnout Inventory - General Survey (MBI-GS). Based on the notion that emotional exhaustion, depersonalization and personal accomplishment can be broadened beyond the interpersonal domain that is characteristic for the human services, they included three more generic burnout dimensions that were labeled exhaustion, cynicism and professional efficacy, respectively. Clearly, these MBI-GS subscales parallel those of the original MBI-HSS. However, contrary to slight adaptations in the wording of items in earlier studies, the MBI-GS includes different items that refer to more general, non-social aspects of the job. Several studies have supported the invariance of the MBI-GS factor structure across various occupational groups (Bakker, Demerouti, and Schaufeli, 2002; Leiter and Schaufeli, 1996), and across nations (Richardson and Martinussen, 2004; Schutte, Toppinen, Kalimo and Schaufeli, 2000). Moreover, the studies with the MBI-GS suggest that the phenomenon and process of burnout takes the same form in occupations within and outside human service professions (Leiter and Harvie, 1998; Leiter, Harvie and Frizzell, 1998; Leiter and Schaufeli, 1996).

Unfortunately, the MBI-GS did not overcome one important psychometric shortcoming of the original version of the MBI, namely that the items in each subscale are all framed in the same direction. Accordingly, all exhaustion and cynicism items are phrased negatively, whereas all professional efficacy items are phrased positively. From a psychometric point of view, such one-sided scales are inferior to scales that include both positively and negatively worded items (Price and Mueller, 1986). It can, for instance, lead to artificial factor solutions in which positively and negatively worded items are likely to cluster (cf., Doty and Glick, 1998). Indeed, some authors (Demerouti and Nachreiner, 1996; Lee and Ashforth, 1990) have criticized the MBI at this point. In addition, Lee and Ashforth (1990) have argued that the item wording can be seen as problematic since it offers an alternative explanation for the strong associations of exhaustion and depersonalization with psychological strain (generally negatively worded), and of personal accomplishment with perceptions of performance (generally positively worded).

THE OLDENBURG BURNOUT INVENTORY

In the present chapter, we propose an alternative measure of burnout, which has originally been constructed and validated among different German occupational groups (Demerouti, 1999; Demerouti and Nachreiner, 1998). This new instrument – the OLdenburg Burnout Inventory (OLBI) – includes positively and negatively framed items to assess the two core dimensions of burnout: *exhaustion* and *disengagement (from work)*. Exhaustion is defined as a consequence of intense physical, affective and cognitive strain, i.e. as a long-term consequence of prolonged exposure to certain job demands. This conceptualization corresponds closely to other definitions of exhaustion (e.g., Aronson, Pines and Kafry, 1983; Shirom, 1989). Contrary to exhaustion as operationalized in the original MBI or MBI-GS, the OLBI covers not only affective aspects of exhaustion but also physical and cognitive aspects. This facilitates the application of the instrument to those workers who perform physical work and those whose job is mainly about processing information.

Whereas depersonalization in the original MBI refers to distancing oneself emotionally from service recipients (e.g., becoming impersonal, callous, hardening), cynicism refers mainly to (lack of) interest in the job and job meaningfulness. In a similar vein, disengagement in the OLBI refers to distancing oneself from one's work in general, work object and work content (e.g., uninteresting, no longer challenging, but also "disgusting"). Moreover, the disengagement items concern the relationship between employees and their jobs, particularly with respect to identification with work and willingness to continue in the same occupation. Disengaged employees endorse negative attitudes toward their work objects, work content, or work in general. In our conceptualization, depersonalization is only one form of disengagement. More similarities exist between the cynicism and disengagement scale. However, the cynicism-items are more restricted in their content than the disengagement-items.

Professional efficacy is not included in the OLBI as a separate burnout dimension because it is not considered as a core dimension of burnout (Bakker, Demerouti and Verbeke, 2004; Green, Walkey and Taylor, 1991; Shirom, 1989), may also be interpreted as a possible consequence of burnout (Koeske and Koeske, 1989; Shirom, 1989), and is suggested to reflect a personality characteristic similar to self-efficacy (Cordes and Dougherty, 1993). The fact that personal accomplishment is the weakest burnout dimension in terms of significant relationships with other variables (cf., Lee and Ashforth, 1996; Schaufeli and Enzmann, 1998) is another indication of the exceptional status of this particular burnout dimension. Note that the negative instead of positive framing of professional efficacy items, which has been proposed in two recent MBI-studies (Bresó, Salanova, and Schaufeli, 2007; Schaufeli and Salanova, 2007), does not change the established finding that the professional efficacy dimension falls outside the burnout construct.

The factorial validity of the OLBI has been confirmed in studies conducted in Germany (Demerouti, Bakker, Nachreiner, and Ebbinghaus, 2002; Demerouti, Bakker, Nachreiner and Schaufeli, 2001), the United States (Halbesleben and Demerouti, 2005), and Greece (Demerouti et al., 2003). Results of these studies clearly showed that a two-factor structure with exhaustion and disengagement as the underlying factors fitted better to the data of several occupational groups than alternative factor structures. Additionally, the convergent validity of the OLBI and MBI-GS has been confirmed in the United States (Halbesleben and

Demerouti, 2005) and Greece (Demerouti et al., 2003). Following a multi-trait multi-method approach, both studies showed that the estimated correlation between the instruments was higher than $r = .70$. Moreover, the parallel scales of both instruments correlated $r = .48$ or higher. The test-retest reliability of the OLBI has been confirmed for time lags of four months (Halbesleben and Demerouti, 2005). The exhaustion subscale was stable with the auto-correlation being .51, while the correlation between time 1 and time 2 disengagement was somewhat lower ($r = .34$). Comparable test-retest reliabilities have been found for the MBI (Taris, Le Blanc, Schaufeli and Schreurs, 2005).

ASSESSING BURNOUT AND ENGAGEMENT WITH THE OLBI

A distinctive feature of the OLBI compared to the MBI-GS (and the original MBI) is that the OLBI includes both negatively and positively worded items so that not only one end of the continuum, but both ends are represented. In other words, the exhaustion and disengagement subscales include items that refer to their opposites, namely vigor and dedication, respectively. Positively framed items should be reverse-coded if one wants to assess burnout. Alternatively, we propose that researchers interested in assessing *work engagement* can recode the negatively framed items to measure engagement with the OLBI.

Demerouti and her colleagues (2001, 2003) tested the hypothesis that instruments including positively and negatively worded items can produce artificial factor solutions in which items framed in one way are likely to cluster. Specifically, the two OLBI-studies used confirmatory factor analyses techniques to test the fit of a model with two latent factors: a factor indicated by all positively phrased items and a factor indicated by all negative phrased items (independent of whether the items belonged to the exhaustion or disengagement dimensions). In both studies, this factor structure was clearly worse than the structure assuming exhaustion and disengagement as underlying factors. This indicates that the wording of the items does not create artificial factor solutions; rather it forces individuals to read and respond carefully to each individual item. Moreover, since the model with exhaustion and disengagement as underlying factors fitted well to the data, these studies suggest that the OLBI can be used to assess burnout *and* work engagement simultaneously.

Maslach and Leiter (1997) agree with our standpoint that burnout and engagement are two opposite poles of one continuum. They rephrased burnout as an erosion of engagement with the job, whereby energy turns into exhaustion, involvement turns into cynicism, and efficacy turns into ineffectiveness. In their view, engagement is characterized by energy, involvement and professional efficacy, which are the direct (perfectly inversely related) opposites of the three burnout dimensions. However, it should be noted that their MBI includes negative items only. Therefore, low mean levels of exhaustion and cynicism cannot be taken as being representative of vigor and dedication. For example, employees who indicate that they are not fatigued at all need not necessarily be full with energy.

Schaufeli and Bakker (2001, 2004) also assume that work engagement is the positive antithesis of burnout, but define and operationalize the engagement concept in its own right with the Utrecht Work Engagement Scale (UWES; Schaufeli and Bakker, 2003; Schaufeli, Salanova, González-Romá and Bakker, 2002). Work engagement is defined as a positive, fulfilling, work-related state of mind that is characterized by vigor, dedication, and absorption. Vigor refers to high levels of energy and mental resilience while working. Dedication refers to a sense of significance, enthusiasm, inspiration, and pride. Vigor and dedication are the direct positive opposites of exhaustion and cynicism, respectively. The third dimension of engagement is called absorption, which was found to be another constituting element of engagement in 30 in-depth interviews (Schaufeli et al., 2001). Absorption is characterized by being fully concentrated and happily engrossed in one's work, whereby time passes quickly.

González-Romá, Schaufeli, Bakker and Lloret (2006) used the MBI-GS and the UWES to test the hypothesis that items reflecting exhaustion-vigor and cynicism-dedication are scalable on two distinct underlying bipolar dimensions (labelled energy and identification, respectively). Using a non-parametric scaling technique, they showed that these core burnout and engagement dimensions can indeed be seen as opposites of each other along two distinct bipolar dimensions (energy vs. identification). It can be concluded from this study that negatively and positively framed items can be used to assess the core dimensions of burnout *and* engagement.

THE PRESENT STUDY

The central aim of the present study is to examine the psychometric quality of the Oldenburg Burnout Inventory (Demerouti et al., 2003). In addition, we will investigate whether the OLBI can be used to assess both burnout and engagement. We will validate the OLBI in two broad occupational groups: health care professionals and white collar workers. The original definition of burnout included people work as a crucial determinant of burnout, but since the MBI was specifically constructed for the assessment of burnout in this sector, the burnout scores of health care workers could not be compared with other occupations. On the basis of the literature, we formulated the following hypotheses:

Hypothesis 1: The OLBI has a two-factor structure including the dimensions of exhaustion and disengagement.
Hypothesis 2: A factor structure including exhaustion and disengagement fits better to the data than a factor structure including two factors representing positively and negatively framed items.
Hypothesis 3: The factor structure of the OLBI is invariant across health care professionals and white collar workers.
Hypothesis 4: Levels of burnout are higher within the health care sector as compared to white collar workers.

METHOD

Procedure and Samples

The current study was conducted among eight different groups of Dutch employees, working in one of two occupational sectors (health care and white collar occupations). All studies (except one) were part of regular occupational health assessments. After informative meetings with representatives of the management, personnel departments, and/or employee/ employer committees, all employees received an invitation to participate by e-mail. The e-mail briefly explained the goal of the study, and emphasized the confidentiality and anonymity of the answers. Participants could log in on a secured website with a self-constructed password. They then filled in all questions, and received online feedback about their levels of burnout. Participants from the health care sector worked as a physician, in an academic hospital (response rate: 69%), or in one of two health care institutes (72% and 82%). The study among the physicians was not part of a regular occupational health assessment. The online instrument was part of the online service provided to members of the Royal Dutch Association of Doctors. Therefore, we could not calculate the response rate for this group. The white collar workers who participated worked as public administrators (response rate 69%), trainers (70%), bank employees (43%), or at a publisher (56%).

The health care sample included 51.2% women and the mean age was 46 years (SD = 9.39). The most frequently mentioned educational level was high school (34.8%) followed by university (23.5%). Most participants had a partner and child(ren) (55.1%), or had a partner without child(ren) (28.0%). The white collar sample included 32.6% women and the mean age was 44.54 years (SD = 9.98). The majority of the participants had a college degree (53.6%). In total, 47.5% of the participants lived with their partner and child(ren), and 33.2% lived only with their partner.

Measure

The *OLdenburg Burnout Inventory (OLBI)* was originally developed in German. For the present research, the OLBI was translated into Dutch and then back-translated to German. The OLBI measures burnout with two dimensions: exhaustion and disengagement. The eight items of the *exhaustion* sub-scale are generic, and refer to general feelings of emptiness, overtaxing from work, a strong need for rest, and a state of physical exhaustion. Example items are "After my work, I regularly feel worn out and weary", and "After my work, I regularly feel totally fit for my leisure activities" (reversed) (1 = strongly disagree, 4 = strongly agree). *Disengagement* refers to distancing oneself from the object and the content of one's work and to negative, cynical attitudes and behaviors toward one's work in general. This sub-scale also comprises eight items, including "I frequently talk about my work in a negative way", and "I get more and more engaged in my work" (reversed). The answering categories are the same as for exhaustion. For both sub-scales, four items are positively worded and four items are negatively worded.

RESULTS

Both OLBI dimensions were reliable. The reliability for both exhaustion and disengagement .85. There were no substantial differences between the two sectors regarding the internal consistencies of the scales. The bi-variate correlations between the two dimensions of exhaustion and disengagement were for health care and white collar workers .55 ($p < .001$) and .57 ($p < .001$), respectively.

Exploratory Factor Analyses

In order to test our first hypothesis (suggesting a two-factor structure), we first examined the factor structure of the OLBI with exploratory factor analyses (EFA; principal axis factoring using varimax rotation) for both sectors separately. The rotated factor structure for each sector is displayed in Table 1. Several findings of the EFA are worth noting. The OLBI has a clear structure in health care, with exhaustion items forming the first factor and disengagement items forming the second factor. Only item D6 had double loadings on both factors and therefore it is unclear to which factor it belongs. Results for the white collar workers are fairly similar (including the double loading of item D6). The only difference is that the first factor consisted of the disengagement items and the second factor referred to the exhaustion items.

Table 1. OLBI Item/Factor Loadings

	Health care		White collar	
	EX	DE	EX	DE
D1. Interesting aspects		.68		.69
D2: Devaluation of work	.37	-.59	.34	-.55
D3: Mechanical execution		-.59		-.50
D4: Challenging		.73		.76
D5: Inner relationship		-.57		-.68
D6: Sick about work tasks	.49	-.45	-.44	.48
D7: No other occupation		.61		.59
D8: More engaged		.62		.66
E1: Tired before work	.64		.58	
E2: Longer times for rest	.69		.65	
E3: Manageable tasks	-.61		-.62	
E4: Emotionally drained	.58	-.40	.63	-.35
E5: Fit for leisure activities	-.67		-.62	
E6: Worn out	.72		.72	
E7: Tolerable workload	-.50		-.43	
E8: Feel energized	-.50	38	-.47	.36

Note: The items above are not presented in full, but in coded form. The English translation of the OLBI is available from the first author on request. DE = Disengagement Scale, EX = Exhaustion Scale.

Taken together, these EFA-findings indicate that the factor structure of the OLBI is confirmed for both health care and white collar workers providing support for our first hypothesis.

Multi-Group Multitrait-Multimethod Analyses

In a second step, the factor structure of the OLBI in the two sectors was tested by means of multi-group confirmatory factor analysis (CFA) using the AMOS 7 program (Arbuckle, 2006). Specifically, CFA was used to test Hypothesis 2 stating that the responses on the OLBI items underlie the burnout components (exhaustion and disengagement) or the method of item framing (positive and negative item formulation. This relies on the criteria of Campbell and Fiske (1959) for multitrait-multimethod matrices and corresponds to the methodology proposed by Bagozzi (1993). Specifically, we tested the Trait model, which hypothesizes that the variation in the items can be explained fully by the underlying traits (the burnout components) plus errors, and without any differentiation among item framing. The burnout items were included as observed variables and the burnout components as correlated latent factors. Both exhaustion and disengagement were operationalized by eight items.

The method model rests on the assumption that the structure is determined not by the burnout components but by whether items were positively or negatively formulated. This model does not take into consideration the different burnout components. It includes the 16 burnout items and two correlated latent method factors. The third model represents the multitrait-multimethod (MTMM) model or the correlated trait / correlated method model (Eid, 2000). This model combines both previous models. It includes again all burnout items and two categories of latent factors: (a) the two burnout components (traits) that are correlated; and (b) the two methods, which also correlate with each other. However, correlations between burnout components and methods were not included. Each item has therefore two loadings: one on a burnout dimension and one on a method factor. In the way we should be better able to uncover the factors that influence responses to the OLBI items than by considering them in separate models.

Table 2 displays the overall fit indices of the competing models for the multi-group MTMM analysis. In general, all models have large chi-squares in relation to the degrees of freedom indicating a poor fit. This is not unexpected because the chi-square is dependent on sample size.

The MTMM model had a satisfactory fit to the data (fit indices > .92 and RMSEA = .05) and proved to be superior to both the Trait and the Method model, Delta χ^2 (51) = 933.53, p < .001 and Delta χ^2 (51) = 1845.80, p < .001, respectively. This means that the fit of the MTMM model became poorer when the burnout dimensions were eliminated from the MTMM model (cf., the Method model), than when the two method factors, namely positive and negative wording factors, were eliminated (cf., the Traits model). In a similar vein, the proposed Trait model including the dimensions of exhaustion and disengagement was better than the Method model including the positively and negatively wording factors (its χ^2 value is 912.21 points higher with equal degrees of freedom).

Table 2. Indices of Overall Fit for Alternative Factor Structures of the OLBI for Health Care (N = 979), and White Collar Workers (N = 644)

Model	χ^2	df	p	GFI	RMSEA	NFI	CFI	IFI
Traits	1663.90	206	.001	.88	.07	.84	.86	.86
Method	2576.17	206	.001	.76	.08	.75	.76	.77
MTMM	730.37	172	.001	.95	.05	.93	.95	.95
Equal correlations	730.97	174	.001	.95	.05	.93	.94	.95
Equal loadings - burnout	936.98	186	.001	.93	.05	.91	.93	.93
Equal loadings - method	761.99	186	.001	.94	.04	.93	.94	.94
Null	10281.68	240	--	.34	.16	--	--	--

Note. χ^2 = chi-square; df = degrees of freedom; p = significance level; GFI = goodness-of-fit index; RMSEA = root mean square error of approximation; NFI = normed fit index; CFI = comparative fit index; IFI = incremental fit index.

Thus, while differentiation between both the burnout dimensions and the item formulation seems to be substantial, the differentiation between the burnout dimensions is more important. This substantiates Hypothesis 2. Additionally, for health care employees, all items had significant loadings on both types of latent factors, the burnout dimensions and the method factors. For white collar workers, we found that all items loaded on both kinds of latent factors save two exceptions: E4 and E7 had non-significant loadings on the exhaustion factor. In general, the pattern of factor loadings suggests that the loadings were somewhat higher for the two method factors than for the two burnout dimensions.

In order to test Hypothesis 3 (i.e. the factor invariance of the OLBI across health care and white collar workers), we imposed three types of constraints in the MTMM model, representing three different nested models. Specifically the first model contained equal correlations between the latent factors for both sectors, the second model contained equal factor loadings on the burnout dimensions and the third model contained equal factor loadings on the method factors for both sectors. As can be seen in Table 2, constraining the correlations between the factors to be equal in both groups did not impair the fit of the model to the data, Delta χ^2 (2) =.60, *n.s.* Similarly, constraining the factor loadings on the burnout factors to be equal for both sectors did not result in a worse model fit, Delta χ^2 (14) = 6.61, *n.s.* However, constraining the factor loadings on the method factors to be equal resulted in a worse model fit, Delta χ^2 (14) = 31.62, *p < .01*. These findings indicate that the factor structure of the OLBI is similar for both health care and white collar workers. Both sectors differ, however, in the influence that item framing has on the responses to the OLBI items.

Mean Score Differences

The two sectors differed significantly (at *p < .001*) in their mean scores on the OLBI dimensions. Specifically, health care workers experienced significantly higher levels of exhaustion (mean= 2.53) and disengagement (mean = 2.38) than white collar workers (mean for exhaustion = 2.28; mean for disengagement = 2.21). This substantiates Hypothesis 4. Inspection of the mean scores on the item level showed that compared to white collar workers, health care workers more frequently agreed with item E1 and less frequently agreed with item D8. Additionally, compared to white collar workers, health care workers more frequently agreed with items E4 and D6 and disagreed with the items E3 and D1.

DISCUSSION

This study is important in that it provides evidence for the validity of an alternative burnout measure for health care and white collar workers. Instead of testing the levels and the factor structure of burnout within health care only, we examined simultaneously workers from a related sector which provided useful insights regarding the levels of burnout, the factor structure of the OLBI and the underlying factors explaining responses to OLBI items in the different sectors.

The findings clearly indicate that the OLBI is a reliable instrument including two moderately high correlating dimensions. The reliability was both for exhaustion and disengagement $\alpha = .85$. Results further confirmed that both sectors differed significantly in the levels of burnout. Health care workers experienced significantly higher levels of burnout (both exhaustion and disengagement) than white collar workers. This corresponds with the findings of Demerouti (1999), who found that health care workers reported higher levels of disengagement than white collar workers (air traffic controllers). These differences may be due to the worse working conditions that health care workers are exposed to compared to white collars. In comparison to white collar workers, health care professionals reported to be more frequently tired before going to work and after finishing work. This suggests that their job demands are so high that they cannot recover during off-job time. Moreover, they experience a kind of disillusionment towards their work in general because they do not find interesting aspects in their job any more and they stop feeling engaged in what they do. Demerouti's (1999) study indicated that health care workers are confronted with higher physical and emotional demands and lower job resources including task variety, feedback and participation in decision making than white collar workers. The combination of high job demands and low job resources has been found to be related to high exhaustion and disengagement (Bakker and Demerouti, 2007; Demerouti et al., 2001; Peterson et al., in press).

Results of the EFA and the CFA confirmed that the OLBI has a two-factor structure in both sectors. For both health care and white collar workers, exhaustion and disengagement emerged as clear factors with all items loading on the intending factor except for D6. This item had double loadings and therefore cannot be clearly classified in one of the two burnout dimensions. Future studies with the OLBI within these sectors could drop this item since the scale would have a clearer factor structure and would still remain reliable (with Cronbach's alpha = .84). An important finding of the CFA was not only the confirmation of the suggested two-factor structure for both health care and white collar workers, but also that the factor structure was *invariant* because the factor loadings did not differ between the sectors. Also Demerouti (1999) found that the factor loadings of the OLBI items did not differ substantially between a variety of health care, production and white collar workers.

Perhaps the most interesting question answered by the present study is whether scales that include both positively and negatively formulated items to operationalize the same dimensions include two types of factors, namely the theoretical dimensions and the dimensions concerning the wording of the items. Results suggest that both types of factors influence item responses (at least regarding the OLBI). Failing to differentiate between the exhaustion and disengagement factor resulted in a very unsatisfactory model fit which was substantially worse than failing to differentiate between positively and negatively wording factors. Thus, the underlying, theoretical dimensions of the OLBI were confirmed. However, the results of the MTMM model showed that both kinds of factors are important and that eliminating the method factors resulted in a worse fit of the model to the data. Moreover, the OLBI items had significant loadings on both kinds of factors. This suggests that individuals do not only respond to the content of the items but are also sensitive to how the content is presented (the positive or negative framing of the items).

González-Romá et al. (2006) offer a statistical explanation for this finding. Accordingly, negatively framed items are not highly and linearly related to positively framed items but show high linear relationships with other negatively framed items. This is particularly the case when Likert-type scales are used. The consequence is that two clusters of highly linearly related items can emerge. Therefore, it is suggested to use non-parametric ways of analyses in future studies with the OLBI, instead of (confirmatory) factor analysis. By applying Mokken analysis, González-Romá et al. (2006) were able to find that exhaustion-vigor and cynicism-dedication were bipolar dimensions, called energy and identification dimensions respectively.

The implication of this discussion is that using one-sided scales makes things simpler because we can never investigate the influence of factors like item framing on the individual responses. However, following such an approach we can never recover the problem that we find relationships between constructs simply because their items are framed the same way. Since the OLBI includes items that measure the whole continuum for both dimensions ranging from vigor to exhaustion and from dedication to disengagement it can be used to measure both burnout and its opposite, work engagement. Energy scores can be obtained adding the four positive, vigor items and the four recoded, exhaustion items. A high score on energy indicates a high level of vigor, whereas a low score on energy indicates a high level of exhaustion. Analogously, identification scores can be obtained by adding the four positively framed engagement items and the four recoded disengagement items. A high score on identification indicates a high level of dedication, whereas a low score on identification indicates a high level of disengagement.

CONCLUSION

In conclusion, this study provided validation evidence for the Oldenburg Burnout Inventory, a measure that is designed to overcome shortcomings of the Maslach Burnout Inventory. While additional validation research is warranted, the present study among a variety of health care and white collar organizations finds support for the internal consistency and factorial validity of the OLBI. Moreover, the present study contributes to the discussion regarding the measurement of burnout and its hypothetical opposite state of work engagement. Our results suggest that the OLBI is able to capture the core dimensions of burnout and its opposite. The differentiation between the dimensions of vigor-exhaustion and dedication-disengagement is more crucial than the differentiation between positively and negatively worded items (that the existing measurement instruments use to measure work engagement and burnout respectively). In our view, this is an important contribution to the literature, as it offers researchers an alternative measure of burnout *and* work engagement with balanced item wording and expanded conceptualization of exhaustion and disengagement/cynicism. The instrument can be used for virtually every job, including health care, and is sensitive enough to uncover differences between jobs. Our study confirms that the classical burnout occupations can be found in health care. Health care professionals experience higher levels of burnout than the broader human service sector with different types of white collar work.

REFERENCES

Arbuckle, J.L. (2006). *Amos 7.0 User's Guide*. Chicago, IL: SPSS Inc.

Aronson, E., Pines, A.M., and Kafry, D. (1983). *Ausgebrannt. Vom Überdruß zur Selbstentfaltung*. [Burnout: From tedium to personal growth]. Stuttgart: Klett-Cotta.

Bagozzi, R.P. (1993). An examination of the psychometric properties of measures of negative affect in the PANAS-X scales. *Journal of Personality and Social Psychology, 65,* 836-851.

Bakker, A.B., and Demerouti, E. (2007). The Job Demands-Resources model: State of the art. *Journal of Managerial Psychology, 22,* 309-328.

Bakker, A.B., Demerouti, E., and Schaufeli, W.B. (2002). The validity of the Maslach Burnout Inventory – General Survey: An Internet study. *Anxiety, Stress, and Coping, 15,* 245-260.

Bakker, A.B., Demerouti, E., and Verbeke, W. (2004). Using the Job Demands – Resources model to predict burnout and performance. *Human Resource Management, 43,* 83-104.

Bresó, E., Salanova, M., and Schaufeli, W.B (2007). In search of the 'third dimension' of burnout: Efficacy or inefficacy? *Applied Psychology: An International review, 56,* 460-478.

Campbell, D.T., and Fiske, D.W. (1959). Convergent and discriminant validation by the multitrait-multimethod matrix. *Psychological Bulletin, 56,* 81-105.

Cordes, C., and Dougherty, T.W. (1993). A review and an integration of research on job burnout. *Academy of Management Review, 18,* 621-656.

Demerouti, E. (1999). *Burnout: Eine Folge Konkreter Abeitsbedingungen bei Dienstleistungs und Produktionstdtigkeiten*. (Burnout: A consequence of specific working conditions among human service and production tasks). Frankfurt/Main: Lang.

Demerouti, E., Bakker, A.B., Nachreiner, F., and Ebbinghaus, M. (2002). From mental strain to burnout. *European Journal of Work and Organizational Psychology, 11,* 423-441.

Demerouti E., Bakker, A.B., Nachreiner, F., and Schaufeli, W.B. (2001). The Job Demands - Resources model of burnout. *Journal of Applied Psychology, 86,* 499-512.

Demerouti, E., Bakker, A.B., Vardakou, I., and Kantas, A. (2003). The convergent validity of two burnout instruments: A multitrait-multimethod analysis. *European Journal of Psychological Assessment, 18,* 296-307.

Demerouti, E., and Nachreiner, F. (1996). Reliability and validity of the Maslach Burnout Inventory: A critical approach. *Zeitschrift für Arbeitswissenschaft, 52,* 82-89.

Demerouti, E. and Nachreiner, F. (1998). Zur Spezifität von Burnout für Dienstleistungsberufe: Fakt oder Artefakt? [The specificity of burnout in human services: Fact or artifact?]. *Zeitschrift für Arbeitswissenschaft, 52*, 82-89.

Doty, D.H., and Glick, W.H. (1998). Common methods bias: Does common methods variance really bias results? *Organizational Research Methods, 1*, 374-406.

Eid, M. (2000). A multitrait-multimethod model with minimal assumptions. *Psychometrika, 65*, 241-261.

González-Romá, V., Schaufeli, W.B., Bakker, A.B., and Lloret, S. (2006). Burnout and work engagement: Independent factors or opposite poles? *Journal of Vocational Behavior, 68*, 165-174.

Green, D.E., Walkey, F.H., and Taylor, A.J.W. (1991). The three-factor structure of the Maslach Burnout Inventory. *Journal of Social Behavior and Personality, 6*, 453-472.

Halbesleben, J.R.B., and Demerouti, E. (2005). The construct validity of an alternative measure of burnout: Investigating the English translation of the Oldenburg Burnout Inventory. *Work and Stress, 19*, 208-220.

Koeske, G.F., and Koeske R.D. (1989). Construct validity of the Maslach Burnout Inventory: A critical review and reconceptualization. *Journal of Applied Behavioral Science, 25*, 131-144.

Lee, R.T., and Ashforth, B.E. (1990). On the meaning of Maslach's three dimensions of burnout. *Journal of Applied Psychology, 75*, 743-747.

Lee, R.T., and Ashforth, B.E. (1996). A meta-analytic examination of the correlates of the three dimensions of job burnout. *Journal of Applied Psychology, 81*, 123-133.

Leiter, M.P., and Harvie, P.L. (1998). Conditions for staff acceptance of organizational change: Burnout as a mediating construct. *Anxiety, Stress and Coping, 11*, 1-25.

Leiter, M.P., Harvie, P.L. and Frizzell, C. (1998). The correspondence of patient satisfaction and nurse burnout. *Social Science and Medicine, 37*, 1-7.

Leiter, M.P. and Schaufeli, W.B. (1996). Consistency of the burnout construct across occupations. *Anxiety, Stress and Coping, 9*, 229-243.

Maslach, C., and Jackson, S.E. (1981). The measurement of experienced burnout. *Journal of Occupational Behavior, 2*, 99-113.

Maslach, C. and Jackson, S.E. (1986). *Maslach Burnout Inventory: Second Edition.* Palo Alto, CA: Consulting Psychologists Press.

Maslach, C., and Leiter, M.P. (1997). *The truth about burnout.* San Francisco: Jossey-Bass.

Maslach, C., Jackson, S.E., and Leiter, M.P. (1996). *Maslach burnout inventory manual* (3rd edn.). Palo Alto, CA: Consulting Psychologists Press.

Maslach, C., Schaufeli, W.B., and Leiter, M.P. (2001). Job burnout. *Annual Review of Psychology, 52*, 397-422.

Peterson, U., Demerouti, E., Bergström, G., Åsberg, M., and Nygren, A. (in press). Work characteristics and sickness absence in burnout and non burnout groups: A study of Swedish health care workers. *International Journal of Stress Management.*

Price, J.L., and Mueller, C.W. (1986). *Handbook of organizational measurement.* Marshfield, MA: Pitman.

Richardsen, A.M., and Martinussen, M. (2004). The Maslach Burnout Inventory: Factorial validity and consistency across occupational groups in Norway. *Journal of Occupational and Organizational Psychology, 77*, 1–20.

Schaufeli, W.B., and Bakker, A.B. (2001). Werk en welbevinden: Naar een positieve benadering in de Arbeids- en Gezondheidspsychologie [Work and well-being. Towards a positive approach in Occupational Health Psychology]. *Gedrag and Organisatie, 14,* 229-253.

Schaufeli, W.B., and Bakker, A.B. (2003). *UWES – Utrecht Work Engagement Scale: Test Manual.* Unpublished Manuscript: Department of Psychology, Utrecht University.

Schaufeli, W.B., and Bakker, A.B. (2004). Job demands, job resources and their relationship with burnout and engagement: A multi-sample study. *Journal of Organizational Behavior, 25,* 293-315.

Schaufeli, W.B., and Enzmann, D. (1998). *The burnout companion to study and practice.* London: Taylor and Francis.

Schaufeli, W.B., Leiter, M.P., Maslach, C., and Jackson, S.E. (1996). The Maslach Burnout Inventory-General Survey. In C. Maslach, S.E. Jackson, and M.P. Leiter (Eds.), *Maslach Burnout Inventory.* Palo Alto, CA: Consulting Psychologists Press.

Schaufeli, W.B., and Salanova, M. (2007). Efficacy or inefficacy, that's the question: Burnout and work engagement and their relationship with efficacy beliefs. *Anxiety, Stress and Coping, 20,* 177-196.

Schaufeli, W.B., Salanova, M., González-Romá, V., and Bakker, A.B. (2002). The measurement of engagement and burnout: A two sample confirmatory factor analytic approach. *Journal of Happiness Studies, 3,* 71-92.

Schutte, N., Toppinen, S., Kalimo, R., and Schaufeli, W. (2000). The factorial validity of the Maslach Burnout Inventory-General Survey (MBI-GS) across occupational groups and nations. *Journal of Occupational and Organizational Psychology, 73,* 53-67.

Shirom, A. (1989). Burnout in work organizations. In C.L. Cooper and I. Robertson (Eds.), *International Review of Industrial and Organizational Psychology* (pp. 25-48). New York: Wiley.

Taris, T.W., Le Blanc, P.M., Schaufeli, W.B., and Schreurs, P.J.G. (2005). Are there causal relations between the dimensions of the Maslach Burnout Inventory? A review and two tests. *Work and Stress, 19,* 238-255.

In: Handbook of Stress and Burnout in Health Care
Editor: Jonathon R. B. Halbesleben

ISBN 978-1-60456-500-3
© 2008 Nova Science Publishers, Inc.

Chapter 7

CROSS-CULTURAL ISSUES IN STRESS AND BURNOUT

Sharon Glazer[*]
San Jose State University

The study of occupational stress across cultures is rare; most typical are one-culture studies or comparisons of two cultures, which is insufficient for understanding cultural differences (Hofstede, 2001). The mere fact that in Chinese the word "stress" is translated with two characters that represent the words 'crisis' and 'opportunity' (Hashim and Zhiliang, 2003) and that in Hebrew the word stress is translated into either "pressure" or "tension" (Glazer, 2002) demonstrates the elusiveness of the concept. In this chapter, I use the word 'stress' to define an area of study. It is a process in which stressors relate to strains. Stressors are environmental demands or constraints that may yield negative responses. Strains are negative responses that arise when one is unable to cope successfully with stressors. The relationship between stressors and strains is at the core of "stress." Across cultures, reported perceptions of stressors and strains differ and implications of the same stressors on strains differ, as do types of stressors influencing the same strains (Glazer and Beehr, 2005). Thus, culture is the greater context in which stress occurs and implications of culture on stress need to be better understood. This chapter presents a framework (see Figure 1) for conducting stress research across cultures substantiated with a comprehensive review of literature from different countries and cross-cultural studies.

Crompton and Lyonette (2006) highlight the importance of cultural context in their comparative study of work-life balance in Finland, Norway, Britain, France, and Portugal. Employment of women, state support for mothers' employment, and child-caring responsibilities differ among these countries and influence work-life balance. For example, in Finland and Norway women and men are given cash for care and up to a year of work leave with pay for having children. In these countries there is little work-life conflict. In contrast, in France, incongruence between (a) a liberal policy for women's employment and (b)

---

[*] Tel: (408) 924-5639; E-mail: sglazer@email.sjsu.edu

traditional division of household labor might be a cultural attribute influencing French workers' work-role conflict.

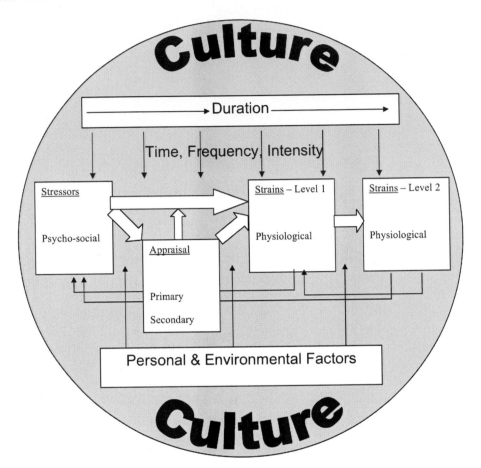

Figure 1. Cultural Context for Occupational Stress.

In this chapter I make a case for studying stress across cultures, explain why nurses are the focal group for this chapter, define culture, and then elaborate on the stress framework.

WHY EXAMINE STRESS OR BURNOUT ACROSS CULTURES?

Economic globalization has created greater interdependence among countries, as evident in the exchange of goods and services, money, and knowledge (Leung, Bhagat, Buchan, Erez, and Gibson, 2005). In the healthcare sector, goods and services, as well as knowledge are exchanged through programs such as "Doctors Without Borders," and the 'import' of healthcare providers from different countries (e.g., Filipino nurses to the USA; American health care, 2006).

With an influx of immigrants and problems with discrimination within country, ethnic differences must also be examined. For example, in the USA, African American high-tech employees report lower levels of well-being than most other ethnic groups in the same occupation and in Israel, female high-tech employees report lower levels of well-being than their male counterparts (Mor Barak, Findler, and Wind, 2003). On the interface of work and nonwork life, Cohen and Kirchmeyer (2005) show that, in Israel, having more children leads to greater turnover intention among Muslim women, but less turnover intention among Jewish women.

The purpose of cross-cultural occupational stress research is to understand *how, when, and why* culture impacts occupational stress at each point of the framework (see Figure 1), including social, legal, political, and economic situations that give rise to stressors, coping strategies and display of reactions to them, and the formal programs that might be effective or considered appropriate to reduce stressors and strains.

NURSES AS FOCAL GROUP FOR CROSS-CULTURAL OCCUPATIONAL STRESS RESEARCH

Nurses, unlike any other healthcare provider in the hospital setting, are at the forefront of providing care to patients, including monitoring patient well-being, listening to patients' needs throughout the shift, serving as a liaison between patient and physician, as well as pharmacy and lab technicians, and interacting with family and friends of patients. Their basic job requirements are also fairly similar across countries, as are the problems of recruitment and turnover (Cimiotti, Aiken, and Poghosyan, present volume; Coomber and Barriball, 2007). This is not to say that nursing has a higher level of work-related burnout than midwives or hospital physicians (at least not in Britain - Anderson, Cooper, and Willmott, 1996 and Denmark - Kristensen, Borritz, Villadsen, and Christensen, 2005), rather they confront somewhat similar work-related demands (e.g., Lambert et al., 2004). And despite these similar work-related demands, nurses experience differing levels of these stressors and even some unique ones (Glazer and Gyurak, in review).

Defining Culture

Culture goes mostly unseen and it often takes being removed from the culture or being an outsider to actually "see" it. Culture is influenced by language, role expectations, customs, symbols, feelings, attitudes, thinking patterns, traditions, beliefs, values, and norms. It is shared among a group of people and it is passed down from one generation to the next. People do not need to live in the same country to share the same culture. In most countries there are multiple cultures and each culture may be found in multiple countries. Countries, religions, gender, ethnicities, organizations, professions, and neighborhoods, each have distinct cultures. The organization's culture must function symbiotically within the country's culture, following the country's laws and regulations of trade and commerce. The organization is further influenced by social, economic, political, technological, and legal contexts of the environment within which the organization is embedded and these contexts are influenced by and influence country cultural norms, values, and general beliefs (Erez and Gati, 2004).

Several frameworks characterize cultures on the basis of social and ecological factors, but no one framework captures the whole of culture. These frameworks include, but are not limited to values (i.e., guiding principles that cultures reinforce its members to uphold; Hofstede, 2001; House, Hanges, Javidan, Dorfman, and Gupta, 2004; Schwartz, 1999; Triandis, 1995), social axioms (i.e., general beliefs that are influenced by one's social surroundings, Leung et al., 2005), ecological differences (e.g., political, economic, environment, growth/death rate; Georgas and Berry, 1995), and tightness and looseness (i.e., "the strength of social norms and the degree of sanctioning within societies," Gelfand, Nishii, and Raver, 2006, p. 1225). People who will engage in cross-cultural research are strongly encouraged to consider as many cultural indicators as possible (and not just cultural values).

Methodological Issues

Numerous methodological issues are of concern when conducting cross-cultural studies, in general, and occupational stress, specifically. One issue is whether the research focus is on discovery of culture-specific aspects of stress from within each culture (i.e., emic studies) or if one is imposing a perspective well-founded in one culture onto another culture (i.e., imposed etic studies). A second concern is with language. Not only is stress an elusive concept to define internationally, it is also inconsistently defined and used in U.S. literature (see review by Jex, Beehr, and Roberts, 1992). This problem is compounded by the use of translated versions of questionnaires developed in one country, typically USA, Canada, or UK. Problems associated with this technique include concerns over conceptual equivalence (i.e., the variable studied is defined the same way across cultures, e.g., intelligence), functional equivalence (i.e., the concept studied serves the same purpose, e.g., smoking in Mexico carries status symbolism), and measurement equivalence (i.e., the way of assessing the concept is the same and understood the same way). Often the appropriateness and the meaning of translated items are lost due to cultural differences in interpretation of the same items/questions and even measurement approach. Literal translations may be understood, but interpreted differently. Connotations of translated words must be addressed. For example, South Asians (but not European Americans) do not interpret depressive emotional symptoms as illness, but as life problems, which require problem-solving coping strategies or avoidance coping (Karasz, 2005).

Burnout has been validated with some success across countries, particularly burnout as measured with Maslach's Burnout Inventory (MBI) (e.g., Armstrong-Stassen, Al-Ma'Aitah, Cameron, and Horsburgh, 1994 in Jordanian Arabic; Ahola et al., 2006 in Finland; Aluja, Blanch, and Garcia, 2005 in Spain's Catalan region; Green, Walkey, and Taylor, 1991 in Great Britain, Estonia, New Zealand, and Ireland; Schaufeli and Janczur, 1994 in Netherlands and Poland; and Söderfeldt, Söderfeldt, Warg, and Ohlson, in Sweden; also see review by Golembiewski, Scherb, and Boudreau, 1993) or cultures (Savicki, 2002 in Australia, Austria, Anglo-Canada, Franco-Canada, Denmark, England, East Germany, West Germany, Israel, Poland, Scotland, Slovakia, and USA). However, numerous MBI items do not resonate well with people of certain cultures, because items are misinterpreted (i.e., it lacks *functional equivalence*). For example, Danish human service workers were upset or angry with the wording of some times (Kristensen, Borritz, Villadsen, and Christensen, 2005). Söderfeldt et al. (1996) also noted that Swedish health service workers flagged certain items as not meaningful among Swedish respondents. Thus, although people are able to respond to translated surveys, it is important to ensure that (1) attitudinal items are written in a culturally appropriate way, (2) descriptive behaviors are written in a way that is consistent with behaviors that might be exhibited in a given culture, and (3) cognitive states or beliefs are culturally feasible.

A third concern is with regard to sample equivalence. In cross-cultural research, subjects within cultures must share similar characteristics with subjects of other cultures on nearly all things but culture (Hofstede, 2001). This way any differences between groups will mostly reflect cultural differences. Included in ensuring sample equivalence is controlling for the level of education or training required of people to perform in a certain occupation. Kim's (2007) study of psychotherapists in Korea and USA shows that Americans, who have higher degrees than their Korean counterparts, also have less role ambiguity.

FRAMEWORK FOR STUDYING OCCUPATIONAL STRESS ACROSS CULTURES

The transactional framework (Lazarus and Folkman, 1984) offers the most comprehensive guide for studying occupational stress without placing limitations on the types of variables that will be included. Culture is added to this framework in a way that demonstrates that culture influences all aspects of 'stress.' Figure 1 illustrates the relationships amongst stressors, strains, time, personal factors, environmental factors, and appraisal and coping, all influenced by culture. No one variable can be separated from culture (Cohen and Kirchmeyer, 2005). Presence, perception, and interpretation of stressors, availability and use of coping resources and strategies, and manifestation, interpretation, and display of strains are all culture-bound. Although it is not depicted here, it is important to recognize that people are embedded within numerous cultures (Erez and Gati, 2004), and they are influenced by these cultures, as well as cultures with which they once interacted (e.g., a different organization or country) or identify (e.g., ethnic group).

Culture is intimately a part of both the person and the environment (Hofstede, 2001). People's attitudes, behaviors, and cognitions are, in part, a product of the cultural milieu. At the same time people's attitudes, behaviors, and cognitions shape culture. As a part of the environment, culture influences stressors that will be presented, coping resources available to moderate the relationship between stressors and strains, as well as first level strains with second level strains. As part of the person, culture influences perceptions and experiences of work-related stressors, coping strategies used, and strains that are manifested, displayed, and defined as strains. Time (duration and frequency) suggests that (1) stress-related events unfold over time and (2) the duration of 'stress' relates to the likelihood and severity of its consequences. However, even the meaning of time differs across cultures (Levine and Norenzayan, 1999).

Stressors

In different cultures different types of stressors present themselves. When the same stressors present themselves, interpretation or perception of the stressors is culturally influenced (Glazer and Beehr, 2005). Thus, whether an environmental condition even constitutes a stressor is in the eye of the beholder (influenced by culture). There are three basic types of stressors, social, psychological, and physical. In organizational psychology, psycho-social stressors are typically examined, though physical stressors undoubtedly influence employees' psychological well-being in the workplace. Psycho-social stressors reflect perceptions of one's place in the social environment. For example, role stressors are based on the perception that members of one's role set are placing unduly demands on the focal person. Physical stressors are objective situational constraints, such as lighting, noise, temperature, etc. that may be threatening to one's well-being.

Stressors have been studied across different countries, including, but not limited to USA, Canada, the Caribbean, Israel, Jordan, Germany, Sweden, Hungary, Italy, Holland, Mexico, Singapore, Japan, Taiwan, South Korea, Thailand, Northern Ireland, and Great Britain. Results from these studies indicate that strain may result from *physical stressors*, such as lack of resources, unfamiliarity with equipment, technology changes, poor pay/benefits, shiftwork, workplace structure, and staff shortages, and *psycho-social stressors*, including empowerment, lack of job control, decision-making opportunities, nurse-physician collaborations, team cohesion, leadership, poor quality of nursing and medical staff, difficult patients or patients' family members, satisfaction with supervisor and job, social support, workload, role conflict, role ambiguity, and communication difficulties (Armstrong-Stassen et al., 1994; Baba, Galperin, and Lituchy, 1999; Coomber and Barriball, 2007; Fang, 2001; Glazer, 2005; Glazer and Beehr, 2005; Glazer and Gyurak, in review; Jowett, 2003; Lambert et al., 2004; Lambert and Lambert, 2001; Lavanco, 1997; Yin and Yang, 2002). Unfortunately, most of these stressors have not changed much over the course of at least a decade (Jowett, 2003), indicating little environmental improvement for nurses. Moreover, these stressors are not necessarily invariant across cultures; only some stressors are reported in all countries, though at different frequencies. For example, British and Dutch nurses do not differ on most reported stressors, including those intrinsic to the job, organizational role, relationship with others, and career and achievement pressure (Broers, Evers, and Cooper, 1995). Exceptions include less pressure from the organizational climate, but more home/work interface pressure for the Dutch than the British nurses.

Cultural differences are also attributed to ethnicity. For example, Asian nurses in the USA, the UK, or Ireland report language and communication problems, different nursing practices, and discrimination as causing them "stress" (Xu, 2007). In general, Allan (2007) reports that nurses, trained overseas, experience more overt and covert discrimination and lack of social and organizational support than non-White British nurses.

Strains

Strains refer to individual responses to stressors. The level of similar strains, type of strains, interpretation of strains, manifestation of strains, and signs of strains differ across cultures (Karasz, 2005). Strains are placed into three categories — physiological, psychological, and behavioral. Each of these three categories can be further divided into two directives, whether the strain is directly impacting the individual or the organization. Moreover, some strains develop as a result of other strains. For example, turnover intention follows anxiety in a study of nurses in Hungary, Italy, UK, and USA (Glazer and Beehr, 2005).

Physiological responses that have direct impact on the organization are absences due to illness, use of healthcare providers, and compensation claims. Physiological responses directly affecting the individual include elevated blood pressure, headaches, coronary heart disease, sleeplessness, agitation, bodily twitches, and more. Work-related stressors (e.g., shift patterns or patient care demands) are found to increase U.S. and Italian nurses' problems with their menstrual cycles (Hatch, Figa-Talamanca, and Salerno, 1999). This suggests that the manifestation of objective physiological responses might be culturally invariant. In contrast, self-reported physiological strain might differ across cultures; people in collectivist cultures report greater physiological strains than people in individualistic cultures (Liu, Spector, and Shi, 2007; Liu and Spector, 2005). However, Spector et al.'s (2002) study of managers in 24 countries shows that the correlations between locus of control and physical well-being vary, but individualism-collectivism does not explain the differences. Something else about culture might be influencing physiological responses to stressors.

Psychological responses that have a direct impact on the organization are low organizational commitment, turnover cognition, and low job satisfaction. Psychological responses directly affecting the individual include depression and anxiety. Relationships between role stressors, anxiety, organizational commitment, and high intention to leave among nurses are invariant across four countries, though the magnitudes of the relationships differ across these countries (Glazer and Beehr, 2005). In Spector et al.'s (2002) study the greater one's external locus of control the lower one's job satisfaction across 23 countries, but not France. Similarly, Perrewé et al. (2002) show that role ambiguity influences burnout in all countries (i.e., USA, Germany, Brazil, Israel, Japan, Hong Kong, China, and Fiji), but France. In contrast, the role conflict-burnout relationship differs across the countries Perrewé et al. studied.

Liu and Spector (2005) also conclude variance in psychological responses. They state that people in collectivist countries report more psychological strains than people in individualistic cultures. In a study of teachers in Hong Kong, Leung and Lee (2006) show that as emotional exhaustion increases, sense of personal accomplishment increases. This is in contrast to established theory whereby increased exhaustion should decrease sense of personal accomplishment. That Asian respondents report psychological strains, but also personal accomplishment may be due to a value for work, obedience, and endurance in Asian societies.

In other studies (Golembiewski et al., 1993; Savicki, 2002), despite invariance in reported stressors, burnout levels differ across cultures. For example, British and Dutch nurses have similar levels of stressors, but Dutch nurses (vs. British nurses) report more satisfaction with job; achievement, value, and growth; organization's design and structure; and organizational processes, and less mental and physical ill-health (Broers et al., 1995). Similarly, correlations between work-related stressors and burnout do not differ between Polish and Dutch nurses, but Polish nurses have more burnout (Schaufeli and Janczur, 1994). There is no indication if the samples differed on mean level of work stressors.

There is also inconsistency as to which aspects of burnout occur first, second, third, or simultaneously, why, and what the relationships are between these components. For example, among Hong Kong teachers, emotional exhaustion leads to a sense of personal accomplishment as opposed to lack of personal accomplishment (Leung and Lee, 1996). Researchers debate the placement of burnout components, as well as a general measure of burnout. Burnout might be a consequence of strain (e.g., Perrewé et al., 2002; Pomaki, Supeli, and Verhoeven, 2007), a mediator of stressor-strain relationships (e.g., Ahola et al., 2006; Armstrong-Stassen et al., 1994; Baba et al., 1999), or a predictor of strains (Leung and Lee, 2006). In this framework, burnout most likely fits under the first level strain category.

Studies on burnout need to examine its etiology. More specifically, why do people in different countries develop it and how does it develop? Pines (2004b) suggests that existentialism (i.e., one's need to find life meaningful and important, Pines, 2004a) and greater social support partly explain why Israeli nurses, managers, and teachers experience less burnout than their American counterparts, regardless of occupation.

These results are found despite similar work requirements, lower salaries in Israel, and closer, less hierarchical relationships between nurses and physicians in Israel. People in Israel (vs. USA) know each other and each others' families; people help each other without expectation of pay or having to wait to be seen (Pines, 2004b). Thus, less burnout is associated with a feeling of meaningfulness and significance in life, further suggesting that those who have greater burnout feel that they are failing in making a contribution toward a meaningful life (Pines, 2004a; 2004b).

Behavioral strains directed at the organization include general turnover rate, absenteeism rate and frequency, and sabotage of company assets. Behavioral responses directly affecting the individual include turnover intention, absenteeism, turnover, smoking, alcohol consumption, and overeating.

In a study of Pakistani and Malaysian employees of a multinational firm located in the respective countries, correlations between work overload, work conflict, and work ambiguity with performance, turnover intentions, and absenteeism are mostly the same (Jamal, 2007), but the mean scores may be statistically different. Unfortunately, Jamal did not conduct a test for statistical difference between countries and did not offer cultural explanations for the differences. In Singapore, supervisor satisfaction negatively relates with Singaporean nurses' turnover intention, but not turnover cognition (i.e., thinking about leaving, but not declaring an intention to leave) (Fang, 2001). Again, there is no cultural context from which to explain the findings.

Coping and the Role of Personal and Environmental Factors

Coping is an action-oriented or emotion-oriented way of dealing with stressors that are perceived as threatening one's homeostasis (primary appraisal). If the individual believes he or she has the resources to cope with the stressors (secondary appraisal) then the resources will likely be used. Coping resources include various sources and types of social support, a variety of problem-solving tactics, and emotion-focused strategies. There is also little research to suggest which ways of coping are most likely used and useful (or effective) in different cultures. Cultures endorse appropriate ways of interpreting and coping with stressors, even when people are faced with the same exact stressors. In some cultures, expressing emotions is acceptable, whereas in other cultures controlling emotions and using cognitive rational thinking (assuming what is rational is culture-laden in itself) is endorsed (Liu and Spector, 2005). In addition, some cultures endorse maintaining relationships when coping with stressors and others endorse adherence to rules and procedures. For example, a nurse who cries when faced with a stressor might be seen as weak in the USA, just as an Israeli nurse working in the USA, who goes to a U.S. physician that she works with to assess a wound would be perceived as breaking the rules and protocol (Pines, 2004b). Other studies summarized by Liu and Spector show that Americans use direct coping strategies, whereas Chinese prefer indirect coping strategies. Comparing two countries is insufficient for understanding how direct Americans are in their coping strategies. It is only with data from more than two countries, for example from USA, Israel, and China, that one can determine how direct or indirect Americans are in their coping strategies.

Given that some coping strategies might be seen as unacceptable among members of certain cultural groups, it is plausible that different coping strategies create conflict in the workplace. Conflict arising because a person has broken normative rules for behavior creates anxiety. At the culture level of analysis, Hofstede (2001) showed that countries higher on Uncertainty Avoidance (i.e., they have more rules of behavior) have higher levels of uncertainty and stress (e.g., Japan). In addition, interdependent cultures (where members care for each other, e.g., Israel) promote well-being, whereas independent cultures (where individuals look out for themselves, e.g., USA) create psychological stress (Mor Barak et al., 2003).

Lambert et al.'s (2004) study, examining ways of coping among nurses in Thailand, Japan, South Korea, and USA, demonstrates that the most utilized ways of coping are self-control (i.e., not showing negative emotions and feelings), seeking social support from others, working with others toward problem-resolution, and positive reappraisal of the stress-producing environment. Lambert et al. explain that these ways of coping are in concert with harmony value emphasized in Asian or Asian-influenced cultures. Likewise, Indians and Americans use support coping and control more than Europeans (in Sweden, UK, and Bulgaria; Bernin et al., 2003).

According to Cohen and Kirchmeyer (2005), withdrawal behaviors may be a way of coping. They suggest that withdrawal among Arab women when faced with *family* demands may be a proactive coping mechanism that ensures work and family balance, whereas among Jewish women with a great deal of *work* demands, absenteeism is a reactive coping mechanism.

Environmental Factors. One potential moderator is social support. In a study by Glazer, Bowling, and Anderson (in review), culture (i.e., autonomy, mastery, or hierarchy cultures) appears to influence the extent to which role ambiguity relates with organizational satisfaction regardless of the level of supervisor emotional support. However, Berlin and Glazer (2007) assert that the only way support would relate to satisfaction is if the type and source (organizational instrumental support) of support matches the satisfaction facet (e.g., organizational satisfaction). Consistent with Beehr and Glazer's (2001) propositions regarding culture and social support, people in conservative cultures (Arab Israelis) report more support available than those in autonomous cultures (USA) (Pines, Ben-Ari, Utasi, and Larson, 2002). Moreover, social support network reduces burnout among human service professionals in India, particularly for Indian men (vs. women) (Brown, Prashantham, and Abbott, 2003). Brown et al. conjecture that work-related support is more accessible to men than to women. Thus, country and gender cultures affect the extent to which social support (sources and types) alleviates strains.

Personal Factors. Personality factors, such as hardiness (Lambert and Lambert, 2001), Type A behavior pattern, and locus of control (Glazer, Stetz, and Izso, 2004), and organizational commitment (Siu, 2002) relate to stress. However, results of moderating stressor-strain relationships are equivocal with little cultural explanations. Another personal coping resource is healthy habits. Pomaki et al.'s (2007) study concludes that health promoting behaviors buffers the effects of role conflict on both emotional exhaustion and depressive symptoms in a sample of Dutch university hospital physicians.

FUTURE RESEARCH DIRECTION

At this point of research development, it is not enough to test Western (mostly North American) theories of occupational stress in different cultural contexts. The general portability of stress frameworks, relating stressors to strains, is confirmed (e.g., Baba et al., 1999; Glazer and Beehr, 2005; Jamal, 2007; Lambert and Lambert, 2001; Liu et al., 2007; Pomaki et al., 2007). Now it is time to discover *why, how, and when* culture influences the magnitude of these relationships (Leung et al., 2005). Specifically, (1) What are potential environmental constraints across cultures? (2) When and why are these demands perceived and reported as stressors? (3) How often (frequency) and strong (intensity) are the stressors presented? (4) What meaning do people in different countries attach to stressors, strains, and different coping styles? (5) When are strains interpreted and experienced (manifested), and why? (6) How does culture influence explanations for the manifestations of stress? (7) How does culture influence conditions that affect a person's susceptibility to, perception of, manifestation of, and signs of 'stress' (including stressors, strains, and coping strategies)? What are natural signs of the onset of strain? (8) How intense are those strains in reality and in relation to self-reports?

For the most part, studies on occupational stress in the healthcare sector, and nursing, in particular, have conducted comparative studies using cultural values as possible explanations for findings. One cultural attribute that has largely been ignored is that of the perception of time. Pines (2004a) asserts that how people perceive time, as in the past, present, or future, might affect the extent to which burnout is manifested. Given that a major stressor for nurses is workload, it makes sense that how people in different cultures perceive time would clarify also the meaning of workload.

Two major problems in occupational stress research, in general, include lack of physiological strain measures and little indication of the frequency, intensity, and duration of stressors. The threshold for stress and, thus, some physiological strains are influenced by culture. In addition, information about frequency, intensity, and duration of stressors provides a basis on which to interpret the meaning of 'stress' across cultures.

A fourth area for further investigation is how individuals' values are associated with work-related stress. Little research exists regarding the role of values in the framework of occupational stress. For example, Sagiv and Schwartz (2000) demonstrate that certain values, such as achievement, self-direction, and stimulation positively correlate with well-being, whereas values related to security, conformity, and tradition negatively correlate with well-being. Further, value congruence, between organizational and personal or societal values yields less strain (e.g., Buchanan and Glazer, 2005; Joiner, 2001), including burnout (Maslach, 2000). A question that arises is how does culture impact effects of value congruence on 'stress?'

The perception and status of the nursing profession needs further assessment cross-culturally. This need is precipitated by the fact that nursing shortage and turnover is a big problem worldwide, despite general satisfaction with the profession (e.g., in Jordan and Canada, Armstrong-Stassen et al., 1994). For example, turnover intention is lower among Australian nurses who are satisfied with the status of their profession (Cowin, 2002) and turnover cognition is lower among Singaporean nurses who are committed to their profession (Fang, 2001). Thus, continuing in line with Hegney, Plank, and Parker's (2006) study of Australian nurses, researchers should ask how important nursing is, why people think there is a shortage of nurses, and how they think this shortage could be fixed? These questions should be asked of non-healthcare professionals to obtain a true indication of how nursing is perceived by the public and better understanding of what aspects of the nursing image need improvement.

Another relevant question related to the problem of turnover is whether there are cross-cultural differences in the return of nurses to the profession after a period of absence? Given that (1) most nurses are women, (2) many probably begin their careers prior to having children, (3) the values that would entice women to become nurses are likely the same values that would make them decide to stay home with families, and (4) laws pertaining to parental leave of absence from work differs across countries, the rate of turnover needs to also take into account the rate of return. Also, if nurses are not returning, where are they going instead?

It would also be interesting to study what strains are manifested as a result of similar stressors and how they are manifested. For example, death and dying is a particularly salient stressor for nurses in Hungary and staff shortage is a salient stressor for English nurses (Glazer and Gyurak, in review). The most likely response to either of these stressors, respectively, might be anxiety, yet anxiety might not be the response English nurses would have to 'death and dying' nor the likely response Hungarian nurses would have to 'staff shortage.'

CONCLUSION

The study of stress across cultures, particularly in healthcare, is in its early phase. Researchers are still testing the basic process of relationships between stressors and strains. It is now time to move beyond, because the core process of stress has been established as universal, but there are differences in magnitudes of relationships that need deeper contextual investigation. This review of literature demonstrates that culture's influence on stress cannot be separated from the phenomenon itself. Therefore, in order to interpret results of studies, researchers are urged to fully describe the context within which their studies are done. The next phase for cross-cultural research in occupational stress among healthcare professionals is to provide concrete evidence for *why, when, and how* culture impacts stress. With this information, management and practitioners will be equipped to modify the workplace and their own actions toward people of different cultural backgrounds, and provide training to healthcare practitioners on stress management strategies that fit well within the cultural context of the organization and do not compromise healthcare providers' cultural identities.

REFERENCES

Ahola, K., Honkonen, T., Kivimäki, M., Virtanen, M., Isometsä, E., Aromaa, A., and Lönnqvist, J. (2006). Contribution of burnout to the association between job strain and depression: The Health 2000 Study. *Journal of Occupational and Environmental Medicine, 48*, 1023-1030.

Allan, H. (2007). Mobbing behaviors encountered by nurse teaching staff. *Nursing Ethics, 14*, 463-465.

Aluja, A., Blanch, A., and Garcia, L. F. (2005). Dimensionality of the Maslach Burnout Inventory in school teachers: A study of several proposals. *European Journal of Psychological Assessment, 21*, 67-76.

American health care depends on immigrant nurses. (29 March, 2006). *The Regents of the University of Michigan*, Ann Arbor, MI. Retrieved on July 31, 2007, http://www.ns.umich.edu/htdocs/releases/story.php?id=189.

Anderson, W. J. R., Cooper, C. L., and Willmott, M. (1996). Sources of stress in the National Health Service: A comparison of seven occupational groups. *Work and Stress, 10*, 88-95.

Armstrong-Stassen, M., Al-Ma'Aitah, R., Cameron, S., and Horsburgh, M. (1994). Determinants and consequences of burnout: A cross-cultural comparison of Canadian and Jordanian nurses. *Healthcare for Women International, 15*, 413-421.

Baba, V. V., Galperin, B. L., and Lituchy, T. R. (1999). Occupational mental health: A study of work-related depression among nurses in the Caribbean. *International Journal of Nursing Studies, 36*, 163-169.

Beehr, T. A., and Glazer, S. (2001). A cultural perspective of social support in relation to occupational stress. In P. Perrewé, D. C. Ganster, and J. Moran (Eds.), *Research in Occupational Stress and Well-Being* (pp. 97-142). Greenwich, CO: JAI Press.

Berlin, J., and Glazer, S. (2007, July). *Social support and job satisfaction across 13 countries*. Paper presentation submitted for the International Association for Intercultural Research conference, Groningen, Netherlands.

Bernin, P., Theorell, T., Cooper, C. L., Sparks, K., Spector, P. E., Radhakrishnan, P., and Russinova, V. (2003). Coping strategies among Swedish female and male managers in an international context. *International Journal of Stress Management, 10*, 376-391.

Broers, P., Evers, A., and Cooper, C. L. (1995). Differences in occupational stress in three European countries. *International Journal of Stress Management, 2*, 171-180.

Brown, N. C., Prashantham, B. J., and Abbott, M. (2003). Personality, social support and burnout among human service professionals in India. *Journal of Community and Applied Social Psychology, 13*, 320-324.

Buchanan, T., and Glazer, S. (2005, April). *Values as moderators of role stressor and physiological strain relationships*. Poster presented at the Society for Industrial and Organizational Psychology conference, Los Angeles, CA.

Cohen, A., and Kirchmeyer, C. (2005). A cross-cultural study of the work/nonwork interface among Israeli nurses. *Applied Psychology: An International Review, 54*, 537-567.

Coomber, B., and Barriball, K. L. (2007). Impact of job satisfaction components on intent to leave and turnover for hospital-based nurses: A review of the research literature. *International Journal of Nursing Studies, 44*, 297-314.

Cowin, L. (2002). The effects of nurses' job satisfaction on retention: An Australian perspective. *Journal of Nursing Administration, 32*, 283-291.

Crompton, R., and Lyonette, C. (2006). Work-life 'balance' in Europe. *Acta Sociologica, 49*, 379-393.

Erez, M., and Gati, E. (2004). A dynamic, multi-level model of culture: From the micro level of the individual to the macro level of a global culture. *Applied Psychology: An International Review, 53*, 583-598.

Fang, Y. (2001). Turnover propensity and its causes among Singapore nurses: An empirical study. *International Journal of Human Resource Management, 12*, 859-871.

Gelfand, M. J., Nishii, L. H., and Raver, J. L. (2006). On the nature and importance of cultural tightness-looseness. *Journal of Applied Psychology, 91*, 1225-1244.

Georgas, J., and Berry, J. W. (1995). An ecocultural taxonomy for cross-cultural psychology. *Cross-Cultural Research, 29*, 121-157.

Glazer, S. (2002). Past, present, and future of cross-cultural studies in Industrial and Organizational psychology. In C. Cooper and I. T. Robertson *International Review of Industrial and Organizational Psychology* (Vol. 17, pp. 145-185*)*. Chichester, UK: Wiley.

Glazer, S., and Beehr, T.A. (2005). Consistency of the implications of three role stressors across four countries. *Journal of Organizational Behavior, 26*, 467-487.

Glazer, S., Bowling, N. A., and Anderson, D. (in review). The role of culture in moderating effects of supervisor support on the relationship between role ambiguity and organizational satisfaction: A 19-country study. *Journal of Organizational Behavior.*

Glazer, S., and Gyurak, A. (in review). A qualitative assessment of sources of occupational stress among nurses in five countries.

Glazer, S., Stetz, T. A., and Izso, L. (2004). Individual difference variables and subjective job stress across five countries. *Personality and Individual Differences, 37*, 645-658.

Golembiewski, R. T., Scherb, K., and Boudreau, R. A. (1993). Burnout in cross-national settings: Generic and model-specific perspectives. In W. Schaufeli, B. Wilmar, C. Maslach, and T. Marek (Eds.), *Professional burnout: Recent developments in theory and research* (pp. 217-236). Philadelphia, PA: Taylor and Francis.

Green, D. E., Walkey, F. H., and Taylor, A. J. W. (1991). The three-factor structure of the Maslach Burnout Inventory: A multicultural, multinational confirmatory study. *Journal of Social Behavior and Personality, 6*, 453-472.

Hashim, I. H., and Zhiliang, Y. (2003). Cultural and gender differences in perceiving stressors: A cross-cultural investigation of African and Western students in Chinese colleges. *Stress and Health, 19*, 217-225.

Hatch, M. C., Figa-Talamanca, I., and Salerno, S. (1999). Work stress and menstrual patterns among American and Italian nurses. *Scandinavian Journal of Work, Environment and Health, 25*, 144-150.

Hegney, D., Plank, A., and Parker, V. (2006). Extrinsic and intrinsic work values: Their impact on job satisfaction in nursing. *Journal of Nursing Management, 14*, 271-281.

Hofstede, G. (2001). *Culture's consequences: Comparing values, behaviors, institutions, and organizations across nations (2nd Ed.). Thousand Oaks,* CA: Sage.

House, R. J., Hanges, P. J., Javidan, M., Dorfman, P., and Gupta, V. (2004). *GLOBE, Cultures, Leadership, and Organizations: GLOBE Study of 62 Societies*. Newbury Park, CA: Sage.

Jamal, M. (2007). Job stress and job performance controversy revisited: An empirical examination in two countries. *International Journal of Stress Management, 14*, 175-187.

Jex, S. M., Beehr, T. A., and Roberts, C. K. (1992). The meaning of occupational stress items to survey respondents. *Journal of Applied Psychology, 77*, 623-628.

Joiner, T. A. (2001). The influence of national culture and organizational culture alignment on job stress and performance: Evidence from Greece. *Journal of Managerial Psychology, 16*, 229-242.

Jowett, S. (2003). Comments on "Occupational stress in nursing." *International Journal of Nursing Studies, 40*, 567-569.

Karasz, A. (2005). Cultural differences in conceptual models of depression. *Social Science and Medicine, 60*, 1625-1635.

Kim, E. (2007). Occupational stress: A survey of psychotherapists in Korea and the United States. *International Journal of Stress Management, 14*, 111-120.

Kristensen, T. S., Borritz, M., Villadsen, E., and Christensen, K. B. (2005). The Copenhagen Burnout Inventory: A new tool for the new assessment of burnout. *Work and Stress, 19*, 192-207.

Lambert, V. A., and Lambert, C. E. (2001). Literature review of role stress/strain on nurses: An international perspective. *Nursing and Health Sciences, 3*, 161-172.

Lambert, V. A., Lambert, C. E., Itano, J., Inouye, J., Kim, S., Kuniviktikul, W., et al. (2004). Cross-cultural comparison of workplace stressors, ways of coping and demographic characteristics as predictors of physical and mental health among hospital nurses in Japan, Thailand, South Korea, and the USA (Hawaii). *International Journal of Nursing Studies, 41*, 671-684.

Lavanco, G. (1997). Burnout syndrome and Type A behavior in nurses and teachers in Sicily. *Psychological Reports, 81*, 523-528.

Lazarus, R. S., and Folkman, S. (1984). *Stress appraisal and coping*. New York: Springer.

Leung, D. Y. P., and Lee, W. W. S. (2006). Predicting intention to quit among Chinese teachers: Differential predictability of the components of burnout. *Anxiety, Stress, and Coping, 19*, 129-141.

Leung, K., Bhagat, R. S., Buchan, N. R., Erez, M., and Gibson, C. B. (2005). Culture and international business: Recent advances and their implications for future research. *Journal of International Business Studies, 36*, 357-378.

Levine, R. V., and Norenzayan, A. (1999). The pace of life in 31 countries. *Journal of Cross-Cultural Psychology, 30*, 178-205.

Liu, C., and Spector, P. E. (2005). International and cross cultural issues. In J. Barling, K. Kelloway, and M. Frone (Eds.), *Handbook of Work Stress* (pp. 487-515). Thousand Oaks, CA: Sage.

Liu, C., Spector, P. E., and Shi, L. (2007). Cross-national job stress: A quantitative and qualitative study. *Journal of Organizational Behavior, 28*, 209-239.

Maslach, C. (2000). A multidimensional theory of burnout. In Cary L. Cooper (Ed.). *Theories of organizational stress* (pp. 68-85). New York: Oxford University Press.

Mor Barak, M. E., Findler, L., and Wind, L. H. (2003). Cross-cultural aspects of diversity and well-being in the workplace: An international perspective. *Journal of Social Work Research and Evaluation, 4*, 145-169.

Perrewé, P. L., Hochwarter, W. A., Rossi, A. M., Wallace, A., Maignan, I., Castro, S. L., et al. (2002). Are work stress relationships universal? A nine-region examination of role stressors, general self-efficacy, and burnout. *Journal of International Management, 8*, 163-187.

Pines, A. M. (2004a). Adult attachment styles and their relationship to burnout: A preliminary, cross-cultural investigation. *Work and Stress, 18*, 66-80.

Pines, A. M. (2004b). Why are Israelis less burned out? *European Psychologist, 9*, 69-77.

Pines, A. M., Ben-Ari, A., Utasi, A., and Larson, D. (2002). A cross-cultural investigation of social support and burnout. *European Psychologist, 7*, 256-264.

Pomaki, G., Supeli, A., and Verhoeven, C. (2007). Role conflict and health behaviors: Moderating effects on psychological distress and somatic complaints. *Psychology and Health, 22*, 317-335.

Sagiv, L., and Schwartz, S. H. (2000). Value priorities and subjective well-being: Direct relations and congruity effects. *European Journal of Social Psychology, 30*, 177-198.

Schwartz, S. H. (1999). A theory of cultural values and some implications for work. *Applied Psychology: An International Review, 48*, 23-47.

Siu, O. (2002). Occupational stressors and well-being among Chinese employees: The role of organizational commitment. *Applied Psychology: An International Review, 51*, 527-544.

Söderfeldt, M., Söderfeldt, B., Warg, L., and Ohlson, C. (1996). The factor structure of the Maslach Burnout Inventory in two Swedish human service organizations. *Scandinavian Journal of Psychology, 37*, 437-443.

Spector, P. E., Cooper, C. L., Sanchez, J. I., O'Driscoll, M., Sparks, K., et al. (2002). Locus of control and well-being at work: How generalizable are western findings? *Academy of Management Journal, 45*, 453-466.

Triandis, H.C. (1995) *Individualism and collectivism.* Boulder, CO: Westview Press.

Xu, Y. (2007). Adaptation strategies of Asian nurses working in western countries. *Home Health Care Management and Practice, 19*, 146-148.

Yin, J. C. T., and Yang, Y. P. A. (2002). Nursing turnover in Taiwan: A meta-analysis of related factors. *International Journal of Nursing Studies, 39*, 573-581.

In: Handbook of Stress and Burnout in Health Care   ISBN 978-1-60456-500-3
Editor: Jonathon R. B. Halbesleben   © 2008 Nova Science Publishers, Inc.

Chapter 8

STRESS IN ENTRANTS TO THE HEALTH CARE SYSTEM: NATURE, MEASUREMENT AND MANAGEMENT

Martyn Jones[*1] *and Steven Pryjmachuk*[2]

[1]NursingSchool of Nursing and Midwifery
University of Dundee, 11 Airlie Place, Dundee, DD1 4HJ
[2]School of Nursing, Midwifery and Social Work
The University of Manchester, Gateway House
Piccadilly South, Manchester M60 7LP

Concerns regarding the mental and physical well-being of student nurses are reported across the world. High levels of sickness absence and attrition during the educational program mean that this topic is of interest to both the health care systems in which the student will practice and the higher education institute in which the entrant pursues his or her studies. This chapter will examine student nurse stress, distress and coping from a range of theoretical frameworks, including transactional and other relevant interactive models of stress. It will detail the broad categories of situational stress reported by student nurses, high levels of distress they report and examine how students cope.

The literature on stress management in student nurses will be critically evaluated both at the individual student level using cognitive behavioral approaches, the interface between student and organization involving managerial support from clinical and academic sources and at the organizational level, for example, in terms of curriculum change. Where relevant, comparisons will be made with other types of health care student or those in higher education.

---
[*] Email: m.c.jones@dundee.ac.uk

WHAT IS THE SCOPE OF THE PROBLEM FOR
STUDENT NURSES?

Being a student can be a stressful experience. In the UK, typically around a third of students experience high levels of stress (Roberts, Golding, Towell, and Weireb, 1999), with reporting rates of 30 and 40% seen in social work and psychology students, respectively (Tobin and Carson, 1994) and between 17 and 19 per cent for the general population within the UK (Borrill et al. 1988).

Preparing to become a health care professional is also reported as a stressful experience (Morrissette, 2004; Powell, 2004; Tully, 2004). Some 30 to 40 % of nursing (Baldwin, Dodd, and Wrate, 1998; Pryjmachuk and Richards 2007) and around a third of medical students report significant emotional distress (Firth, 1986; Moffat, McConnachie, Ross, and Morrison, 2004). Student nurses are exposed to a wide range of academic and clinical demands early in their course which may result in some settings of up to 67% of student nurses reporting significant levels of distress (Jones and Johnston, 1997). Such issues are of international, global concern within nurse education (Davitz, 1972; Hamill, 1995; Morrissette, 2004; Suserud, 1993; Williams, Hagerty, Murphy-Weinberg, and Wan, 1995).

THEORETICAL APPROACHES TO THE STUDY OF
STUDENT NURSES STRESS, DISTRESS AND COPING

A range of theoretical approaches can be found in the general occupational stress literature linking the work environment and well being (House, 1981; Karasek, 1979; Lazarus and Folkman, 1984; Siegrist, 1996). However, the nature of occupational stress for student nurses has been described almost exclusively from a transactional perspective. Comparatively little is known about the effect of the work environment on student well-being and performance, with key exceptions (Jones and Johnston 2005; Parkes, 1986).

*Transactional model of stress (Lazarus and Folkman, 1984; Cox et al, 2000).*The transactional model has defined stress as, "a particular relationship between the person and the environment which is appraised by the person as taxing or exceeding his or her resources and endangering his or her well-being" (Lazarus and Folkman, 1984, p. 19). With stress viewed as a continuous series of interactions, adjustments or transactions between person and environment, and described in terms of the cognitive processes and emotional reactions arising from person-environment transactions, or as an over demand. The central construct of this model, cognitive appraisal, weighs perceived demand against perceived availability of individual resources, and following appraisal of the control opportunities present in a situation, the enactment of considered coping behaviour has the potential to alleviate or worsen the subjective impact of a situation (Folkman, 1984).

The experience of stress is defined by an individual's '… realisation that they are having difficulty coping with demands and threats to their well-being … [and by a realisation] that coping is important and the difficulty in coping worries or depresses them'(Cox, Griffiths, and Rial-Gonzales, 2000, p. 42).

WHAT DO STUDENTS WORRY ABOUT?

Current evidence suggests that student nurses experience high levels of stress arising from a range of sources during the early parts of their training (Jones and Johnston, 1997, 1999, 2006). The literature identifies four main sources of stress including academic, clinical sources, personal/social and interface sources.

Academic sources of stress consistently reported in the literature include examinations and assessments (Baldwin, Dodd, and Wrate, 1998; Beck and Srivastava, 1991; Clarke and Ruffin, 1992; Jones and Johnston, 1997; Kipping, 2000; Lindop, 1991; Howard 2001); workload (Clarke and Ruffin, 1992; Jones and Johnston, 1997; Lo 2002) and the fear of failure (Jones and Johnston 1997; Parkes 1985). Similar reports regarding the salience of workload and examination stressors are seen in generic higher education students (University of Leicester, 2002).

Clinical sources of stress feature consistently in student reports. Items include placements (Kipping, 2000; Snape and Cavanagh 1995); the fear of making mistakes (Clarke and Ruffin, 1992; Kleehammer, Hart, and Keck, 1990); the initial clinical experience (Jones and Johnston 1997; Kleehammer et al. 1990); and issues related to death and dying (Rhead 1995; Snape and Cavanagh 1995). Concerns regarding interpersonal relationships with other staff, particularly negative and hostile attitudes from superiors are common (Howard 2001; Kirkland 1988; Kleehammer et al. 1990; Lindop, 1991).

Personal/social sources of stress consistently reported include finances (Baldwin et al. 1998; Beck and Srivastava 1991; Brown and Edelmann 2000; Jones and Johnston 1997; Kirkland 1988; Lo 2002; Timmins and Kaliszer 2002) and issues relating to the home-college interface such as a lack of free time (Baldwin et al. 1998). Demands representing the interface between work and home environments are relevant for men and women generally, and for nursing students in particular (Jones and Johnston, 1997).

Several measures of student nurse stressors exist (Beck and Srivastava, 1991; Clarke and Ruffin, 1992; Rhead, 1995), however the factor structures of such measures have not been sufficiently explored with sufficient participants and none of these measures were validated across independent samples of student nurses. The Student Nurse Stress Index (Jones and Johnston, 1999), however, has a reliable 22 variable solution with a simple oblique, (i.e., correlated) structure. This factor structure was obtained in this initial sample of 235 first year student nurses, and confirmed at an exploratory level in a further independent validation sample of 188 first year students. Factors include; *Academic load* including amount, difficulty of class work, examinations and grades, fear of failing; *Clinical concerns* focusing on relationships with other professionals, too much responsibility, patient attitudes, teaching climate in clinical setting, relations with clinical staff; *Personal problems* including personal health problems, physical health of family members, relationships with parents, other problems; *Interface worries* including peer competition, lack of free time, school response, lack of performance feedback, no time for entertainment or family. This measure is currently in use in a range of international settings and has been used to characterize student nurse stress in a range of studies (Jones and Johnston 2006; Morrissette, 2004; Pryjmachuk and Richards, 2007; Tully, 2004).

How Has Distress Been Conceptualized and Measured?

Stress has been operationalized using a broad range of subjective and objective measures, the range of measures reflecting the complexity of the concept. Objective measures have tended to focus largely on the physiological aspects of the stress-response and have included measures of blood pressure, heart rate and galvanic skin response as well as levels of the so-called 'stress hormones' adrenaline, noradrenaline and cortisol in saliva, urine or blood (Payne, 1999).

In examining the impact of preparing to become a student nurse, the majority of studies have used self-report, context-free measures of affect. The State-Trait Anxiety Inventory (Spielberger, Gorsuch, and Luchene, 1983) purports to measure anxiety, both 'trait' (dispositional) and 'state' (situational) anxiety. The General Health Questionnaire (Goldberg and Williams, 1988) produces either a general index of psychological distress or categorisation into the dichotomy 'case' vs. 'normal', depending on how the scale is scored and cut-off determined. Using this approach, entrants to the health care environment generally report difficulties in adjustment, with up to 68% of student nurses reporting significant levels of affective distress within 6 months of entry (Jones and Johnston, 1997) Of the few studies examining burnout in student nurses (Constantini, Solano, Di Napoli, and Bosco, 1997; Schaufeli, van Direndonck, and van Gorp, 1996), one has suggested that a key feature of the phenomenon, i.e. "*depersonalization*" is not seen in students early in their training (Schaufeli et al., 1996). Various developmental models of burnout have also been proposed and tested (Schaufeli, et al., 1996), with job stress leading to "*emotional exhaustion*", which in turn leads to "*depersonalization*" (Keijsers, Schaufeli, Le Blanc, Zwerts, and Miranda, 1995) . Burnout in turn may lead to student attrition (Deary, Watson, and Hogston, 2003). Studies reporting job satisfaction reported by student nurses are rare (e.g., Jones and Johnston, 2005).

How Do Student Nurses Cope?

Early research the coping of student nurses has been carried out by Katherine Parkes in the 1980's in initial educational and practice settings (Parkes, 1984; 1986). This involved the amendment of a version of the Ways of Coping questionnaire (Coyne, Aldwin, and Lazarus, 1981), and its presentation to 171 student nurses in their first year of study, over a four year period (Parkes, 1984). The 44 item amendment was comprised of a general and two bipolar factors named, "*general*", "*direct*", and ""*suppression*"" coping, respectively.

"*General*" coping reflected student tendencies to use cognitive and behavioral coping strategies in difficult situations, and was described initially as representing student coping repertoire. "*Direct*" coping combines the use of rational problem-focused strategies to change, or manage the stressful situation, and avoidance of emotionally based items such as *fantasy, wishful thinking* and *hostility*. "*Suppression*" coping, reflects coping effort aimed at suppressing thoughts of the situation, inhibiting action and carrying on as if nothing has happened. Including both problem-focused and emotion-focused strategies, "*direct*" and "*suppression*" coping are both potentially adaptive strategies.

Student nurses reporting high distress with low direct coping scores generally use "wishful thinking", "escape", "fantasy" and "hostility" to cope with difficult situations Student nurses experiencing low levels of distress on the GHQ 30 showed a tendency to use problem solving strategies in preference to using "fantasy" and "hostility" (Jones and Johnston, 1997; 2006).

Other recent studies of coping in student nurses (e.g., Pryjmachuk and Richards, 2007), have used the *Coping Inventory for Stressful Situations* (CISS;Endler and Parker 1990). The CISS-Adult is a 48-item measure of dispositional (as opposed to situational) coping that yields three factors. Two of the factors, 'task-oriented' coping (coping that employs cognitive or behavioral problem-solving techniques) and 'emotion-oriented' coping (coping that employs emotional techniques, such as fantasy or self-preoccupation) are comparable, respectively, to the problem- and emotion-focused scales found in other widely used coping scales, including the WCQ. A third factor, 'avoidance-oriented' coping, involves avoidance of the stressful situation by either engaging in a distracting task or by seeking out other people. Using this approach, differences in coping between branches of nursing have emerged (Pryjmachuk and Richards, in press). Mental health nursing students tend to use fewer emotion-focused coping strategies than adult students, which may be a product of the mental health students' use of 'direct coping.' Alternatively, such differences between branches of student nurses may also be explained by differences in hardiness between groups. Hardiness is thought to buffer stress (Cox, 1993; Pagana, 1990; Sawatzky, 1998) although the evidence for this is not particularly overwhelming. Mental health nurses may also perceive potential stressors as challenges rather than threats, and feel more in control.

WHAT CAN BE DONE ABOUT STRESS IN STUDENT NURSES?

There is a recognized need for interventions at an organizational level to reduce work stress and improve staff well-being in general and health-related work settings (Couzins et al., 2004). While there is considerable evidence regarding the general concerns reported by student nurses, the design and evaluation of stress management interventions with randomised controlled trials are very rare. Cox et al. (2000) states that stress can be tackled on a primary, secondary or tertiary level, levels and can be loosely described, respectively, as prevention, timely reaction and rehabilitation.

Primary approaches. Primary approaches to dealing with stress – prevention – generally involve what Cox et al. (2000) call 'hazard control', such as controlling particular sources of stress. Although it is often impossible to remove some stressors, concessions from an organizational perspective can sometimes be made. Reviewing the assessment load when designing curricula is, for example, one way of tacking the anxiety associated with examinations. Other considerations could include a reduction in unnecessary coursework (Lo, 2002) or the use of befriending or 'buddy' systems to help students settle in (Monk and Mahmood, 1999). Alternatively, examining the effects of managerial support on student well-being offers the opportunity to develop an organizational level intervention (Jones and Johnston, 2005).

The positive effect of organizational change in the form of introducing a student-centred, problem-based learning curriculum on student well-being, demonstrated for some time in medical students (Kiessling, Schubert, Scheffner, and Burger, 2004; Moore-West, Harrington, Mennin, Kaufman, and Skipper, 1989), has only recently been shown in nursing students (Jones and Johnston, 2006). Students on an innovative student centred course based around problem-based learning reported lower levels of distress at comparable time points in the first year of the course and reported fewer academic, clinical and personal worries than students in the previous more traditional course. Students on the more student centred program were more likely to report using adaptive direct, problem-solving coping at week 50, see Table 1. In this setting, curriculum innovation was associated with positive changes in student well-being. However, such positive changes were not mirrored by any improvement in academic performance or reductions in sickness absence.

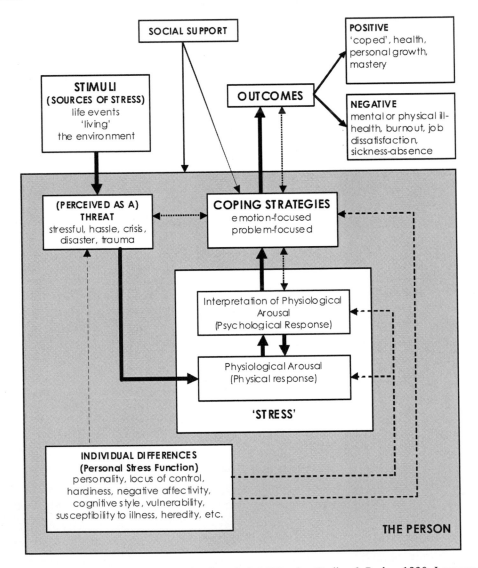

Figure 1. A transactional model of stress (Pryjmachuk 2003, after Endler & Parker 1990; Lazarus & Folkman 1984; Payne 1999).

Table 1. Comparative levels of distress in student nurses on traditional and innovative courses

Traditional scheme of nurse education	Student centred scheme of nurse education
Week 24, n=197. 67.5% distressed	Week 25, n=340. 38.8% distressed
Week 40, n=194. 58.2% distressed	Week 50, n=291. 33.7% distressed

Few studies have examined the role of managerial support in the adaptation of health care entrants (Olk and Friedlander, 1992). Little is known about the general effect of managerial support on entrant well-being (Jones and Johnston, 2000a) and how this may affect sickness absence and attrition (Deary, Watson, and Hogston, 2003).

Recent research has shown that support from both academic and clinical sources has an indirect influence on student nurse job satisfaction, but by differing mechanisms (Jones and Johnston, 2005). Managerial support at an academic level has its positive association with satisfaction via role clarity (accounting for 5% of the variance in satisfaction, see Figure 2). The mediation of clinical support on satisfaction is because of the increased role clarity and job control reported by entrants (see Figure 3). The influence of an academic tutor/clinical preceptor support on satisfaction results in increased perceived role clarity and control. Managerial support from clinical sources seems to be particularly important to facilitating entrant perceptions of control, particularly as the course progresses. This approach also revealed that emotional distress had an indirect association with sickness absence, via somatic health.

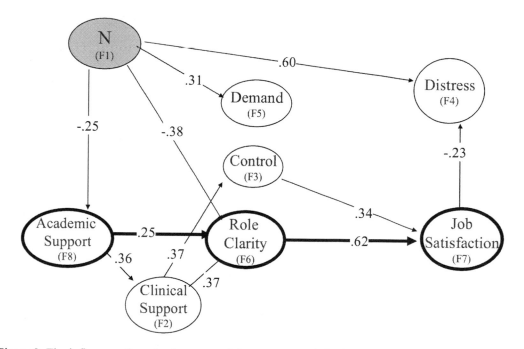

Figure 2. The influence of academic managerial support on satisfaction.

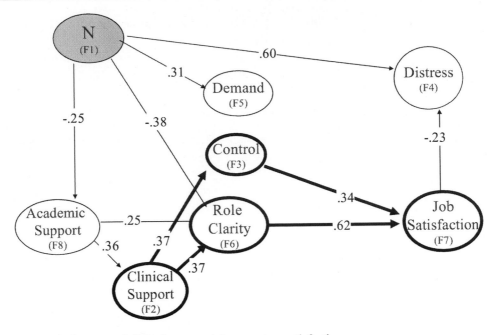

Figure 3. The influences of clinical managerial support on satisfaction.

Secondary approaches. Secondary approaches to dealing with stress – timely reaction – generally involve training programs and initiatives designed to help individuals manage stress or the sources of stress. While there is a considerable literature examining the effects of stress management in general work settings (Michie and Williams, 2003) and in trained nurses (Mimura and Griffiths, 2003) there are far fewer stress management interventions targeting student nurses. Since 1990 there have been only three randomized controlled trials targeting student nurses with a range of stress management interventions (see Table 2 for design details). Further detail regarding additional quasi-experimental and pre-experimental studies are identified by Jones and Johnston(2000b).

The focus of the majority of worksite studies involving student nurses has been at an individual level, with preventive interventions delivered to groups of unselected, non-distressed participants. The sole exception to this being the intervention described by Jones and Johnston (2000c), which targeted student nurses showing significant levels of emotional distress. The design, content and outcome of this intervention are described below.

The evidence for the effectiveness of such studies has been mixed. Many studies have had little adaptive impact. This absence of treatment effect may have been related to power issues in some studies, with insufficient participants in each treatment group, e.g. Russler, (1991). The success of these studies has been largely quantified in terms of reductions in state anxiety for treatment groups (Johansson, 1991; Jones and Johnston, 2000b). Reductions in trait anxiety following training have also been found (Jones and Johnston, 2000b). The impact of stress reduction/management programs targeting student nurses have been demonstrated at both interface and organizational levels, with reductions in *"domestic"* and *"vocational dissatisfaction"* for those receiving the program (Jones and Johnston, 2000c).

Table 2. Methodological characteristics of worksite stress reduction and management interventions targeting student nurses 1990-2006 (Jones and D. Johnston, 2000b; Ruotsalainen and Verbeek, 2006)

Source	Subjects	Design	Training Methods	Programme format	Response Measures	Results		Comments
						Post training	Follow-up	
1. Johansson (1991).	42 sophomore, 34 senior nursing students.	Experimental, no-treatment control, pretest-post test design, with stratified random allocation. Measures taken weekly on three occasions pre/post intervention, averaged to give a single pre/post treatment score.	Stress inoculation approach (education/ training/ application). Breathing exercises, progressive muscular autogenic relaxation.	6, 50 minute sessions, 2 sessions a week. Treatment given in groups.	State and Trait Anxiety; Institute for Personality and Ability Testing (IPAT) Depression Scale.	Found a treatment group main-effect with a 2 x 2 ANOVA, with E/C time 2 data, and year 1/2 as between group factors. No effect of year, or group x year interaction for Anxiety and Depression.	No further evaluation.	Volunteers not selected for recent distress.
2. Jones and Johnston, (2000)	73 student nurses.	Experimental, pre-test, post-test, 3 month follow-up, with a wait-control group. Repeated measures design, with evaluation at individual, interface and organizational levels. Intervention took place during a second series of hospital placements. Intervention set at individual and interface levels.	Didactic presentation of information augmented with applied relaxation, problem solving (individual and group), time and self management skills, and the alteration of lifestyle and health behaviours.	6, 2 hour, weekly sessions. Intervention provided in a group setting. 3 experimental groups, with a maximum of 14 participants in each.	General Health Questionnaire (30 item version), State and Trait Anxiety Inventory (STAI), Beck Depression Inventory (BDI), Derogatis Stress Profile, Beck and Srivastava Stress Inventory (BSSI), Ways of Coping Questionnaire (Parkes, 1984), Objective performance measures.	Overall treatment x time interactions found with GHQ, STAI, BDI and emotional response domain from Derogatis Stress Profile. In addition, a similar effect was seen with Direct coping, and BSSI.	Adaptive changes in antecedent, process and outcome variables following intervention were maintained to 3 month follow-up for experimental group. Participants receiving intervention reported lower anxiety prior to examination at 3 and 18 month follow-up.	Participants selected in terms of the significant levels of distress experienced during their initial series of hospital placements. Some 53% of adaptive changes in GHQ scores attributable to the intervention.
3. Russler, (1991).	57 first year baccalaureate nursing students.	Experimental, pre-test post-test, placebo group, control group design.	Stress Inoculation with relaxation, assertiveness skills and didactic content for experimental group. Self-awareness training for placebo control.	16 hours of contact on two consecutive Saturdays for experimental and placebo control groups.	State and Trait Anxiety; Reported Emotions Survey; Ways of Coping; Coopersmith Self Esteem Inventory; Schedule of Recent Experience.	Time main effects for State Anxiety, Reported Emotions and Coping. Intervention had no effect.	No longer term follow-up.	Unselected, non-distressed volunteers recruited to this preventive study.

A recently completed systematic review of stress management interventions of prevention of occupational stress in health care workers has not identified any further stress management interventions targeting student nurses and suggests that there is a continuing need to evaluate the effect of such interventions with larger and better quality trials (Ruotsalainen and Verbeek, 2006).

Jones and Johnston (2000c) provided an outline for stress management programs. This intervention adopted a transactional conceptualisation of the stress process (Lazarus and Folkman, 1984) to guide the design and implementation of the informational and skill acquisition content of the worksite-based coping intervention. In addition, the heuristic framework suggested by Ivancevich, et al., (1990) guided the design, implementation and evaluation of the intervention. According to Ivancevich, et al., (1990) a work site stress management intervention can target and attempt to:

(a) Reduce the intensity or number of situational stressors faced by the individual;
(b) To help the individual modify their appraisal of potentially stressful situations; and
(c) To help the individual cope more effectively with the consequences of stress.

This multi-modal stress management intervention was comprised of six, two-hour sessions held in a School of Nursing and Midwifery. Sessions were additional to the routine curriculum. Each session incorporated a brief 15 minute didactic presentation of information related to the practise of specific coping skills. The coping skills presented included self-monitoring of distress symptoms (Session 1), the use of problem solving strategies to change situations (D'Zurrilla, 1990) (Session 2), the use of the cognitive technique of situational reappraisal (Session 3), and the development of time and self-management skills to improve personal effectiveness in the academic setting and to increase health protecting behaviour use (Schafer, 1992) (Session 4). Experiential learning was a central teaching strategy which encouraged the application of these techniques to personally relevant clinical, academic and home/work settings. Individual and group reflection followed practice in both classroom and real-life settings. Sessions 5 and 6 enabled the application of previously attained generic stress management skills to situations of current concern. Students formulated their own plans to amend or adapt to problematic situations arising from the course. In particular, participants were required to develop strategies to manage academic demands including coping with examinations within a scenario context, and concerning their own forthcoming examinations.

A six session relaxation intervention formed a major component of the series of six workshops, (Johnston et al., 1993; Ost, 1987). The aim of the relaxation program was to enable the student to relax in a non-threatening situation in 30 seconds, and for the student to generalise this "applied relaxation" coping skill in real life situations. The process of "applied relaxation" skill acquisition involved introducing the student to a sequence of progressive muscular relaxation (Session 1), release-only relaxation (Session 2), rapid relaxation training (Session 4), and practice in the application of rapid relaxation in real life situations (Sessions 5 and 6). The techniques of autogenic relaxation and meditation were introduced in Session 3.

The intervention had a positive impact on affective outcomes including General Health Questionnaire-30, see Figure 4, State and Trait Anxiety Inventory, Beck Depression Inventory, and a measure of domestic satisfaction. The intervention also led to an increase in Direct Coping use, see Figure 5. The overall intervention produced changes in coping use across time, with an increase in rational task-orientated coping following the intervention reported by the experimental group alone. This within-group effect was apparent at three month follow-up. State Anxiety immediately preceding two important examinations, i.e. at three- and 18-month follow-up, was lower for students receiving stress management. These reductions were directly attributable to treatment.

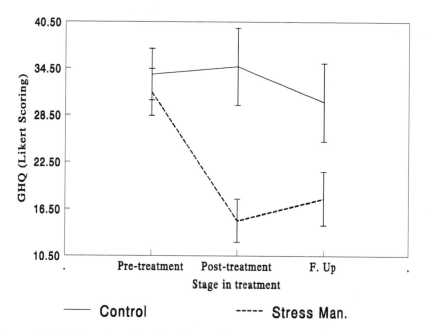

Figure 4. General Health Questionnaire, the effects of stress management (Jones and Johnston, 2000).

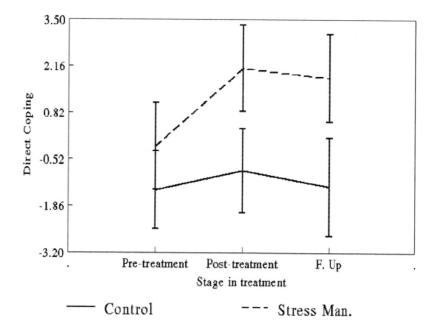

Figure 5. Direct Coping, the effects of stress management (Jones and Johnston, 2000).

The six session treatment produced no detectable effects on the organizational outcomes of sickness, absence, and academic performance of participants. In this study, there was no relationship between initial distress, sickness, absence and academic performance prior to the intervention, a finding confirmed in a later study with independent cohorts (Jones and Johnston, 2005). This study was designed to improve uptake of managerial support in clinical and academic settings. Such strategies are rarely included in worksite stress management interventions targeting student nurses. In addition, using participant experience as a focus, a problem solving approach in a group setting (Sessions 2-6) was used to reduce of work-family conflict.

Tertiary approaches. Tertiary approaches to dealing with stress – rehabilitation – are generally concerned with counselling or, in an occupational environment, with what are often termed 'employee assistance programs' (EAPs). In terms of outcomes such as sickness-absence and self-reported psychological health, evaluations of EAPs/workplace counselling have generally been positive in a general work setting (Cox et al. 2000; McLeod 2001) although there has been little work into what the 'active ingredient' of these programs might be. Such interventions are rarely reported targeting student nurses. However, the consortium of Health Promoting Universities in the UK (HEFC, 2001; University of Leicester, 2002) now offers counselling to all students and provides Employee Assistance Programmes where necessary.

CONCLUSION

Student nurse stress is a concern worldwide. While there is a growing literature that clarifies the nature of student concerns, coping and distress levels, there is still very little robust evidence about what to do to remedy the situation. Of the limited research carried out, most is restricted to the individual level, helping the person to adjust, ignoring the organizational determinants that contribute to the problem. There is virtually no evaluation of primary (organizational) or tertiary level interventions targeting entrants to the health care services, such as student nurses. There is an urgent need to undertake a program of research to explore the organizational and personal determinants of occupational stress in health care entrants, such as student nurses, and to develop and evaluate such multi-level interventions at primary, secondary and tertiary levels using randomized controlled designs.

REFERENCES

Baldwin, P., Dodd, M., and Wrate, R. (1998). *Nurses: Training, Work, Health and Welfare: A Longitudinal Study 1994-1998*. (No. K/OPR/2/2D172). Edinburgh: CSO.

Beck, D. L., and Srivastava, R. (1991). Perceived Level and Sources of Stress in Baccalaureate Nursing Students. *Journal of Nursing Education, 30*(3), 127-133.

Borrill, C. S., Wall, T. D., West, M. A., Hardy, G. E., Shapiro, D. A., Haynes, C. E., Stride, C. B., Woods, D., and Carter, A. (1998). *Stress among Staff in NHS Trusts: Final Report*. Sheffield/Leeds: Institute of Work Psychology, University of Sheffield/Psychological Therapies Research Centre, University of Leeds.

Brown, H., and Edelmann, R. (2000). Project 2000: a study of expected and experienced stressors and support reported by students and qualified nurses. *Journal of Advanced Nursing, 31*(4), 857-864.

Burke, R. J. (1993). Organizational Level Interventions to Reduce Occupational Stressors. *Work and Stress, 7*, 77-87.

Clarke, V. A., and Ruffin, C. L. (1992). Perceived Sources of Stress among Student Nurses. *Contemporary Nurse: A Journal for the Australian Nursing Profession, 1*(1), 35-40.

Constantini, A., Solano, L., Di Napoli, R., and Bosco, A. (1997). Relationship between Hardiness and Risk of Burnout in a Sample of 92 Nurses Working in Oncology and AIDS Wards. *Psychotherapy and Psychosomatics, 66*, 78-82.

Couzins, R., Mackay, C., Clark, S., Kelly, C., Kelly, P., and Mccaig, R. (2004). 'Management Standards' and work-related stress in the UK: Practical development. *Work and Stress, 18*, 113-136.

Cox, T. (1993). *Stress Research and Stress Management: Putting Theory to Work* (No. No 61). London: HSE Contract Research Report, HMSO.

Cox, T., Griffiths, A., and Rial-Gonzales, E. (2000). *Research on work related stress.* Luxembourg: European Agency for Safety and Health at Work.

Coyne, J. C., Aldwin, C., and Lazarus, R. S. (1981). Depression and Coping in Stressful Episodes. *Journal of Abnormal Psychology, 90*(5), 439-447.

Davitz, L. J. (1972). Identification of Stressful Situations in a Nigerian School of Nursing. *Nursing Research, 21*(4), 352-357.

D'Zurrilla, T. J. (1990). Problem Solving Training For Effective Stress Management and Prevention. *Journal of Cognitive Psychotherapy: An International Quarterly, 4*(4), 327-354.

Deary, I., Watson, R., and Hogston, R. (2003). A Longitudinal Cohort Study of Burnout and Attrition in Nursing Students. *Journal of Advanced Nursing, 43*(1), 71-81.

Endler, N. S. and Parker, J. D. A. (1990). Multi-dimensional assessment of coping: a critical evaluation. *Journal of Personality and Social Psychology, 58*(5), 844-854.

Firth, Jenny A. (1986). Levels and Sources of Stress in Medical Students. *British Medical Journal, 292*, 1177-1180.

Folkman, S. (1984). Personal Control and Stress and Coping Processes: A Theoretical Analysis. *Journal of Personality and Social Psychology, 46*(4), 839-852.

Goldberg, D., and Williams, P. (1988). *A Users Guide to the General Health Questionnaire.* Windsor: NFer-Nelson.

Hamill, C. (1995). The Phenomenon of Stress as Perceived by Project 2000 Student Nurses: A Case Study. *Journal of Advanced Nursing, 21*, 528-536.

Higher Education Funding Council. (2001). *Occupational Stress in Higher Education Institutions*: University of Plymouth http://www.ihs.plymouth.ac.uk/~stresshe.index.htm Accessed February 2005.

House, J. S. (1981). *Work Stress and Social Support.* London: Addison-Wesley Publishing Company.

Howard, D. A. (2001). Student nurses' experience of Project 2000. *Nursing Standard, 15*(48), 33-38 (15 August).

Ivancevich, J. M., Matteson, M. T., Freedman, S. M., and Phillips, J. S. (1990). Worksite Stress Management Interventions. *American Psychologist, 45*(2), 252-261.

Johansson, N. (1991). Effectiveness of a Stress Management Program in Reducing Anxiety and Depression in Nursing Students. *Journal of American College Health, 40*, 125-129.

Jones, M. C., and Johnston, D. W. (1997). Distress, Stress and Coping in First-Year Student Nurses. *Journal of Advanced Nursing, 26*, 475-482.

Jones, M. C., and Johnston, D. W. (1999). The Derivation of a Brief Student Nurse Stress Index. *Work and Stress, 13*(2), 162-181.

Jones, M., and Johnston, D. (2000a). A Critical Review of the Relationship Between Perception of the Work Environment, Coping and Mental Health in Trained Nurses, and Patient Outcomes. *Clinical Effectiveness in Nursing, 4*, 75-85.

Jones, M., and Johnston, D. (2000b). Reducing Distress in First Level and Student Nurses: A Review of the Applied Stress Management Literature. *Journal of Advanced Nursing, 32*(1), 66-74.

Jones, M. C., and Johnston, D. W. (2000c). Evaluating the Impact of a Worksite Stress Management Programme for Distressed Student Nurses: A Randomised Controlled Trial. *Psychology and Health, 15*(5), 689-706.

Jones, M. C., and Johnston, D. W. (2005). Exploring the Michigan Model: The relationship of personality, managerial support and organisational structure with health outcomes of entrants to the healthcare environment. *Work and Stress, 19*, 1-22.

Jones, M. C., and Johnston , D. W. (2006). Is the introduction of a student-centred, problem-based curriculum associated with improvements in student nurse well-being and performance? An observational study of effect. *International Journal of Nursing Studies, 43*, 941-952.

Karasek, R. A. (1979). Job Demands, Job Decision Latitude and Mental Strain: Implications for Job Redesign. *Administrative Science Quarterly, 24*, 285-308.

Keijsers, G. J., Schaufeli, W. B., Le Blanc, P. M., Zwerts, C., and Miranda, D. R. (1995). Performance and Burnout in Intensive Care Units. *Work and Stress, 9*(4), 513-527.

Kiessling, C., Schubert, B., Scheffner, D., and Burger, W. (2004). First year medical students' perceptions of stress and suppport: A comparision between reformed and traditional track curricula. *Medical Education, 38*, 504-509.

Kipping, C. (2000). Stress in mental health nursing. *International Journal of Nursing Studies, 37*, 207-218.

Kleehammer, K., Hart, A. L., and Keck, J. F. (1990). Nursing Students' Perceptions of Anxiety-Producing Situations in the Clinical Setting. *Journal of Nursing Education, 29*, 183-187.

Lazarus, R. S., and Folkman, S. (1984). *Stress, appraisal and coping.* New York: Springer Publishing Company.

Lindop, E. (1991). Individual Stress Among Nurses in Training: Why Some Leave While Others Stay. *Nurse Education Today, 11*, 110-120.

Lo, R. (2002). A longitudinal study of perceived level of stress, coping and self-esteem of undergraduate nursing students: an Australian case study. *Journal of Advanced Nursing, 39*(2), 119-126.

McLeod, J. (2001). *Counselling in the workplace: The facts. A systematic study of the research evidence.* Rugby: British Association for Counselling and Psychotherapy.

Michie, S., and Williams, S. (2003). Reducing work related psychological ill-health and sickness absence: A Systematic literature review. *Occupational and Environmental Medicine, 60*, 3-9.

Moffat, K., McConnachie, A., Ross, S., and Morrison, J. (2004). First year medical student stress and coping in a problem-based learning medical curriculum. *Medical Education, 38,* 482-491.

Monk, E. M., and Mahmood, Z. (1999). Student mental health: a pilot study. *Counselling Psychology Quarterly, 12*(2), 199-210.

Mimura, C., and Griffiths, P. (2002). The effectiveness of current approaches to workplace stress management in the nursing profession: An evidence-based literature. *Occupational and Environmental Medicine, 60,* 10-15.

Morrissette, P. (2004). Promoting psychiatric student nurse well-being. *Journal of Psychiatric Mental Health Nursing, 11,* 534-540.

Olk, M., and Friedlander, M. (1992). Trainees' experiences of role conflict and role ambiguity in supervisory relationships. *Journal of Counseling Psychology, 39*(3), 389-397.

Ost, L. G. (1987). Applied relaxation: description of a coping technique and review of controlled studies. *Behavioural Research Therapy, 25*(5), 397-409.

Pagana, K. D. (1990). The relationship of hardiness and social support to student appraisal of stress in an initial clinical nursing situation. *Journal of Nursing Education, 29*(6), 255-261.

Parkes, K. (1984). locus of control, cognitive appraisal, and coping in stressful episodes. *Journal of Personality and Social Psychology, 46,* 655-668.

Parkes, K. (1986). Coping in stressful episodes: The role of individual differences, environmental factors, and situational characteristics. *Journal of Personality and Social Psychology, 51,* 1277-1292.

Payne, R. (1999). Stress at work: a conceptual framework. In J. Firth-Cozens and R. Payne (eds.) *Stress in Health Professionals: Psychological and Organisational Causes and Interventions.* Chichester: John Wiley and Sons.

Pryjmachuk, S. (2003). *Sources of stress, stress and coping in a population of pre registration nursing and midwifery students.* Unpublished PhD Thesis. Manchester: The University of Manchester.

Pryjmachuk, S., and Richards, D. (2007). Predicting stress in pre-registration nursing students. *British Journal of Health Psychology, 12,* 125-144.

Pryjmachuk, S., and Richards, D. A. (in press). Mental health nursing students differ from other nursing students: Some observations from a study on stress and coping. *International Journal of Mental Health Nursing.*

Rhead, M. M. (1995). Stress Among Student Nurses: Is it Practical or Academic? *Journal of Clinical Nursing, 4*(6), 369-376.

Roberts, R., Golding, J., Towell, T.,and Weireb, I. (1999). The effects of economic circumstances on British students' mental and physical health. *Journal of American College Health, 48,* 103-109.

Ruotsalainen, M., and Verbeek, S. (2006). Preventing occupational stress in healthcare workers. *Cochrane Database of Systematic Reviews, 2006*(4), Art No.: CD002892. DOI: 002810.001002/14651858.CD14002892.pub14651852.

Russler, M. F. (1991). Multidimensional stress management in nursing education. *Journal of Nursing Education, 30*(8), 341-346.

Sawatzky, J. (1998). Understanding nursing students' stress: A proposed framework. *Nurse Education Today, 18,* 108-115.

Schafer, W. (1992). *Stress Management for Wellness* (Second ed.). Fort Worth: Harcourt Brace Janovich.

Schaufeli, W. B., van Direndonck, D., and van Gorp, K. (1996). Burnout and reciprocity: Towards a dual-level social exchange model. *Work and Stress, 10*, 225-237.

Siegrist, J. (1996). Adverse health effects of high-effort/low-reward conditions. *Journal of Occupational Health Psychology, 1*, 27-41.

Snape, J. and Cavanagh, S. (1995). The problems facing students of nursing. *Education Today: Journal of the College of Teachers, 45*(2), 10-15.

Spielberger, C., Gorsuch, R., and R, L. (1983). *The State-Trait Inventory: Test Manual for Form Y*. Palo Alto, California: Consulting Psychologists Press.

Suserud, B.-O. (1993). Acting at a disaster site: Views expressed by swedish nursing students. *Journal of Advanced Nursing, 18*, 613-620.

Tobin, P. J., and Carson, J. (1994). Stress and the student social worker. *Social Work and Social Sciences Review, 5*(3), 246-255.

Timmins, F., and Kaliszer, M. (2002). Absenteeism among student nurses: Fact or fiction. *Journal of Nursing Management, 10*, 251-264.

Tully, A. (2004). Stress, sources of stress and ways of coping among psychiatric nursing students. *Journal of Psychiatric Mental Health Nursing, 11*, 43-47.

University of Leicester. (2002). *Student psychological health project: Undergraduate student survey results - Report of findings from research conducted in 2001 and 1998.*: Leicester: University of Leicester Educational Development and Support Centre. Available from www.le.ac.uk/edsc/sphp. Accessed July 2007.

Williams, R. A., Hagerty, B. M., Murphy-Weinberg, V., and Wan, J. (1995). Symptoms of depression among female nursing students. *Archives of Psychiatric Nursing, 9*(5), 269-278.

In: Handbook of Stress and Burnout in Health Care
Editor: Jonathon R. B. Halbesleben

ISBN 978-1-60456-500-3
© 2008 Nova Science Publishers, Inc.

Chapter 9

CROSSOVER OF BURNOUT AMONG HEALTH CARE PROFESSIONALS

Mina Westman[1] and Arnold B. Bakker[2]
[1]Tel Aviv University
Faculty of Management, Tel Aviv, Israel
[2]Erasmus University Rotterdam,
Dept. of Work and Organizational Psychology
Rotterdam, the Netherlands

There is a growing interest in the psychosocial work environment of health care professionals (e.g., physicians, nurses) since they are at high risk for burnout. Take for example the work of intensive care nurses. Traditionally, they have heavy workloads and extensive responsibilities, they must care for unstable patients, do accurate routines, and react to extremely urgent matters (Erlen and Sereika, 1997), although their decision latitude is often insufficient to cope effectively with these demands (Sawatzky, 1996). Such working conditions form the breeding ground for job stress. According to the demand-control model (DCM; Karasek, 1979), jobs that combine high job demands with low job control evoke psychological and physical distress ('high strain' jobs). These working conditions eventually deplete nurses' emotional resources and may initiate the burnout syndrome (e.g., Bourbonnais, Comeau and Vézina, 1999; DeRijk, LeBlanc, Schaufeli and DeJonge, 1998).

While job stress perspectives like the DCM try to explain how strain and burnout originate in the work environment, the present chapter takes a different perspective by looking at the social nature of work. Specifically, we will discuss research showing that burnout and other work-related states may *transfer* among individuals at the workplace. The notion that burnout may cross over from one employee to another is not new. Several authors have used anecdotal evidence to argue that job-induced strain and burnout may transfer between colleagues (e.g., Cherniss, 1980; Edelwich and Brodsky, 1980; Schwartz and Will, 1953). We will describe recent, more systematic studies that have provided empirical evidence for this phenomenon.

Two streams of literature will be combined, namely research on *crossover* and *emotional contagion*. Crossover research has traditionally focused on the crossover of stress and strain from employees to their *partners* and vice versa. Emotional contagion research originated in the laboratory, and has been applied to the transference of burnout from employees to their *colleagues*. Thus crossover research focuses mainly on the dyads while emotional contagion research focuses mainly on the team. Before we discuss the phenomena of crossover and emotional contagion, we will first introduce the concept of burnout, since many crossover and contagion studies have used this state as the focal variable of interest.

BURNOUT

Burnout has been defined as a specific kind of occupational stress among human service professionals, as a result of the demanding and emotionally charged relationships between caregivers and their recipients (Maslach and Jackson, 1981; see also Demerouti and Bakker, this volume). Feelings of emotional exhaustion are generally considered a core symptom of the burnout syndrome (Shirom, 1989). In addition, two other central characteristics of burnout have been documented: the development of negative, cynical attitudes towards the recipients of one's service or care (depersonalization), and the tendency to believe that one is no longer effective in working with patients (reduced personal accomplishment) (Maslach and Jackson, 1981).

Recently, Bakker and Demerouti (2007a) have proposed the Job Demands – Resources model to explain how the combination of various types of (high) job demands and various types of (low) job resources may combine to produce burnout (see, e.g., Bakker, Demerouti and Euwema, 2005), also among health care professionals (Bakker, Demerouti, Taris, Schaufeli, and Schreurs, 2003; Demerouti and Bakker, this volume; Demerouti, Bakker, Nachreiner, and Schaufeli, 2001). Moreover, their psychological strain, including burnout, may also affect their spouses and their team members in a process of crossover or emotional contagion.

Research on the symptomatology of burnout has shown that the syndrome may manifest itself in various ways. Schaufeli and Enzmann (1998) counted more than one-hundred burnout symptoms in the literature, including such highly visible symptoms as hyperactivity, physical fatigue, and enhanced irritability. Moreover, researchers have identified several "social symptoms" of burnout, most notably negative or cynical attitudes toward clients and work (see Burisch, 1989, for an overview). Such negative attitudes may take the form of reduced empathy, cynicism, black humor, and stereotyping. Burnout symptoms expressed by health care professionals may therefore transfer to colleagues when they socialize with one another on the job or in informal meetings. In addition, professionals may communicate their burnout complaints to their intimate partners once they come home and talk about the stress they experience at work.

CROSSOVER

Crossover is the term used to describe the interpersonal process that occurs when job stress or psychological strain (stress reactions) experienced by one person affect the level of strain of another person in the same social environment (Bolger, Delongis, Kessler, and Wethington, 1989). Some researchers have focused on the crossover of job stress from the individual to the spouse, others have examined the process whereby job stress of the individual affects the *strain* of the spouse, and yet others have studied how psychological strain of one partner affects the strain of the other (see Westman, 2001). Most studies have investigated and found the crossover of psychological strains such as anxiety (Westman, Etzion, and Horovitz, 2004a), burnout (e.g., Bakker and Schaufeli, 2000), distress (Barnett, Raudenbush, Brennan, Pleck, and Marshall, 1995), depression (Howe, Levy, and Caplan, 2004), adjustment (Takeuchi, Yun, and Teslu, 2002), work-family conflict (e.g., Hammer, Allen, and Grigsby, 1997; Westman and Etzion, 2005), and marital dissatisfaction (Westman, Roziner, Hamilton, and Roziner, 2004). A few studies investigated crossover of health complaints and perceived health between partners (Gorgievski-Duijvesteijin, Giesen and Bakker, 2000; Westman, Keinan, Vinokur and Benyamini, in press). Some studies focused on unidirectional crossover from husbands to wives, whereas others looked for bi-directional crossover, from husbands to wives and from wives to husbands but detected only uni-directional crossover.

To elaborate, there are several studies exclusively showing *unidirectional* crossover effects (only from one spouse to the other but not vice versa), or no crossover at all. For instance, several studies have found unique effects of husbands' job stress on the well-being of their wives (Burke, Weir, and DuWors, 1980; Jackson and Maslach, 1982; Rook, Dooley, and Catalano 1991). These studies, however, did not distinguish between working and non-working wives and did not control for wives' levels of job or life stress. Other studies have investigated the impact of women's mere employment, but not their specific job stress, and found negative effects of wives' employment on their husbands' strain (Haynes, Eaker, and Feinleib, 1983; Rosenfield, 1992; Staines, Pottic, and Fudge, 1986). Note that these studies neither specified which element of wives' employment was responsible for the crossover, nor did they control for men's job stress levels. In a more elaborated study, Jones and Fletcher (1993) found transmission of husbands' job demands on wives such that males' job demands crossed over to females' anxiety and depression after controlling for females' job stress, particularly among men working in highly stressful jobs. They did not find such an effect from wives to husbands. Similarly, Westman, Etzion and Danon (2001) found crossover of burnout only from husbands to wives but not from wives to husbands. Finally, Westman, Vinokur, Hamilton, and Roziner (2004) demonstrated crossover of marital dissatisfaction from husbands to wives, but no crossover from wives to husbands in their study of Russian officers and their wives .

Several crossover studies have investigated bi-directional crossover processes and found evidence for *symmetric* crossover effects between partners; from husbands to wives and from wives to husbands (e.g., Barnett et al., 1995; Demerouti, Le Blanc, Bakker, and Schaufeli, 2005; Hammer et al., 1997; Hammer, Bauer, and Grandey, 2003; Westman and Etzion, 1995; Westman and Etzion, 2005; Westman and Vinokur, 1998). To illustrate, Westman and Etzion (1995) demonstrated the crossover of burnout (i.e. physical, emotional and mental exhaustion) of a similar magnitude from army career officers to their spouses and vice versa, after controlling for their own and the partners' job demands and sense of control.

Hammer et al. (1997) found evidence for bi-directional crossover of work-to-family conflict from husbands to wives and vice versa, after controlling for own work salience, work schedule flexibility and family involvement. Furthermore, Westman and Vinokur (1998) found a direct crossover effect of depression from husbands to their spouses and vice versa after controlling for life events and social undermining. Tacheuchi, Yun and Teslu (2002) found bi-directional crossover of partner's general cross-cultural adjustment among expatriates. Westman, Keinan, Roziner, and Benyamini, (in press) studying a large sample of Russian couples, found a bi-directional crossover of similar magnitude between spouses' health perceptions. Similarly, Westman and Etzion (2005) found a bidirectional crossover of work family conflict between air force women and their spouses.

In a recent study, Bakker, Demerouti, and Schaufeli (2005) tested the hypothesis that burnout and *work engagement* may cross over from husbands to wives and vice versa among couples working in a variety of occupations. The results provided evidence for the crossover of burnout (exhaustion and cynicism) and work engagement (vigor and dedication) among partners. The crossover relationships were significant and about equally strong for both partners, after controlling for important characteristics of the work and home environment.

The bi-directional crossover effect has also been supported in studies using a longitudinal design. For example, Barnett et al. (1995) demonstrated that changes in distress (i.e., anxiety and depression) of one partner were mirrored in the changes in distress of the other. Westman and Vinokur (1998) found bidirectional crossover of distress and Westman, Etzion, and Horovitz (2004), depression, and anxiety from husbands to wives and from wives to husbands using longitudinal designs.

CROSSOVER IN THE WORKPLACE

The study of crossover thus far has been limited mostly to the crossover of stress and strain between spouses. Westman (2001) has suggested adding crossover at the workplace to crossover research. As previous crossover research was based on the work-family interface, researchers have focused particularly on the family as the "victim" of the job incumbent's stress. However, when we base the crossover construct on role theory, we can broaden the scope of research and investigate the crossover of stress among role senders in the work environment. Moreover, in the latter case, we can broaden the conceptualization of the unit of study from dyads to the work team. This approach is consistent with Moos' (1984) theory that people are part of social systems and we need to understand them within these systems. Each member in the system is linked to other members and, presumably, change in one will affect change in others. Edelwich and Brodsky (1980) were the first to relate to the possibility of crossover of burnout at work: "If burnout only affected individuals in isolation, it would be far less important and far less devastating in its impact than it is. Burnout in Human Services Agencies is like an infection in hospitals; it gets around. It spreads from clients to staff, from one staff member to another, and from staff back to clients. Perhaps it ought to be called staff infection." (p. 25).

Thus, a person's stress generated at the workplace may transmit to others in the work team. Individuals in the work team who share the same environment may start a crossover chain of stressors and strain among themselves whether the source of stress is in the family or at the workplace. The shared environment which is crucial to the crossover process characterizes workplaces where job incumbents work in close cooperation. Clearly, the study of crossover should be extended to the workplace.

Westman and Etzion (1999) conducted the first crossover field study in the workplace. They found a crossover of job-induced strain from school principals to teachers and vice versa. However, the findings relate to crossover between a manager and subordinates and not among the teachers. The next step is to investigate crossover among team members following Edelwich and Brodsky (1980) insight. This has been done in emotional contagion research.

EMOTIONAL CONTAGION

Emotional contagion has been defined as "The tendency to automatically mimic and synchronize facial expressions, vocalizations, postures, and movements with those of another person and, consequently, to converge emotionally" (Hatfield, Cacioppo, and Rapson, 1994; p.5). The emphasis in this definition is on non-conscious emotional contagion. Research has indeed shown that, in conversations, people 'automatically' mimic the facial expressions, voices, postures, and behaviors of others (Bavelas, Black, Lemery, and Mullett, 1987; Bernieri, Reznick, and Rosenthal, 1988), and that people's conscious experience may be shaped by such facial feedback (e.g., Laird, 1984).

There is, however, a second way in which people may 'catch' another's emotions. Contagion may also occur via a conscious cognitive process by 'tuning in' to the emotions of others. This will be the case when a person tries to imagine how they would feel in the position of another, and, as a consequence, experiences the same feelings. Thus, the realization that another person is happy or sad may trigger memories of the times we have felt that way, and these reveries may spark similar emotions (Hsee, Hatfield, Carlson, and Chemtob, 1990). Particularly the attitude of helping professionals to show empathic concern is likely to foster such a process of consciously 'tuning in' to others' emotions.

Regardless of why such contagion might occur, researchers from a wide range of disciplines have described phenomena that suggest that emotional contagion does exist (see Hatfield et al., 1994; and McIntosh, Druckman, and Zajonc, 1994, for overviews). Hsee and his colleagues (Hsee et al., 1990; Uchino, Hsee, Hatfield, Carlson, and Chemtob, 1991) documented convincing evidence for emotional contagion using controlled laboratory studies.

Recently, researchers have begun to investigate affective linkages between team members (e.g., Barsade, 2002; Totterdell, Kellet, Teuchmann, and Briner, 1998). Barsade (2002) in her experimental work demonstrated that emotional contagion does occur in groups and changes people's moods and serves as affective information: people are "walking mood inductors" continuously influencing the moods of others. Other researchers focused on emotional contagion at the workplace viewing contagion as a reciprocal emotional reaction among employees who closely collaborate. Thus, in a field setting, Totterdell et al. (1998) found evidence that the moods of teams of nurses and accountants were related to each other even after controlling for shared work problems.

One may assume that the mechanisms involved in emotional contagion processes are comparable to those involved in burnout contagion processes. Moreover, there is also evidence for contagious depression, and depression is a syndrome that is related to burnout, most notably the emotional exhaustion dimension (Glass, McKnight and Valdimarsdottir, 1993.

Burnout Contagion

The first empirical indication for a socially induced burnout effect came from Rountree (1984), who investigated 186 task groups in 23 local settings of organizations. He found that 87.5% of employees with the highest scores on burnout worked in task groups in which at least 50% of the staff was in a similar advanced burnout phase. Low scoring, less burned-out employees showed a similar but less marked tendency to cluster. Rountree concluded that "...the affinity of work groups for extreme scores seems substantial" (p. 245). Thus, individuals with very high or very low burnout scores can often be found within one task group, suggesting the possibility that task group members "infect" each other with the burnout-"virus". After reviewing similar additional studies, Golembiewski, Munzenrider and Stevenson (1986, p. 184) concluded that: "Very high and very low scores on burnout tend to concentrate to a substantial degree." They added that "these findings suggest 'contagion' or 'resonance' effects" (p. 185).

However, this concentration of burnout in particular work groups may also be explained by a negative change in the working conditions, because burnout has been related to a wide range of detrimental behaviors. For example, Freudenberger (1974) observed that burned-out individuals do not perform efficiently, independently of how hard they try. Indeed, it has been found that they make more on-the-job mistakes, misuse work breaks, and have higher absenteeism rates (e.g., Bakker, Demerouti, De Boer, and Schaufeli, 2003b; Kahill, 1988). In a team, each of these behaviors may increase the workload of the other team members, as they will have to compensate for the inefficient or disruptive behaviors of their burned-out colleagues.

To rule out the third variable explanation, Bakker and his colleagues set up a series of studies including measures of working conditions, burnout and/or work engagement. Evidence for direct *and* indirect routes of socially induced burnout was found in a study that included nurses from eighty European intensive care units (Bakker, Le Blanc and Schaufeli, 1997; see also Bakker, Le Blanc and Schaufeli, 2005). In addition to a *direct* effect from unit burnout to individual nurses' burnout, unit burnout had an *indirect* effect through its influence on individual nurses' workload and job autonomy. More specifically, unit burnout had a positive influence on the workload reported by individual nurses, and a negative impact on their autonomy. These changed working conditions, in turn, had a significant impact on their experience of burnout. That is, workload had a positive, and job autonomy had a negative influence on individual nurses' feelings of exhaustion, depersonalization (a specific form of cynicism), and reduced personal accomplishment (i.e., professional efficacy). This indirect influence of unit burnout on individual burnout can be explained by assuming that individual nurses had more work to do because of the impaired job performance of their burned-out colleagues. Conceptually similar findings have been reported by Bakker, Demerouti and Schaufeli (2003a) among a sample of employees of a large banking and insurance company.

They showed that burnout at the team level is related to individual team members' burnout scores, both directly and indirectly – through its relationship with individual members' job demands, job control and perceived social support.

Bakker, Van Emmerik and Euwema (2006) investigated the crossover of burnout and *work engagement* among Dutch constabulary officers. On the basis of theories on crossover and emotional contagion, they hypothesized that both types of work-related feelings and attitudes may transfer from teams to individual team members. The results of multilevel analyses confirmed this crossover phenomenon by showing that team level burnout and work engagement were related to individual team members' burnout (i.e., exhaustion, cynicism and reduced professional efficacy) and work engagement (vigor, dedication, and absorption), after controlling for individual members' job demands and resources.

A CLOSER LOOK AT THE CROSSOVER PROCESS

Hatfield et al. (1994) have argued that there are several circumstances under which people should be especially likely to catch others' emotions. Emotional contagion is particularly likely, for example, if individuals pay close attention to others, and if they construe themselves as interrelated to others rather than as independent and unique. Given the increased models of teamwork in modern organizations, it is likely that employees indeed experience higher levels of interdependence, and therefore are more sensitive to the emotional states of their colleagues. Furthermore, a number of studies have shown that there exist stable individual differences in people's susceptibility to emotional stimuli (Doherty, Orimoto, Singelis, Hatfield and Hebb, 1995; Stiff, Dillard, Somera, Kim, and Sleight, 1988), and that these individual differences are good predictors of the extent to which people catch positive and negative emotions from others. What are the conditions under which the crossover of burnout among health care professionals is most likely?

Empathy. Westman and Vinokur (1998) have argued that empathy can be a moderator of the crossover process. Literally, the root meaning of the word empathy is "feeling into". Starcevic and Piontek (1997) define empathy as interpersonal communication that is predominantly emotional in nature. It involves the ability to be affected by the other's affective state, as well as to be able to read in oneself what that affect has been. Similarly, Lazarus (1991) defined empathy as "sharing another's feelings by placing oneself psychologically in that person's circumstances" (p. 287). The core relational theme for empathy would have to involve a sharing of another person's emotional state, distressed or otherwise. Accordingly, strain in one partner produces an empathic reaction in the other that increases his or her own strain, by way of what may be called *empathic identification*. Social learning theorists (e.g., Bandura, 1969; Stotland, 1969) support this view, and have explained the transmission of emotions as a conscious processing of information. They suggested that individuals imagine how they would feel in the position of another – empathic identification – and thus come to experience and share the other's feelings. Eckenrode and Gore (1981) suggested that the effect of one's strain on the spouse's distress might be the result of empathy as expressed in reports such as "We feel their pain is our own" (p. 771).

Bakker and Demerouti (2007b) tested Westman and Vinokur's (1998) hypothesis that empathy moderates the crossover of work engagement – the direct opposite of burnout. They reasoned that empathy may best be considered as a set of related constructs including both emotional and non-emotional components (cf. Davis, 1980, 1983; Deutsch and Madle, 1975). One empathy component in their study was perspective taking, that is "the spontaneous tendency of a person to adopt the psychological perspective of other people – to entertain the point of view of others" (Davis, 1983, p. 169). This component clearly refers to the non-emotional or cognitive type of empathy. The second component of interest was empathic concern, which refers to "an individual's tendency to experience feelings of warmth, compassion, and concern for others" (p. 169). Thus, in contrast to perspective taking, empathic concern is clearly an indicator of emotional responsivity. Bakker and Demerouti (2007b) collected data among Dutch working couples. As hypothesized, results clearly showed that perspective taking (but not empathic concern) moderated the relationship between women's and men's work engagement. The crossover of engagement was strongest when men were characterized by high (vs. low) levels of perspective taking.

Susceptibility. Bakker, Schaufeli, Sixma, and Bosveld (2001) observed that general practitioners' individual susceptibility to emotional contagion was positively related to burnout. That is, they were most vulnerable to catching the negative emotions expressed by their patients, such as fear, anxiety, depressed mood, and worry. Interestingly, and in line with Hatfield et al.'s (1994) predictions, susceptibility to the emotions of others particularly showed a relationship with burnout when doctors reported many colleagues with burnout symptoms. That is, practitioners who perceived burnout complaints among their colleagues *and* who were susceptible to the emotions expressed by their colleagues reported the highest emotional exhaustion scores. A similar finding was reported by Bakker and Schaufeli (2000), who found that teachers who were most vulnerable to the emotions and negative attitudes expressed by their colleagues were most likely to become burned-out.

Frequency of exchanging views. In their study among teachers, Bakker and Schaufeli (2000) also found that teachers who frequently talked with their burned-out colleagues about problematic students had the highest probability of catching the negative attitudes expressed by their colleagues. In repeatedly trying to understand the problems their colleagues were facing, teachers presumably had to tune in to the negative attitudes expressed by their colleagues (about themselves as well as about students). This creates a condition under which central or systematic processing of information is likely to occur (Petty and Cacioppo, 1986; Stroebe, 1999). The result is negative attitude change, particularly when the burned out colleague (the 'source') has evidence or strong arguments to bolster their frustration and uncaring attitudes.

Similarity with the source. Classic social comparison theory regards uncertainty as the main motive for social comparison activity (Festinger, 1954; Schachter, 1959). Festinger argued that when objective sources of information for self-evaluation are lacking, people would turn to others in their environment. Schachter (1959) stated that when individuals feel uncertain about the appropriateness of their emotions, they tend to reduce this uncertainty by socially comparing and by adjusting their emotional reactions to those of others. Indeed, Groenestijn, Buunk and Schaufeli (1992) found that nurses who perceived burnout complaints among their colleagues and who felt a strong need for social comparison were more susceptible to burnout compared to those who had a low need for social comparison.

In addition, an important assumption in Festinger's (1954) theory is that others who are similar will be preferred for comparison, because information about similar others is most informative for self-evaluation (see also Tesser, 1988; Tesser, Millar and Moore, 1988). Keinan, Sadeh and Rosen (2003) investigated the attitudes and reactions to media coverage of terrorist acts. They suggested that the experience of stress responses in reaction to media coverage stems from identification with the victims of violence, and this identification is related to the degree of similarity between the media consumer and the victim: The greater the number of shared characteristics, the greater the probability of identifying with the victim.

Bakker, Westman and Schaufeli (2007) tested this hypothesis in the context of burnout crossover among a sample of soldiers. The participants were randomly exposed to a videotape of a burned-out or an engaged colleague who was either similar in profession and status (soldier), or who had a considerably higher status (squadron leader). The results confirmed the crossover of burnout from the stimulus soldier to the group. In addition, a significant interaction effect for cynicism revealed that the crossover of burnout was moderated by similarity with the stimulus person. Soldiers were particularly susceptible to the negative attitudes endorsed by those who were similar in rank.

Avenues for Future Research

So far, the crossover of employee well-being has been studied exclusively in field studies or in the laboratory, using between-subjects designs. An innovation would be to study crossover among health care professionals using a within-subjects design in which respondents are followed closely during their working day, for instance by asking them to keep an electronic diary (Van Eerde, Holman, and Totterdell, 2005). In doing so, crossover might be studied from a slightly broader perspective of emotional labor (Hochschild, 1983). Furthermore, the reviewed crossover literature shows only one experiment in crossover research (Bakker et al., 2007). The methodological gap in crossover research should be filled by using experimental designs employed in a natural field setting.

Another way to gain more insight into the crossover process is conducting qualitative studies. Long interviews with physicians and nurses in specified teams will shed light on the crossover process. It is especially important among team members as it will show who initiates the process and what are the mechanisms involved.

Another aim is to move beyond self-report measures conventionally used in crossover research. Such self-reports have been the only method of assessing the extent to which emotions cross over between partners. However, emotional experiences are well documented to affect cognitive processes, so that negative affect leads to poor task performance (e.g., Mandler, 1993), whereas positive affect holds beneficial effects for cognitive processes (e.g., Isen, 1999). Such effects of negative vs. positive emotions have been substantiated with many cognitive processes including attention, creative thinking, and memory (for a review see Isen, 1999). Future research should include objective measures of cognitive tasks alongside traditional self-report measures, under the rationale that negative crossover can be indicated by decreased cognitive performance and positive crossover can be indicated by enhanced cognitive performance. If we think of a laboratory experiment, we can have negative and positive stimulus persons talking to a team of nurses. We assume that the team that is confronted with the negative stimulus will show negative crossover and the other team will exhibit positive crossover. In addition to collecting data on burnout/work engagement and negative affectivity, researchers could provide the nurses with cognitive tasks (e.g. creativity task adapted from the *Torrance Tests of Creative Thinking* (Torrance, 1984) where participants are asked to list as many uses as they can think of for an ordinary object.

Several mediating and moderating variables have been identified in the crossover process: empathy, susceptibility to crossover, frequency of interactions, conflictual interactions, and similarity. Some of these suggested variables and processes should be investigated more thoroughly and additional processes should be identified. Traditionally, emotional labor has been studied in relation to customers or clients (Heuven and Bakker, 2003), but linking it to our notion of emotional contagion would open the possibility to study how employees manage the emotions of other employees they are working with.

Another interesting avenue for research would be to investigate the relative impact of negative and positive emotional contagion. So far, the contagious nature of burnout and work engagement has been studied separately. Only two exceptions exists in which both are studied simultaneously; one of these studies was on working couples (Bakker, Demerouti and Schaufeli, 2005; Bakker, Van Emmerik, and Euwema, 2006). Westman (2001) maintains that if the crossover process operates via empathy, one would expect to find not only negative crossover but positive crossover as well. Thus, empathy could just as easily involve the sharing of another's positive emotions and the conditions that bring them about. Thus, positive events and emotions may also cross over to the partner and team members and have a positive impact on their well-being.

So it remains to be seen if the effect of negative emotions on burnout levels of team members is equally strong as the effect of positive emotions on engagement. Based on arguments from evolutionary psychology, one could argue that negative contagion effects might be stronger than positive effects because the former have greater survival value compared to the latter (Fredrickson, 1998). That is, negative emotions signal danger, damage or threat and thus a potential assault on one's mental integrity. Hence, they have greater immediate relevance for survival than positive emotions that broaden one's scope and initiate learning and development (Frederickson, 2001). The investigation of positive crossover can add to theoretical thinking and broaden the current boundaries of crossover models.

GENERAL CONCLUSIONS

The review of the literature shows that burnout is a risk factor for health care professionals because their job is characterized by high demands and low resources. Furthermore we demonstrated that burnout is contagious and doctors and nurses transfer their burnout and other psychological strains to their team members with whom they interact. As health care professionals are characterized by high empathy and frequent interactions between team members, the process of crossover is more intense in their case. This process leads to burned-out teams. Crossover of burnout among team members is detrimental in any profession. However, crossover of burnout in health care professions can create an additional hazard except for psychological and physiological price, namely, errors in judgment and mistreatment of patients. Therefore serious measures should be taken to combat burnout and stop this vicious cycle, to decrease burnout by augmenting resources and dealing with demands. The next step is to develop engagement, enhancing positive team atmosphere and facilitate positive crossover.

REFERENCES

Bakker, A.B., and Demerouti, E. (2007a). The Job Demands-Resources model: State of the art. *Journal of Managerial Psychology, 22,* 309-328.

Bakker, A.B., and Demerouti, E. (2007b). *The crossover of work engagement: A closer look at the role of empathy*. Manuscript submitted for publication.

Bakker, A.B., Demerouti, E., and Euwema, M.C. (2005). Job resources buffer the impact of job demands on burnout. *Journal of Occupational Health Psychology, 10,* 170-180.

Bakker, A.B., Demerouti, E., and Schaufeli, W.B. (2003a). The socially induced burnout model. In S.P. Shohov (Ed.), *Advances in Psychology Research* (Vol. 25; p. 13-30). New York: Nova Science Publishers.

Bakker, A.B., Demerouti, E., and Schaufeli, W.B. (2005). Crossover of burnout and work engagement among working couples. *Human Relations, 58,* 661-689.

Bakker, A.B., Demerouti, E., De Boer, E., and Schaufeli, W.B. (2003b). Job demands and job resources as predictors of absence duration and frequency. *Journal of Vocational Behavior, 62,* 341-356.

Bakker, A.B., Demerouti, E., Taris, T., Schaufeli, W.B., and Schreurs, P. (2003). A multi-group analysis of the Job Demands - Resources model in four home care organizations. *International Journal of Stress Management, 10,* 16-38.

Bakker, A.B., Le Blanc, P.M., and Schaufeli, W.B. (1997). *Burnout contagion among nurses who work at intensive care units*. Paper presented at the fifth European conference on organizational psychology and health care, Utrecht, The Netherlands.

Bakker, A.B., Le Blanc, P.M., and Schaufeli, W.B. (2005). Burnout contagion among nurses who work at intensive care units. *Journal of Advanced Nursing, 51,* 276-287.

Bakker, A.B., and Schaufeli, W.B. (2000). Burnout contagion processes among teachers. *Journal of Applied Social Psychology, 30,* 2289-2308.

Bakker, A.B., Schaufeli, W.B., Sixma, H., and Bosveld, W. (2001). Burnout contagion among general practitioners. *Journal of Social and Clinical Psychology, 20,* 82-98.

Bakker, A.B., Van Emmerik, IJ.H., and Euwema, M.C. (2006). Crossover of burnout and engagement in work teams. *Work and Occupations, 33,* 464-489.

Bakker, A.B., Westman, M., and Schaufeli, W.B. (2007). Crossover of burnout: An experimental design. *European Journal of Work and Organizational Psychology, 16,* 220-239.

Bandura, A. (1969). *Principles of behavior modification*. New York: Holt, Rinehart, and Winston.

Barnett, R, C., Raudenbush, S.W., Brennan, R. T., Pleck, J. H., and Marshall, N. L. (1995). Changes in job and marital experience and change in psychological distress: A longitudinal study of dual-earner couples. *Journal of Personality and Social Psychology, 69,* 839-850.

Barsade, S. (2002). The ripple effect: emotional contagion and its influence on group behavior. *Administrative Science Quarterly*, 47, 644-677.

Bavelas, J.B., Black, A., Lemery, C.R., and Mullett, J. (1987). Motor mimicry as primitive empathy. In N. Eisenberg and J. Strayer (Eds.), *Empathy and its development* (pp. 317-338). New York: Cambridge University Press.

Bernieri, F.J., Reznick, J.S., and Rosenthal, R. (1988). Synchrony, pseudosynchrony, and dissynchrony: Measuring the entrainment process in mother-infant interactions. *Journal of Personality and Social Psychology, 54*, 1242-1253.

Bolger, N., DeLongis, A., Kessler, R., and Wethington, E. (1989). The contagion of stress across multiple roles. *Journal of Marriage and the Family, 51*, 175-183.

Burisch, M. (1989). *Das burnout-syndrom: Theorie der inneren Erschöpfung* [The burnout syndrome: A theory of inner exhaustion]. Berlin: Springer-Verlag.

Bourbonnais, R., Comeau, M., and Vézina, M. (1999). Job strain and evolution of mental health among nurses. *Journal of Occupational Health Psychology, 4*, 95-107.

Burke, R. J., Weir, T., and DuWors, R. E. (1980). Work demands on administrators and spouse well-being. *Human Relations, 33*, 253-278.

Cherniss, C. (1980). *Professional burnout in human service organizations.* New York: Praeger.

Davis, M.H. (1980). A multidimensional approach to individual differences in empathy. *JSAS Catalog of Selected Documents in Psychology, 10*, 85.

Davis, M.H. (1983). Measuring individual differences in empathy: Evidence for a multidimensional approach. *Journal of Personality and Social Psychology, 44*, 113-126.

Demerouti, E., and Bakker, A.B. (2007 – this volume). The Oldenburg Burnout Inventory: A good alternative to measure burnout (and engagement). In J. Halbesleben (Ed.). *xxxx*. Nova Sciences.

Demerouti, E., Bakker, A.B., Nachreiner, F., and Schaufeli, W.B. (2001). The job demands-resources model of burnout. *Journal of Applied Psychology, 86*, 499-512.

Demerouti, E., Le Blanc, P., Bakker, A.B., and Schaufeli, W.B. (2005). The costs of 'working through' sickness: A three-wave study on presenteeism. *Manuscript submitted for publication.*

Deutsch, F., and Madle, R. (1975). Empathy: Historic and current conceptualizations, measurement, and a cognitive theoretical perspective. *Human Development, 18*, 267-287.

Doherty, R.W., Orimoto, L., Singelis, T.M., Hatfield, E., and Hebb, J. (1995). Emotional contagion: Gender and occupational differences. *Psychology of Women Quarterly, 19*, 355-371.

Eckenrode, J., and Gore, S. (1981). Stressful events and social support: The significance of context. In B. Gottlieb (Ed.), *Social networks and social support* (pp. 43-68). Beverly Hills, CA: Sage.

Edelwich, J., and Brodsky, A. (1980). *Burnout: Stages of disillusionment in the helping professions.* New York: Human Sciences Press.

Erlen, J.A. and Sereika, S.M. (1997). Critical care nurses, ethical decision-making and stress. *Journal of Advanced Nursing, 26*, 953-961.

Festinger, L. (1954). A theory of social comparison processes. *Human Relations, 7*, 117-140.

Fredrickson, B.L. (2001). The role of positive emotions in positive psychology: The broaden-and-build theory of positive emotions. *American Psychologist, 56*, 218-226.

Fredrickson, B.L. (1998). What good are positive emotions? *Review of General Psychology*, *2*, 300-319.

Freudenberger, H.J. (1974). Staff burn-out. *Journal of Social Issues, 30*, 159-166.

Glass, D.C., McKnight, D., and Valdimarsdottir, H. (1993). Depression, burnout, and perceptions of control in hospital nurses. *Journal of Consulting and Clinical Psychology*, *61*, 147-155.

Golembiewski, R.T., Munzenrider, R.F., and Stevenson, J.G. (1986). *Stress in organizations: Towards a phase model of burnout*. New York: Praeger.

Gorgievski-Duijvesteijin, M. J., Giesen, C, W., and Bakker, A, B.(2000). Financial problems and health complaints among farm couples: Results of a 10-yr follow-up study. *Journal of Occupational Health Psychology. 5*, 359-373.

Groenestijn, E., Buunk, B.P., and Schaufeli, W.B. (1992). Het besmettingsgevaar bij burnout: De rol van sociale vergelijkingsprocessen [The danger of burnout contagion: The role of social comparison processes]. In R.W. Meertens, A.P. Buunk, P.A.M. van Lange, and B. Verplanken (Eds.), *Sociale psychologie and beïnvloeding van intermenselijke en gezondheidsproblemen* (pp. 88-103). The Hague, The Netherlands: VUGA.

Hammer, L. B., Allen, E., and Grigsby, T. D. (1997). Work-family conflict in dual-earner couples: Within individual and crossover effects of work and family. *Journal of Vocational Behavior, 50*, 185-203.

Hammer, L. B., Bauer, T., and Grandey, A. (2003). Work-family conflict and work-related withdrawal behaviors. *Journal of Business and Psychology, 17*, 419-436.

Howe, G., Levy, M., and Caplan, R. (2004). Job loss and depressive symptoms in couples: Common stressors, stress transmission, or relationship disruption? *Journal of Family Psychology, 18*, 639-650.

Hatfield, E., Cacioppo, J.T., and Rapson, R.L. (1994). *Emotional contagion*. New York: Cambridge University Press.

Haynes, S.G., Eaker, E. D., and Feinleib, M. (1983). Spouse behavior and coronary heart disease in men: Prospective results from the Framingham heart study. *American Journal of Epidemiology, 118*, 1-22.

Heuven, E., and Bakker, A.B. (2003). Emotional dissonance and burnout among cabin attendants. *European Journal of Work and Organizational Psychology, 12*, 81-100.

Hobfoll, S. E. (2002). Social and psychological resources and adaptation. *Review of General Psychology, 6*, 307-324.

Hochschild, A.R. (1983). *The managed heart. Commercialization of human feeling*. Berkeley, CA: University of California Press.

Hsee, C.K., Hatfield, E., Carlson, J.G., and Chemtob, C. (1990). The effect of power on susceptibility to emotional contagion. *Cognition and Emotion, 4*, 327-340.

Isen, A. M. (1999). Positive affect. In T. Dagleish and M. Power (Eds.), *Handbook of cognition and emotion* (pp. 521 – 539). Sussex, England: Wiley.

Jackson, S. E., and Maslach, C. (1982). After-effects of job-related stress: Families as victims. *Journal of Occupational Behavior, 3*, 63-77.

Kahill, S. (1988). Symptoms of professional burnout: A review of the empirical evidence. *Canadian Psychology, 29*, 284-297.

Karasek, R.A. (1979). Job demands, job decision latitude, and mental strain: Implications for job design. *Administrative Science Quarterly, 24*, 285-308.

Keinan, G., and Sadeh, A., and Rosen, S. (2003). Attitudes and reaction to media coverage on terrorist acts. *Journal of Community Psychology, 31,* 149-168.

Laird, J.D. (1984). The real role of facial response in the experience of emotion: A reply to Tourangeau and Ellsworth, and others. *Journal of Personality and Social Psychology, 47,* 909-917.

Lazarus, R.S. (1991). *Emotion and adaptation.* New York: Oxford.

Mandler, G. (1993). Thought, memory and learning: Effects of emotional stress. In: L. Goldberger and S. Breznitz (Eds.), *Handbook of stress* (pp. 40-55). New York: The Free Press.

Maslach, C. and Jackson, S.E. (1981). The measurement of experienced burnout. *Journal of Occupational Behavior, 2,* 99-113.

McIntosh, D.N., Druckman, D., and Zajonc, R.B. (1994). Socially induced affect. In D. Druckman and R.A. Bjork (Eds.), *Learning, remembering, believing: Enhancing human performance* (pp. 251-276). Washington, DC: National Academy Press.

Moos, R. (1984). Context and coping: Toward a unifying conceptual framework. *American Journal of Community Psychology, 12,* 5-25.

Petty, R.E., and Cacioppo, J.T. (1986). The elaboration likelihood model of persuasion. In: L. Berkowitz (Ed). *Advances in experimental social psychology* (Vol. 19; pp. 124-205). Orlando, FL: Academic Press.

Rook, S. K., Dooley, D., and Catalano, R. (1991). Stress transmission: The effects of husbands' job stressors on emotional health of their wives. *Journal of Marriage and the Family, 53,* 165-177.

Rosenfield, S. (1992). The cost of sharing: Wives employment and husbands' mental health. *Journal of Health and Social Behavior, 33,* 213-225.

Rountree, B.H. (1984). Psychological burnout in task groups. *Journal of Health and Human Resources Administration, 7,* 235-248.

Sawatzky. J.V. (1996). Stress in critical care nurses: Actual and perceived. *Heart and Lung, 25,* 409-417.

Schachter, S. (1959). *The psychology of affiliation.* Palo Alto, CA: Stanford University Press.

Schaufeli, W.B. (2005). The future of occupational health psychology. *Applied Psychology: An International Review, 53,* 502-517.

Schaufeli, W.B., and Enzmann, D. (1998). *The burnout companion to research and practice: A critical analysis.* London: Taylor and Francis.

Schwartz, M.S., and Will, G.T. (1953). Low morale and mutual withdrawal on a hospital ward. *Psychiatry, 16,* 337-353.

Shirom, A. (1989). Burnout in work organizations. In C. L. Cooper and I. Robertson (eds.) *International Review of Industrial and Organizational Psychology* (pp. 26-48), Wiley, New York.

Staines, G. L., Pottic, K. G., Fudge, D. A. (1985). The effects of wives' employment on husbands' job and life satisfaction. *Psychology of Women Quarterly, 9,* 190-201

Starcevic, V., and Piontek, C.M. (1997). Empathic understanding revisited: Conceptualization, controversies, and limitations. *American Journal of Psychotherapy, 51,* 317-328.

Stiff, J.B., Dillard, J.P., Somera, L., Kim, H., and Sleight, C. (1988). Empathy, communication, and prosocial behavior. *Communication Monographs, 55,* 198-213.

Stotland, E. (1969). Exploratory investigations of empathy. In L. Berkowitz (Ed.), *Advances in experimental social psychology* (vol. 4, pp. 271-314). New York: Academic Press.

Stroebe, W. (1999). The return of the one-track mind. *Psychological Inquiry, 10*, 173-176.

Takeuchi, R., Yun, S., and Teslu, P. T. (2002). An examination of crossover and spillover effects of spouse and expatriate cross-cultural adjustment on expatriate outcomes. *Journal of Applied Psychology, 85*, 655-666.

Tesser, A. (1988).Towards a self-evaluation maintenance model of social behavior. In L. Berkowitz (Ed.), *Advances in experimental social psychology* (Volume 21; pp. 181-227). San Diego: Academic Press.

Tesser, A., Millar, M., and Moore, J. (1988). Some affective consequences of social comparison and reflection processes: The pain and pleasure of being close. *Journal of Personality and Social Psychology, 54*, 49-61.

Torrance, E. P., and Ball, O. E. (1984). *Torrance Tests of Creative Thinking (revised) Manual.* Bensenville: Scholastic Testing Service Inc.

Totterdell, P., S. Kellet, K. Teuchmann, and R. B. Briner (1998). Evidence of mood linkage in work groups. *Journal of Personality and Social Psychology, 74*, 1504-1515.

Uchino, B., Hsee, C.K., Hatfield, E., Carlson, J.G., and Chemtob, C. (1991). *The effect of expectations on susceptibility to emotional contagion.* Unpublished manuscript, University of Hawaii.

Van Eerde, W., Holman, D., and Totterdell, P. (2005). Editorial: Diary studies in work psychology. *Journal of Occupational and Organizational Psychology, 78*, 151-154.

Westman, M. (2001). Stress and strain crossover. *Human Relations, 54*, 557-591.

Westman, M., and Etzion, D. (1995). Crossover of stress, strain and resources from one spouse to another. *Journal of Organizational Behavior, 16*, 169-181.

Westman, M., and Etzion, D. (1999). The crossover of strain from school principals to teachers and vice versa. *Journal of Occupational Health Psychology, 4*, 269-278.

Westman, M., and Etzion, D. (2005). The crossover of work-family conflict from one spouse to the other. *Journal of Applied Social Psychology. 35*, 1936-1957.

Westman, M, Etzion, D., and Danon, E. (2001). Job insecurity and crossover of burnout in married couples. *Journal of Organizational Behavior, 22*, 467-481.

Westman, M., Etzion, D., and Horovitz, S. (2004). The toll of unemployment does not stop with the unemployed. *Human Relations, 57*, 823-844.

Westman, M. Keinan, G., and Roziner, R., and Benyamini (in press). The crossover of perceived health between couples: A theoretical model. *Journal of Occupational Health Psychology.*

Westman, M., and Vinokur, A. (1998). Unraveling the relationship of distress levels within couples: Common stressors, emphatic reactions, or crossover via social interactions? *Human Relations, 51*, 137-156.

Westman, M., Vinokur, A., Hamilton, L., and Roziner, I. (2004). Crossover of marital dissatisfaction during military downsizing among Russian army officers and their spouses. *Journal of Applied Psychology, 89*, 769-779.

In: Handbook of Stress and Burnout in Health Care
Editor: Jonathon R. B. Halbesleben

ISBN 978-1-60456-500-3
© 2008 Nova Science Publishers, Inc.

Chapter 10

WORK SCHEDULES AND STRESS AMONG HEALTH PROFESSIONALS

Jeanne Geiger-Brown, Valerie E. Rogers,
Alison M. Trinkoff and Victoria Selby
Work and Health Research Center
University of Maryland, Baltimore

Adverse work schedules are common for health care workers (HCWs). By necessity, they provide around-the-clock coverage, thus shiftwork is often an unavoidable component of the work schedule. In addition to shift work, extended work shifts, quick returns or a break of only 8 hours when changing from one shift to another, mandatory overtime, on-call, and working without breaks are common to maintain staffing levels among registered nurses (RNs). Physicians also have severely extended workdays during their training years. The effect of these schedules is often physical and mental fatigue, which has both short- and long-term effects on the health and safety of HCWs, as well as consequences for patient safety. This chapter will describe the relationship between work schedules and adverse outcomes in HCWs, including the role of both person and system factors in moderating the scheduling effects, and will describe the role of sleep as the critical mechanism for reducing the impact of adverse work schedules on outcomes (Figure 1).

WORK SCHEDULES

Shiftwork

Humans have a strong circadian drive to sleep at night, and when sleep opportunity is restricted, all physiological and behavioral systems are affected. An extensive body of literature has accumulated that details the effects of various permutations of shiftwork including speed of shift rotation, direction (clockwise versus counterclockwise), regularity of rotation, shift start and end times, and predictability/control over shift schedules.

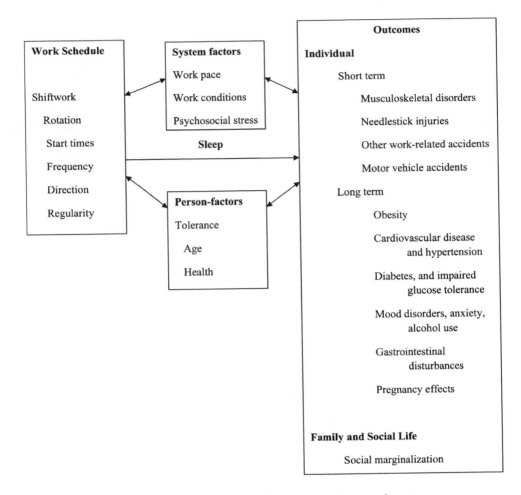

Figure 1. Work schedules and outcomes moderated by person and system factors.

Evidence-based guidelines are available for choosing a good shift system (Wedderburn, 1998), however these guidelines are helpful only to the extent that workers have control over their work schedule. Monk (2005) points out that coping with shiftwork is influenced by a complex interaction of circadian, sleep, and domestic factors. It is possible for some workers to adjust to the night shift, although this process is slow, taking about five to six days to fully transition to an eight-hour change in sleep schedule. However, circadian rhythms for body temperature, hormone production, cell division, urinary excretion, and respiratory rate do not fully adjust. Rather than reversing schedule to accommodate the day-night reversal, the circadian curves for physiologic functions flatten (Harrington, 2001). One of the barriers to adaptation for night workers is that on weekends and days off they often revert to a daytime schedule, which very rapidly realigns their circadian clock to its normal rhythm. In addition, zeitgebers—environmental factors that helps to set the circadian clock such as daylight, noise and activity levels, and social clues—stimulate the body to maintain a daytime orientation. Simply walking to a parked car in daylight after a night shift is a sufficiently potent zeitgeber to alter melatonin secretion and reduce nocturnal orientation. Harrington (2001) points out that the effect of shift work is like working in San Francisco and returning to London for rest days. Furthermore, the body's ability to tolerate night shiftwork decreases with aging, even for experienced night shift devotees, and individuals with "morning-lark" traits often cannot make the adjustment to night shift at all.

A common complaint among night shiftworkers is that of short sleep duration, with awakenings during daytime sleep. They are in a state of partial sleep deprivation most of the time. Even in ideal sleep circumstances, most night shiftworkers get about 10 hours less sleep per week as compared to those working day shifts. In a study of RNs' sleep by shift and domestic situation, night shiftworkers averaged five to six hours of sleep per night as compared with seven to nine hours of sleep for those working other shift arrangements, with nurses having child care responsibilities showing the least sleep (Clissold, Smith, and Acutt, 2001). Furthermore, their sleep architecture differs, with less total rapid eye movement (REM) sleep, and problems with sleep maintenance. Consequently, night shiftworkers experience sleepiness, often during the work shift, and dangerously, while driving home. Altered sleep patterns also produce strain on workers' domestic lives, as their families must try to avoid arousing the sleeping person with normal household noise. Adequate recovery sleep can lessen the detrimental effects of an occasional night of acute sleep deprivation associated with shiftwork if the recovery sleep period is of sufficient length. When shiftwork is associated with chronic sleep deprivation, increasing duration of shiftwork (years to decades) is associated with lower cognitive abilities, which return to normal only after four years of normal work times (Rouch, Wild, Ansiau, and Marquie, 2005).

Extended and Compressed Work Hours

Extended work hours can occur through higher number of hours worked per day, working more days per week or working shifts in a compressed manner with less time between shifts. Although definitions vary, extended work hours are generally considered to be more than 48 hours per week (Harrington, 2001). Both the International Labour Organization (ILO) and European countries (European Directive on Working Hours) have tried to limit working hours to reduce adverse health effects. In the United States (US), the American College of Graduate Medical Education (ACGME) mandated a limit to total and extended work hours, This effort has reduced only the most extreme schedules, but has not produced a paradigm shift for physicians in training. Lockley, Landrigan, Barger, and Czeisler (2006) describe both acute and chronic sleep deprivation when physicians-in-training work extended work schedules. They provide compelling evidence for an increased risk of post-call motor vehicle crashes and serious medical errors, concluding that "all sleep hours and all wake hours are not equal." There have been numerous studies comparing performance and physician quality of life before and after the 2003 ACGME work hour regulation. Although nearly all suffer from poor rigor, residents' quality of life generally appears to be better under the new work hour regulations (Fletcher et al., 2005). No work hours regulations have been promulgated for nurses, however the Institute of Medicine, in its recent report "Improving Patient Safety: Transforming the Work Environment of Nurses" suggests that nurses should work no more than 12 hours per day and no more than 60 hours per week (Institute of Medicine, 2004). Geiger-Brown and Trinkoff believe that working 60 hours per week increases the risk of musculoskeletal disorders and needlestick injuries to RNs, thus may still be excessively long

(Trinkoff, Le, Geiger-Brown, and Lipscomb, 2007; Trinkoff, Geiger-Brown, Brady, Lipscomb, and Muntaner, 2006; Trinkoff, Le, Geiger-Brown, Lipscomb, and Lang, 2006).

Health care workers often consider fatigue a normal part of their job and may not make the association between fatigue and later impaired health. Fatigue-associated impairment is the performance equivalent of alcohol intoxication. A study of pediatric residents, for example, showed psychomotor vigilance decrements, omissions in a continuous performance test, and impaired driving in a simulator following four weeks of heavy call to be equivalent to performance with a blood alcohol concentration of 0.04 to 0.05 g%BAC (Arnedt, Owens, Crouch, Stahl, and Carskadon, 2005). As these are common work schedules among all HCWs, inadequate sleep, sleepiness and fatigue have the potential to affect the long-term health of a substantial portion of the millions of health care workers in the US, as well as the patients that they serve.

PERSON FACTORS

The influence of work schedules on health and safety outcomes is not equal among all HCWs. Several factors have been identified that modify the scheduling effect, with aging and work-home conflict both prominent among these. In high demand jobs, aging workers are known to have reduced functional capacities (Sluiter, 2006), although there is significant inter-individual variation in decline. Older workers show a circadian shift to "morningness," an earlier acrophase and a shorter sleep with more sleep disruption, making them more vulnerable to circadian effects and sleep loss when working shifts (Reid and Dawson, 2001; Reilly, Waterhouse, and Atkinson, 1997). In a laboratory simulation, older workers were less able to maintain performance over 12-hour shifts, however in real employment situations there is extensive self-selection of shiftwork among HCWs based on their tolerance for it (Reid and Dawson, 2001). Early in the careers of both physicians and nurses, shiftwork is common. Physicians, however, select specialties that mesh with their tolerance to working non-daytime hours, and after their initial postgraduate training do far less shiftwork. Furthermore, physicians are moving to a care-delivery model that includes less on-call and more in-house physician coverage in hospital specialties. Nurses, on the other hand, may still be doing shiftwork late into their careers unless they move into management or ambulatory care settings, thus the need to accommodate aging workers remains an issue in this profession.

Shiftwork, extended work hours, and compressed work weeks (CWWs) disrupt the family and social life of health care professionals, causing additional stress. Employees are largely favorable to working CWWs because they afford more days off. As expected, on the days during which these shifts are worked, less time is spent in social activities and with spouses and children. During days off, however, no more time is spent in these activities (Barton Cunningham, 1989) than would have occurred during a traditional daytime work schedule, so that the effect is a net loss of time spent with family and in recreation.

Shiftwork further contributes to a loss of social and family time because the overlap of family members' leisure time (White and Keith, 1990) is reduced and effectively prevents social interaction among family members. Presser aptly refers to this interaction as the "'glue' that binds them together" (Presser, 2000, p. 94)—a glue that helps forge strong marital and family commitments, but which is decreased in families of shiftworkers. Work-family conflict develops as a result of social isolation (Holland, 2006) caused by schedules out of synchrony with most family daily routines (Simon, 1990), worker fatigue from poor quality sleep (Rotenberg, Moreno, Portela, Benedito-Silva, and Menna-Barreto, 2000), depressed mood and declining well-being (Smith and Folkard, 1993), all of which place stress on both the worker and the family.

Marital disruption, including separation and divorce, is frequently associated with shift work (Presser, 2000; White and Keith, 1990). Examining data from a longitudinal study of 1,668 married men and women interviewed three years apart, for example, White and Keith (1990) found that shift work increased the probability of divorce from 7% to 11%. Similarly Presser, in a sample of 3,476 married couples drawn from the National Survey of Families and Household, found that among couples married for less than five years where one partner worked the night shift, there was an increased likelihood of marital instability of 41.2% among the men and 35.4% among the women. Perhaps not surprisingly, in this study nonstandard work schedules only affected marital stability in couples with dependent children (Presser, 2000).

Moreover, work-family conflict appears to be gendered (Grosswald, 2003), likely as a result of differential societal expectations for men and women. Women continue to retain primary responsibility for domestic work and family care (Fast and Frederick, 1996), working a full time job and coming home to complete household chores, child care and elder care responsibilities. These "second shift" (Hochschild, 1989) responsibilities create stress and result in loss of sleep and fatigue. Child care, in particular, is a potent cause of stress for women. For example, Lee (1992) found in her study of 760 registered nurses, that women under 40 years of age had more frequent awakenings regardless of the shift worked, as a result of child care responsibilities, a finding echoed by other studies (Gottlieb, Kelloway, and Martin-Matthews, 1996) and one that hints at the complexity of the work-family interface as a cause of stress, particularly among women.

Despite the preponderance of studies reporting harmful family and societal outcomes for shift workers, however, they are not uniformly negative. Several investigators have reported either equivalent or improved family and social lives (Barton and Folkard, 1991; Lowden, Kecklund, Axelsson, and Akerstedt, 1998; Mitchell and Williamson, 2000; Rosa, Colligan, and Lewis, 1989) among nontraditional shift workers. Family support (Holland, 2006) and psychological and social conditions in the workplace such as scheduling flexibility, job autonomy (Grosswald, 2004), workload and relations with superiors (Geurts, Rutte, and Peeters, 1999), as well as workplace expectations of work role priority over family role (Hammer, Saksvik, Nytro, Torvatn, and Bayazit, 2004) all influence the development and degree of work-family stress.

SYSTEM FACTORS

Physical and psychological job demands such as excessive work pace contribute to workers' stress. In addition to aspects of the work schedule such as shift work, long hours, overtime and on-call hours, health care work can impair workers' health both acutely and in the long-term. Chronic stress over time is known to increase allostatic load due to excessive demands and a persistent sympathetic (adrenergic) load, negatively affecting the neurologic, immune, and cardiovascular systems (McEwen, 2003; Schnorpfeil et al., 2003) and leading to musculoskeletal injuries/disorders (MSDs) and other injuries, infections, mental health problems and in the longer term, cardiovascular, metabolic, and neoplastic diseases.

Injuries such as needlestick or sharps injuries and musculoskeletal disorders are more likely to occur in HCWs who work longer hours (Trinkoff et al., 2007; Trinkoff, Le, et al., 2006), as a function of both increased exposure and a lack of sufficient time to recuperate away from the workplace. Furthermore, excessive demands contribute to musculoskeletal injury (Bongers, Kremer, and ter Laak, 2002; van den Heuvel, van der Beek, Blatter, Hoogendoorn, and Bongers, 2005) largely related to the physical demands of patient handling (Trinkoff, Lipscomb, Geiger-Brown, Storr, and Brady, 2003). Patients are becoming heavier, and the nursing care workforce is aging (Bleich, Connolly, Davis, Hewlett, and Hill, 2006). It is estimated that in 2003, 66% of the US population was overweight or obese, representing a nearly 20% increase in the past two decades (National Center for Health Statistics, 2003-2004). Patient transfers (e.g. movement from bed to stretcher) require extensive flexion and rotation of the body, increasing the injury risk to HCW's due to a combination of compression, rotation, and shear forces (Forde, Punnett, and Wegman, 2002).

Extended work hours, similar to night shiftwork, may reduce the time available for sleep leading to sleep deprivation or disturbed sleep and incomplete recovery from work (Sparks, Cooper, Fried, and Shirom, 1997; Spurgeon, Harrington, and Cooper, 1997; van der Hulst, 2003). Alertness requires not only adequate length of sleep, but is also dependent on obtaining an adequate duration of quality sleep (Knowlton, 1999). Acute or chronic sleep loss is associated with deficits in neurobehavioral functioning such as reduced vigilance, reaction time, memory, psychomotor coordination, information processing and decision making ability (Dinges et al., 1997; Rosa, 1995; Rosekind et al., 1997; Van Dongen, Maislin, Mullington, Dinges, and Dinges, 2003). O'Shea (1999) found that nurses ranked distraction and being tired/exhausted in the top three perceived causes of medication errors. In an assessment of psychological job demands by hospital nurses, 75% said their job requires periods of intense concentration, yet 80% said that tasks are often interrupted (Institute of Medicine, 2004). Interruptions were found to be a major contributor to errors in health care (Kohn, Corrigan, and Donaldson, 2000). Furthermore, high-noise environments, such as those worked by critical care nurses (Hale, 1996), are known to induce fatigue.

The relationship of physical and psychological demands to injury is also important (Ijzelenberg, Molenaar, and Burdorf, 2004) as both demands occur extensively in health care work. Health care work is physically and psychologically demanding, with few breaks taken during the shift (Lipscomb, Trinkoff, Geiger-Brown, and Brady, 2002; Trinkoff, Geiger-Brown, et al., 2006; Trinkoff, Brady, and Nielsen, 2003; Trinkoff, Storr, and Lipscomb, 2001). Because the pace of the work is externally driven, many HCWs cannot slow down or allocate the work to preserve their endurance, an important factor in preventing adverse consequences (Wellens and Smith, 2006). This rapid work pace is a critical factor in the need for rest and recovery away from work (Sonnentag, 2006; van Veldhoven and Broersen, 2003).

Psychological demands may detract from physical health through an increase in muscle strain, muscle contraction, fatigue, intolerance of physical discomfort, and anxiety (Bongers, de Winter, Kompier, and Hildebrandt, 1993; Forde et al., 2002). In fact, it has been demonstrated that psychological risk factors increased EMG activity independent of physical load, and accentuated muscle tension when physical load was present (Lundberg et al., 1994).

In jobs that require high physical demand, psychological demands had an even greater impact on MSD (Devereux, Vlachonikolis, and Buckle, 2002). Other studies validate the contribution that psychological and physical demands place on one another in terms of symptoms and/or injury (Bongers et al., 1993; Devereux et al., 2002; Forde et al., 2002; Ijzelenberg et al., 2004).

As we have described, the work schedule and job demands can lead to fatigue, illness and impaired performance. Furthermore, to prevent injury or illness, adequate rest and recuperation time is required to heal and recover. Improvements in work scheduling and reduction of job demands should be studied further as means to promote health and reduce adverse consequences among HCWs.

OUTCOMES

Adverse work schedules, in addition to the hazards of health care work itself, can have both short term and long term negative outcomes for the HCW. In the short term, schedule-related sleep loss and excessive periods of wakefulness are associated with sleepiness, which can cause both job performance problems and work-related injuries (Caruso, Hitchcock, Dick, Russo, and Schmit, 2004). In the longer term, working without adequate recovery between shifts can lead to fatigue, which has added long-term negative health effects for the worker. Inadequate sleep increases the risk for cardiovascular disease and hypertension, diabetes and impaired glucose tolerance, obesity, anxiety and depression, alcohol use, and adverse pregnancy outcomes.

Short-Term Outcomes

HCWs suffer adverse short term health consequences such as needlestick injuries, motor vehicle accidents and MSDs as a result of shiftwork and extended work hours. In a large population-based prospective study of RNs, Trinkoff et al. (Trinkoff et al., 2007) found a 50% to 60% increase in the relative risk of needlestick injuries for hospital nurses working extended work hours or shiftwork as compared to those working 8-hour day shifts. Physician needlestick injury risk factors were similar, with fatigue following extended work hours cited as an important contributor (Ayas et al., 2006). Motor vehicle accidents pose a significant hazard for physicians in training, with more than double the odds of being involved in a crash after working greater than 24 hours. With repeated bouts of extended hours such as taking call every third night, the risk of a crash increased to 162% after one month (Barger et al., 2005). Working extended days, working during off-shifts and working weekends all increase the relative risk for MSDs for nurses (Trinkoff, Le, et al., 2006), with the mechanisms for injury including increased exposure to physical demands and reduced time off for recovery.

Long-Term Outcomes

Long-term health effects of adverse work schedules have been identified from several large epidemiologic cohort studies of workers. Shiftwork is associated with an increased risk of cardiovascular diseases including hypertension, myocardial disease and cerebrovascular disease, with a consistent finding across studies of a 40% increase in relative risk (Boggild and Knutsson, 1999). Mechanisms for this effect include sympathetic overactivity, changes in lipids and fibrinogen levels, increased blood pressure, and decreased glucose tolerance, with sleep duration acting as a mediating factor (Ayas et al., 2003). Similarly, gastrointestinal (GI) complaints are common in shift workers, the mechanisms of which are thought to include altered GI motility and acid-base balance, as well as changes in the gastric mucosa and inflammatory intestinal systems (Caruso, Lusk, and Gillespie, 2004).

Metabolic functioning also changes when HCWs work shifts. Both experimental and epidemiologic evidence suggest an increased risk for glucose intolerance and the development of diabetes mellitus among shiftworkers. Young healthy males showed a 40% reduction in the speed of clearance of a experimental test dose of IV glucose, and a 30% decrease in acute insulin response to glucose after four days of laboratory sleep deprivation (Spiegel, Leproult, and Van Cauter, 1999). In the large prospective Sleep Heart Health Study, the odds of having diabetes mellitus if sleeping five or fewer hours per night was 2.5 when compared to those getting seven to eight hours of sleep per night (Gottlieb et al., 2005). In a prospective study, the age-adjusted rate of diabetes among nurses increased with increasing years of shiftwork (Kawachi et al., 1995), and the incidence of Type 2 diabetes over 6 years of follow-up was increased (RR=1.23) in nurses working more than 41 hours per week, as compared to those working 21 to 40 hours per week (Kroenke et al., 2006). Thus, shiftwork is a risk factor for the development of diabetes, which can also contribute to the risk for heart disease.

When shiftwork and extended work hours interfere with sleep, mood deteriorates. A meta-analysis of 19 studies examined the effect of sleep deprivation on performance (Pilcher and Huffcutt, 1996) and determined that partial sleep deprivation had a large negative effect on mood. Residents in their first two years of medical training average under 6 hours of sleep per night, with surgical residents having less sleep than other specialties (Baldwin and Daugherty, 2004). Medical residents report emotional exhaustion and an aversion to patients (Biaggi, Peter, and Ulich, 2003), moodiness and short temper (Baldwin and Daugherty, 2004) and increased burnout with longer work hours and insufficient time off (Martini, Arfken, and Balon, 2006; Tzischinsky, Zohar, Epstein, Chillag, and Lavie, 2001). This is also true of less skilled workers. In a large study of nursing assistants working in nursing homes, depression was more prevalent in those working two or more double-shifts per month, or working six to seven days per week (Geiger-Brown, Muntaner, Lipscomb, and Trinkoff, 2004).

However, control over the work schedule and hours worked positively predicted job satisfaction and negatively predicted burnout in a sample of OB-GYN residents (Keeton, Fenner, Johnson, and Hayward, 2007). In another study, among female physicians, those working full-time had better job satisfaction irrespective of the quality of their home life, but for physicians working reduced-hours, the quality of their family life greatly influenced their career satisfaction (Barnett, Gareis, and Carr, 2005). Nurses are often stressed when required to do mandatory overtime or on-call, usually with minimal notice (Geiger-Brown et al., 2004; Trinkoff, Geiger-Brown, et al., 2006). As 95% of nurses are women, unplanned work interferes with their "second job" of caring for their families, including child care and elder care.

Both early and late-term pregnancy difficulties are more common among shiftworkers. The Nurses' Health Study, a large prospective cohort study, provided evidence for effects of both shiftwork and extended work hours on adverse pregnancy outcomes. Nurses working the night shift exclusively (RR=1.6, 95% CI 1.3-19), or working more than 40 hours per week (RR=1.5, 95% CI 1.3-1.7) during the first trimester of pregnancy had increased risk of spontaneous abortion (Whelan et al., 2007). Although the mechanism for this is not known, the authors speculate that hormonal changes associated with circadian rhythm disruption or stress may alter the balance of cellular immune responses necessary to maintain a pregnancy. Similar findings for night work were found for late gestational fetal loss in a large Danish cohort study of workers (Zhu, Hjollund, Andersen, and Olsen, 2004). Low birth weight and preterm births are also more prevalent in shiftworkers (Knutsson, 2003).

Implications for Health Care Workers

Because health care services need to be delivered around the clock, HCWs will always be exposed to adverse work schedules to some degree. However, there are a number of areas where these workers can be protected from the stressors of shiftwork and extended work hours. In other safety-sensitive industries, strong regulations have been promulgated to protect the public, and when enforced have also improved the lives of the workers including truck drivers, nuclear power plant operators, pilots, and others. For physicians-in-training, the ACGME approach to limiting work hours has removed only the most egregious of schedules, with excessive hours still the norm. Similarly, the IOM recommendations for nurses' work schedules will likely not produce much improvement. Work schedules of HCWs are not known by the public, but if reportable as a quality monitor, might begin to change to improve patient safety.

These authors support an incremental approach to regulation, first moving to exclude the most vulnerable workers (pregnant, over 40, diabetic, cardiovascular disease, sleep disorders) from shiftwork as a matter of course, with others able to opt out based on demonstrated intolerance for this schedule. In addition, sufficient staff should be hired to make excessive work hours rare. This economic decision will require health care institutions to value their workers' health and safety in meaningful ways, while developing safe hand-off procedures to ensure that patients are safely cared for. Other fatigue countermeasures such as naps during shifts are worth researching in the US. Safe transportation options should be made available for night shiftworkers who find themselves too tired to drive home safely. HCWs need education to understand the importance of sleeping during off-time and the choosing of sensible work schedules. Solutions to HCW health and safety outcomes will require interventions at the individual, institutional, and regulatory level but will be important to protect both the workers and the patients that they serve.

REFERENCES

Arnedt, J. T., Owens, J., Crouch, M., Stahl, J., and Carskadon, M. A. (2005). Neurobehavioral performance of residents after heavy night call vs after alcohol ingestion. *JAMA, 294,* 1025-1033.

Ayas, N. T., Barger, L. K., Cade, B. E., Hashimoto, D. M., Rosner, B., Cronin, J. W., et al. (2006). Extended work duration and the risk of self-reported percutaneous injuries in interns. *JAMA, 296,* 1055-1062.

Ayas, N. T., White, D. P., Manson, J. E., Stampfer, M. J., Speizer, F. E., Malhotra, A., et al. (2003). A propective study of sleep duration and coronary heart disease in women. *Archives of Internal Medicine, 163,* 205-209.

Baldwin, D., and Daugherty, S. (2004). Sleep deprivation and fatigue in residency training: results of a national survey of first- and second year residents. *Sleep, 27,* 217-223.

Barger, L. K., Cade, B. E., Ayas, N. T., Cronin, J. W., Rosner, B., Speizer, F. E., et al. (2005). Extended work shifts and the risk of motor vehicle crashes among interns. *New England Journal of Medicine, 352,* 125-134.

Barnett, R., Gareis, K., and Carr, P. (2005). Career satisfaction and retention of a sample of women physicians who work reduced hours. *Journal of Women's Health, 14,* 146-153.

Barton Cunningham, J. (1989). A compressed shift schedule: Dealing with some of the problems of shift-work. *Journal of Organizational Behavior, 10,* 231-245.

Barton, J., and Folkard, S. (1991). The response of day and night nurses to their work schedules. *Journal of Occupational Psychology, 64,* 207-218.

Biaggi, P., Peter, S., and Ulich, E. (2003). Stressors, emotional exhaustion and aversion to patients in residents and chief residents - what can be done? *Swiss Medical Weekly, 133,* 339-346.

Bleich, M. R., Connolly, C., Davis, K., Hewlett, P. O., and Hill, K. S. (2006). *Wisdom at work: The importance of the older and experienced nurse in the workplace.* Retrieved January 19, 2007, from http://www.rwjf.org/files/publications/other/wisdomatwork.pdf.

Boggild, H., and Knutsson, A. (1999). Shift work, risk factors and cardiovascular disease. *Scand J. Work Environ Health, 25,* 85-99.

Bongers, P. M., de Winter, C. R., Kompier, M. A., and Hildebrandt, V. H. (1993). Psychosocial factors at work and musculoskeletal disease. *Scandinavian Journal of Work, Environment and Health, 19,* 297-312.

Bongers, P. M., Kremer, A. M., and ter Laak, J. (2002). Are psychosocial factors, risk factors for symptoms and signs of the shoulder, elbow, or hand/wrist? A review of the epidemiological literature. *American Journal of Industrial Medicine, 41,* 315-342.

Caruso, C. C., Hitchcock, E. M., Dick, R. B., Russo, J. M., and Schmit, J. M. (2004). *Overtime and extended work shifts: Recent findings on illnesses, injuries, and health behaviors.* Retrieved. July 31, 2007, from http://www.cdc.gov/niosh/docs/2004-143/pdfs/2004-143.pdf.

Caruso, C. C., Lusk, S. L., and Gillespie, B. W. (2004). Relationship of work schedules to gastrointestinal diagnoses, symptoms, and medication use in auto factory workers. *American Journal of Industrial Medicine, 46,* 586-598.

Clissold, G., Smith, P., and Acutt, B. (2001). The impact of unwaged domestic work on the duration and timing of sleep of female nurses working full-time on rotating 3-shift rosters. *Journal of Human Ergology., 30*, 345-349.

Devereux, J. J., Vlachonikolis, I. G., and Buckle, P. W. (2002). Epidemiological study to investigate potential interaction between physical and psychosocial factors at work that may increase the risk of symptoms of musculoskeletal disorder of the neck and upper limb. *Occupational and Environmental Medicine, 59*, 269-277.

Dinges, D. F., Pack, F., Williams, K., Gillen, K. A., Powell, J. W., Ott, G. E., et al. (1997). Cumulative sleepiness, mood disturbance, and psychomotor vigilance performance decrements during a week of sleep restricted to 4-5 hours per night. *Sleep., 20*, 267-267.

Fast, J. E., and Frederick, J. A. (1996). *Working arrangements and time stress* (No. 11-008-XPE): Statistics Canada.

Fletcher, K. E., Underwood III, W., Davis, S. Q., Mangrulkar, R. S., McMahon, L. F., and Saint, S. (2005). Effects of work-hour reduction on residents' lives: a systematic review. *JAMA, 294*, 1088-1100.

Forde, M. S., Punnett, L., and Wegman, D. H. (2002). Pathomechanisms of work-related musculoskeletal disorders: Conceptual issues. *Ergonomics, 45*, 619-630.

Geiger-Brown, J., Muntaner, C., Lipscomb, J. A., and Trinkoff, A. (2004). Demanding work schedules and mental health among nursing assistants working in nursing homes. *Work and Stress, 18*, 292-304.

Geurts, S., Rutte, C., and Peeters, M. (1999). Antecedents and consequences of work-home interference among medical residents. *Social Science and Medicine, 48*, 1135-1148.

Gottlieb, B. H., Kelloway, E. K., and Martin-Matthews, A. (1996). Predictors of work-family conflict, stress, and job satisfaction among nurses. *Canadian Journal of Nursing Research, 28*, 99-117.

Gottlieb, D., Punjabi, N., Newman, A., Resnick, H., Redline, S., Baldwin, C., et al. (2005). Association of sleep time with diabetes mellitus and impaired glucose tolerance. *Archives of Internal Medicine, 165*, 863-868.

Grosswald, B. (2003). Shift work and negative work-to-family spillover. *Journal of Sociology and Social Welfare, 30*, 31-56.

Grosswald, B. (2004). The effects of shift work on family satisfaction. *Families in Society: The Journal of Contemporary Social Services, 85*, 413-423.

Hale, D. R. (1996). Noise in the hospital: A quality improvement approach. *Journal of Nursing Administration, 26*(3), 4.

Hammer, T. H., Saksvik, P. O., Nytro, K., Torvatn, H., and Bayazit, M. (2004). Expanding the psychosocial work environment: Workplace norms and work-family conflict as correlates of stress and health. *Journal of Occupational Health Psychology, 9*, 83-97.

Harrington, J. M. (2001). Health effects of shift work and extended hours of work. *Occupational and Environmental Medicine, 58*, 68-72.

Hochschild, A. (Ed.). (1989). *The second shift*. New York: Avon Books.

Holland, D. W. (2006). The effect of shiftwork related fatigue on the family life of train operators: Implications for safety and health professionals. *Work, 26*, 115-121.

Ijzelenberg, W., Molenaar, D., and Burdorf, A. (2004). Different risk factors for musculoskeletal complaints and musculoskeletal sickness absence. *Scandinavian Journal of Work, Environment and Health, 30*, 56-63.

Institute of Medicine. (2004). *Keeping Patients Safe. Transforming the Work Environment of Nurses*. Washington, DC: National Academy Press.

Kawachi, I., Colditz, G., Stampfer, M. J., Willett, W., Manson, J. E., Speizer, F., et al. (1995). Prospective study of shift work and risk of coronary heart disease in women. *Circulation, 92*, 3178-3182.

Keeton, K., Fenner, D. E., Johnson, T. R., and Hayward, R. A. (2007). Predictors of physician career satisfaction, work-life balance, and burnout. *Obstetrics and Gynecology, 109*, 949-955.

Knowlton, L. (1999). Neurobehavioral consequences of sleep dysfunction. *Psychiatric Times, 16*, 99.

Knutsson, A. (2003). Health disorders of shift workers. *Occupational Medicine (Oxford), 53*, 103-108.

Kohn, L. T., Corrigan, J. M., and Donaldson, M. S. (Eds.). (2000). *To err is human: Building a safer health system*. Washington, D.C.: Institute of Medicine.

Kroenke, H., Spiegelman, D., Manson, J. E., Schernhammer, E., Colditz, G., and Kawachi, I. (2006). Work characteristics and incidence of Type 2 diabetes in women. *American Journal of Epidemiology, 165*, 175-183.

Lee, K. (1992). Self-reported sleep disturbances in employed women. *Sleep, 15*, 493-498.

Lipscomb, J. A., Trinkoff, A. M., Geiger-Brown, J., and Brady, B. (2002). Work-schedule characteristics and reported musculoskeletal disorders of registered nurses. *Scandinavian Journal of Work, Environment and Health., 28*, 394-401.

Lockley, S. W., Landrigan, C. P., Barger, L. K., and Czeisler, C. A. (2006). When policy meets physiology. The challenges of reducing resident work hours. *Clinical Orthopaedics and Related Research, 449*, 116-127.

Lowden, A., Kecklund, G., Axelsson, J., and Akerstedt, T. (1998). Change from an 8-hour shift to a 12-hour shift, attitudes, sleep, sleepiness and performance. *Scandinavian Journal of Work, Environment and Health., 24(Suppl 3)*, 69-75.

Lundberg, U., Kadefors, R., Melin, B., Palmerud, G., Hassmen, P., Engstrom, M., et al. (1994). Psychophysiologic stress and EMG activity of the trapezius muscle. *International Journal of Behavioral Medicine, 1*, 354-370.

Martini, S., Arfken, C., and Balon, R. (2006). Comparison of burnout among medical residents before and after the implementation of work hours limits. *Academic Psychiatry, 30*, 352-355.

McEwen, B. S. (2003). Mood disorders and allostatic load. *Biological Psychiatry, 54*, 200-207.

Monk, T. H. (2005). Shift work: Basic principles. In M. Kryger, T. Roth and W. C. Dement (Eds.), *Principles and practice of sleep medicine* (4th ed., pp. 673-679). Philadelphia: Elsevier Saunders.

National Center for Health Statistics. (2003-2004). Prevalence of overweight and obesity among adults: United States, 2003-2004. Retrieved July 31, 2007, from http://www.cdc.gov/nchs/products/pubs/pubd/hestats/overweight/overwght_adult_03.htm

O'Shea, E. (1999). Factors contributing to medication errors: A literature review. *Journal of Clinical Nursing, 8*, 496-504.

Pilcher, J. J., and Huffcutt, A. I. (1996). Effects of sleep deprivation on performance: A meta-analysis. *Sleep, 19*, 318-326.

Presser, H. (2000). Nonstandard work schedules and marital instability. *Journal of Marriage and the Family, 62*, 93-110.

Reid, K., and Dawson, D. (2001). Comparing performance on a simulated 12 hour shift rotation in young and older subjects. *Occupational and Environmental Medicine, 58*, 58-62.

Reilly, T., Waterhouse, J., and Atkinson, G. (1997). Aging, rhythms of physical peformance, and adjustment to changes in the sleep-activity cycle. *Occupational and Environmental Medicine, 54*, 812-816.

Rosa, R. R. (1995). Extended workshifts and excessive fatigue. *Journal of Sleep Research, 4(Supplement 2)*, 51-56.

Rotenberg, L., Moreno, C., Portela, L. F., Benedito-Silva, A. A., and Menna-Barreto, L. (2000). The amount of diurnal sleep, and complaints of fatigue and poor sleep, in night-working women: The effects of having children. *Biological Rhythm Research, 31*, 515-522.

Rouch, I., Wild, P., Ansiau, D., and Marquie, J. (2005). Shiftwork experience, age and cognitive performance. *Ergonomics, 48*, 1282-1293.

Schnorpfeil, P., Noll, A., Schulze, R., Ehlert, U., Frey, K., and Fischer, J. E. (2003). Allostatic load and work conditions. *Social Science and Medicine, 57*, 647-656.

Simon, B. L. (1990). Impact of shift work on individuals and families. *Families in Society: The Journal of Contemporary Social Services, 71*, 342-348.

Sluiter, J. K. (2006). High-demand jobs: Age-related diversity in work ability? *Applied Ergonomics, 37*, 429-440.

Smith, L., and Folkard, S. (1993). The perceptions and feelings of shiftworkers' partners. *Ergonomics, 36*, 299-305.

Sonnentag, S. (2006). Psychological detachment from work during off-job time: The role of job stressors, job involvement and recovery-related self-efficacy. *European Journal of Work and Organizational Psychology, 15*, 197-217.

Sparks, K., Cooper, C., Fried, Y., and Shirom, A. (1997). The effects of hours of work on health: A meta-analytic review. *Journal of Occupational and Organizational Psychology, 70*, 391-408.

Spiegel, K., Leproult, R., and Van Cauter, E. (1999). Impact of sleep debt on metabolic and endocrine functions. *Lancet, 354*, 1435-1439.

Spurgeon, A., Harrington, J. M., and Cooper, C. L. (1997). Health and safety problems associated with long working hours: A review of the current position. *Occupational and Environmental Medicine, 54*, 367-375.

Trinkoff, A., Geiger-Brown, J., Brady, B., Lipscomb, J., and Muntaner, C. (2006). How long and how much are nurses now working? *American Journal of Nursing, 106*, 60-71.

Trinkoff, A. M., Brady, B., and Nielsen, K. (2003). Workplace prevention and musculoskeletal injuries in nurses. *Journal of Nursing Administration, 33*, 153-158.

Trinkoff, A. M., Le, R., Geiger-Brown, J., and Lipscomb, J. (2007). Work schedule, needle use, and needlestick injuries among registered nurses. *Infection Control and Hospital Epidemiology, 28*, 156-164.

Trinkoff, A. M., Le, R., Geiger-Brown, J., Lipscomb, J., and Lang, G. M. (2006). Longitudinal relationship of work hours, mandatory overtime, and on-call to musculoskeletal problems in nurses. *American Journal of Industrial Medicine, 49*, 964-971.

Trinkoff, A. M., Lipscomb, J. A., Geiger-Brown, J., Storr, C. L., and Brady, B. A. (2003). Perceived physical demands and reported musculoskeletal problems in registered nurses. *American Journal of Preventive Medicine, 24*, 270-275.

Trinkoff, A. M., Storr, C. L., and Lipscomb, J. A. (2001). Physically demanding work and inadequate sleep, pain medication use, and absenteeism in registered nurses. *Journal of Occupational and Environmental Medicine, 43*, 355-363.

Tzischinsky, O., Zohar, D., Epstein, R., Chillag, N., and Lavie, P. (2001). Daily and yearly burnout symptoms in Israeli shift work residents. *Journal of Human Ergology, 30*, 357-362.

van der Hulst, M. (2003). Long work hours and health. *Scandinavian Journal of Work, Environment and Health, 29*, 171-188.

Wedderburn, A. (1998). *Best Bulletin. Continuous Shift Systems*. Retrieved 5/30/2007. from http://www.eurofound.europa.eu/publications/htmlfiles/ef9802.htm.

Wellens, B. T., and Smith, A. P. (2006). Combined workplace stressors and their relationship with mood, physiology, and performance. *Work and Stress, 20*, 245-258.

Whelan, E., Lawson, C., Grajewski, B., Hibert, E., Spiegelman, D., and Rich-Edwards, J. (2007). Work schedule during pregnancy and spontaneous abortion. *Epidemiology, 18*, 350-355.

White, L., and Keith, B. (1990). The effect of shift work on the quality and stability of marital relations. *Journal of Marriage and the Family, 52*, 453-462.

Zhu, J. L., Hjollund, N. H., Andersen, A. M., and Olsen, J. (2004). Shift work, job stress, and late fetal loss: The National Birth Cohort in Denmark. *Journal of Occupational and Environmental Medicine, 46*, 1144-1149.

In: Handbook of Stress and Burnout in Health Care   ISBN 978-1-60456-500-3
Editor: Jonathon R. B. Halbesleben   © 2008 Nova Science Publishers, Inc.

Chapter 11

PHYSICIAN BURNOUT AS PREDICTED BY SUBJECTIVE AND OBJECTIVE WORKLOAD AND BY AUTONOMY

Arie Shirom[*1], *Nurit Nirel*[2] *and Amiram D. Vinokur*[3]

[1]Faculty of Management,
Tel-Aviv University
[2]Meyers-JDC-Brookdale Institute,
Jerusalem
[3]University of Michigan,
Institute for Social Research

Burnout is an affective state, comprised of the feelings of emotional exhaustion, physical fatigue and cognitive weariness, which denotes the depletion of energetic resources resulting from cumulative exposure to chronic work and life stresses (cf. Melamed, Shirom, Toker, Berliner, and Shapira, 2006). Accumulating evidence indicates that burnout is associated with negative health consequences, primarily increased risk of cardiovascular disease (Melamed et al., 2006). Physicians have reported that depletion in their energetic resources tended to lead to the provision of less than optimal patient care (e.g., Firth-Cozens and Greenhalgh, 1997). Additionally, physicians' level of burnout was found to be positively related to the likelihood of their making medical errors (West et al., 2006). Previous research consistently found that one's level of burnout may affect one's co-workers, including within teams of physicians (Bakker, Schaufeli, Sixma, and Bosveld, 2001). Recent studies have documented a growing prevalence of physicians' burnout in many countries (Kushnir, Levhar, and Cohen, 2004; Visser, Smets, Oort, and De Haes, 2003). Despite the rising prevalence rates of burnout among physicians, its objective and subjective antecedents have yet to be systematically investigated, with very few exceptions (e.g., Panagopoulou, Montgomery, and Benos, 2006). Following this rationale, our study focuses on burnout and its objective and subjective antecedents among physicians.

---

[*] Please address future correspondence regarding this study to Arie Shirom, Faculty of Management, Tel Aviv University, Ramat Aviv, PO Box 39010, Tel Aviv 69978, ISRAEL, or email to: ashirom@post.tau.ac.il.

Our first objective in the current research was to test specific expectations considering the extent to which physicians' objective and subjective workload predict global burnout among specialists. The second objective was to examine the extent to which perceived workload and autonomy mediated the relationships between indicators of physicians' objective workload and their levels of burnout. Our theoretical model was based on the Person-Environment Fit (P-EF) theory (French, Caplan, and Harrison, 1982). P-EF theory has been extensively used in occupational stress research (Hart and Cooper, 2001). It makes the conceptual distinction between the objective environment and the subjective or perceived environment, represented in our study by physicians' caseload and work hours and by perceived workload and autonomy, respectively. Two basic premises of P-EF theory are that the objective environment is an imperfect determinant of its subjective counterpart due to perceptual distortions and cognitive biases and that the effects of the objective environment on strain and mental health are mediated at least in part by its subjective counterpart (Edwards, Caplan, and Van Harrison, 1998).

Conceptualizing Burnout. Based on Conservation of Resources [COR] theory (Hobfoll, 1989, 2002), we conceptualized burnout as a multidimensional construct whose three facets were physical fatigue, emotional exhaustion, and cognitive weariness, for several theoretical reasons. First, physical, emotional, and cognitive energy are individually possessed and are expected to be closely interrelated (Hobfoll and Shirom, 2000). The COR theory postulates that personal resources affect each other and exist as a resource pool - lacking one is often associated with lacking another. Further, COR theory argues that these resources represent a set of resources internal to the self that facilitates the development and use of other resources (Hobfoll, 2002; Hobfoll and Shirom, 2000). For the above reasons, our basic assumption was that any change in them reflects a change in the underlying latent construct of global burnout, an assumption supported by previous studies (cf. Melamed et al., 2006).

Perceived workload and burnout. In the theory of job demands-resources, Demerouti and her colleagues (Demerouti, Bakker, Nachreiner, and Schaufeli, 2001) refer to job demands as those physical, psychological and organizational aspects of the job that require sustained physical, emotional and cognitive efforts. Job demands often turn into stressors when meeting the demands requires sustained efforts (Demerouti et al., 2001), and are closely related to psychological and physiological strains, including burnout (Schaufeli and Bakker, 2004). Based on meta-analytic evidence (Lee and Ashforth, 1996; Schaufeli and Enzmann, 1998) workload was consistently found to be is a major predictor of burnout, including among physicians (Deckard, Meterko, and Field, 1994). High workload was also found to be widespread among physicians in healthcare systems (Visser et al., 2003). Consequently, we predicted that perceived workload would be positively linked with global burnout (Hypothesis 1).

Autonomy and burnout. A major proposition of the Job Demands-Resources model (Demerouti et al., 2001) is that burnout develops when certain job demands are high and certain job resources are limited. Job autonomy represents a job-related resource that potentially enables employees to cope more effectively with stressful situations they experience at work because they could use their available coping resources and skills more flexibly (Fried and Ferris, 1987). Several studies reported that lack of job autonomy was negatively associated with all dimensions of burnout (cf. Bakker, Demerouti, and Euwema, 2005), and that high levels of job autonomy ameliorated the effects of job-related stresses on the core content of burnout (cf. Peeters and Rutte, 2005). Therefore, we expected autonomy to be a negative predictor of global burnout as representing the common variance of its three facets (Hypothesis 2).

Objective workload and perceived workload. Workload may be defined by a variety of measures, including employees' reports of hours worked and number of people served or worked for (Spector, Dwyer, and Jex, 1988). Among physicians, the number of work hours worked was consistently found to be a positive predictor of both perceived stress and workload. For example, Linzer and colleagues (Linzer et al., 2001) investigated the antecedents of stress using a nationally-representative sample of US physicians and found that the number of work hours was closely associated with perceived stress, after controlling for age, gender, medical specialty, and practice setting. Following this evidence, we hypothesized (Hypothesis 3) that both number of work hours and patient load would positively predict perceived workload.

Perceived workload as a mediator. Based on the aforementioned major propositions of PE-F theory we expected that perceived workload would mediate the relationships between objective workload and burnout. Based on their meta-analysis of the relations between work hours and health, Sparks and her colleagues (Sparks, Cooper, Fried, and Shirom, 1997) and subsequently Spurgeon and his colleagues (Spurgeon, Harrington, and Cooper, 1997) found that perceived stress mediated the relations between work hours and strain. In a longitudinal study of U.S. residents (Hillhouse, Adler, and Walters, 2000) posttest burnout was not predicted by baseline work hours but only by baseline perceived workload. In the same vein, a more recent study (Panagopoulou, Montgomery, and Benos, 2006) of the predictors of specialists and residents' burnout in Greece found that perceived working conditions were of considerable importance in explaining the variance in burnout relative to work hours, while, in contrast, work hours did not emerge as a significant predictor. These two studies did not test any mediational hypothesis. We expected full mediation because it represented the most parsimonious model (cf. James, Mulaik, and Brett, 2006). We hypothesized that work hours and patient load would affect burnout and physical fatigue only indirectly, with their effects fully mediated by perceived workload (Hypothesis 4).

Control Variables. Gender, age and seniority were included in our model as control variables because they were consistently found in previous studies to be negatively associated with several of our predictors and with burnout (Brewer and Shapard, 2004). Seniority was found in several meta-analytic studies to be associated with different facets of job performance (Sturman, 2003) and burnout (Brewer and Shapard, 2004). Congruent with these meta-analytic results, a recent study (Shanafelt, Bradley, Wipf, and Back, 2002) found relatively high levels of burnout among specialists early in their career. Collective bargaining agreements covering the work conditions of the primarily salaried physicians under study stipulate a reduction in their weekly work hours after they reach specific levels of seniority. Therefore, we expected seniority to negatively predict work hours and number of patients regardless of age. Seniority was also expected to negatively predict perceived workload because senior physicians are more experienced and consequently cope better; hence, they may report lower levels of overload relative to their junior colleagues. A positive impact of seniority on autonomy was suggested by several previous studies (cf. Perrone, Zaheer, and McEvily, 2003). We also added academic affiliation, indicating that the specialist has a clinical academic appointment in one of the country's medical schools, as yet another control variables, because having such an appointment is likely to add to the specialists other duties the additional duty of teaching medical students and residents in hospitals.

METHOD

Sample

The sampling frame consisted of all the country's specialists working in six areas of medical specialization - six areas which represent specialty medicine provided in community clinics. The medical specializations chosen were ophthalmology, dermatology, otolaryngology and gynecology, mostly providing care in community clinics, and general surgery and cardiology, mostly providing care in acute-care hospitals' outpatient clinics. We constructed the sampling frame based on the service manuals of the four health plans or sick funds, similar to health maintenance organizations in the U.S., and the list of specialists compiled by the Israeli Ministry of Health for the year 2001. A 50% random probability sample was drawn from each of the six specialties, after excluding from the sampling frame those who either lived abroad or were 65 years of age or older at the time of the study.

About 80% of the specialists in the study were men. The proportion of women was particularly small among general surgeons (5%) and cardiologists (13%), and relatively large among dermatologists (44%) and ophthalmologists (30%). All respondents were MDs; 54% had completed medical school in Israel. Of the remainder, 17% had completed medical school in the former Soviet Union. Concerning their educational attainment, 59% were certified specialists in their area of specialization, 30% reported having an additional sub-specialization in their area of specialization, and the remainder had, in addition to their MD degree and certified specialist status, either a Master's degree in medicine or a PhD. Thirty-one percent of the respondents held an academic appointment. Median age and seniority were 52 and 12 (SD = 7.2, 7.7), respectively.

Procedure

The study's questionnaire was mailed to 1,410 specialists, of whom 890 - representing a response rate of 63% - completed it. The questionnaire was accompanied by a letter, which explained the importance of the study and included a guarantee of confidentiality, as well as the endorsement of the Ministry of Health and the Israel Medical Association. The non-respondents, namely those who either refused or failed to respond, did so despite two mailings and a follow-up telephone reminder. We systematically compared those who responded (N=890) with the non-respondents (N=304) regarding differences in medical specialty; no significant difference was found. Using logistic regression, we also systematically compared the extent to which any socio-demographic variable significantly predicted those who replied early (to our first mailing), as opposed to those who replied late, and found a slight tendency for younger physicians and physicians who had been trained in the former Soviet Union to be late respondents. A recent meta-analysis (Schalm and Kelloway, 2001) concluded that non-response is not likely to result in substantial bias in the results of a survey in this area of research.

Measures

Measures were formed following a confirmatory factor analysis (CFA) of the questionnaire items related to each of the multi-item variables under study. Following the confirmation of the expected measurement model in the respective CFA, we calculated the reliability of each resulting measure by Cronbach's internal consistency reliability index, alpha (α). We calculated each respondent's score as the average of his or her responses to the items included in the respective measure.

Burnout was gauged by the Shirom-Melamed Burnout Measure [SMBM][4]. A series of studies conducted over the past ten years, on a diverse range of occupational groups, has generally confirmed the expected relationships between the SMBM and certain physiological variables, thus lending support to its predictive validity (cf. Melamed et al., 2006). Other aspects of the construct validity of the SMBM were recently compared with those of the MBI with favorable results (Shirom and Melamed, 2006). Responses to the 12 items in the measure were gauged using a 7-point scale ranging from 1 (almost never) to 7 (almost always). Confirmatory factor analysis[5] confirmed the theoretically expected SMBM three-factor structure and led to our constructing three subscales, each representing one of the factors, and also a total burnout scale representing all three factors ($\alpha = .93$). The three subscales, with sample items for each, were as follows: the physical fatigue factor (six items) – the frequency of feeling tired, physically drained, and physically exhausted ($\alpha = .93$); the cognitive weariness factor (three items) – the frequency of feeling difficulty in concentrating, and slow thinking processes ($\alpha = .91$); and the emotional exhaustion factor (three items) – the frequency of feeling emotionally fatigued and emotionally burned out ($\alpha = .89$). For our SEM analyses the global burnout measure was modeled as a second-order factor with each of the three components as first-order factors. The emotional exhaustion factor was indicated by three items; the cognitive weariness factor by three items and the physical fatigue factor by three indices- each was the mean of two items.

Perceived workload was gauged based on the overload scale used in the French et al. study (French, Caplan, and Harrison, 1982), with additional physician-specific items adopted from a study which had investigated overload among physicians (Sutherland and Cooper, 1992). Respondents rated their work load using a five-point scale that ranged from 1 (not at all) to 5 (to a very great extent). The nine-item measure ($\alpha = .92$) included items gauging quantitative overload (worked too many hours, worked too hard, had too many patients), and qualitative overload (found it difficult to divide his or her available time between work and family). We used the mean of these nine items for correlational analyses, and the two subscales of quantitative and qualitative workload as two indicators of the overload latent factor for our SEM analyses.

Autonomy was assessed by a measure constructed to reflect physicians' professional autonomy and perceived control over key aspects of caring for their patients (Schulz, Greenley, and Peterson, 1983), a measure used in several previous studies (cf. Schulz, Greenley, and Brown, 1995). The ten-item measure asked respondents to assess on a five-point scale the extent to which they had control over professional issues including prescribing medications, adopting new modes of care, updating themselves, number and types of patients

---

[4] The SMBM, its norms, and instructions concerning its use are in the public domain and are downloadable from the following site: http://www.tau.ac.il/~ashirom/

[5] Detailed results of this analysis are available from the authors upon request.

they cared for, and deciding on their order of priorities in providing care to patients. The measure had an alpha coefficient of .82. The 10 items were randomly divided into two subscales that served as indicators of the autonomy latent factor.

Objective workload was assessed by the self-reported total number of weekly work hours, and by the total number of patients to whom he or she provides care during a typical workday. Self-reports on hours of work were found to have high correlations with supervisory reports (Spector, 1992; Spector, Dwyer, and Jex, 1988), and self-reports on caseload were found to have high correlations with employers' records (Spector, 1992). Therefore, we have used these two variables as indicators of objective workload. Seniority was assessed by the total number of years a physician has been working in his or her field of specialty. Academic affiliation was a dichotomy with the value of 1 representing having a clinical appointment in one of the country's medical schools, while the value of 0 was assign to those responding that they did not hold such an appointment.

Data Analysis

Our main analyses involved the testing of the model representing our hypotheses by using structural equation modeling (SEM) with EQS software (Bentler, 2002). Following widely- accepted recommendations for SEM analysis (McDonald and Ho, 2002), we report three goodness-of-fit indices: the normed fit index (NFI), the non-normed fit index (NNFI, also known as TLI) and the comparative fit index (CFI). We also report the misfit index known as root mean-square error of approximation (RMSEA). Hu and Bentler (1999) suggested that fit indices close to or above .95 combined with RMSEA below .06 could be considered indicative of good approximate fit. In our analysis we first tested the measurement model for the second order factor model of burnout and found that it fit the data very well with χ^2 (17, 890) = 34.67, NFI, NNFI, CFI all = .99, and RMSEA = .034, relative to each of the two-factor and the one-factor solutions which resulted in unacceptable values of the same fit indexes[2]. We next estimated the measurement model of all latent variables, and after which we tested two structural models, the theoretical model embodying all our hypotheses and the alternative model in which the arrow implied by Hypothesis 1a, from perceived overload to the physical fatigue facet of total burnout, was omitted.

RESULTS

Descriptive Results

Table 1 provides the product moment correlations among the study variables, as well as their means and standard deviations. The more hours a physician worked per week (at all of his or her jobs), the more likely he or she was to experience job overload. In addition, the more years of seniority a physician had, the smaller the chance that he or she would experience overload.

Table 1. Product Moment Correlations, Means and Standard Deviations among the Study factors (1-6) and variables (8-10)

	(1)	(2)	(3)	(4)	(5)	(6)	(7)	(8)	(9)	(10)
(1) Burnout, General	1.00									
(2) Physical fatigue	.94	1.00								
(3) Cognitive weariness	.83	.67	1.00							
(4) Emotional exhaustion	.74	.51	.57	1.00						
(5) Workload, subjective	.57	.60	.45	.31	1.00					
(6) Autonomy	-.26	-.22	-.24	-.23	-.11	1.00				
(7) Work hours, total	.14	.17	.09	.05	.33	.01	1.00			
(8) No. of patients	-.03	-.02	-.02	-.04	.03	-.07	.02	1.00		
(9) Seniority	-.05	-.04	-.07	-.02	-.08	-.14	-.07	-.14	1.00	
(10) Academic affil. (0=no)	-.01	-.02	.03	.01	-.17	-.20	-.14	.17	-.11	1.00
(11) Gender (0=males)	-.08	-.06	-.06	-.12	-.13	-.13	-.17	.06	-.07	.15
Mean	2.78	3.38	2.15	2.23	3.02	3.57	44.2	28.8	12.5	.71
SD	1.07	1.33	1.10	1.13	0.93	0.66	13.2	15.8	7.7	.45

Note. N= 890. A correlation coefficient lower than .06 is not significant at the p < .05 level.

Testing the Measurement and the Structural Models

We first tested the structural model for all the latent factors presented in Figure 1. The results demonstrated a good fit with χ^2 (95, n = 890) = 358.6; Normed, Non-normed and Comparative fit indexes were .96, .95 and .97, respectively, and RMSEA = .056 (90% confidence interval for RMSEA ranged from .051 to .065).

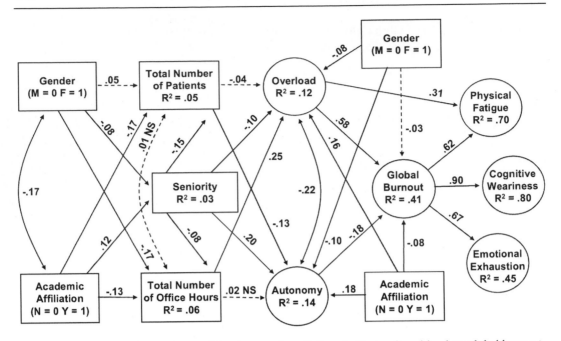

Figure 1. Standardized coefficients of the direct and mediational effects of workload on global burnout. X2 (95, N = 890) = 358.6. NFI, NNFI and CFI = .96, .95, and .97, respectively. RMSEA = .06. Solid lines and curves represent statistically significant paths at p < .05. Double arrow curves represent correlations between variables or disturbances (residuals). Gender and academic affiliation appear twice to improve the clarity of their paths to other constructs.

Our hypothesized model with the standardized beta coefficients along the paths is presented in Figure 1. As expected in Hypotheses 1, in the theoretical model (see Figure 1), perceived overload had a significantly strong positive impact on global burnout, β = .58 (p < .01), and on physical fatigue, β = .31 (p < .01). Autonomy was a negative predictor of the criterion (β = -.18), thus supporting Hypothesis 2. Hypothesis 3 was only partly supported in that the number of work hours was found to be a significant positive predictor of perceived workload (β = .26); in contrast, the number of patients was not a significant predictor of perceived workload. The number of patients and the number of work hours were not correlated (r = .01). The number of patients was negatively linked with autonomy (β = -.13). Figure 1 also provides support for our choice of control variables in that seniority was positively associated with autonomy (β = .20) and, as expected, was a negative predictor of perceived workload (β = -.10). Additionally, academic affiliation was a negative predictor of number of patients and work hours (β = -.17, β = -.13, respectively) and also was found to be a negative predictor of global burnout (β = -.08) and a positive predictor of autonomy (β = .18). Gender (men=0, women=1), used as a control variable, was found to be a significant negative predictor of work hours (β = -.17) and workload (β = -.18).

In conclusion, the major hypotheses of the study regarding the prediction of global burnout by perceived workload and autonomy, as well as the hypothesized linkage of work with perceived workload, were supported by the statistically significant path coefficients within a model that provided a good fit to the data.

Testing Full Mediation of Objective Workload Linkages with Burnout

Perceived overload could be considered as fully mediating the influence of work hours and number of patients on global burnout and on physical fatigue if the indirect paths from the two indicators of objective workload to the criteria are significant (MacKinnon, Fairchild, and Fritz, 2007; MacKinnon, Lockwood, Hoffman, West, and Sheets, 2002). For perceived workload to carry the influence of work hours and number of patients to global burnout and physical fatigue, the two indicators of objective workload must significantly affect perceived workload. As evident from Figure 1, number of patients did not significantly predict perceived workload, thereby disconfirming this part of Hypothesis 4. However, as noted, work hours significantly predicted perceived workload. Furthermore, our SEM model indicated that the prediction of global burnout and of physical fatigue by work hours is insignificantly different from zero, thus lending support to our hypothesized full mediation model. We therefore proceeded to test if work hours had significant indirect effects on global burnout and on physical fatigue. For testing the significance of the hypothesized indirect effects, we used the Sobel test because it performed best in a Monte Carlo study and was found to converge with the Goodman test for sample sizes > 50 (MacKinnon, Warsi, and Dwyer, 1995), and also because using it, given our sample size, yielded power over .8 to our mediation tests (Fritz and MacKinnon, 2007). We found that both indirect effects via the mediator of perceived workload, from work hours to global burnout and from work hours to physical fatigue, were significant (Sobel's Z= 6.51 and 5.47, respectively, both significant at the p< .001 level). On an explorative basis, we also tested if the number of patient had an indirect effect on global burnout via the mediator of autonomy; indeed, this indirect effect was found to be significant (Sobel's Z= 2.35, p< .02). Therefore, the number of patients exerted an indirect effect on global burnout but this indirect effect was transmitted via the full mediation of autonomy rather than perceived workload.

DISCUSSION

Stress and burnout experienced by specialists in their work environment have been shown to have an impact on both their mental and physical health (Deary et al., 1996; Deckard, Meterko, and Field, 1994), as well as on their performance and quality of care (Shirom, Nirel, and Vinokur, 2006; A. Spurgeon and Harrington, 1989). Still, the objective antecedents of burnout, like number of patients and number of work hours, have hardly been investigated. As indicated, when these objective indicators of workload were considered in past research, the possibility that their effects on burnout is fully mediated by perceived job-related demands or resources have not been investigated. The current research contributes to our understanding of these relationships by investigating them in a representative sample of Israeli specialists. With some exceptions discussed below, our conceptual model received considerable support. It had a very good fit to the data and explained 41% of the variance of global burnout, thus favorably comparing with other studies that predicted burnout (cf. Halbesleben and Buckley, 2004; W. B. Schaufeli and Enzmann, 1998). As expected, we found that perceived workload completely mediated the linkage between work hours, global burnout, and physical fatigue (as a facet of global burnout). We consider this set of findings, based on a large and representative sample of the country's specialists, as having significant implications with regard to both future researches investigating the antecedents of physician burnout and those involved in formulating policies designed to limit physician work hours; these implications are discussed below.

Perceived workload did not mediate the linkage between number of patients and burnout; more specifically, number of patients was not found to be a significant predictor of perceived workload. What could possibly account for our failure to support this part of Hypothesis 4? This may be due to the inadequacy of the measure used, which confounds caseload with the type, intensity and duration of client contacts. These dimensions of caseload probably vary within and between the medical specialties included in our sample. In addition, we would like to suggest that the quality of the interaction with patients, for example whether or not it is laden with conflict or tension, is a particularly relevant dimension of a physician-patient interaction. Therefore, we suggest that future examinations of the effects of caseload on burnout will include improved operationalization of this objective indicator of workload, including quantitative measures such as duration of average contact and qualitative measures like intensity and nature of contact (Jackson, Schwab, and Schuler, 1986). As noted, number of patients did affect burnout, but only indirectly, through the full mediation of autonomy.

Limitations. Though we did find that the data fit our model very well, this provides only support, and not confirmation, for our model and hypotheses. Other models, not considered here, could be equally compatible with the data. We recommend that future research in this area will replicate our model and test additional alternative models on new samples. As in any other cross-sectional study, the direction of causality is an open question. Generally, longitudinal designs adhere to the positivist view of causation in that the cause precedes the effect over time. However, temporal precedence is a necessary, but not a sufficient, condition for causation (Rogosa, 1980).

Gathering self-reports on stress, burnout, and self-rated performance in the same questionnaire could lead to artifacts such as priming and consistency effects associated with the bias of common method variance. Common method variance is expected to inflate the correlations between self-reported measures in our questionnaire (Spector and Brannick, 1995). From Table 1, it is obvious that there are non-significant and zero-level correlations among the percept –percept variables included in our study; this fact militates against the existence of a pervasive common method bias (Williams and Brown, 1994). As suggested by both meta-analytic and qualitative reviews of the area, common method bias may indeed exist, but not at a level that would typically invalidate substantive conclusions (Crampton and Wagner, 1994; Doty and Glick, 1998). These reviews of the literature on common method variance have led one author to refer to it as an urban legend (Spector, 2006). Specifically relating to our measure of global burnout and its three facets, modeling both the first- and second-order factors of burnout is advantageous in that our facet-specific findings are probably less prone to confound substance with method effect.

Implications. Our findings carry several implications for future research and policy making on specialists' work lives. Recall that we found that seniority was negatively related to number of patients, number of work hours, and perceived workload, and positively associated with autonomy. Having an academic affiliation was found to be a negative predictor of global burnout and perceived workload, and a positive predictor of autonomy. Additionally, having an academic affiliation predicted lower hours of work and number of patients. Therefore, based on our set of results, we would like to recommend that future researchers consider the addition of these variables to their research design, possibly adding additional aspects of physicians' work experience (Tesluk and Jacobs, 1998).

As indicated above, specialists' burnout was found in past research to be associated with the quality of their health care to patients, their patients' satisfaction, and to the health and well-being of these physicians. The number of physicians' work hours has often been linked to the same set of negative outcomes. Accumulated evidence suggests that the variable representing this aspect of physicians' objective workload, work hours, is associated with the number of medical errors, patients safety, and physicians' quality of life (cf. Barger et al., 2006; Vidyarthi, Auerbach, Wachter, and Katz, 2007). In the European Union, the USA and Canada, among other countries, concerns about the effects of excessive physician work hours upon patient safety led to legislation on duty-hour restrictions. For example, the European Working Time Directive, which became law in the U.K. in 1998, determines that the maximum period that may be spent as a resident in hospitals is 56 hours per week and that after August 2009 this maximal period of stay would drop to 48 hours per week (Douglas, 2005). A number of researchers have suggested that critical mediators linking work hours with maladaptive outcomes like medical errors and reduced patient safety are physician subjective workload and burnout (Deckard, Meterko, and Field, 1994; Shirom, Nirel, and Vinokur, 2006; Spickard, Gabbe, and Christensen, 2002). Our study could provide a plausible explanation why these work hours reforms failed to have an appreciable effect on physician burnout because it was designed to investigate a plausible causal path leading from work hours to perceived workload and subsequently to burnout.

We found a full mediation of the linkage between number of work hours and burnout by perceived workload. This finding is yet another demonstration of the dictum long suggested by Kurt Lewin, namely that behavior cannot be properly explained if one does not understand the way in which individuals view the world in which they live. Additionally, there is also a practical implication that arises from the finding that work hours were not directly related to global burnout or physical fatigue. It has been established that the effect of work hours on affective and behavioral outcomes, such as burnout and job performance, operate through multiple and sustained paths of influence, including increases in physiological arousal, sleep disturbances, and changes in health-related behaviors (Sparks et al., 1997). Efforts to reduce physicians' workload have traditionally focused on work hours since they reflect exposure to stress that can be easily ameliorated by lowering the level of exposure. As our findings suggest, work hours have direct and relatively strong impact on perceived workload, and therefore the focus on reducing them seems justified. However, the results of our study cast some doubt over the effectiveness of this policy in terms of the possible effects on physicians' burnout. We would like to argue, based on our study, that work hours may impact burnout, and possible other important outcomes, only indirectly, through its effects on mediators such as perceived workload. Perceived workload, long known to be the most potent predictor of burnout (Schaufeli and Enzmann, 1998), should be considered as a focal variable in future interventions designed to reduce the levels of burnout among physicians. We reached this conclusion because it appears to transmit the effects of work hours onto burnout.

ACKNOWLEDGEMENT

The authors wish to thank the National Institute for Health Policy and Health Services Research, Israel, for financial support to this research, and the physicians who volunteered their time to complete the questionnaire. Both made this study possible.

REFERENCES

Bakker, A. B., Demerouti, E., and Euwema, M. C. (2005). Job resources buffer the impact of job demands on burnout. *Journal of Occupational Health Psychology, 10*(2), 170-180.

Bakker, A. B., Schaufeli, W. B., Sixma, H. J., and Bosveld, W. (2001). Burnout contagion among general practitioners. *Journal o Social and Clinical Psychology, 20*(1), 82-98.

Barger, L. K., Ayas, N. T., Cade, B. E., Cronin, J. W., Rosner, B., Speizer, F. E., et al. (2006). Impact of extended-duration shifts on medical errors, adverse events, and attentional failures. *Plos Medicine, 3*(12), 2440-2448.

Bentler, P. M. (2002). *EQS 6 structural equation program manual.* Encino, CA: Multivariate Software Inc.

Brewer, E. W., and Shapard, L. (2004). Employee burnout: A meta-analysis of the relationship between age and years of experience. *Human Resource Development Review, 3*, 102-123.

Deary, I. J., Blenkin, H., Agius, R. M., Endler, N. S., Zealley, H., and Wood, R. (1996). Models of job-related stress and personal achievement among consultant doctors. *British Journal of Psychology, 87*(1), 3-29.

Deckard, G., Meterko, M., and Field, D. (1994). Physician burnout: An examination of personal, professional, and organizational relationships. *Medical Care, 32*, 745-754.

Demerouti, E., Bakker, A. B., Nachreiner, F., and Schaufeli, W. B. (2001). The Job Demands-Resources Model of burnout. *Journal of Applied Psychology, 86*(3), 499-512.

Douglas, N. J. (2005). Sleep, performance, and the European Working Time Directive. *Clinical Medicine, 5*(1), 95-96.

Edwards, J. R., Caplan, R. D., and Van Harrison, R. (1998). Person-Environment Fit Theory: Conceptual foundations, empirical evidence, and directions for future research. In C. L. Cooper (Ed.), *Theories of organizational stress* (pp. 28-68). New York City, N.Y.: Oxford University Press.

Firth-Cozens, J., and Greenhalgh, J. (1997). Doctors' perceptions of the links between stress and lowered clinical care. *Social Science and Medicine, 44*(7), 1017-1022.

French, J. R. P., Caplan, R. D., and Harrison, R. V. (1982). *The mechanisms of job stress and strain.* Chichester, U.K: John Wiley and Sons.

Fried, Y., and Ferris, G. R. (1987). The validity of the Job Characteristics Model: A review and meta-analysis. *Personnel Psychology, 40*(2), 287-322.

Halbesleben, J. R. B., and Buckley, M. R. (2004). Burnout in organizational life. *Journal of Management, 30*(6), 859-879.

Hart, P. M., and Cooper, C. L. (2001). Occupational stress: Toward a more integrated framework. In N. R. Anderson, D. S. Ones, H. K. Sinangil and C. Viswesvaran (Eds.), *Handbook of industrial, work and organizational psychology* (Vol. 2, pp. 93-115). London, U. K.: Sage Publications.

Hillhouse, J. J., Adler, C. M., and Walters, D. N. (2000). A simple model of stress, burnout and symptomatology in medical residents: a longitudinal study. *Psychology, Health and Medicine, 5*(1), 63 - 73.

Hobfoll, S. E. (1989). Conservation of resources: A new attempt at conceptualizing stress. *American Psychologist, 44*(3), 513-524.

Hobfoll, S. E. (2002). Social and psychological resources and adaptation. *Review of General Psychology, 6*(4), 307-324.

Hobfoll, S. E., and Shirom, A. (2000). Conservation of resources theory: Applications to stress and management in the workplace. In R. T. Golembiewski (Ed.), *Handbook of organization behavior* (2nd Revised ed., pp. 57-81). New York: Dekker.

Hu, L. T., and Bentler, P. M. (1999). Cutoff criteria for fit in covariance structure analysis. *Structural Equation Modeling, 6*, 1-55.

Jackson, S. E., Schwab, R. K., and Schuler, R. S. (1986). Toward an understanding of the burnout phenomenon. *Journal of Applied Psychology, 71*(4), 630-640.

Kushnir, T., Levhar, C., and Cohen, A. H. (2004). Are burnout levels increasing? The experience of Israeli primary care physicians. *Israel Journal of Medical Science, 6*, 451-455.

Lee, R. T., and Ashforth, B. E. (1996). A meta-analytic examination of the correlates of the three dimensions of job burnout. *Journal of Applied Psychology, 81*(2), 123-133.

Linzer, M., Visser, M. R. M., Oort, F. J., Smets, E. M. A., McMurray, J. E., and de Haes, H. C. J. M. (2001). Predicting and preventing physician burnout: results from the United States and the Netherlands. *The American Journal of Medicine, 111*(2), 170-175.

MacKinnon, D. P., Fairchild, A. J., and Fritz, M. S. (2007). Mediation analysis. *Annual Review of Psychology, 58*(1), 593-614.

MacKinnon, D. P., Lockwood, C. M., Hoffman, J. M., West, S. G., and Sheets, V. (2002). A comparison of methods to test mediation and other intervening variables effects. *Psychological Methods, 7*(1), 83-103.

McDonald, R. P., and Ho, M. R. (2002). Principles and practices in reporting structural equation analyses. *Psychological Methods, 7*(1), 64-82.

Melamed, S., Shirom, A., Toker, S., Berliner, S., and Shapira, I. (2006). Burnout and risk of cardiovascular disease: Evidence, possible causal paths, and promising research directions. *Psychological Bulletin, 132*(3), 327-353.

Panagopoulou, E., Montgomery, A., and Benos, A. (2006). Burnout in internal medicine physicians: Differences between residents and specialists. *European Journal of Internal Medicine, 17*(3), 195-200.

Peeters, M. A., and Rutte, C. G. (2005). Time management behavior as a moderator for the job demand-control interaction. *Journal of Occupational Health Psychology, 10*(1), 64-75.

Perrone, V., Zaheer, A., and McEvily, B. (2003). Free to be trusted? Organizational constraints on trust in boundary spanners. *Organization Science, 14*(4), 422-439.

Schalm, R. L., and Kelloway, E. K. (2001). The relationship between response rate and effect size in occupational health psychology. *Journal of Occupational Health Psychology, 6*(2), 160-163.

Schaufeli, W. B., and Bakker, A. B. (2004). Job demands, job resources, and their relationship with burnout and engagement: A multi-sample study. *Journal of Organizational Behavior, 25*(3), 293-315.

Schaufeli, W. B., and Enzmann, D. (1998). *The burnout companion to study and practice: A critical analysis.* Washington, DC: Taylor and Francis.

Schulz, R., Greenley, J. R., and Brown, R. (1995). Organization, management, and client effects on staff burnout. *Journal of Health and Social Behavior, 36*(4), 333-345.

Schulz, R., Greenley, J. R., and Peterson, R. W. (1983). Management, cost, and quality of acute inpatient psychiatric services. *Medical Care, 21*(4), 911-928.

Shanafelt, T. D., Bradley, K. A., Wipf, J. E., and Back, A. L. (2002). Burnout and self-reported patient care in an internal medicine residency program. *Annals of Internal Medicine, 136*, 358-367.

Shirom, A., and Melamed, S. (2006). A comparison of the construct validity of two burnout measures in two groups of professionals. *International Journal of Stress Management, 13*(2), 176-200.

Shirom, A., Nirel, N., and Vinokur, A. (2006). Overload, autonomy, and burnout as predictors of physicians' quality of care. *Journal of Occupational Health Psychology, 11*(4), 328-342.

Sparks, K., Cooper, C. L., Fried, Y., and Shirom, A. (1997). The effects of hours of work on health: A meta-analytic review. *Journal of Occupational and Organizational Psychology, 70*(4), 391-408.

Spector, P. E. (1992). A consideration of the validity of and meaning of self-report measures of job conditions. In C. L. Cooper and I. T. Robertson (Eds.), *International Review of Industrial and Organizational Psychology* (pp. 123-151). England: Wiley.

Spector, P. E. (2006). Method variance in organizational research: Truth or urban legend? *Organizational Research Methods, 9*(2), 221-232.

Spector, P. E., Dwyer, D. J., and Jex, S. M. (1988). Relation of job stressors to affective, health, and performance outcomes: a comparison of multiple data sources. *Journal of Applied Psychology, 73*(1), 11-19.

Spickard, A., Gabbe, S. G., and Christensen, J. F. (2002). Mid-career burnout in generalist and specialist physicians. *JAMA, 288*(12), 1447-1450.

Spurgeon, A., and Harrington, J. M. (1989). Work performance and health of junior hospital doctors: A review of the literature. *Work and Stress, 3*, 117-128.

Spurgeon, A., Harrington, J. M., and Cooper, C. L. (1997). Health and safety problems associated with long working hours: A review of the current position. *Occupational and Environmental Medicine, 54*, 367-375.

Sturman, M. C. (2003). Searching for the inverted U-shaped relationship between time and performance: A meta-analysis of the experience-performance, tenure-performance, and age-performance relationships. *Journal of Management, 29*(4), 609-640.

Sutherland, V. J., and Cooper, C. L. (1992). Job stress, satisfaction, and mental health among general practitioners before and after introduction of a new contract. *British Medical Journal, 304*, 1545-1548.

Tesluk, P. E., and Jacobs, R. R. (1998). Toward an integrated model of work experience. *Personnel Psychology, 51*(4), 321-355.

Vidyarthi, A. R., Auerbach, A. D., Wachter, R. M., and Katz, P. P. (2007). The impact of duty hours on resident self reports of errors. *Journal of General Internal Medicine, 22*(2), 205-209.

Visser, M. R. M., Smets, E. M. A., Oort, F. J., and De Haes, J. C. J. M. (2003). Stress, satisfaction and burnout among Dutch medical specialists. *Canadian Medical Association Journal, 168*(3), 271-275.

West, C. P., Huschka, M. M., Novotny, P. J., Sloan, J. A., Kolars, J. C., Habermann, T. M., et al. (2006). Association of perceived medical errors with resident distress and emapthy: A prospective longitudinal study. *JAMA, 296*(9), 1071-1078.

In: Handbook of Stress and Burnout in Health Care
Editor: Jonathon R. B. Halbesleben

ISBN 978-1-60456-500-3
© 2008 Nova Science Publishers, Inc.

Chapter 12

BURNOUT AND CONSEQUENCES: A REVIEW OF HEALTH PROFESSIONAL MALTREATMENT OF THE PATIENT

Jean-Pierre Neveu
Human Resource Management, University Montesquieu, France

This chapter is about the relatively deserted issue of burnout consequences, with a specific, yet characteristic, focus on health professions. Data collected in the two main bibliographical searches available to date (Boudreau and Nakashima, 2002[6]; Kleiber and Enzmann, 1989) indicate that out of a cumulated 4434 references listed between 1968 and 2002, less than 50 empirical studies have sought to evaluate the link between burnout and occupational performance. The overwhelming majority of investigations still concentrate on burnout etiology, determining factors and correlates, thus leaving scant attention to the "right end"/output stage of the process model.

The following pages address a double challenge. First, they seek to integrate burnout outcomes within a functional perspective. Our purpose is to help reconcile consequences to the disphoric symptom through the prism of quality management. In the context of health professions, staff burnout may thus substantiate a "service-performance gap" (Zeithaml, Parasuraman, and Berry, 1990), where burnout-induced behaviors would affect quality care to the patients (Mawji et al., 2002). Second, their aim is to assess a problematic issue to pave the way for further empirical developments. Specifically, it is interested in staff burnout as a source of patients' maltreatment[7]. Burnout is thus viewed as a dysfunctional factor to patients' well-being.

---

[6] This work provides a detailed yet non-exhaustive list of burnout citations for the period under review. Additional references are included in the present chapter.

[7] Maltreatment is first defined by three criteria: intent, a cognitive process, and a resulting harm (Rippon, 2000). Yet, in the context of professional care, unintentional harmful behavior or attitude should also be considered, as caregivers may fail to provide assistance without any intention to hurt (NCEA & Westat, 1998).

BURNOUT AS A QUALITY SERVICE PROBLEM

Typically, research on burnout outcomes has identified three targets of dysfunctional consequences, the burned-out individual, the interactions between co-workers, and the organization (Burke and Richardsen, 1993; Cordes and Dougherty, 1993). In relation to health professions, the first level would include investigations on both physical and emotional consequences (Maslach and Pines, 1977), the second, on problems of work climate (McManus, Keeling, and Paice, 2004), and the third, on various types of organizational withdrawal attitudes and behaviors, from lessened job involvement to higher absenteeism or lower performance (Parker and Kulik, 1995). Far fewer studies, however, have analyzed the impact of occupational burnout on outside stakeholders such as clients. In some sense, the consumer has been the missing target of not only burnout research but also of workplace aggression literature (Hershcovis et al., 2007). This situation has become all the more problematic as in service sectors such as health, patients are to be considered directly concerned by a (failed) quality of care potentially determined by poor professional well-being.

From an organizational standpoint, occupational burnout of health professionals stands as a strategic concern that relates to service quality to the patient / customer. Health structures are open institutions whose missions blur the lines between work conditions service quality, two areas traditionally distinct in organization structures. The former is usually considered relevant to human resource management, while the latter more in tune to consumer marketing. Nowadays, however, the experience of care is intrinsically dyadic. It corresponds to a daily co-production between reaching-out health professionals and "prosummer" (Tofler, 1980) patients who actively participate in the caring process (Crawford et al., 2002). Hence, in a perspective of service quality, a functional understanding of occupational burnout among caregivers cannot dissociate the professional's view from service-seeking patient perceptions. Although clinically observed (Berland, 1990; Cherniss, 1995; Pines and Maslach, 1978), the link between burnout as a depletion of individual resources and quality service remains relatively under-investigated with still few statistically significant findings.

In compounding two bibliographical surveys (Boudreau and Nakashima, 2002; Kleiber and Enzmann, 1989), only one empirical study emerged that investigated the link between burnout and quality of nursing care (McCarthy and Frieze, 1999), while another tackled with burnout and quality of nurse work (Allen and Kraft, 1981). Similar paucity of empirical evidence was also evidenced concerning staff burnout related to patients' satisfaction (three studies: Kendrick, 1988; Leiter, Harvie, and Frizzell, 1998), and to patients' care (four studies: Maslach, 1979; Shanafelt, Bradley, Wipf, and Back 2002; Wamsley, 1996; Wimbusch, 1983)[8].

Poorly investigated, the field also yields mixed results. For instance, in their milestone review of burnout research, Schaufeli and Enzmann (1998) considered that, on average, burnout correlated to self-rated performance for only about 5% with emotional exhaustion, 4% with depersonalization, and 6 % with reduced personal accomplishment (indiscriminate occupational samples, including health professionals). As for supervisor-rated performance, findings were deemed both "inconsistent and disappointing" (1998: 92). Such a mixed assessment, however, should be tempered. First, it should be noted that out of the 11

---

[8] More recent studies still acknowledge such a research deficit (Vahey, Aiken, Sloane, Clarke, and Delfino, 2004).

empirical studies identified by Schaufeli and Enzmann, only a minority of them did effectively concern health professionals. Second, more studies tend to confirm the negative relationship between burnout, positive staff attitudes and organization-rated service quality to the patient (Aström, Nilsson, Norberg, Sandman, and Winblad, 1991; Kennedy, 2005). Ross et al. (2002) even uncovered an interesting negative correlation between emotional exhaustion and a rarely used MBI dimension called "involvement". As a degree of proximal solicitude between the care-giver and his recipient(s), this 3-item optional burnout dimension of the MBI questionnaire (Maslach and Jackson, 1981) can indeed be considered a measure of service quality. Conversely, the positive relationship between emotional exhaustion and reduced performance has been verified using an alternative to the MBI (data obtained on cross-occupational population with health professionals sub-sample) (Bakker, Demerouti, and Verbeke, 2004).

From a patient's perspective, service quality has been found to relate to the state of caregivers' burnout (Shanafelt et al., 2002). Yet, and contrary to the stress often put upon the role of tangible symptoms such as staff / patient ratios (Rafferty et al., 2007) or technical quality of health care procedures (Eriksen, 1987), the perception of service quality is mainly contingent upon the nature of relational links between caregivers and care recipients. Glass (1991) acknowledges such a distinction between *care*, that focuses on medical / nursing skills and appropriateness, and *caring*, more interested in staff / patient interactions. For instance, nursing home residents would define quality as being partially contingent on the state of affective relationships experienced with caregivers (Bowers, Fibich, and Jacobson, 2001; Charles et al., 1994; Miller-Bader, 1998; Taylor, Hudson, and Keeling, 1991). Leiter et al. (1998) showed a highly significant negative correlation between hospital patients' rating of care and competence and nurses' exhaustion and cynicism (indiscriminate nursing occupation sample). Similar evidence was presented in mental illness units where MBI components related significantly to multiple facets of recipients' satisfaction, e.g. physical environment, therapists' accessibility and professionalism, treatment protocol, and post-treatment rehabilitation (Garman, Corrigan, and Morris, 2002).

MALTREATMENT AS A SYMPTOM OF OCCUPATIONAL BURNOUT

A majority of studies have focused on the role of patients' aggressiveness in nurses' burnout (Büssing and Höge, 2004; Evers, Tomic, and Brouwers, 2002; Goodridge, Johnston, and Thomson, 1996). For example, investigating among 2,354 hospital staff, Arnetz and Arnetz (2001) found that 78% of the total variance for predicting quality of care was explained by violence and patient's ratings of the staff work. Yet, 96% of such violence originated from patients and patients' relatives. Consequently, the reality of patients' aggressiveness and of its impact on burnout has prompted a debate over coercive institutional policies to better preserve the psychological wellbeing of health professionals (Whittington and Higgins, 2002). Research, however, has highlighted that such a situation was not as clearcut as it may seem. For instance, uncooperative behaviors of patients were considered at the root of staff abuse by 64% of a large sample of nurses surveyed in Ontario (College of Nurses of Ontario, 1993). Indeed, findings have evidenced a circular relationship where patients' aggressiveness was fueled by poor quality of care resulting from patients' own abusive behavior on staff (Winstanley and Whittington, 2002). This would indicate that there is more to professional abuse than a mere aggressor to victim linear relationship, and that maltreatment ought to be considered from an interactionist perspective involving the patient, the caregiver, the work institution, and both cultural and social environment.

Research relating patients' maltreatment to health professionals' burnout is fairly scarce. In theory, patient abuse has been admitted to mirror a state of emotional exhaustion among nurses (Heine, 1986; Wierucka and Goodridge, 1996). Empirically, however, there is a definite dearth of results. To be sure, a number of studies have sought to verify such a hypothesis but they often consider non-professionals such as family caregivers (Homer and Gilleard, 1990; Pillemer and Suitor, 1992). To our knowledge, the only explicit empirical evidence is limited to nursing home staff. The survey-based study conducted by Pillemer (Pillemer and Bachman-Prehn, 1991; Pillemer and Moore, 1989; Pillemer and Moore, 1990) stands as the landmark research to the point that more recent reports on the subject keep listing it as basically the sole available empirical justification (Gibbs and Mosqueda, 2004; Spencer and Beaulieu, 1994). Conducted among 577 nursing home caregivers dispatched in 32 long-term care facilities, the study showed that the frustration of humanistic concerns for help strongly correlated to mistreatment, both physical and psychological.

Other studies may exist but methodological side-effects may hinder proper identification. For instance, Harris and Benson (1999) have established an empirical link between nursing home theft and negative feelings of staff toward patients. Yet, it appears that the three-item scale they use to evaluate such feelings appears quite synonymous to MBI's three dimensions, including "Most patients are more trouble than they are worth" (emotional exhaustion), "I treat patients as if they are family" ((reverse) depersonalization), and "Most patients don't appreciate what I do for them" (lack of personal accomplishment) (Harris and Benson, 1999, p. 80). Finally, some additional information is provided by qualitative research (Foner, 1994; Kayser-Jones, 1990). These ethnographic approaches, however, suggest or describe more than explicitly expose and analyze the relation between staff emotional exhaustion and patients' abuse. A recourse to psychoanalysis stands as a possible solution to such a shortcoming as a recent study linked patients' abuse to a pervert climax of burned-out caregivers' sense of power (Daloz, Bénony, Frénisy, and Chahraoui, 2005).

When presenting their state of the art on burnout research, Cordes and Dougherty (1993) acknowledged that "despite the extensive literature on burnout to date, strategies other than the existing ones may offer a significant benefit to this fields" (p. 649). Paradoxically, we could paraphrase such an assessment and conversely state that due to the paucity of empirical evidence on burnout-induced maltreatment to date, the field is wide open to a variety of possible research strategies.

RESEARCH PERSPECTIVES

Basically, most themes to be addressed for future investigations can be grouped under the two main headings constituted by theory and methodology. These two broad issues congregate within themselves a number of research tracks that, taken together, should help confer maturity to research not only in health professions, but also to the broader issue of customer abuse by burned-out employees in service occupations.

A Need for Theorizing

Anticipating Shirom's (2005) call for theory building in burnout research, McDonald and Collins (2000) observed that existing literature on abuse and neglect of older adults assimilates theoretical explanations to risk factors of abuse. Specifically, and as exemplified by Pillemer's (1988) early model, burnout is construed as an antecedent risk variable that determines patient maltreatment. Although Pillemer defended himself from providing a definite theoretical model but rather some sort of a working guide (Pillemer, 1988, p. 230), research has conveniently shunned away from solid conceptual frameworks. Consequently, maltreatment is investigated outside of any specific theorizing, as one of many other outcomes of burnout, such as absenteeism or turnover. This theoretical blank is mirrored by the near absence of adequate reference to burnout in the aggression/violence literature. Instead of burnout, correlates such as negative affectivity and trait anger stand as the most investigated, and validated, individual predictors of workplace aggressiveness (El Akremi and Sassi, 2007; Hershcovis et al., 2007).

To help overcome this situation, we now propose to assess a possible integration of maltreatment within specific theory-based burnout models that draw from a variety of approaches.

Track One: the social exchange perspective. Social exchange theory (Blau, 1964) offers a conceptual framework that may provide a first answer to integrating maltreatment to burnout modeling. In essence, Blau's theory posits that the value of a reciprocal exchange is determined by a socioemotional cost/benefit analysis held by respective stakeholders, an interplay between competing attachments and open-ended obligations. In the case of a perceived balanced outcome, the exchange is deemed equitable. Applying this process to helping professions, Schaufeli et al. (1996) have proposed to associate burnout to the demanding relationships experienced with care recipients. As such, burnout would surface as a symptom of inequitable discrepancies between what the helper feels he contributed to and what he eventually considers getting in return. From the standpoint of the caregiver, maltreatment would thus to be viewed as an outcome resulting from a perceived inequity between the cost of attending and the benefit of self-rewarding activity, an implicit attempt to reduce cognitive dissonance.

A main advantage to the social exchange perspective is that it has already gained empirical support. Studies have validated the relevance of Brickman's (Brickman et al., 1982) medical model of helping to account for burnout emergence among nurses (Truchot and Deregard 2001; Van Yperen, 1996). Cropanzano et al. (2003) have successfully showed how social exchange theory could be used to analyze the negative link between emotional exhaustion and job performance among hospital employees. Longitudinal analysis confirmed the mediating impact of perceived inequity among general practitioners (Bakker, Schaufeli, Sixma, Bosveld, and Dierendonck, 2000). Under such a scenario, maltreatment could then be viewed as conditioned by the level of tolerance of health professionals, relative to the satisfaction needs held by the patients. Notwithstanding its value, however, a social exchange approach to burnout and maltreatment would still have to answer some challenging issues.

First, perceived (in)equity may proceed differently as varying health care situations may necessitate alternative helping models. The context of wards treating somatic illness and wounds, where unable patients are bound to passively accept staff expertise, proved appropriate for validating a medical model (Truchot and Deregard, 2001). Long-term nursing institutions with patients suffering from dementia or Alzheimer's could also be analyzed through a similar helping model. Other types of units, however, could conceivably be better studied using other models. For instance, a compensatory model of helping that emphasizes patient's responsibility for handicap recovery could be more appropriate for maternity wards, while moral models of helping could be used in the context of toxicology. A second challenge to the social exchange proposition is more conceptual. In its application to the burnout process, the issue of inequity has mainly been addressed from the standpoint of staff perception. Specifically, the source of inequity is located in patient's excessive demands (Bakker et al., 2000). Consequently, it could be expected that maltreatment reflect a somewhat legitimate symptom of the caregiver whose burnout stems from the failure to establish a satisfactory reciprocal exchange with the recipient. Obviously, the problem with such a scenario is its insensitivity to the demands for quality-service that is typical of health and care institutions. More research should then be designed from the standpoint of patients' equity perceptions. Finally, a third challenge lies in the static nature of the social exchange perspective. This theory aptly describes and analyzes current situations. It gives no workable clues to management, however, as to how to anticipate possible problems with equity perceptions.

Track Two: the job demands-resources perspective. The job demands-resources (JD-R) theory has been acknowledged as one of the dominant burnout model to date (Halbesleben and Buckley, 2004). According to this perspective, conceptually indebted to Karasek's (1979) stress model, burnout is a resulting symptom of a perceived imbalance between job demands and resources (Bakker et al., 2004; Demerouti, Bakker, Nachreiner, and Schaufeli, 2001). Demands are associated with such psychological costs as occupational burnout. Conversely, in reducing job demands, and therefore burnout, resources associate to personal growth and engagement (Schaufeli and Bakker, 2004).

The JD-R model has received ample empirical support, including among health care professionals (Bakker, Demerouti, Taris, Schaufeli, and Schreurs, 2003; Bakker, Demerouti, and Euwema, 2005; Demerouti et al., 2001; Demerouti, Bakker, Nachreiner, and Ebbinghaus 2002). It has highlighted the distinctive role of such job demands as workload and time pressure to understanding burnout formation while such job resources as autonomy would facilitate commitment and wellbeing. Yet, few points of the model still need to be clarified. For instance, results are still conflicting concerning a supposed buffering effect of job resources between job demands and dysfunctional outcomes (Bakker et al., 2004; Bakker et al., 2005). Nevertheless, and as already mentioned, the JD-R proposition seems to deserve serious consideration to further develop an integrated process-theory of burnout.

So far, however, the main challenge to the JD-R theory is to transcend its investigations on burnout etiology. Its sophistication seems to focus mainly on burnout antecedents, while seemingly neglecting a coherent link with relevant outcomes. As it stands now, the JD-R adds nothing especially new to understanding the process of consequences and the rationale that would animate the process between emotional exhaustion and the development of specific negative consequences. As such, maltreatment would undergo a non-specific analysis as it stands theoretically lumped to a bundle of other dysfunctional outcomes, generically related to job demands. It is symptomatic that when including a recipient contact variable in a test among nurses, JD-R investigators include this variable as a job demand factor, and not as a burnout outcome (Bakker et al., 2003; Demerouti et al., 2001). This raises a number of concerns. First, and as previously mentioned, the literature shows how the contact with patients can also be source of pleasure for the caregiver, and thus be considered as a job resource. Second, recipient contact is not necessarily to be exclusively treated as an organizational factor. Within a perspective of service-quality, patients could rather be viewed as situational factors (Maslach, Schaufeli, and Leiter, 2001), and thus be considered differently from their role as potential stressors. The patient stands mostly as a given, hardly susceptible to be "changed", as could either be the employee or the organization (Maslach et al., 2001). Finally, the linear and cumulative approach suggested by the JD-R theory may fall short to properly account for the qualitative nature of the staff-patients interactive process.

Track Three: the conservation of resources perspective. Synthetically, the COR concept posits that burnout is function of a resource depletion process (Hobfoll, 1989; Hobfoll and Shirom, 1993). Hobfoll (2001) discusses a classification of such resources depending on whether or not these are held by individuals (i.e., personal characteristics) or conditioned by others (i.e. tangibles). At the heart of the theory is the loss of, or perceived threat of losing, resources deemed valuable: "the basic tenet of COR theory is that individuals strive to obtain, retain, protect, and foster those things that they value" (Hobfoll, 2001: 341). Unlike most stress and burnout conceptualizations that keep rooted in Selye's (1956) homeostatic assumption, the COR proposition is fundamentally a motivation theory (Halbesleben and Bowler, 2007) where demands are second to a basic drive for resources development.

Although COR theory has provided a conceptual base for a variety of empirical situations, it is not exempt from challenging limitations, for example regarding the nature and relative importance of resources (Hobfoll, 2001). Nevertheless, its motivational nature makes it a potentially powerful alternative for theorizing the link from occupational burnout to negative consequences. Hence, maltreatment may be viewed as an outcome of resource frustration that is expressed under more or less active and direct forms. Frustration and powerlessness have been found to be rampant among nurses unable to carry out their mission among demented patients (Eriksson and Saveman, 2002).

The hypothesis of a fundamental drive for resources preservation to prevent burnout and adverse consequences finds support in the immunity notion developed by Conlin-Shaw (1998). Specifically, Conlin-Shaw underscored the role of such resources as home / work balance, compensation, and professional competence, in preserving psychological resistance, *sustaining immunity*, not only against both patients' aggressiveness but also in prevention of their own abusing behaviors. Consequently, professionals may use maltreatment as a form of coping aimed at preserving their own personal valued resources (Goergen, 2001). Further support for such a hypothesis can be found in empirical studies that give evidence of the role of MBI's depersonalization as a defensive withdrawal from the anticipated, or effective, loss of resources (Lee and Ashforth, 1996). In a snowball effect, such a strategy leads to poorer service that, in turn, fuels adverse reactions from patients towards health professionals (Bakker et al., 2000).

Another type of findings that can also plea in favor of a COR-based research perspective is that of the role and nature of patient's demands. Typically, patients' aggressiveness is only viewed as a determining factor of burnout. Empirical data, however, have shown that this is not invariably the case, with significant differences among nurses even working within the same institution. Caregivers' familiarity with patients' personal characteristics, and their expectations about recovery evolution, also play an important role in determining the occurrence of burnout and maltreatment. For instance, a comparative study showed that burnout levels were lower among better-trained caregivers working in general hospital geriatric wards than in regular nursing homes (Cocco, Gatti, Mendonça Lima, and Camus, 2002). In long-term facilities such as psychiatric (Melchior et al., 1997), geriatric (Hare and Pratt, 1988; Wang, 2005), or acute care (Hare and Pratt, 1988) settings, maltreatment was found to be significantly related to inappropriate training, a type of resources whose frustration, or depletion, has been identified as a condition to burnout (Hobfoll, 1989).

Competence has not been the only resource to be evidenced by research. Rafii et al. (2004), showed how the quality of care could vary depending on nurses' social and spiritual values, both instances of personal resources. Interestingly, this research indicates that job demands could therefore be understood as inhibitors of resources, that they exert a moderating role on an antecedent strive for competence utilization.

A Challenging Methodology

The field of burnout to maltreatment must address a number of issues pertaining to research implementation. Two main challenges of uneven difficulty appear to be facing the methodological protocol: sampling and measuring.

The sampling challenge. Research on staff maltreatment is conducted overwhelmingly among nurses. Whether aides, Licensed Practical, or Registered, the availability and accessibility of such a personnel makes it the backbone of empirical investigations. This is a clear reflection of the vast number of studies traditionally interested in burnout among health professions (Boudreau and Nakashima, 2002; Kleiber and Enzmann, 1989). In contrast, other health occupations attract marginal interest. To be sure, anecdotal evidence has been presented early, as in Maslach (1982) who reported the aggressive behavior of burned-out surgeons. Yet, a recent bibliographical search spanning a period from 1984 to 2001 on physician burnout (Chopra, Sotile, and Sotile, 2004) was able to identify only one quantitative study linking emotional exhaustion to effective suboptimal patient care (Shanafelt et al., 2002). Adding one more research to this survey (Deckard, Meterko, and Field, 1994) should not invalidate the general conclusion on a paucity of sample diversity.

Another typical problem of the field is that almost all studies concern one type of health setting (i.e., geriatric wards or institutions). From the standpoint of what we know about the interaction between the formation of burnout and the dynamics of attachment between caregivers and recipients, it makes sense to focus professional relations experienced in such facilities as nursing homes. Yet, significant and promising results linking burnout to occupational performance in other health environments (e.g. intensive care, operating rooms, psychiatrics, medicine / surgery; Keijsers, Schaufeli, LeBlanc, Zwerts, and Miranda, 1995; Parker and Kulik, 1995), burn centers (Rafii, Oskouie, and Nikravesh, 2004), and AIDS units (Vahey et al., 2004), may be worth extending to the particular theme of maltreatment.

The measurement challenge. Measuring maltreatment is a tricky endeavor for no perpetrator would easily recognize, or enact, abusing behaviors in front of a researcher. Moreover, unlike other burnout outcomes such as turnover and absenteeism, little reliable official information can be registered in administrative records. In fact, the difficulty of measuring professional maltreatment may go beyond what is commonly faced when investigating aggressive behaviors for we are dealing with a sector whose core mission is precisely about helping and caring. Nevertheless, a number of issues may be addressed that illustrate some typical methodological challenges.

First, the study of healthcare maltreatment may be either qualitative or quantitative. The clinical origin of burnout studies has consolidated a qualitative research tradition about the link with maltreatment. For example, grounded theory has been invoked to underline the impact of burnout on the quality of caring (Conlin-Shaw, 1998; Rafii et al., 2004). A similar approach has been undertaken by Foner (1994) who used a rare longitudinal in-depth anthropological approach to uncover those daily routines that may, or may not, lead to staff burnout and maltreatment of nursing home residents. More recently, Sandvide et al. (2006) relied on narrative data and positioning theory to analyze the systemic perception of violence between one health professional and older residents. Finally, Daloz et al., (2006) followed a psycho-analytical framework to analyze interviews conducted among more than 100 health care professionals.

A second set of measurement issues is related to the quantitative nature that makes the bulk of studies. A number of methodologies are used to apprehend the link between burnout and maltreatment. The most common is to associate already validated self-report questionnaires. Concerning burnout, there is an hegemony of the MBI, notwithstanding the alternative use of other scales such as Pines et al.'s Burnout Measurement (1981) (Aström et al., 1991) or Jones' (1980) Staff Burnout Scale for Health Professionals (Goodridge et al., 1996). The measurement of consequent staff maltreatment, however, clearly remains problematic with a number of unsettled issues, including standardization of measurement, and intrinsic reliability of data obtained by investigators. A first type of research uses already existing questionnaires. For instance, Pillemer and Moore (1989) administered a telephone survey to evaluate staff attitudes toward patients. Questions asked were adapted from the Conflict Tactics Scale (Straus, 1979) and applied to physical and psychological maltreatment situations. Aström et al. (1991) preferred using their own validated Attitudes towards Dementia Patient Scale (ADPS), a 20-item measurement. A second type of empirical studies relies on ad-hoc questionnaires. In their landmark study, Pillemer and Moore (1990) designed three original questions to assess hostile staff attitudes toward patients. Shanafelt, et al. (2002) developed two self-reporting scales, one about "suboptimal patient care practiced at least monthly" (5 items), the other about "suboptimal patient care attitudes experienced at least monthly" (3 items). In order to assess theft in nursing homes, Harris and Benson (1999, 2006) utilized a combination of original instruments, including a self-report questionnaire asking staff respondents to report on their own robberies, an observation report on colleagues' behavior, and a family questionnaire.

Clearly, more effort should be devoted to designing and validating relevant and manageable maltreatment scales. Among a number to alternative paths, it is first suggested that when using the MBI, the depersonalization dimension be used as a measure of neglect toward the patient. To the extent that research has evoked depersonalization as a form of coping, it could rightfully be viewed as a form of passive maltreatment on the part of care recipients. The protection of one may be akin to the rejection of the other. MBI's depersonalization scale, or Jones' (1980) *"Unprofessional Patient Relationship"* dimension of his Staff Burnout Scale for Health Professionals, could therefore be contrasted to, and applied against, other subscales of such burnout measurements. For instance, in a rare study conducted among HMO physicians, Deckard et al. (1994) found that the two most significant variables regressing on depersonalization were patients' reactions and quality of care. These results corroborate qualitative findings presented by Lee-Treweek (1994) showing how patients who precisely refused to be treated like objects would increase their vulnerability to staff maltreatment.

Another methodological possibility could be to adapt existing questionnaires, originally constructed to assess the reality and the nature of maltreatment among incoming patients from family caregivers, to institutional abusers (for instance, the Verbal Abuse Scale (Manderino and Banton, 1994) or the Violent Incident Form (Arnetz, 1998)).

Last but not least, there remains the possibility of direct asking to patients and fitting their own responses to burnout questionnaires distributed to caregivers. So far, studies interested in staff burnout do not seek direct information about recipients' perceptions, while quality tools used among patients do not bridge the gap with professionals' psychological health. To the extent that relevant questionnaires exist that assess patients' perceptions of quality service (Corrigan and Jakus, 1993; Leiter et al., 1998; Pakdil and Harwood, 2005; Vahey et al., 2004), it would seem very promising to engage into empirical investigations on the edge of human resource management and service marketing.

CONCLUSION

The study of maltreatment and of its relation to burnout comes as a telling illustration of the relative dearth of research devoted to burnout outcomes. Whether from the standpoint of quality seeking care recipients or that of worn-out health professionals, this issue has surprisingly attracted far less scientific attention than a widespread social concern would have otherwise suggested. Probably due to divisions between a plurality of relevant academic research fields, each one focusing on "their part of the story" (health psychology, medicine, management studies, etc.), and also to some cultural hesitation to consider professional caregivers as potential sources of aggression, little evidence is still available that validates a causal link from burnout to patient maltreatment. In this chapter, a review of existing literature did nevertheless demonstrate significant and promising results that justify the relevance of the core hypothesis. Yet, much effort was also found to be needed to bring about a sound conceptual framework and a validated methodology, both conditions to consolidate a body of knowledge that could otherwise rate as little more than anecdotal significance.

REFERENCES

Allen, R.F., and Kraft, C. (1981). From burnout to turn-on: Improving the quality of hospital work. *Hospital Forum*, 24(3), 18-20, 23-24, 27-28.

Arnetz, J.E.(1998). The Violent Incident Form (VIF): A practical instrument for the registration of violent incidents in the health care workplace. *Work and Stress*, 12(1), 17-28.

Arnetz, J.E., and Arnetz, B.B. (2001). Violence toward health care staff and possible effects on the quality of patient care. *Social Science and Medicine*, 52, 417-427.

Aström, S., Nilsson, M., Norberg, A., Sandman, P.O., and Winblad, B. (1991). Staff burnout in dementia care-relations to empathy and attitudes. *International Journal of Nursing Studies*, 28(1), 65-75.

Bakker, A.B., Demerouti, E., and Verbeke, W. (2004). Using the job demands-resources model to predict burnout and performance. *Human Resource Management*, 43(1), 83-104.

Bakker, A.B., Schaufeli, W.B., Sixma, H.J., Bosveld, W., and Dierendonck, A.D. van (2000). Patient demands, lack of reciprocity, and burnout: A five-year longitudinal study among practitioners. *Journal of Organizational Behavior*, 21, 425-441.

Bakker, A.B., Demerouti, E., Taris, T.W., Schaufeli, W.B., and Schreurs, P.J.G. (2003). A multigroup analysis of the Job Demands-Resources model in four home care organizations. *International Journal of Stress Management*, 10(1), 16-38.

Bakker, A.B., Demerouti, E., and Euwema, M.C. (2005). Job resources buffer the impact of job demands on burnout. *Journal of Occupational Health Psychology*, 10(2), 170-180.

Berland, (1990). Controlling workload. *Canadian Nurse*, 86(5), 36-38.

Blau, P.M. (1964). *Exchange and power in social life.* New York : Wiley.

Boudreau, R., and Nakashima, J. (2002). *A bibliography of burnout citations, 1990-2002.* ASAC: Winnipeg.

Bowers, B.J., Fibich, B., and Jacobson, N. (2001). Care-as-service, care-as-relating, care-as-comfort: Understanding nursing home residents' definitions of quality. *Gerontologist*, 41, 539-545.

Brickman, P., Rabinowitz, V.C., Karuza, J., Coates, D., Cohn, E., and Kidder, L. (1982). Models of helping and coping. *American Psychologist*, 37(4), 368-384.

Burke, R.J., and Richardsen, A.M (1993). Psychological burnout in organizations. In R.T. Golembiewski (Ed.), *Handbook of Organizational Behavior* (pp. 263-298). New York: Dekker.

Büssing, A., and Höge, T. (2004). Aggression and violence against home care workers. *Journal of Occupational Health Psychology*, 9(3), 206-219.

Charles, C., Gauld, M., Chambers, L., O'Brien, B., Haynes, R.B., and Labelle, R. (1994). How was your hospital stay? Patients' reports about their care in Canadian hospitals. *Canadian Medical Association Journal*, 150, 1813-1822.

Cherniss, C. (1995). Beyond burnout. New-York: Routledge.

Chopra, S.S., Sotile, W.M., and Sotile, M.O. (2004). Physician burnout. *Journal of American Medical Association*, 291(5), 633.

Cocco, E., Gatti, M., Mendonça Lima, C.A., and Camus, V. (2002). A comparative study of stress and burnout among staff caregivers in nursing homes and acute geriatric wards. *International Journal of Geriatric Psychiatry*, 18, 78-85.

College of Nurses of Ontario (1993). Abuse of clients by RN and RNA's. *Report to Council on Results of Canada Health Monitor Survey of Registrants*, 1-11.

Conlin-Shaw, M.M. (1998). Nursing home resident abuse by staff: Exploring the dynamics. *Journal of Elder Abuse and Neglect*, 9(4), 1-21.

Cordes, C.L., and Dougherty, T.W. (1993). A review and an integration of research on job burnout. *Academy of Management Review*, 18, 621-656.

Corrigan, P.W., and Jakus, M.R. (1993). The Patient Satisfaction Interview for partial hospitalization programs. *Psychological Reports*, 72, 387-390.

Crawford, M., Rutter, D., Manley, C., Weaver, T., Bhui, K., Fulop, N., and Tyrer, P. (2002). Systematic review of involving patients in the planning and development of health care. *British Medical Journal*, 325, 1263-1268.

Cropanzano, R., Rupp, D.E., and Byrne, Z.S. (2003). The relationship of emotional exhaustion to work attitudes, job performance, and organizational citizenship behaviors. *Journal of Applied Psychology*, 88(1), 160-169.

Daloz, L., Bénony, H., Frénisy, M.-C., and Chahraoui, K. (2005). Burnout et maltraitance dans la relation soignante. *Annales Médico-Psychologiques*, 163, 156-160.

Deckard, G., Meterko, M., and Field, D. (1994). Physician burnout: An examination of personal, professional, and organizational relationships. *Medical Care*, 32(7), 745-754.

Demerouti, E., Bakker, A.B., Nachreiner, F., and Schaufeli, W.B. (2001). The job-demands-resources model of burnout. *Journal of Applied Psychology*, 86, 499-512.

Demerouti, E., Bakker, A.B., Nachreiner, F., and Ebbinghaus, M. (2002). From mental strain to burnout. *European Journal of Work and Organizational Psychology*, 11(4), 423-441.

El Akremi, A., and Sassi, N. (2007). *Workplace aggression: A conceptual typology*. 13th European Association of Work and Organizational Psychology, Stockholm.

Eriksen, L.R. (1987). Patient satisfaction: An indicator of nursing care quality? *Nursing Management*, 18(7), 31-35.

Eriksson, C., and Saveman, B.-I. (2002). Nurses' experiences of abusive/non abusive caring for demented patients in acute care settings. *Scandinavian Journal of Caring Sciences*, 16, 79-85.

Evers, W., Tomic, W., and Brouwers, A. (2002). Aggressive behaviour and burnout among staff of homes for the elderly. *International Journal of Mental Health Nursing*, 11, 2-9.

Foner, N. (1994). Nursing home aides: Saints or monsters? *The Gerontologist*, 34, 245-250.

Garman, A.N., Corrigan, P.W., and Morris, S. (2002). Staff burnout and patient satisfaction: Evidence of relationships at the care unit level. *Journal of Occupational Health Psychology*, 7(3), 235-241.

Gibbs, L.M., and Mosqueda, L. (2004). Confronting elder mistreatment in long-term care. *Annals of Long-Term Care*, 12(4), 30-35.

Glass, A.P. (1991). Nursing home quality: A framework for analysis. *The Journal of Applied Gerontology*, 10(1), 5-19.

Goergen, T. (2001). Stress, conflict, elder abuse and neglect in German nursing homes: A pilot study among professional caregivers. *Journal of Elder Abuse and Neglect*, 13(1), 1-26.

Goodridge, D.M., Johnston, P., and Thomson, M. (1996). Conflict and aggression as stressors in the work environment of nursing assistants: Implications for institutional elder abuse. *Journal of Elder Abuse and Neglect*, 8(1), 49-67.

Halbesleben, J.R.B., and Bowler, Wm.M. (2007). Emotional exhaustion and job performance: The mediating role of motivation. *Journal of Applied Psychology*, 92, 93-106.

Halbesleben, J. R. B., and Buckley, M. R. (2004). Burnout in organizational life. *Journal of Management, 30*, 859-879.

Hare, J., and Pratt, C.C. (1988). Burnout: Differences between professional and paraprofessional nursing staff in acute care and long-term care health facilities. *Journal of Applied Gerontology*, 7(1), 60-72.

Harris, D.K., and Benson, M.L. (1999). Theft in nursing homes: An overlooked form of elder abuse. *Journal of Elder Abuse and Neglect*, 11(3), 73-90.

Harris, D.K., and Benson, M.L. (2006). *Maltreatment of patients in nursing homes – There is no safe place*. New York: Haworth Pastoral Press.

Heine, C.A. (1986). Burnout amon,g nursing home personnel. Journal of Gerontological Nursing, 12(3), 14-18.

Hershcovis, S., Turner, N., Barling, J., Arnold, R.A., Dupré, K.E., Inness, M., LeBlanc, M.M., and Sivanathan, N. (2007). Predicting workplace aggression: A meta-analysis. *Journal of Applied Psychology*, 92(1), 228-238.

Hobfoll, S.E. (1989). Conservation of resources: A new attempt at conceptualizing stress. *American Psychologist*, 44, 513-524.

Hobfoll, S.E. (2001). The influence of culture, community, and the nested-self in the stress process: Advancing conservation of resources theory. *Applied Psychology: An International Review*, 50, 337-421.

Hobfoll, S. E. and Shirom, J. (1993). Stress and burnout in the workplace: Conservation of resources. In R. T. Golembiewski (Eds.), *Handbook of Organizational Behavior* (pp. 41-60). New York: Dekker.

Homer, A.C., and Gilleard, C. (1990). Abuse of elderly people by their carers. *British Journal of Medicine*, 301, 1359-1362.

Jones, J. W. (1980). *The staff Burnout Scale for Health Professionals*. Park Ridge, ILL: London House Press.

Karasek, R. A. (1979). Job demands, job decision latitude, and mental strain: Implications for job redesign. *Administrative Science Quarterly*, 24, 285-308

Kayser-Jones, J.S. (1990). *Old, alone, and neglected – Care of the aged in Scotland and the United States*. Berkeley: University of California Press.

Keijsers, G.J., Schaufeli, W.B., LeBlanc, P.M., Zwerts, C., and Miranda, D.R. (1995). Performance and burnout in intensive care units. *Work and Stress*, 9(4), 513-527 ?

Kendrick, S.J. (1988). Job burnout in nurses and patient satisfaction with nursing care. *Master Abstract International*, 27(1), 97 (Order N° MA1333241).

Kennedy, B.R. (2005). Stress and burnout of nursing staff working with geriatric clients in long-term care. *Journal of Nursing Scholarship*, fourth quarter, 381-382.

Kleiber, D., and Enzmann, D. (1989). *Burnout : An annotated bibliography*. Göttingen: Verlag-Hogrefe.

Lee, R.T., and Ashforth, B.E. (1996). A meta-analytic examination of the correlates of the three dimensions of job burnout. *Journal of Applied Psychology*, 81(2), 23-133.

Lee-Treweek, G. (1994). Bedroom abuse: The hidden work in a nursing home. *Generations Review*, 4(1), 2-4.

Leiter, M.P., Harvie, P., and Frizzell, C. (1998). The correspondance of patient satisfaction and nurse burnout. *Social Science and Medicine*, 47(10), 1611-1617.

Manderino, M.A., and Banton, S. (1994). Evaluation of the Verbal Abuse Scale. Unpublished manuscript.

Maslach, C. (1979). The burn-out syndrome and patient care. In C.A. Garfield (Ed.), *Stress and survival: The emotional realities of life-threatening illness* (pp. 111-120). St. Louis, Mosby.

Maslach, C. (1982). *Burnout: The cost of caring*. New York: Prentice Hall.

Maslach, C., and Jackson, S.E. (1981). The measurement of experienced burnout. *Journal of Occupational Behaviour*, 2, 99-113.

Maslach, C., and Pines, A.M. (1977). The burn-out syndrome in the daycare setting. *Child Care Quarterly*, 6(2), 100-113.

Maslach, C., Schaufeli, W., and Leiter, M.P. (2001). Job burnout. *Annual Review of Psychology*, 52, 397-422.

Mawji, Z., Stillman, P., Laskowski, R., Lawrence, S., Karoly, E., Capuano, T., and Sussman, E. (2002). First do no harm: Integrating patient safety and quality improvement. *Joint Commission Journal on Quality Improvement*, 28(7), 373-386.

McCarthy, W.C., and Frieze, I.H. (1999). Negative aspects of therapy: Client perceptions of therapists' social influence, burnout, and quality of care. *Journal of Social Issues*, 55(1), 33-50.

McDonald, L., and Collins, A. (2000). *Abuse and neglect of older adults: A discussion paper*. Ottawa: Family Violence Prevention Unit, Health Issues Division, Promotion and Programs Branch, Health Canada.

McManus, I.C., Keeling, A., and Paice, E. (2004). Stress, burnout and doctors' attitudes to work are determined by personality and learning style: A twelve year longitudinal study of UK medical graduates. *BMC Medicine*, 18, 2:29.

Melchior, M.E.W., Berg, A.A. van den, Halfens, R., Huyer Abu-Saad, H., Philipsen, H., and Gassman, P. (1997). Burnout and the work environment of nurses in psychiatric long-stay care settings. *Social Psychiatry and Psychiatric Epidemiology*, 32, 158-164.

Miller-Bader, M.M. (1988). Nursing care behaviours that predict patient satisfaction. *Journal of Nursing Quality Assurance*, 2, 11-17.

NCEA (National Center on Elder Abuse), and Westat, Inc (1998). *The National Elder Abuse Incidence Study*. Report for the Administration on Aging and Administration for Children and Families. Washington, D.C.: NCEA.

Pakdil, F., and Harwood, T.N. (2005). Patient satisfaction in a preoperative assessment clinic: An analysis using SERVQUAL dimensions. *Total Quality Management*, 16(1), 15-30.

Parker, P.A., and Kulik, J.A. (1995). Burnout, self- and supervisor-rated job performance, and absenteeism among nurses. *Journal of Behavioral Medicine*, 18(6), 581-599.

Pillemer, K. (1988). Maltreatment of patients in nursing homes: Overview and research agenda. *Journal of Health and Social Behavior*, 29, 227-238.

Pillemer, K., and Moore, D.W. (1989). Abuse of patients in nursing homes: Findings from a survey of staff. *The Gerontologist*, 29(3), 314-320.

Pillemer, K., and Moore, D.W. (1990). Highlights from a study of abuse of patients in nursing homes. *Journal of Elder Abuse and Neglect*, 2(1/2), 5-29.

Pillemer, K., and Suitor, J. (1992). Violence and violent feelings: What causes them among family caregivers ? *Journal of Gerontology*, 47(4), 165-172.

Pillemer, K., and Bachman-Prehn, R. (1991). Helping and hurting: Predictors of maltreatment of patients in nursing homes. *Research on Aging*, 13, 74-75.

Pines, A., and Maslach, C. (1978). Characteristics of staff burnout in mental health settings. *Hospital and Community Psychiatry*, 29(4), 233-237.

Pines, A., and Aronson, E., and Kafry, D. (1981. *Burnout from tedium to personal growth*. New York: Free Press.

Rafferty, A.M., Clarke, S.P., Coles, J., Ball, J., James, P., McKee, M., and Aiken, L.H. (2007). Outcomes of variation in hospital nurse staffing in English hospitals: cross sectional analysis of survey data and discharge records. *International Journal of Nursing Studies*, 44(2).

Rafii, F., Oskouie, F., and Nikravesh, M. (2004). Factors involved in nurses' responses to burnout: a grouded theory study. *BMC Nursing*, 3, 1-10.

Rippon, T.J. (2000). Aggression and violence in health care professions. *Journal of Advanced Nursing*, 31(1), 452-460.

Ross, M. M., Carswell, A., and Dalziel, W. B. (2002). Staff burnout in long-term care facilities. *Geriatrics Today*, 5, 132-135.

Sandvide, A., Fahigren, S., Norberg, A., and Saveman, B.-I. (2006). From perpetrator to victim in a violent situation in institutional care for elderly persons: Exploring a narrative from one involved care provider. *Nursing Inquiry*, 13(3), 194-202.

Schaufeli, W.B., and Bakker, A.B. (2004). Job demands, job resources, and their relationships with burnout and engagement: A multi-sample study. *Journal of Organizational Behavior*, 25, 293-315.

Schaufeli, W.B., and Enzmann, D. (1998). *The burnout companion to study and practice: A critical analysis*. London: Taylor and Francis.

Schaufeli, W.B.,Van Dierendonck, D., and Van Gorp, K. (1996). Burnout and reciprocity: Towards a dual-level social exchange model. *Work and Stress*, 10, 225-237.

Selye, H. (1956). *The Stress of life*. New York: McGraw-Hill

Shanafelt, T.D., Bradley, K.A., Wipf, J.E., and Back, A.L. (2002). Burnout and self-reported patient care in an internal medicine residency program. *Annals of Internal Medicine*, 136(5), 358-367.

Shirom, A. (2005). Commentary: Reflexions on the study of burnout. *Work and Stress*, 19(3), 263-270.

Spencer, C., and Beaulieu, M. (June 1994). *Abuse and neglect of older adults in institutional settings – An annotated bibliography*. Ottawa: Health Division, Health Services Directorate, Health Canada.

Straus, M.A. (1979). Measuring intra-family conflict and violence: The conflict tactics (CT) scales. *Journal of Marriage and the Family*, 41, 75-88.

Taylor, A.G., Hudson, K., and Keeling, A. (1991). Quality nursing care: The consumers' perspective revisited. *Journal of Nursing Quality Assurance*, 5, 23-31.

Tofler, A. (1980). *The Third Wave*. New York: Bantam Books.

Truchot, D., and Deregard, M. (2001). Perceived inequity, communal orientation and burnout: The role of helping models. *Work and Stress*, 15(4), 347-356.

Vahey C.C., Aiken, L.H., Sloane, D.M., Clarke, S.P., and Vargas, D. (2004). Nurse burnout and patient satisfaction. *Medical Care*, 42(2), 57-66.

Van Yperen, N.W. (1996). Communal orientation and the burnout syndrome among nurses: A replication and extension. *Journal of Applied Social Psychology*, 26-338-354.

Wamsley, L.M. (1996). Stress, stress related depression, and burnout: Their effects on nurses and holistic patient care. *Dissertation Abstracts International: Section B: The Sciences and Engineering*. 56(10-B): 5412.

Wang, J.J. (2005). Psychological abuse behavior exhibited by caregivers in the care of elderly and correlated factors in long-term care facilities in Taiwan. *Journal of Nursing Research*, 13(4), 271-280.

Whittington, R., and Higgins, L. (2002). More than zero-tolerance ? Burnout and tolerance for patient aggression amongst mental health nurses in China and the UK. *Acta Psychiatrica Scandinavica*, 106 (Supplement), 37-40.

Wierucka, D., and Goodridge, D. (1996). Vulnerable in a safe place: Institutional elder abuse. *Canadian Journal of Nursing Administration,* September-October, 82-103.

Wimbusch, F.B. (1983). Nurse burnout: Its effect on patient care. *Nursing Management*, 14(1), 55-57.

Winstanley, S., and Whittington, R. (2002). Anxiety, burnout and coping styles in general hospital staff exposed to workplace aggression: A cyclical model of burnout and vulnerability to aggression. *Work and Stress*, 16(4), 302-315.

Zeithaml, V.A., Parasuraman, A., and Berry, L.L. (1990). *Delivering quality service – Balancing customer perceptions and expectations*. New York: Free Press.

In: Handbook of Stress and Burnout in Health Care   ISBN 978-1-60456-500-3
Editor: Jonathon R. B. Halbesleben   © 2008 Nova Science Publishers, Inc.

Chapter 13

STRESS AND PATIENT SAFETY

Achim Elfering[1] and Simone Grebner[2]
[1]Department of Psychology,
University of Bern, Switzerland
[2]Department of Psychology,
Central Michigan University

In the late 1990s, consulting firms promoted 'restructuring' of care modalities to reduce the costs of patient care. Since then, work of health care personnel has changed dramatically. Downsizing and especially staff reduction (i.e. registered nurses) provoked studies that related nurse staffing (the nurse-to-patient-ratio) to patient outcomes. It was the work of Linda Aiken and colleagues that reliably showed nurse staffing to be related to both well-being and injuries of nurses and patient outcomes (e.g., Aiken, Clarke, Sloane, Sochalski, and Silber, 2002; Clarke, Rockett, Sloane, and Aiken, 2002; Curtin, 2003; Joint Commission on Accreditation of Health Care Organizations, 2001; Lang, Hodge, Olson, Romano, and Kravitz, 2004; Hickam et al., 2003; Mark, Harless, McCue, and Xu, 2004; National Audit Office, 2005; Needleman, Buerhaus, Mattke, Stewart, and Zelevinsky, 2002; Rafferty et al., 2007; Stewart, and Zelevinsky, 2002; Unruh, 2003; Whitman, Kim, Davidson, Wolf, and Wang, 2002). Numerous studies found strong evidence for non-fatal adverse outcomes such as newly acquired infections (e.g., Needleman et al., 2002). Evidence for the relation between staffing and patient mortality is mixed. Some studies do find a relation (e.g., Aiken et al., 2002), others do not (e.g. Needleman et al., 2002). There is also evidence that education of personnel is associated with patient safety. In surgical patients, a negative association between the degree of nurse education and patient mortality was found (Callahan, 2004). Moreover, a study by Unruh (2003) confirmed that *registered nurse hours of care* impact the level of adverse events patients suffer from.

Working conditions that are associated with nurse staffing which include overtime, frequent work interruptions, distractions, and conflicting task requirements have been found to be the risk factors most likely to decrease patient safety (Hickam et al., 2003). These work characteristics were also reliably linked to stress and burnout among health care personnel (Schaufeli and Enzmann, 1998). However, the link between nurses' stress and patient safety so far is inconclusive (Hickam et al., 2003) because models or theories are lacking that could help us to understand that link. Hence, this chapter discusses evidence concerning the association of stress and patient safety. Moreover, evidence is explained using action regulation theory (e.g., Frese and Zapf, 1994).

ASSOCIATIONS BETWEEN WORKING CONDITIONS, STRESS, BURNOUT, AND PATIENT SAFETY

According to a seminal report by the Institute of Medicine (IOM, 2004), poor management practices and unfavorable working conditions are major threats to patient safety in the US. In Canada, a study found that 36.9% of the reported adverse events would have been highly preventable if nurses would have had better working conditions (Baker, Norton, and Flintoft, et al., 2004). A recent study in the UK (Rafferty et al., 2007) showed that the quartile of hospitals with highest patient-to-nurse ratio had 26% higher mortality. Moreover, nurses in hospitals with highest patient-to-nurse ratios reported higher levels of burnout and job dissatisfaction. In addition, they reported lower quality of working conditions compared to the quartile of hospitals with lowest patient-to-nurse ratios. Aiken and co-workers (2002) found similar associations in the US.

In health care, stressful events are frequently safety-related (Elfering, Semmer and Grebner, 2006). When nurses were asked to report stressful situations while working, it turned out that 20% of all events reported were coded as being safety-related. It is plausible to assume that the number of safety-related events is underreported, since reporting may be associated with anxiety and shame (Davidoff, 2002; Firth-Cozens, 2002). Overall, there is good agreement that stress at work contributes to impaired health and well-being (e.g., Kahn and Byosiere, 1992; Semmer, McGrath, and Beehr, 2005; Sonnentag and Frese, 2003). Nevertheless, the association between work stress and safety (e.g., patient safety) is less well investigated (Mäkinen, Kivimäki, Elovainio, and Virtanen, 2003). It does seem to be likely that, under stress, hospital staff are more likely to make mistakes that can contribute to the emergence of accidents, because high stress levels can impair the level of concentration, cognitive information processing, decision-making, and work behavior (Furney, 1986). Moreover, work stress, especially work overload, has been shown to be associated with occupational accidents (e.g., Frone, 1998; Zohar, 2000) and medical malpractice (Jones et al., 1988). On the other hand, resources such as job control are positively related to health and productivity as well as safe working practices (Parker, Axtell, and Turner, 2001). We suggest an action regulation theory framework to model the link between work conditions, stress, and patient safety. For instance Greiner, Krause, Fischer, and Ragland (1998) employed observational job analysis based on action regulation theory among transit driving operators. For operators with high work barriers (i.e. poor technical organizational design), a relative risk of 3.8 was found concerning sickness absence; for operators with high time pressure and medium time-control, an elevated risk for work accidents was reported.

ACTION REGULATION THEORY

A theory based classification of task characteristics, is provided by *action regulation theory,* a general cognitive theory of (work) behavior (e.g., Frese and Zapf, 1994; Hacker, 1998; Oesterreich and Volpert, 1986). Stress-related task characteristics are classified according to necessities and possibilities of cognitive action regulation. Moreover, conditions which interfere with information processing, and therefore impede goal directed action, are considered. Such conditions include, for instance, interruptions by co-workers or unclear instructions of supervisors. Task conduct at work is regarded as conscious and goal-directed behavior. According to the rationale of action regulation theory, task characteristics are distinguished with regard to the *action regulatory function of cognition*s in (a) *quality of work task,* which include *regulation requirements* (i.e. decision necessities) and *regulation possibilities* (i.e. decision possibilities), and (b) *regulation obstacles* (i.e. stressors), which interrupt the action process and impede, or even thwart, goal attainment.

Regulation Requirements

Regulation requirements can be differentiated into *task complexity, variety, social requirements, requirements to collaborate* and *completeness of actions* (cf. Frese and Zapf, 1994; Semmer and Mohr, 2001). A highly complex task implies the necessity of many decisions. However, *complexity* depends on requirements of the situation as well as on the skill level of the person. *Variety* of tasks is defined as the number of distinguishable actions required by tasks. *Social requirements* include emotion work and the requirement to comply to emotional display rules defined by the organization (e.g., Zapf, 2002).

Requirements to ollaborate include the necessity to bring task conduct into agreement with co-workers (cf. Semmer, Zapf, and Dunckel, 1995). Finally, *completeness of action* is defined as completeness of action process and hierarchy of action regulation. Because goals are mostly defined by supervisors, maximal completeness of actions is scarce in work life (Volpert, 1974). Regulation requirements are considered to act as a 'double-edged sword.' A high as well as a low level of complexity can be detrimental, whereas a medium level is considered to contribute positively to well-being, health, and performance (Frese and Zapf, 1994). Of course, complexity of tasks has to be considered in relation to the skill level of an employee.

Regulation possibilities. Regulation possibilities (i.e. resources, cf. Frese and Zapf, 1994) can be differentiated into *job control* (e.g., Karasek, 1979; Terry and Jimmieson, 1999) and *possibilities to collaborate* and *communicate* with others (Semmer and Mohr, 2001). *Control* is defined as the extent of influence over task *content* (goals and plans), *way of task conduct* (sequence of action steps) and *time frame* of task conduct (time point, succession and duration of actions). Possibilities to collaborate are defined as freedom to decide about working solitary or with others, and the possibility to select preferred co-workers, and possibilities to communicate as freedom to decide about timing and quantity of interpersonal communication at work including work as well as non-work related issues. Regulation possibilities contribute in general positively to well-being, health, and performance (e.g., Frese and Zapf, 1994, Kahn and Byosiere, 1992; Sonnentag and Frese, 2003). Moreover, it can plausibly be assumed that job control is a job characteristic that is positively related to patient safety.

Regulation problems. Stress may either develop if actions are disrupted by a change of the action process, or if actions themselves generate stress (Semmer, 1984). Stressors are defined as situational characteristics affecting goal setting, planning, and levels of regulation. Regulation problems include three types of stressors. First are *regulation obstacles*, which impede or even thwart pursuit and attainment of a goal. They are divided into *regulation difficulties* (e.g., difficulty in obtaining sufficient information, or to move), and *interruptions,* which are generated by unpredictable external events, such as by other persons, technical problems, and organizational problems (e.g., deficient material or tools). Regulation obstacles require additional effort (to start again, to repeat parts of the action process, or to enhance physical strength etc.), or even the use of more risky actions (c.f. Frese and Zapf, 1994; Leitner et al., 1987). The second type, *regulation uncertainty*, is defined as a lack of knowledge about the ways to achieve a goal, usefulness of plans, and types of feedback (c.f. Semmer, 1984), for instance, due to high complexity. Role conflict and role ambiguity (e.g., Kahn and Byosiere, 1992) can be regarded as subcategories of regulation uncertainty (cf. Frese and Zapf, 1994; Semmer, 1984). The third type, *overtaxing regulations* (overload), are related to the speed and intensity of information processing requirements. High *speed* (time pressure) of information processing may require deviation from the original action plan. On the other hand, high *intensity* of information processing may lead to information overload of the short-term working memory, for instance, due to the necessity of working using high levels of concentration over a long period of time (cf. *role overload*, e.g., Kahn and Byosiere, 1992). Overtaxing regulations are supposed to lead to high physiological arousal and exhaustion of mental and physical capacities. Regulation problems contribute, in general, negatively to well-being and health. However, recent research suggests that regulation problems can be separated into challenge and hindrance stressors (e.g., conflicts), both contributing to impaired well-being and health. although challenge stressors (e.g., overtaxing regulations) were related positively to performance (LePine, Podsakoff, and LePine, 2005). It is important to note that, so far, it is not well investigated whether this applies to all types of tasks. We assume that hindrance as well as challenge stressors might be detrimental when patient safety is considered such as during instances when speeding up decision-making might lead to errors (see below).

Stress Induced Change of Cognitive Strategies in Task Fulfillment

According to Hacker (2003), three levels of consciousness of the cognitive processes and representations that regulate work activities can be distinguished: An automated, unconscious mode of regulation, a knowledge-based and possibly conscious mode, and a strictly conscious intellectual mode. The levels are organized in a top-down hierarchy. Higher and controlled levels include, and determine, lower and more automatic levels. However, lower levels are thought to have regulative autonomy and the possibility of a bottom up impact on higher levels. Under stress, individuals tend to regress to lower uncontrolled levels of action regulation following the principle of cognitive economy in terms of using basic heuristics in order to reduce mental effort. Hence, employees tend to redefine (Hackman, 1970) tasks under stress. For instance, under conditions of understaffing, geriatric nurses tend to redefine their task and to change work strategies. Nurses no longer use time-consuming programmes in order to stimulate elderly patients, but rather change to sedate patients using medication. As a consequence, overload is reduced and economic goals are met, but the humane aspects of patient care are neglected (Hacker, 2003).

A second stress induced change in the regulation of actions is reduction of effort with regard to secondary tasks such as double-checking, documenting, and preventive maintenance. Secondary tasks may be carried out less attentively, resulting in reduced monitoring (cf. Hockey, 1997; Matthews, Davies, Westerman, and Stammers, 2000; Schönpflug and Battmann, 1988). Reduction of effort in fulfilment of secondary tasks may have an impact, not only on one's own health, but also on the health of others (e.g., patients: see Aiken et al., 2002).

A third mechanism to reduce effort and/or to save time in task fulfilment is to accelerate decision-making with changed judgmental effects (Elfering, 2005) and use of more basic cognitive heuristics in task fulfilment. Maintaining performance under pressure is often only possible by relying on more basic functioning. Employees use heuristics that help to save mental energy and work in most instances. Such heuristics, however, increase the probability of errors and failure in exceptional cases. These heuristics are automatically activated in stress-situations. Regression towards more basic heuristics is obvious in decision-making, such as in medical diagnostics. Human factors that threaten reliability of medical diagnoses are *cognitive errors* that include failures in perception (e.g., non-detection in medical image analysis), failed heuristics (e.g., satisfaction of search –error: the tendency to stop searching for disease causes after finding one), and biases (e.g., confirmation bias: the tendency to look for confirming evidence to support a diagnosis rather than look for disconfirming evidence to refute it, despite the latter often being more persuasive and definitive). Collectively, these cognitive error have been referred to as *cognitive dispositions to respond* (CDRs; for a comprehensive overview of CDR in medical decision-making, see Croskerry, 2003).

COGNITIVE FUNCTIONING AS THE LINK BETWEEN STRESS AND PATIENT SAFETY

Reason (2000) defines human error as a failure of achieving the intended outcome in a planned sequence of mental or physical activities in cases when that failure is not due to chance. Errors are divided into slips and mistakes (Reason, 2002): (1) slips result from incorrect execution of a correct action sequence, and (2) mistakes result from the correct execution of an incorrect action sequence. Zhang, Patel, Johnsson, and Shortliffe (2004) developed an action regulation based approach to medical errors that maintained the differentiation of slips and mistakes while adding an action theory approach according to the work of Norman (1986). Slips and mistakes can be identified within seven different phases of the action cycle (i.e. pursuit of behaviour from planning via executing, up to evaluation of action results). As an example, Zhang et al. (2004) report the application of an infusion: "…any action has seven stages of activities: (1) establishing the goal (e.g., "set volume to be infused at 1000 cc"), which is abstract and independent of the system or concrete setting; (2) forming the intention (e.g., "use keypad to enter 1000"), which is concrete and dependent on the actual system or concrete setting; (3) specifying the action specification (e.g., "press 1 0 0

0''), which is the formation of the sequence of actions to be carried out; (4) executing the action (e.g., "physically pressing 1 0 0 0"), which is physically carrying out the actions; (5) perceiving the system state (e.g., "volume: 1000 cc, with 1000 highlighted"), which is to detect and recognize any changes in system state; (6) interpreting the state, which means to make sense of the information perceived from the perception stage (e.g., "1000 cc is displayed, but what does the highlighting mean? Has the pump accepted the value, or do I have to press another button?"); and (7) evaluating the system state with respect to goals and intentions (e.g., "determine if the system has accepted the volume, i.e., press key to start infusion"), which is to check if the original goal has been completed."(p. 196).

A major advantage of action regulation theory is that it gives insight into work-related cognitive processes, and explains why slips and mistakes occur. For example, a typical slip during action evaluation would be to start the infusion but to forget to open the clamp on the hose, resulting in no drug being infused (example from Zhang et al., 2004). Saving working memory capacity should therefore be a primary goal in task design. For instance, retention and reactivation of future goals consumes much of the capacity of working memory (i.e. prospective memory; Hacker, 2003). When future goals and activities are time-based, for example, "start infusions at 7 a.m.," nurses typically redefine time-based orders into event-based orders (e.g., "start infusions after breakfast") in order to reduce cognitive load of self-initiated retrieval.

THE ROLE OF REGULATION POSSIBILITIES

The IOM report (1999) noted that quality of patient care is related to the degree to which nurses are active and empowered participants in making decisions about their patient's plan of care and by the degree to which they have an active and central role in organizational decision-making. Interestingly, regulation resources seem to have decreased in the working population in recent decades (Kompier, 2005). Moreover, looking at young nurse's first four years of occupational practice, nurses were shown to have lower levels of job control compared to other occupations in the service sector (e.g., bank clerks) (Semmer, Tschan, Elfering, Kälin, and Grebner, 2005). Moreover, while job control did increase with job experience in bank clerks, salesman, cooks, and mechanics, job control decreased among nurses, which might be a risk factor for patient safety (Semmer et al., 2005). Taris, Stoffelsen, Bakker, Schaufeli, and van Dierendonck, (2005) showed that differences in occupational levels of job control are inversely related to levels of burnout.

Why are regulation possibilities so important with respect to patient safety? The most compelling answer is that they enable health care personnel to cope successfully with *conflicting task demands* that arise often from the goal to increase cost effectiveness while offering the best and safe care. For instance, nurses who have control with respect to sequence and priority of tasks (i.e. time control), and who can decide how care is administered (i.e. method control) are more able to react to unforeseen events and increasing work load. Rationalisation of care (e.g., understaffing, limited competencies) in terms of preventing nurses from meeting their own performance standards is associated with job dissatisfaction, injuries, and burnout (Bourgeault et al., 2001; Schubert et al., 2004) and indicators of patient's safety (Schubert et al., 2004). Hence, lack of resources impedes task fulfillment and goal attainment, and therefore, success experiences and subjective meaningfulness of work (Hacker, 2003). Increasing work pressure directly reduces resources. First, self-regulation may be impaired (Baumeister, Faber and Wallace, 1999), which may lead to less competent interpersonal behavior. Moreover, increased time pressure impedes giving and receiving of social support at work and increases the probability of role conflict (Hacker, 2003). Supporting evidence was found in analyses of the Scandinavian health care system (Lindström, Kiviranta, Bach, Bast-Peterson and Toomingas, 1994). Second, increased time pressure may also prevent continuing education, that is considered to be necessary for high performance. Moreover, when people work under high demands (e.g., high concentration demands) and low control, events that endanger safety are experienced as more familiar, and more likely to recur (Elfering et al., 2006).

THE ROLE OF TRAINING AND EDUCATION

In terms of action regulation theory, training and education improves the mental model of the task, such as expertise in attending to those signals that are important for anticipation of problems and to successfully avoid them. Therefore, training will augment expertise as another resource that allows one to work efficiently while maintaining all health quality and safety standards. Training of novice nurses should address the association between workload and patient safety and the processes behind these, and educate nurses in self-management strategies for stressful situations. Some special emphasis should be laid on cognitive heuristics. For instance, Croskerry (2003) proposed a cognitive fallacy training (Table 1).

Semmer and Regenass (1999) argued, based on an action regulation theory approach, that, in reference to training, more emphasis should be laid on collecting data with regard to actual practices, real dilemmas (e.g., conflicting goals in stress situations), and decisions. Hence, the authors propose a situation-related training approach, in which participants are confronted with dilemma that stem from conflicting social norms and various costs and benefits associated with different types of behaviour.

Stress is certainly not always avoidable in health care (e.g., emergency situations). Since many procedures are team or group-based, simulation-trainings of highly stressful situations such as emergencies are recommended for individuals as well as teams. In particular, training of communication and leadership skills ensure a shared mental model of a specific work situation that is a prerequisite for successful work performance (for a action regulation based group training approach, see Tschan, Semmer, Gautschi, Hunziker, Spychiger, and Marsch, 2006).

Table 1. Training/Intervention Strategies to Reduce Errors from Cognitive Dispositions to Respond (adopted from Croskerry, 2003)

Accountability: Establish clear accountability and follow-up for decisions made.

Cognitive forcing strategies: Develop generic and specific strategies to avoid predictable bias in particular clinical situations.

Consider alternatives: Encourage routinely asking the question: What else might this be? Decrease reliance on working memory: Improve the accuracy of judgments through cognitive aids: mnemonics, clinical practice guidelines, algorithms, etc..

Feedback: Provide as rapid and reliable feedback as possible to decision makers so that errors are immediately appreciated, understood, and corrected, resulting in better calibration of decision makers

Make task easier: Provide more information about the specific problem to reduce task difficulty and ambiguity. Make available rapid access to concise, clear, well-organized information. Reduce dual-tasking.

Metacognition: Train for a reflective approach to problem solving: stepping back from the immediate problem to examine and reflect on the thinking process.

Minimize time pressures: Provide adequate time for quality decision making.

Simulation: Develop mental rehearsal, "cognitive walkthrough" strategies for specific clinical scenarios to allow cognitive biases to be made and their consequences to be observed. Construct clinical training videos contrasting incorrect (biased) approaches with the correct (debiased) approach.

Strategy Mechanism/Action Develop insight/ awareness: Provide detailed descriptions and thorough characterizations of known cognitive biases, together with multiple clinical examples illustrating their adverse effects on decision-making.

BURNOUT AS AN ANTECEDENT OF REDUCED PATIENT SAFETY

The coincidence of burnout in nurses and deficits in patient safety is often found (Aiken et al, 2002). However, there exists little evidence concerning tests of specific relations between burnout and patient safety (e.g., main effects). Burke (2001) analyzed the responses of nurses to restructuring finding that cynical, as well as fearful, responses were found to be associated with negative perceptions of hospital functioning and effectiveness. Maslach (2006) showed workload and emotional exhaustion to be related to objective injury rates in the following year among employees in the administrative service sector. Moreover, emotional exhaustion mediated the relationship between workload and injuries. An international study by Laschinger (2006) confirmed the mediator hypothesis. The study measured quality of nurses work life (i.e. involvement of staff in policy development, staffing levels, support for a nursing model of care, and physician/nurse relationships), burnout as a mediator, and patient safety outcomes (i.e. reports of medication errors, patient falls, infections, and number of patient complaints). Staffing level showed a direct as well as an indirect effect on patient safety. According to Sonnentag (2005), depersonalisation, disengagement, and cynicism can be considered as ways of coping with stress at work. However, this may result in a distancing from work that could lower job performance: "for example, the client is seen in a depersonalized way and one's tasks are accomplished "mechanically" (p.272). Future studies should investigate these proposed mediation models and associated change in cognitive strategies in health care workers who suffer from burnout.

CONSEQUENCES FOR WORK INTERVENTION IN HEALTH CARE

In 2002, the UK Department of Health and the Design Council commissioned a study in order to gain practical recommendations to reduce the risk of medical error and improve patient safety across the National Health Service (NHS). An important result was the "need to better understand the healthcare system, including the users of that system, as the context into which specific design solutions must be delivered. Without a broader understanding there can be no certainty that any single design will contribute to reducing medical error and the consequential costs thereof" (Clarkson et al., 2004, p.123). Action regulation theory suggests using task analysis as the basic information for ways to improve patient safety. Of course, solutions should be tailored to organizational settings and single tasks. There is, however evidence that regulation possibilities play a crucial role in delivering safe care (Elfering et al., 2006). Efforts should be made in order to increase and maintain nurses' autonomy in making decisions at the bedside, nursing involvement in determining the nursing work environment, professional education, career development, and nursing leadership. The "Magnet Hospital" standards, defined by over 65 standards developed by the American Nurses Credentialing Center (ANCC, Armstrong, and Laschinger, 2006), address these regulation possibilities. It is important to note, that work redesign in terms of enhancing regulation possibilities does not contradict economic reasoning as O'Brien-Pallas, Thomson, Alksnis, and Bruce (2001) concluded. They proposed to (a) employ sufficient nursing staff to meet the needs of patients in order to avoid overtime that may impair nurse health and patient outcomes, (b) examine roles and activities of front-line nurses to determine ways to increase the time available for patient care, and (c) invest in training of managers and nurse leadership. Moreover, the plea is to stop substituting nursing aids for registered nurses. Gaining expertise is crucial in novice nurses who require "consistent availability of expertise in light of workload unpredictability, the social climate regarding expectations of novice performers, realistic expectations of novice decision making, ability during complex situations even up to a year after graduation, and strategies to recognize and intervene when novices are at risk for error" (Ebright, Urden, Patterson, and Chalko, 2004, p.531).

OUTLOOK

Beside the unspecific call for prospective intervention studies, some points emerged that relied on action regulation theory as the framework to model the relation between work stress and patient safety. First, research should take a situation-based view to address the types, frequency, and severity of stressors in safety-sensitive areas in health care. Incidents of medical error should be analyzed for preventable precursors, especially concerning conflicting task requirements, interruptions, and distractions. Further research should evaluate the unique and joint effects of situation-related interventions (e.g., job design) and person-related interventions (e.g., training) on patient safety. In particular, the role of cognitive functioning should be investigated in terms of a link between work stress and patient safety.

Second, there is a need to test the main and buffering effects of resources like job control, social support, and expertise in intervention studies. Research should include tests of mediator, as well as moderator, effects of burnout dimensions for the relation between stress and patient safety. Turnover rates are high among nurses (Hasselhorn, Tackenberg, and Müller, 2003) and related to burnout (Hasselhorn, Tackenberg, Peter, and the Nurses Early Exit [NEXT]-Study Group, 2004). Moreover, Gelinas and Bohlen (2002) reported that low turnover organizations showed lowered risk adjusted mortality scores as well as lower severity-adjusted length of stay compared to hospitals with higher turnover rates. Hence, turnover should be included in model tests in terms of an antecedent as well as consequences of reduced patient safety.

Finally, there is a need for a closer collaboration of nursing science and (Occupational Health) Psychology. Previous psychological research on the relationship of stress and patient safety often used weak measures of patient safety, while research in nursing science so far has tended to disregard work related stress theory and theories of occupational safety.

REFERENCES

Aiken, L. H., Clarke, S. P., Sloane, D. M., Sochalski, J., and Silber, J. H. (2002). Hospital nurse staffing and patient mortality, nurse burnout, and job dissatisfaction. *Journal of the American Medical Association, 288*, 1987-1993.

American Nurses Credentialing Center (ANCC). http://www.nursecredentialing.org/

Armstrong, K.J., and Laschinger, H. (2006). Structural empowerment, magnet hospital characteristics, and patient safety culture: Making the link. *Journal of Nursing Care Quality, 21*, 1242-131.

Baker, G. R., Norton, P. G., Flintoft, V., Blais, R., Brown, A., Cox, J., Etchells, E., Ghali, W. A., Hébert, P., Majumdar, S. R., O'Beirne, M., Palacios-Derflingher, L., Reid, R. J., Sheps, S., and Tamblyn, R. (2004). The Canadian adverse events study: The incidence of adverse events among hospital patients in Canada. *Canadian Medical Association Journal, 170*, 1678 – 1686.

Baumeister, R. F., Faber, J. E., and Wallace, H. M. (1999). Coping and ego depletion. In C. R. Snyder (Ed.), *Coping: The psychology of what works* (pp. 50-69). New York: Oxford University Press.

Bourgeault, I. L., Armstrong, P., Armstrong, H., Choiniere, J., Lexchin, J., Mykhalovskiy, E., Peters, S., and White, J. (2001). Everyday experiences of implicit rationing: Comparing the voices of nurses in California and British Columbia. *Sociology of Health and Illness, 23*, 633-653.

Burke, R. J. (2001). Nursing staff survivor responses to hospital restructuring and downsizing. *Stress and Health, 17*, 195–205.

Callahan, M. A. (2004). Surgical patient are at lower risk of death in hospitals with more degree-educated nurses. *Evidence-Based Healthcare, 8*, 67–68.

Clarke, S. P., Rockett, J. L., Sloane, D.M., and Aiken, L. H. (2002). Organizational climate, staffing and safety equipment as predictors of needlestick injuries and near-misses in hospital nurses. *American Journal of Infection Control, 30*, 207–16.

Clarkson, P. J., Buckle, P., Coleman, R., Stubbs, D., Ward, J., Jarrett, J., Lane, R., and Bound, J. (2004). Design for patient safety: A review of the effectiveness of design in the UK health service. *Journal of Engineering Design, 15*, 123–140.

Croskerry, P. (2003). The importance of cognitive errors in diagnosis and strategies to minimize them. *Academic Medicine, 78*, 775-780.

Curtin, L. (2003). An integrated analysis of nurse staffing and related variables: Effects on patient outcomes. *Online Journal of Issues in Nursing, 8* (3). Available: http://nursingworld.org/ojin/keynotes/speech3.htm

Davidoff, F. (2002). Shame: the elephant in the room. *British Medical Journal, 324*, 623-624.

Ebright, P. R., Urden, L., Patterson, E., and Chalko, B. (2004). Themes surrounding novice nurse near—miss and adverse-event situations. *Journal of Nursing Administration, 34*, 531-538.

Elfering, A. (2005). Human factors in matching images to standards: Assimilation and time order error. *International Journal of Occupational Safety and Ergonomics, 11*, 399-407.

Elfering, A., Semmer, N. K., and Grebner, S. (2006). Work stress and patient safety: Observer-rated work stressors as predictors of characteristics of safety-related events reported by young nurses. *Ergonomics, 49*, 457-469.

Firth-Cozens, J. (2002). Anxiety as a barrier to risk management. *Quality and Safety in Health Care, 11*, 115-115.

Frese, M., and Zapf, D. (1994). Action as the core of work psychology: A German approach. In Dunnette, M. D., Hough L. M., and Triandis, H. C. (Eds.), *Handbook of Industrial and Organizational Psychology*, Vol. 4 (pp. 271-340). Palo Alto, CA: Consulting Psychologists Press.

Gelinas, L., and Bohlen, C. (2002). The business case for retention. *Journal of Clinical Systems Management*, 4, 14–16.

Greiner, B. A., Krause, N., Fisher, J. M., and Ragland D. R. (1998). Objective stress factors, accidents, and absenteeism in transit operators: A theoretical framework and empirical evidence. *Journal of Occupational Health Psychology, 3*, 130-146.

Hacker, W. (1998). *Allgemeine Arbeitspsychologie: Psychische Regulation von Arbeitstätigkeiten* [General industrial psychology]. Bern: Huber.

Hacker, W. (2003). Action regulation theory: A practical tool for the design of modern work processes. *European Journal of Work and Organizational Psychology, 12*, 105-130.

Hackman, J. R. (1970). Task and task-performance in research on stress. In J. E. McGrath (Ed.), *Social and psychological factors in stress* (pp. 202-237). New York: Holt, Rimhart and Winston.

Hasselhorn, H. M., Tackenberg, P., and Müller, B. H. (2003). Vorzeitiger Berufsausstieg aus der Pflege in Deutschland als zunehmendes Problem für den Gesundheitsdienst – eine Übersichtsarbeit [Premature Departure from Nursing in Germany as a Growing Problem for the Health Care System - a Review]. *Das Gesundheitswesen, 65*, 40-46.

Hasselhorn, H. M., Tackenberg, P., Peter, R., and the NEXT-Study Group (2004). Effort-reward-imbalance among nurses in stable countries and in countries in transition. International *Journal of Occupational and Environmental Health, 10*, 401-408.

Hickam, D. H., Severance, S., Feldstein, A., Ray, L., Gorman, P., Schuldheis, S., Hersh, W. R., Krages, K. P., and Helfand, M., (2003). The effect of health care working conditions on patient safety. *Evidence Report/Technology Assessment Number 74*. (Prepared by Oregon Health and Science University under Contract No. 290-97-0018.) AHRQ Publication No. 03-E, Rockville, MD: Agency for Healthcare Research and Quality.

Hockey, G. R. J. (1997). Compensatory control in the regulation of human performance under stress and high workload: A cognitive-energetical framework. *Biological Psychology, 45*, 73-93.

Institute of Medicine (1999). To err is human. Building a safer health system. Washington, DC: National Academic Press. Available at: http://www.iom.edu/Object.File/ Master/4/117/ToErr-8pager.pdf. Retrieved August 25, 2007.

Institute of Medicine (2004). *Keeping patients safe: Transforming the work environment of nurses*. Washington, DC: The National Academies Press.

Joint Commission on Accreditation of Health Care Organizations (2001). *Sentinel Events Alert 2001*. Retrieved on October 10, 2007 from http://www.jointcommission.org/SentinelEvents/SentinelEventAlert/

Kahn, R. L., and Byosiere, P. (1992). Stress in organizations. In M. D. Dunnette and L. M. Hough (Eds.), Handbook of Industrial and Organizational Psychology (2nd ed., pp. 571-650). Palo Alto, CA: Consulting Psychologists Press.

Kompier, M. (2005). Dealing with workplace stress. In C. L. Cooper (Ed.), *Handbook of Stress Medicine and Health* (2nd ed.) (pp. 349-374). Boca Raton: CRC.

Lang, T. A., Hodge, M., Olson, V., Romano, P. S., and Kravitz, R. L. (2004). Nurse-patient ratios: A systematic review on the effects of nurse staffing on patient, nurse employee and hospital outcomes. *Journal of Nursing Administration, 34*, 326–37.

Laschinger, H. K. S. (2006, March). Nursing environments and patient safety: the mediating role of burnout. APA/NIOSH Conference: Work, Stress, and Health 2006: Making a Difference in the Workplace Conference, Miami, FL.

Lindström, K., Kiviranta, J., Bach, E., Bast-Pettersen, R. and Toomingas, A. (1994). *Research on work organization and well-being among health care personnel*. Helsinki: Nordic Seminar Working Papers.

Mäkinen, A., Kivimäki, M., Elovainio, M., and Virtanen, M. (2003). Organization of nursing care and stressful work characteristics. *Journal of Advanced Nursing, 43*, 197–205.

Mark, B. A., Harless, D. W., McCue, M., and Xu, Y. (2004). A Longitudinal examination of hospital registered nurse staffing and quality of care. *Health Services Research, 39*, 279–300.

Maslach, C. (2006, March). Burnout and workplace injuries: A longitudinal analysis. APA/NIOSH Conference: Work, Stress, and Health 2006: Making a Difference in the Workplace Conference, Miami, FL.

National Audit Office (2005). *A safer place for patients: Learning to improve patient safety. Report by the Controller and Auditor General*. London: The Stationery Office.

Needleman, J., Buerhaus, P., Mattke, S., Stewart, M., and Zelevinsky, K. (2002). Nurse-staffing levels and the quality of care in hospitals. *The New England Journal of Medicine, 346*, 1715–22.

Norman, D. A. (1986). Cognitive engineering. In D. A. Norman and S. W. Draper (Eds.), *User centered system design*. Hillsdale, NJ: Lawrence Erlbaum Associates.

O'Brien-Pallas, L., Thomson, D., Alksnis C., and Bruce, S. (2001). The economic impact of nurse staffing decisions: time to turn down another road? *Hospital Quarterly, 4*, 42-50.

Oesterreich, R., and Volpert, W. (1986). Task analysis of action regulation theory. *Economic and Industrial Democracy, 7*, 503-527.

Rafferty, A. M., Clarke, S. P., Coles, J., Ball, J., James, P., Mckee, M., and Aiken, L. (2007). Outcomes of variation in hospital nurse staffing in English hospitals: Cross-sectional analysis of survey data and discharge records. *International Journal of Nursing Studies, 44*, 175-182.

Reason, J. (2000). Education and debate. Human error: Models and management. *British Medical Journal, 320*, 768-70.

Schaufeli, W. B. and Enzmann, D. (1998). *The burnout companion to study and practice: A critical analysis*. London: Taylor and Francis.

Schönpflug, W., and Battmann, W. (1988). The costs and benefits of coping. In S. Fisher and J. Reason (Eds.), *Handbook of life stress, cognition and health* (pp. 699-713). New York, NY: Wiley.

Semmer, N. (1984). *Stressbezogene Tätigkeitsanalyse* [Stress-oriented task analysis]. Weinheim, Germany: Beltz.

Semmer, N., Zapf, D., and Dunckel, H. (1995). Assessing stress at work: A framework of an instrument. In O. Svane and Ch. Johansen (Eds.), *Work and health - scientific basis of progress in the working environment* (pp. 105-113). Luxembourg: Office for Official Publications of the European Communities.

Semmer, N. (1996). Individual differences, work stress and health. In M. J. Schabracq, J. A. M. Winnubst, and C. L. Cooper (Eds.), *Handbook of work and health psychology* (pp. 53-86). Chichester: Wiley.

Semmer, N. K., Tschan, F., Elfering, A., Kälin, W., and Grebner, S. (2005). Young adults entering the workforce in Switzerland: Working conditions and well-being. In H. Kriesi, P. Farago, M. Kohli, and M. Zarin, (Eds.), *Contemporary Switzerland: Revisiting the special case* (pp. 163-189). Houndmills, UK: Palgrave Macmillan.

Semmer, N., and Mohr, G. (2001). Arbeit und Gesundheit: Konzepte und Ergebnisse der arbeitspsychologischen Stressforschung [Work and health: Concepts and results of stress research in work psychology]. *Psychologische Rundschau, 52*, 150-158.

Semmer, N., and Regenass, A. (1999). Situational assessment of safety culture. In J. Misumi, B. Wilpert, and R. Miller (Eds.). *Nuclear safety: A human factors perspective* (pp. 85-96). London: Taylor and Francis.

Semmer, N. K., McGrath, J. E., and Beehr, T. A. (2005). Conceptual issues in research on stress and health. In C. L. Cooper (Ed.), *Handbook of Stress and Health* (2nd ed., pp. 1-43). New York: CRC Press.

Sonnentag, S. (2005). Burnout research. Adding an off-work and day-level perspective. *Work and Stress, 19*, 271-275.

Sonnentag, S., and Frese, M. (2003). Stress in organizations. In W. C. Borman, D. R. Ilgen, and J. R. Klimoski (Eds.), *Comprehensive handbook of psychology. Industrial and organizational psychology* (Vol. 12, pp. 453-491). New York: Wiley.

Taris, T. W., Stoffelsen, J., Bakker, A. B., Schaufeli, W. B., and van Dierendonck, D. (2005). Job control and burnout across occupations. *Psychological Reports, 97*, 955-961.

Tschan, F., Semmer, N. K., Gautschi, D., Hunziker, M., Spychiger, M., and Marsch, S. U. (2006). Leading to recovery: Group performance and coordinative activities in medical emergency driven groups. *Human Performance, 19*, 277-304.

Unruh, L. (2003). Licensed nurse staffing and adverse events in hospitals. *Medical Care, 41*, 142-152.

Volpert, W. (1974). *Handlungsstrukturanalyse als Beitrag zur Qualifikationsforschung* [Analysis of action structure as contribution to research on qualification]. Köln, Germany: Pahl-Rugenstein.

Wallace, J. C., and Chen, G. (2005). Development and validation of a work-specific measure of cognitive failure: Implications for occupational safety. *Journal of Occupational and Organizational Psychology, 78*, 615–632.

Warr, P. (1987). *Work, unemployment and mental health*. Oxford: Clarendon Press.

Whitman, G. R., Kim, Y., Davidson, L. J., Wolf, G. A., and Wang, S. (2002). The impact of staffing on patient outcomes across specialty units. *Journal of Nursing Administration, 32*, 633–639.

Zapf, D. (2002).Emotion work and psychological well-being. *Human Resource Management Review, 12*, 237-268.

Zhang, J., Patel, V. L., Johnsson, T. R., and Shortliffe, E. H. (2004). A cognitive taxonomy of medical errors. *Journal for Biomedical Informatics*, 37, 193-204.

In: Handbook of Stress and Burnout in Health Care   ISBN 978-1-60456-500-3
Editor: Jonathon R. B. Halbesleben   © 2008 Nova Science Publishers, Inc.

Chapter 14

DISCONNECTING THE STRESS-BURNOUT-TURNOVER RELATIONSHIP AMONG NURSING PROFESSIONALS: A SYNTHESIS OF MICRO AND MACRO HRM RESEARCH

Anthony R. Wheeler
University of Rhode Island

There is little doubt in the health care industry that nurses experience high levels of occupational (Jenkins and Elliot, 2004) and job-related stress (Weyers, Peter, Boggild, Jeppesen, and Siegrist, 2006), and this stress often leads to increased levels of burnout and turnover among nursing professionals (Gelsema, Van Der Doef, Maes, Janssen, Akerboom, and Verhoeven, 2006). The cycle of stress, burnout, and turnover is especially problematic in the nursing profession because there is currently a worldwide shortage of qualified nurses that borders on pandemic (Lucero and Sousa, 2006). Furthermore, the value added by nurses to health care organizations and their patients cannot be underestimated, as nurse staffing levels often strongly predict adverse patient health outcomes (Janiszewski Goodin, 2003; Seago and Ash, 2004). Given that turnover costs range between 70% - 200% of a turned-over employee's salary (Kaye and Jordan-Evans, 2001), turnover among nurses strongly predicts the financial survivability of health care organizations (Brown, Sturman, and Simmering, 2003). Traditionally, human resource management (HRM) professionals commence retention programs aimed at reducing turnover and increasing financial performance; thus HRM scholars and practitioners should devote considerable effort in reducing a key cause of nursing turnover: stress-induced burnout.

This is not to say that HRM and nursing scholars and practitioners have not devoted effort to mitigating the effects of stress on burnout and turnover. Indeed, the extant HRM and nursing literatures are strewn with studies that examine this problem. For example, nursing scholars typically examine employee training programs designed to provide nurses with more efficient coping mechanisms to deal with stress and burnout (Edward and Hercelinskyj, 2007; Tabak and Orit, 2007). Aspects of job design, typically addressed through job analysis by

HRM scholars, permeate the nursing literature as an explanation to why nurses typically experience job role stress and burnout (Gelsema et al., 2006; Lucero and Sousa, 2006; Makinen, Kivimaki, Elovainio, and Virtanen, 2003). The current extant research lacks, at least from a HRM perspective, two fundamental unifying nomological tenets. First, both HRM and nursing scholars lack a common frame of reference for understanding the causes, processes, and outcomes (and therefore HRM solutions) of the problem of reducing stress induced burnout and turnover. Second, both HRM and nursing scholars tend to focus on one level of analysis, typically the employee level, which inhibits understanding of how stress induced burnout affects the total organization.

The first issue, that of a common frame of reference to describing stress induced burnout and turnover from a HRM perspective, can be addressed through the lens of person-environment (PE) fit, which has been applied to stress, burnout, and turnover (Edwards, 1996). PE fit encompasses several conceptualizations of what it means to *fit* within an occupation, organization, general work environment, and job (Kristof, 1996; Wheeler, Buckley, Halbesleben, Brouer, and Ferris, 2005). The unifying process underlying the multiple conceptualizations of PE is *congruence* (Kristof, 1996; Wheeler et al., 2005). That is, does the individual possess the personality type, values, and knowledge, skills, and abilities (KSAs) required by the occupation, organization, and job? The lack of congruence and therefore PE misfit causes stress induced burnout and turnover (Edwards, 1996; Quick, Nelson, Quick, and Orman, 2001).

The second issue, that of single level focus and analysis, is a common, although increasingly addressed, problem within organizational sciences (Schonfeld and Rindskopf, 2007). HRM and nursing scholars and practitioners alike have identified a wide array of tools specifically aimed at reducing the stress, burnout, and turnover resulting from employee misfit; unfortunately, these scholars and practitioners have yet to apply these tools in a consistent and coherent manner that addresses not only employee level outcomes, such as stress, burnout, turnover, and even performance, but also addresses organization level outcomes, such as organization turnover rates, financial and clinical performance, and customer satisfaction. HRM and nursing scholars should examine the problem of nurse stress induced burnout from a multilevel perspective, which requires the infusion of strategic HRM research. Macro level strategic HRM (SHRM) research describes how organizations can increase employee retention, productivity, and organizational financial performance through integrating HRM functions and tying these integrated HRM systems to the organization's strategy (e.g., Huselid, 1995). Logically, health care organizations interested in reducing the stress, burnout, and turnover of nurses should be able to develop integrated, stress reducing HRM systems that directly support the health care organization's mission.

As such, the present chapter seeks to develop a conceptual multilevel HRM solution to the problem of nurse stress induced burnout and turnover. In order to achieve this goal, the present chapter has four goals. First, I briefly summarize the current HRM-related research on nurse stress induced burnout and turnover. Second, I introduce PE fit as a common frame of reference for understanding the process and outcomes of stress induced burnout and turnover. Third, I summarize HRM "best practices" that should reduce stress induced burnout and turnover; moreover and fourth, I then link these best practices into a multilevel, strategic stress reducing work system (SRWS). In doing so, I provide HRM and nursing scholars and practitioners with a solution that not only reduces stress induced burnout among nurses but also provides health care organizations with a solution that increases nursing retention, organization financial and clinical performance, and customer satisfaction.

SUMMARY OF HRM LITERATURE APPLIED TO NURSING

A search of leading nursing (*PubMed*) and HRM (*PsychInfo*) academic literature search engines using keywords like 'stress', 'burnout', 'nurses', 'HRM', and any of the specific HRM functions yields several thousand peer reviewed research and practitioner articles from the last decade alone. While it is impossible to summarize this massive literature, several broad conclusions can be drawn related to the causes of nurse stress induced burnout and turnover. First, the job of a nurse is complex (Shi and Singh, 2004). Second, there is a worldwide shortage of nurses (Buchan and Calman, 2004; Peterson, 2001). Third, as nursing becomes more complex, it becomes increasingly difficult to hire nurses with the requisite KSAs needed to perform the job (Buchan, 1999; Shi and Singh, 2004). Fourth, health care organizations have increasingly turned to complex training and performance management techniques to further develop nurse KSAs and to reduce stress and burnout among nurses (Edward and Hercelinskyj, 2007; Tabak and Orit, 2007). Finally, due to the aforementioned shortage of nurses worldwide, organizations increasingly utilize lead the market pay strategies and costly incentive systems to attract, motivate, and retain nurses (Brown et al., 2003), which in and of itself creates nurse 'job hopping' (Upenieks, 2005). The complexity of the job, the scarcity of qualified nurses, and the worldwide demand for nurses creates a vicious cycle of perpetually understaffed and increasingly stressed and burned out nurses (AbuAlRub, 2004). The outcomes of this cycle include increased turnover rates of nurses, increased hospital costs (Buchan, 1999), and increased deleterious health outcomes among patients (Buchan, 1999).

SUMMARY OF PERSON-ENVIRONMENT FIT LITERATURE

The sheer volume of theoretical, empirical, and practical research conducted around the world on the topic leaves little doubt as to why it appears as though the research on this topic is not unified. From a strictly HRM perspective, the cause of stress relates to PE fit, which encompasses many conceptualizations of fit. Person-Organization (PO) fit describes the congruence between an employee's values, goals, and beliefs and the organization's values, goals, and beliefs (Chatman, 1989). Person-Job (PJ) fit, which is sometimes referred to as the *demands-abilities* component of PE fit (Edwards, 1991), relates to the congruence between an employee's KSAs and the KSAs required by the job (Caldwell and O'Reilly, 1990). Person-Preferences for Culture (PP) fit, which is sometimes referred to as a *needs-supplies* component of PE fit (Edwards, 1991, 1996), describes the congruence between an employees needs (financial, social, esteem, etc.) and what the organization supplies (compensation, promotion, development, etc.) as part of being a member of the organization (Van Vianen,

2000). Person-Vocation (PV) fit, which is sometimes included in the *demands-abilities* component of PE fit (Edwards, 1991, 1996), relates to the overlap between an employee's personality and the personality typically associated with members of the organization in specific jobs (Holland, 1985). PV Fit is often associated with vocational preference in that employees often self-select into vocations, occupations, or careers based upon personality type (Furnham, 2001; Wheeler et al., 2005). For the purpose of clarity in this chapter and consistent with research on the phenomenon of fit (Arthur, Bell, Villado, and Doverspike, 2006), I refer to all of these conceptualizations by the broader conceptualization of 'PE Fit'.

PE Fit and its narrower conceptualizations have been empirically related to employee stress, burnout, and turnover (see Edwards, 1992, 1996; Kristof, 1996; Wheeler et al., 2005). Moreover, much of the empirical nursing research on stress, burnout, and turnover can be interpreted as manifestations of misfit or lack of congruence between nurses and their occupation (Edwards, Guppy, and Cockerton, 2007), organization (Jenkins and Elliott, 2004), job (Xianyu and Lambert, 2006), or general work environment (Akerboom and Maes, 2006). As the lack of congruence and fit causes considerable stress induced burnout and turnover among nursing professionals, the health care organizations employing these nurses should develop and implement HRM practices specifically designed to reduce stress.

DEVELOPMENT OF MULTILEVEL STRATEGIC STRESS REDUCING WORK SYSTEMS

While the independent HRM functions in and of themselves have been found to reduce stress by increasing PE fit, the full impact of HRM on decreasing stress, burnout, and turnover as it increases employee and organization performance cannot be felt until the organization strategically aligns these functions into a coherent system (Boxall, 1996; Huselid, 1995). SHRM research, typically theoretically grounded in Barney's (1991) resource based view (RBV) of the organization, consistently demonstrates that fully integrated and interdependent HRM functions that are directly linked to an organization's strategy will increase employee job performance, productivity, and retention (Lepak and Snell, 2002) while also increasing organization financial performance. Moreover, SHRM research on 'system architecture', that is how organizations bundle HRM functions together, concludes that 'commitment based HRM systems' that "shape desired employee behaviors and attitudes by forging psychological links between organizational and employee goals" (Arthur, 1994, p. 671) most effectively improve performance and retention (Lepak and Snell, 2002). Furthermore, commitment based HRM systems "elicit and reinforce the set of role behaviors" (Lado and Wilson, 1994, p. 699), which helps to increase employee motivation. SHRM researchers call these commitment based HRM systems 'high performing work systems' (HPWS; Huselid, 1995).

SHRM research, however, is at a crossroad. Becker and Huselid (2006) evaluated 15 years of SHRM literature, concluding that while SHRM research generally predicts organizational turnover and financial success, SHRM researchers should examine the impact of HPWS on individual jobs and employees. Indeed, they call for SHRM research to explain how HPWS impact important job categories and how employees holding these jobs "interact with the HR architecture [and] also the level of investment directed to the employees"

(Becker and Huselid, 2006, p. 918). Furthermore, SHRM research "needs to focus more heavily on the workforce component of the firm's strategic capabilities" (Becker and Huselid, 2006, p. 920). That is, a truly strategic HPWS allow organizations to invest resources in individual employees so that employee performance directly links to departmental productivity and then organizational financial performance. With the importance of the job of a nurse in predicting clinical and financial performance within health care organizations, it makes logical sense to examine how HPWS directly affect the mechanisms that increase nurse performance and turnover and how this then ties into the larger context of the organization.

From a practical standpoint in terms of decreasing nurse stress, burnout, and turnover, it stands to reason that health care organizations could in fact develop not just HPWS in general but develop stress reducing work systems (SRWS) that accomplish the same thing as HPWS but with the added benefit of reducing nurse stress and burnout along the way to reducing turnover and increasing performance. In the following section of this chapter, I outline just such a SRWS that includes job analysis, RJP, proper RN staffing ratios, multiple hurdle selection system, ELPs and formal socialization programs, objective performance assessment, job-based training, and progressive compensation systems. Two key elements of these systems are 1) the use of job analysis to integrate the discrete HRM functions into an interdependent system and 2) the conscious linkage of these interdependent systems to the health care organization's overall mission. While nursing researchers consistently note that a main cause of nurse stress is poor job design, SRWS begin with job analysis and function to the extent that health care organizations explicitly state that stress reduction is a crucial mission to the organization. These relatively simple yet organizationally powerful steps should then allow HRM practitioners to design SRWS that decrease nurse stress and burnout while also increasing nurse performance and retention. The effects of such a system would ripple throughout the organization.

There is evidence that health care organizations already understand the utility of SHRM systems. West, Guthrie, Dawson, Borrill, and Carter (2006) found that hospitals can increase beneficial clinical outcomes, such as heart attack survival rates, by increasing the effectiveness of their HRM systems. This research suggests that health care organizations can meet the needs of their patients, employees, and stakeholders by achieving strategic integration. The question is whether or not the unspecified "bundles" of HRM functions are also reducing stress. The purpose of the present chapter was to delineate a conceptual model of SRWS that could indeed achieve increased employee and health care organization performance and retention through decreasing stress. Much like most HRM problems, the solutions appear straightforward. Implementation becomes key.

STRESS REDUCING "BEST PRACTICES"

HRM scholars and practitioners have several stress reducing "best practices" that not only reduce stress, burnout, and turnover but also increase employee job performance. As seen in the nursing stress, burnout, and turnover literature, one of the fundamental causes of stress and burnout among nurses is poor job design. The HRM process of job or work analysis acts as the foundation to any HRM system (Sanchez and Levine, 2001), and if done properly a job or work analysis identifies two key sets of information that allow subsequent HRM functions to operate more efficiently: job description and work specification. A job description identifies the knowledge, skills, abilities, tasks, and functions associated with the job itself; whereas a job specification identifies the human competencies or capabilities required to perform the job as outlined in the job description (Sanchez and Levine, 2001). That is, a job description includes what is done in a job and a job specification includes what human capabilities or characteristics are needed to do that job. These two job or work analysis outcomes cannot be underestimated in their ability to reduce a host of adverse employee and organization outcomes (Sanchez and Levine, 2001). Much of the role stress that nurses experience could be solve through a simple job analysis; moreover, the identification of hidden or erroneous job duties creates a ripple that affects all other HRM functions. While these other HRM functions can also help reduce stress, burnout, and turnover, the process of defining the job and defining the qualities of the employee who will likely succeed in that job must come first. Moreover, the identification of job description and specification information that can be used for selection and training purposes can limit misfit in the demands-abilities dimension of PE Fit. That is, if health care organizations specify the job and the KSAs needed to perform in the job, they will likely hire nurses who fit the demands of the job; thus this initial HRM step potentially alleviates a great source of stress induced burnout and turnover.

In the realm of recruiting and staffing nurses, organizations should adopt two specific HRM practices that should reduce misfit induced nurse stress. First, as stress is created through PE misfit, organizations need awareness of what fit related messages, images, or signals that they send to prospective applications during the attraction phase of recruitment (Saks and Ashforth, 1997). Research conducted on unfulfilled employee expectations points to the early role of recruitment. Organizations begin to shape employee expectations during recruitment through the information transmitted to potential employees (Saks and Ashforth, 1997). Should the organization fail to meet these pre-hire set expectations post-hire, employees become frustrated, dissatisfied, less committed, stressed, burned out, and likely to turnover (Robinson and Rousseau, 1994). This almost sequential process (Demerouti, Bakker, Nachreiner, and Ebbinghaus, 2002), rooted in the violation of expectations, also deleteriously influences employee performance (Robinson and Rousseau, 1994). With this in mind, recruiting scholars point to the use of *realistic job previews* (RJPs) as an invaluable tool that inhibits the unmet expectation process. RJPs essentially give prospective employees as much information, positive and negative, about the job and the organization as possible (Wanous, 1992). While RJPs have been found to cause some otherwise qualified applicants to self select out of the recruitment process (Wanous, 1992), researchers consistently find that employees attracted to organizations through RJPs become more satisfied, more committed, less stressed, less burnout out, more likely to remain with the organization, and higher performing compared to those employees who do not receive RJP-type information during recruitment (Phillips, 1998). RJPs essentially set pre-hire PE fit expectations so that employees who do apply after receiving RJPs likely share the same values, goals, beliefs, KSAs, and preferences for working environment that exists in the organization (Dineen, Ash, and Noe, 2002). Thus, a recruiting tool like RJPs can limit the post-hire stress, burnout, and turnover caused by poor PE Fit.

Second, the issue of nurse staffing levels results in dramatic employee, patient, and organization consequences. Research on nursing staffing levels, relative to the ratio of RNs and licensed nurse practitioners (LPNs), suggests that there is an optimal ratio of RNs to

LPNs that increases positive patient outcomes, such as heart attack survival rates and pneumonia rates (Kovner, Jones, Zhan, Gergen, and Basu, 2002). This optimal ratio is pegged at roughly 6 to 1 (Kovner et al., 2002). Moreover, nursing research suggests that there is an optimal ratio of RNs to patients of about 3 to 1 (Person, Allison, Kiefe, Weaver, Williams, Centor, and Weissman, 2004). Using these two simple ratio analyses, health care organizations can adjust nursing staffing levels based upon the number of patients to provide the optimal number of nurses so that work overload can be reduced. An added benefit to these simple staffing ratios is that the RN to LPN optimal staffing ratio has been found to positively predict hospital productivity (average length of stay), patient health (heart attack survival rates), and hospital financial performance (Brown, 2006; Brown et al., 2003).

Ensuring proper PE Fit between the employee and the job falls not only upon conducting a job analysis but also on an organization selection or hiring processes. Organizations should keep two broad employee selection guidelines, which the United States Supreme Court established, in mind when hiring. First, all selection tests must be job-related, and this is accomplished through a proper job analysis (Sanchez and Levine, 2001). Second, all selection tests must exhibit *criterion validity*, which is to say that a selection must predict job performance (Salgado, Viswesvaran, and Ones, 2001). With these two broad guidelines in place and given the complexity of the nurse job, a fairly straightforward multiple hurdle selection system can be used that satisfied these guidelines with added benefit of increasing PE fit and thus reducing stress related burnout among nurses. IQ, which is defined as an individual's cognitive processing efficiency (Ree, Carretta, and Steindl, 2001), is the best predictor of performance in complex jobs and easily assessed via valid and reliable tests (Salgado et al., 2001). The personality trait of conscientiousness, which describes an individual who is internally motivated, dedicated, and detail oriented, is tested through brief tests and predicts a sizable amount of performance variability (Barrick and Mount, 1991). Emotional stability describes an individual who displays appropriate and fairly stable emotional responses to situations, and tests of this personality trait predict performance in jobs requiring an even emotional keel (Barrick and Mount, 1991). Lastly, while selection tests based upon PE fit have limited criterion validity (Arthur et al., 2006), research has linked PE misfit to stress and turnover (Edwards, 1996). Because interviews tend to predict more PE fit than performance (Salgado et al., 2001), HRM scholars often suggest that organizations limit their sole reliance upon interviewing as a means of selecting employees. However, in the context of nurses and stress, PE fit selection tests, including interviews aimed at assessing PE fit, relate to the job, predict limited job performance, but greatly reduces misfit that can lead to stress, burnout, and turnover (Kristof, 1996; Wheeler et al., 2005). Taken together, this multiple hurdle selection system should reduce nurse stress, burnout, and turnover through increased PE fit.

Once a nurse is hired, organizational socialization, training, performance management, and compensation systems can also reduce stress by increasing fit. Organizational socialization, during which an employee either formally or informally learns what it means to be a member of the organization, typically lasts about 12 – 18 months in duration (Bauer, Morrison, and Callister, 1998). Interestingly, the majority of employee turnover occurs during this time span, as employee pre-hire PE fit expectations are not met post-hire (Cable and Parsons, 2001). Not coincidentally, employees typically report the highest levels of stress and burnout during this time span, as well. Cable and Parsons (2001) found, however, that organizations could increase employee fit through providing employees with strong culture-related content and strong social networking opportunities during formal socialization programs. Similarly, Autry and Wheeler (2005) found that organizational socialization and training programs increased employee perceptions of fit with the job and organization. Some HRM scholars have even found that simply lowering employee expectations during formal socialization programs decreases turnover caused by unmet expectations. Buckley, Fedor, Veres, Wiese, and Carraher (1998) developed *expectation lowering procedures* (ELPs) that simply raise employee awareness of the consequences of inflated expectations. Without even mentioning company culture or job requirements, Buckley et al. (1998) found that ELPs deflate employee initial expectations about the organization and the job by reframing their expectations. The use of ELPs reduced post-hire turnover intentions and increased employee retention.

Stress reducing or stress coping training programs permeate the nursing literature. However, these training programs treat stress as a dispositional issue for employees. That is, these programs try to change employee patterns of behaviors or predetermined responses to stress. This view of stress reduction ignores the work and job contexts; many authors in the stress and burnout intervention literature have turned their emphasis to changing aspects of the environment rather than focusing on the person experiencing the stress (cf., Halbesleben, Osburn, and Mumford, 2006; LeBlanc and Schaufeli, 2008). While surely some employees possess personality traits more suited to coping with stressful jobs and environments, the environment or job itself can still cause stress. If the employee does not possess the requisite KSAs or qualifications to perform the job, that employee will become stressed and burned out regardless of his or her dispositional traits. Thus, for nurses it becomes increasingly important to ensure that nurses possess these requisite KSAs or qualifications. This can be accomplished through employee selection, training, or both. Furthermore, as nursing jobs become more complex through technological and medical advances, nurses need continual training to ensure that they possess the KSAs and qualifications needed to perform the job. Providing this type of support sends signals to employees that the organizations cares about employee well-being (Cropanzano and Mitchell, 2005), and these signals can reinforce employee perceptions of fit.

Performance management in and of itself creates stress (Gabris and Ihrke, 2001; Korsgaard and Roberson, 1995). Employees typically view performance feedback as a negative experience, especially given that employees tend to only receive negative performance feedback (Fedor, Buckley, and Eder, 1990). Moreover, if rater bias or favoritism enters the performance management process, employees develop cynical attitudes toward the process and perceive the process and organization as treating employees in an unfair manner (Tziner and Kopeland, 2002). However, an effective performance management program acts to develop employee KSAs, and thus reduce the PE misfit that can increase stress induced burnout and turnover. As such, organizations can develop more objective performance management systems, such as using behaviorally anchored rating scales combined with rater frame of reference training, to not only improve employee KSAs but also create an environment in which employees perceive that they are being treated fairly (Woehr and Huffcutt, 1994).

Lastly, organizations can gear compensation systems toward increasing PE fit. Much like the nursing training literature, the nursing compensation literature abounds with research that examines the outcomes of nursing compensation, mostly in terms of attracting, motivating, and retaining nurses (Buchan and Calman, 2004). However, aside from attraction, motivation, and retention, PE fit research suggests that employees become stressed in response to the lack of congruence between what employees need in terms of resources compared to what that organization offers (Van Vianen, 2000). This lack of fit extends beyond direct compensation to include incentives, benefits, and work-family balance issues (Van Vianen, 2000). Brown et al. (2003) found that hospitals use lead the market compensation strategies to attract much needed nurses; thus, nurses expect this level of direct compensation support (Upenieks, 2005) and quickly become discontent with their organization should they not receive prevailing market wages. As for indirect forms of compensation, many nurses experience a great amount of stress related to the work-family interface (Duffield, Pallas, and Aitken, 2004). Typically, health care organizations offer nurses compressed work week hours (Havlovic, Lau, and Pinfield, 2002); moreover, many organizations offer several compensatory benefits aimed directly at mitigating any non-work related stress from infiltrating into the job. These benefits include employee assistance programs (Gilbert, 1994), which include counseling, substance abuse, weight loss, adoption, and general wellness programs (Van Den Bergh, 2000).

CONCLUSION

Although reducing stress related burnout and turnover among nurses is complex and may seem a daunting problem to address, both macro and micro HRM scholars and practitioners have identified potential solutions to this problem. First and foremost, health care organizations must acknowledge that the solutions to this problem require more than simple one system solutions. The problem of nurse stress, burnout, and turnover requires an integrated systems solution. Health care organizations should include stress reduction as a platform in its mission and goals, as health care organizations cannot fully meet patient needs if its own strategically critical employees, such as nurses, are ailing from the stress caused by the very nature of these jobs, organizations, and occupations. Once health care organizations understand that their HRM systems can facilitate the meeting of organizational strategies and goals by linking its HRM functions to the organization's mission and by linking the discrete HRM functions together, the seemingly complex and daunting task of reducing nurse stress related burnout and turnover becomes more manageable. In this chapter, I have outlined how health care organizations can use its HRM systems to meet these goals and I have outlined why it is crucial that health care organizations endeavor this system-based solution.

REFERENCES

AbuAlRub, R.F. (2004). Job stress, job performance, and social support among hospital nurses. *Journal of Nursing Scholarship, 36*, 73-78.

Akerboom, S., and Maes, S. (2006). Beyond demand and control: The contribution of organizational risk factors in assessing the psychological well-being of health care employees. *Work and Stress, 20*, 21-36.

Arthur, J.B. (1994). Effects of human resource systems on manufacturing performance and turnover. *Academy of Management Journal, 37*, 670-687.

Arthur, W., Jr., Bell, S.T., Villado, A.J., and Doverspike, D.D. (2006). The use of person-organization fit in employment decision making: An assessment of its criterion-related validity. *Journal of Applied Psychology, 91*, 786-801.

Autry, C.A., Wheeler, A.R. (2005). Post-hire human resource management practices and person-organization fit: A study of warehouse employees. *Journal of Managerial Issues, 17*, 58-75.

Barney, J.B. (1991). Firm resources and sustained competitive advantage. *Journal of Management, 17*, 9-120.

Barrick, M.R., and Mount, M.K. (1991). The Big Five personality dimensions and job performance: A meta-analysis. *Personnel Psychology, 44*, 1-26.

Bauer, T. N., Morrison, E.W., and Callister, R.R. (1998). Organizational socialization: A review and directions for future research. In G.R. Ferris (Ed.), *Research in Personnel and Human Resource Management, Vol.* 6 (pp.149-214), Greenwich, CT: Elsevier Science/JAI Press.

Becker, B.E., and Huselid, M.A. (2006). Strategic human resource management: Where do we go from here? *Journal of Management, 32*, 898-925.

Brown, M. P. (2006). The effect of nursing professional pay structures and pay levels on hospitals' heart attack outcomes. *Health Care Management Review, 31*(3), 1-10.

Brown, M.P., Sturman, M.C., and Simmering, M.J. (2003). Compensation policy and organizational performance: The efficiency, operational, and financial implications of pay levels and pay structure. *Academy of Management Journal, 46*, 752-762.

Boxall, P. (1996). The strategic HRM debate and the resource-based view of the firm. *Human Resource Management Journal, 6*, 59-75.

Buchan, J. (1999). Still attractive after all these years? Magnet hospitals in a changing health care environment. *Journal of Advanced Nursing, 30*, 100-108.

Buchan, J., and Calman, L. (2004). *The global shortage of registered nurses: An overview of issues and actions*. Geneva: International Council of Nurses.

Buckley, M.R., Fedor, D.B., Veres, J.G., Wiese, D.S., and Carraher, S.M. (1998). Investigating newcomer expectations and job-related outcomes. *Journal of Applied Psychology, 83*, 452-461.

Cable, D.M., and Parsons, C.K. (2001). Socialization tactics and person-organization fit. *Personnel Psychology, 54*, 1-23.

Caldwell, D.F., and O'Reilly, C.A. III (1990). Measuring person-job fit with a profile comparison process. *Journal of Applied Psychology, 75*, 648-657.

Chatman, J. (1989). Improving interactional organizational research: A model of person-organization fit. *Academy of Management Review, 14*, 333-349.

Cropanzano, R., and Mitchell, M.S. (2005). Social exchange theory: An interdisciplinary review. *Journal of Management, 31*, 874-900.

Demerouti, E., Bakker, A.B., Nachreiner, F., and Ebbinghaus, M. (2002). From mental strain to burnout. *European Journal of Work and Organizational Psychology, 11*, 423-441.

Dineen, B.R., Ash, S.R., and Noe, R.A. (2002). A web of applicant attraction: Person-organization fit in the context of web-based recruitment. *Journal of Applied Psychology, 87*, 723-734.

Duffield, C., Pallas, L.O., and Aitken, L.M. (2004). Nurses who work outside of nursing. *Journal of Advanced Nursing, 47*, 664-671.

Edward, K.L., and Hercelinskyj, G. (2007). Burnout in the caring nurse: Learning resilient behaviors. *British Journal of Nursing, 16*, 240-242.

Edwards, J.A., Guppy, A., and Cockerton, T. (2007). A longitudinal study exploring the relationships between occupational stressors, non-work stressors, and work performance. *Work and Stress, 21*, 99-116.

Edwards, J.R. (1996). An examination of competing versions of the person-environment fit approach to stress. *Academy of Management Journal, 39*, 292-339.

Edwards, J. R. (1992). A cybernetic theory of stress, coping, and well-being in organizations. *Academy of Management Review, 17,* 238-274.

Edwards, J.R. (1991). Person-job fit: A conceptual integration, literature review, and methodological critique. In C.L. Copper and I.T. Robertson (Eds.), *International review of industrial/organizational psychology* (Vol. 6, pp. 283-357). London: Wiley.

Fedor, D.B., Buckley, M.R., and Eder, R.W. (1990). Measuring subordinate perceptions of supervisor feedback intentions: Some unsettling results. *Educational and Psychological Measurement, 50*, 73-89.

Furnham, A. (2001). Vocational preference and P-O fit: Reflections on Holland's theory of vocational choice. *Applied Psychology: An International Review, 50*, 5-29.

Gabris, G.T., and Ihrke, D.M. (2001). Does performance appraisal contribute to heightened levels of employee burnout? The results of one study. *Public Personnel Management, 30*, 157-172.

Gelsema, T.I., Van Der Doef, M., Maes, S., Janssen, M., Akerboom, S., and Verhoeven, C. (2006). A longitudinal study of job stress in the nursing profession: Causes and consequences. *Journal of Nursing Management, 14*, 289-299.

Gilbert, B. (1994). Employee assistance programs: History and program description. *American Association of Occupational Health Nurses Journal, 42*, 488-493.

Halbesleben, J. R. B., Osburn, H. K., and Mumford, M. D. (2006). Action research as a burnout Intervention: Reducing burnout in the Federal Fire Service. *Journal of Applied Behavioral Science, 42*, 244-266.

Havlovic, S.J., Lau, D.C., and Pinfield, L.T. (2002). Repercussions of work schedule congruence among full-time, part-time, and contingent nurses. *Health Care Management Review, 27*, 30-41.

Holland, J.L. (1985). *Making vocational choices: A theory of careers* (2nd ed.). Englewood Cliffs, NJ: Prentice-Hall.

Huselid, M.A. (1995). The impact of human resource management practices on turnover, productivity, and corporate financial performance. *Academy of Management Journal, 38*, 635-672.

Janiszewski Goodin, H. (2003). The nursing shortage in the United States of America: An integrative review of the literature. *Journal of Advanced Nursing, 43*, 335-350.

Jenkins, R., and Elliot, P. (2004). Stressors, burnout, and social support: Nurses in acute mental health settings. *Journal of Advanced Nursing, 48*, 622-631.

Kaye, B., and Jordan-Evans, S. (2001). Retaining key employees. *Public Management, 83*, 6-12.

Korsgaard, A.M., and Roberson, L. (1995). Procedural justice in performance evaluation: The role of instrumental and non-instrumental voice in performance appraisal discussions. *Journal of Management, 21*, 657-669.

Kovner, C., Jones, C., Zhan, C., Gergen, P.J., and Basu, J. (2002) Nurse staffing and postsurgical adverse events: An analysis of administrative data from a sample of U.S. hospitals, 1990-1996. *Health Services Research, 37*, 611-629.

Kristof, A.L. (1996). Person-organization fit: An integrative review of its conceptualizations, measurement, and implications. *Personnel Psychology, 49*, 1-49.

Lado, A.A., and Wilson, M.C. (1994). Human resource systems and sustained competitive advantage: A competency-based perspective. *Academy of Management Review, 19*, 699-727.

LeBlanc, P. M., and Schaufeli, W. B. (2008). Burnout interventions: An overview and illustration. In J. R. B. Halbesleben (Ed.). *Handbook of stress and burnout in health care.* Hauppauge, NY: Nova Science.

Lepak, D.P., and Snell, S.A. (2002). Examining the human resource architecture: The relationships among human capital, employment, and human resource configurations. *Journal of Management, 28*, 517-543.

Lucero, R.J., and Sousa, K.H. (2006). Participation and change in the nurse work environment. *Journal of Rogerian Nursing Science, 14*, 48-59.

Makinen, A., Kivimaki, Elovainio, M., and Virtanen, M. (2003). Organization of nursing care and stressful work characteristics. *Journal of Advanced Nursing, 43*, 197-205.

Person, S.D., Allison, J.J., Kiefe, C.I., Weaver, M.T., Williams, O.D., Centor, R.M., and Weissman, N.W. (2004). Nurse staffing and mortality for Medicare patients with acute myocardial infarction. *Medical Care, 42*, 4-12.

Peterson, C.A. (2001). In short supply: Around the world, the need grows. *American Journal of Nursing, 101*, 61-64.

Phillips, J.M. (1998). Effects of realistic job previews on multiple organizational outcomes: A Meta-analysis. *Academy of Management Journal, 41*, 673-690.

Quick, J.C., Nelson, D.L., Quick, J.D., and Orman, D.K. (2001). An isomorphic theory of stress: The dynamics of person-environment fit. *Stress and Health: Journal of the International Society for the Investigation of Stress, 17*, 147-157.

Ree, M.J., Carreta, T.R., and Steindl, J.R. (2001). Cognitive ability. In N. Anderson, D.S. Ones, H.K. Sinangil, and C. Viswesvaran (Eds.), *Handbook of Industrial, Work, and Organizational Psychology, Vol. 1 Personnel Psychology* (pp.219-232), Thousand Oaks, CA: Sage Publications.

Robinson, S.L., and Rousseau, D.M. (1994). Violating the psychological contract: Not the exception but the norm. *Journal of Organizational Behavior, 15*, 245-259.

Saks, A.M. and Ashforth, B.E. (1997). A longitudinal investigation of the relationship between job information sources, applicant perceptions of fit, and work outcomes. *Personnel Psychology, 50*, 395-426.

Salgado, J.F., Viswesvaran, C., Ones, D.S. (2001). Predictors used for personnel selection: An overview of constructs, methods and techniques. In N. Anderson, D.S. Ones, H.K. Sinangil, and C. Viswesvaran (Eds.), *Handbook of Industrial, Work, and Organizational Psychology, Vol. 1 Personnel Psychology* (pp.165-199), Thousand Oaks, CA: Sage Publications.

Sanchez, J.I., and Levine, E.L. (2001). The analysis of work in the 20th and 21st centuries. In N. Anderson, D.S. Ones, H.K. Sinangil, and C. Viswesvaran (Eds.), *Handbook of Industrial, Work, and Organizational Psychology, Vol. 1 Personnel Psychology* (pp.71-89), Thousand Oaks, CA: Sage Publications.

Seago, J.A., and Ash, M. 2004. .The effect of registered nurses' unions on heart-attack mortality *Industrial and Labor Relations Review, 57,* 422–442.

Schonfeld, I.S., and Rindskopf, D. (2007). Hierarchical linear modeling in organizational research: Longitudinal data outside the context of growth modeling. *Organizational Research Methods, 10,* 417-429.

Shi, L., and Singh, D. A. (2004). *Delivering health care in America: A systems approach.* Sudbury, MA: Jones and Bartlett.

Tabak, N., and Orit, K. (2007). Relationships between how nurses resolve their conflicts with doctors, their stress, and their job satisfaction. *Journal of Nursing Management, 15,* 321-331.

Tziner, A, and Kopeland, R.E. (2002). Is there a preferred performance rating format?: A non-psychometric perspective. *Applied Psychology: An International Review, 51,* 479-503.

Upenieks, V. (2005). Recruitment and retention strategies: A magnet hospital prevention model. *Nursing Economic$, 21,* 7-13.

Van Den Bergh, N. (2000). Where have we been? Where are we going?: Employee assistance practice in the 21st century. *Employee Assistance Quarterly, 16,* 1-13.

Van Vianen, A.E.M. (2000). Person-organization fit: The match between newcomers' and recruiters' preferences for organizational culture. *Personnel Psychology, 53,* 113-149.

Wanous, J.P. (1992) *Organizational entry.* Reading, MA: Addison-Wesley.

West, M.A., Guthrie, J.P., Dawson, J.F., Borrill, C.S., and Carter, M. (2006). Reducing patient mortality in hospitals: The role of human resource management. *Journal of Organizational Behavior, 27,* 983-1002.

Weyers, S., Peter, R., Boggild, Jeppesen, H.J., and Siegrist, J. (2006). Psychosocial work stress is associated with poor self-rated health in Danish nurses: A test of the effort-reward imbalance model. *Scandinavian Journal of Caring Sciences, 20,* 26-34.

Wheeler, A.R., Buckley, M.R., Halbesleben, J.R., Brouer, R.L., and Ferris, G.R. 2005. "The elusive criterion of fit" revisited: Toward an integrative theory of MDF. In J. Martocchio (Ed.), *Research in Personnel and Human Resource Management* (pp. 265-304), *24,* Greenwich, CT: Elsevier/JAI Press.

Woehr, D.J., and Huffcutt, A.I. (1994). Rater training for performance appraisal: A quantitative review. *Journal Occupational and Organizational Psychology, 67,* 189-205.

Xianyu, Y., and Lambert, V.A. (2006). Investigation of the relationship among workplace stressors, ways of coping, and mental health of Chinese head nurses. *Nursing and Health Sciences, 8,* 147-155.

In: Handbook of Stress and Burnout in Health Care ISBN 978-1-60456-500-3
Editor: Jonathon R. B. Halbesleben © 2008 Nova Science Publishers, Inc.

Chapter 15

BURNOUT INTERVENTIONS: AN OVERVIEW AND ILLUSTRATION

Pascale M. Le Blanc and Wilmar B. Schaufeli
Utrecht University, Department of Social and Organizational Psychology

INTRODUCTION

Over the past decades, the level of job stress and burnout has risen alarmingly worldwide. In the 2000 European Working Conditions Survey (EWCS), job stress was found to be the second most common job-related problem (28%) across the EU Member States (Houtman, 2005). Burnout, a form of chronic job stress, is significantly related to negative outcomes for the individual worker, e.g., depression and psychosomatic distress (Schaufeli and Enzmann, 1998), and for the organization, including absenteeism, turnover, and lowered productivity (Cordes and Dougherty, 1993; Lee and Ashforth, 1996; Schaufeli and Buunk, 2003). The associated costs are high. For example, stress and burnout account for 300 million lost working days and cost American businesses an estimated $300 billion per year (American Institute of Stress, 2002, in Halbesleben, Osburn and Mumford, 2006). So, from the individual, the organizational and the social point of view, efforts to combat (chronic) job stress are urgently needed.

A sector in which workers are most at risk of experiencing job stress and burnout are the so-called human services - such as health care, social services, and education - in which contact with other people plays a central role (Houtman, 2005). Next to stressors that are common to workers in other sectors (e.g., high workload, lack of autonomy), human service providers are confronted with (emotional) stressors that are inherent to the direct interaction with individual patients, clients or pupils. Examples of this type of stressor are patients' pain and suffering, or pupils' aggressive behaviours (Dollard et al., 2003). As the number of workers that are employed in the human services is rapidly growing, studies that yield more insight into ways to prevent or alleviate chronic forms of job stress such as burnout seem especially relevant to this sector. In this chapter, the current research on burnout interventions is summarized, followed by an illustration of a burnout intervention program that was implemented in Dutch hospitals among oncology care providers.

BURNOUT INTERVENTIONS

Despite the relevance of the subject, relatively few well-designed scientific studies have been conducted on the effectiveness of burnout intervention programs. Generally speaking, burnout interventions focus on changing either individual workers or the workplace (Schaufeli and Buunk, 2003). In the following sections, we will first review some research findings on the effectiveness of different types of burnout intervention strategies, followed by a more detailed discussion of a methodology that, in our view, holds promise for burnout intervention, i.e. action research.

Individual Approaches

Even though almost every author on the subject acknowledges that a combination of individual and workplace approaches is likely to be most effective, the vast majority of burnout interventions have been conducted on the individual level (Schaufeli and Buunk, 2003). A recent study in a nationally representative Finnish sample of 3276 employees (Ahola et al, 2007) indeed showed that employees with burnout were less often targets of occupational interventions but participated more in individual-focused interventions when compared with other employees.

Most individual level strategies that are aimed at reducing burnout are well established and have a long and successful history in clinical or health psychology. However, they are often rather general in nature, focusing on managing stress per se rather than combating burnout in particular. Principally, these strategies seek either to increase workers' awareness, or to reduce the high level of (negative) arousal that characterizes stress in general. Examples of awareness-enhancing strategies are: self-monitoring of signs and symptoms of distress, self-assessment of one's personal level of stress or burnout, and didactic stress management providing practical information on (ways of coping with) stress and burnout. Frequently used strategies to reduce negative arousal are: relaxation techniques, promotion of a healthy lifestyle (e.g., physical training), and cognitive-behavioral techniques (e.g., stress inoculation training, rational emotive therapy, cognitive restructuring, and behavioral rehearsal). The latter strategies are particularly relevant, because burnout often includes 'wrong' cognitions such as unrealistic expectations and false hopes (Schaufeli and Enzmann, 1998; Schaufeli and Buunk, 2003).

For some of these individual level strategies, empirical evidence for their effectiveness in reducing burnout has indeed been found. Several studies demonstrated that *skills training*, for example in the form of stress inoculation training (Meichenbaum, 1985), may lead to a reduction in burnout levels by altering the way the individual processes information about stressful situations and identifying cognitive and behavioral coping skills to change unproductive ways of reacting. For example, Freedy and Hobfoll (1994) enhanced nurses' coping skills by teaching them how to use their social support and individual mastery resources, and found a significant reduction in emotional exhaustion in the training group as compared to the non-treated control group after the 5-weeks intervention period. In another study by West, Horan and Games (1984), several coping skills were taught to nurses simultaneously (i.e., relaxation, assertiveness, cognitive restructuring, and time management) which resulted in a significant reduction of emotional exhaustion and an increase in personal accomplishment at the 4-month follow-up. Higgins (1986) showed that learning palliative coping skills (i.e., progressive relaxation and systematic desensitization) was as effective as cognitive and behavioral skills training (i.e., time management, assertiveness training, and rational emotive therapy) in reducing levels of emotional exhaustion among a sample of working women from various helping professions. The same result was found by Van Rhenen et al. (2001), who compared the short- and long-term effectiveness of two brief (i.e., 4 sessions) intervention programs among a sample of Dutch telecommunication workers. One program was cognition-focused, aiming at restructuring irrational beliefs, whereas the other program was physically oriented, aiming at introducing physical and relaxation exercises in daily work activities. Their results showed that both types of interventions were equally effective, revealing a positive impact on burnout scores at short term as well as at 6-month follow up. A study by Corcoran and Bryce (1983) on the effectiveness of interpersonal skills training for social workers, demonstrated that focusing on affective components (i.e., reflective listening, personalization, and empathy) led to a significant decrease in feelings of emotional exhaustion, whereas focusing on cognitive components (i.e., open ended questioning, reflection of feelings, paraphrasing, and summarizing) did not. Finally, Rowe (2000) found that a program in which health care providers were taught proactive coping skills (i.e., using problem-focused strategies for solvable problems and emotion-focused strategies for problems where solutions are not readily available) was effective in reducing feelings of emotional exhaustion and increasing feelings of personal accomplishment. However, subjects who participated in the 6-weeks program reported only temporary decreases in burnout, while those subjects who also received 1-hour refresher sessions at 5, 11, and 17 months showed consistent decreases in burnout across a 2 ½ year period.

In so-called *burnout workshops*, several of the above-mentioned strategies are combined into a comprehensive program. Usually, these workshops rest on two pillars, i.e. increasing participants' awareness of their work-related problems and enhancing their coping resources, e.g. by cognitive and behavioral skills training (Schaufeli and Enzmann, 1998). Pines and Aronson (1983) evaluated a 1-day burnout workshop for employees of two social services that included several individual level strategies: relaxation techniques, cognitive stress management, time management, social skills training, didactic stress management and attitude change. Even though the decrease in participants' level of exhaustion was not significant, satisfaction with co-workers went up significantly in the training group as compared to the control group that did not participate in the workshop. This impact of the workshop was even observable after 6 months. However, when evaluating a similar 3-day workshop for community nurses, Schaufeli (1995) did find a significant decrease in participants' levels of exhaustion, but not in the other two, attitudinal components of burnout (i.e., depersonalization and reduced personal accomplishment) at the 1-month follow-up. These results are in line with those of Enzmann et al. (1992) who evaluated a 3-day burnout workshop for human services professionals (mostly hospice staff) that was spread across 3 weekly intervals. Participants kept a stress diary, had to use their newly developed cognitive and behavioral skills during the weekly intervals, and had to report on their last week's experiences in the next session. The workshop included didactic stress management, relaxation training, coping skills training and interpersonal skills training. At the 2-month follow-up, only levels of emotional exhaustion were significantly lower in the training group as compared to the non-treated control group. Finally, Van Dierendonck, Schaufeli and Buunk (1996) evaluated a cognitive-behaviorally oriented burnout workshop for staff working in direct care for mentally disabled persons that included strategies such as cognitive restructuring, didactic stress management, and relaxation. In addition, a strong emphasis was put on career management, by letting participants analyze their strengths and weaknesses and draw up action plans for the future. After 6 months and 1 year, respectively, follow-up meetings were organized to evaluate these plans. Results showed that participants' level of emotional exhaustion dropped significantly compared to two non-treated control groups, i.e. an internal control group consisting of staff members from the same organization and an external control group consisting of staff members from another, similar organization. However, again, no effects were observed for depersonalization and reduced personal accomplishment.

It can be concluded that the empirical support for the effectiveness of individual level, cognitive-behavioral based burnout interventions – both in isolation and combined in multifaceted workshops – is generally quite strong. However, in most cases, only the core affective symptom of burnout (i.e., exhaustion) is reduced, whereas the other two burnout dimensions are rarely affected. This is not surprising since most techniques that are employed are aimed at reducing negative arousal and not – or to a much lesser extent - at changing attitudes or enhancing professional skills or resources (Schaufeli, 2003). An additional concern is that these programs "do little to change environmental stressors" (Cartwright and Cooper 2005, p.618, in Halbesleben et al., 2006), and as such do not address the underlying cause of the burnout and subsequently do little to actually reduce burnout itself. According to several scholars in the field of burnout (e.g., Golembiewski and Boss, 1992; Maslach, Leiter and Schaufeli, 2001; Halbesleben and Buckley, 2004), a more promising approach to the reduction of burnout is to attempt to make changes in the work environment, as this has a better chance of relieving stress and burnout for employees on a more widespread basis.

Organizational (Workplace) Approaches

There are both philosophical and pragmatic reasons underlying the predominant focus on the individual in burnout intervention, including notions of individual causality and responsibility, and the assumption that it is easier and cheaper to change people than organizations (Maslach and Goldberg, 1998). Nevertheless, this focus on individual-centered solutions is particularly paradoxical, given that the majority of the scientific research has found that social and organizational factors play a much larger role in (the development of) burnout than do individual factors (Maslach, et al., 2001; Schaufeli and Buunk, 2003). Up till now, very little attention has been paid to situational or organizational strategies for burnout prevention; in particular, situational strategies that are geared toward eliminating or modifying work stressors are seldom implemented. This might be due partly to the fact that this kind of organizational interventions are complex because many different people at different levels of the organization are involved and considerable time, effort and money are needed (Maslach et al., 2001). As a result, workplace burnout interventions are even less specifically described in the literature than are individual approaches (Schaufeli and Buunk, 2003).

Job redesign (i.e., job enlargement, job rotation, and job enrichment) is generally considered as a major tool to decrease workload, and thus counteract burnout. Berg, Welander-Hansson and Hallberg (1994) studied the effects of introducing individually planned nursing care – a form of job enrichment – in a Swedish psychogeriatric clinic and found that at 1-year follow up burnout levels of nurses in the experimental wards had dropped significantly compared to the traditional control wards. However, two Dutch studies on job redesign in nursing found less positive effects on burnout. In the first study by Melchior et al. (1996), burnout levels of a group of psychiatric nurses working according to primary nursing (i.e., similar nursing principles as in the Swedish study) were compared with those of a control group that kept on working in the traditional way. During the 2 ½ -years period of this study, no differences in burnout levels between the two groups could be demonstrated. In the other study by Jansen (1996) among community nurses and nurses aides, the introduction of either differentiated practice (i.e., assignment of patients based on complexity of nursing care) or specialization (i.e., assignment of patients based on area of expertise) actually lead to an increase in burnout levels over a 1-year period. The author speculated that that the introduction of these two systems might have lead to an increase in workload, because management had put more emphasis on productivity and efficiency.

Some other programs have focused on co-worker *support* as a key to burnout intervention. Already in 1978, Maslach found that burnout rates were lower in health care workers who actively expressed, analyzed, and shared their personal feelings with their colleagues, e.g. during so-called staff support group-meetings. This interaction between co-workers may also contribute to problem solving by yielding new perspectives on and solutions to job-related problems. However, the empirical evidence on the effectiveness of these peer-support groups is mixed. Studies by Brown (1984) and by Larson (1986) showed that nurses and oncology and hospice workers respectively, who participated in support groups were more satisfied with their supervisors and co-workers. However, their burnout levels were not reduced. On the other hand, in a study among special educators, Cooley and Yovanoff (1996) found that the combination of a 1-month peer-support collaboration program and a stress management workshop lead to significant reductions in levels of emotional exhaustion and depersonalization. These effects were still observable at 6-months and 1-year follow-ups. Finally, Rabinowitz, Kushnir and Ribak (1996) studied the effects of fortnightly Balint groups for nurses, in which they discussed patients about whom they felt concerned and aspects of their work that they found personally troubling. Results showed that nurses who participated in these groups for 10 months displayed less emotional exhaustion at the end of the course.

Another organizational approach to burnout intervention is *career counseling*, since feelings of being 'locked in' to your career can be conducive to burnout (Schaufeli and Buunk, 2003). Gorter et al. (2001) indeed demonstrated that a cognitive-behavioral career counseling program for dentists resulted in statistically significant improvements on both emotional exhaustion and personal accomplishment one month after the program ended. However, dentists in the control group who had self-initiated preventative measures - based on information about their burnout-scores - showed similar improvements. Moreover, at the 1-year follow-up, the program participants showed a relapse, whereas the controls who took action on their own initiative reported a beneficial effect in the long run as well (Te Brake et al., 2001). The authors speculated that perhaps the latter group might have had a more intrinsic motivation for change and/or a heightened perception of being able to control (i.e., adapt) the working environment. Van Dierendonk, Garssen and Visser (2005) showed that a 10-day transpersonal, psychosynthesis-based intervention program was effective in reducing feelings of exhaustion and increasing professional efficacy among mid-career employees who were at risk for burnout. This program focused on personal growth, by exploring the structure of one's own psyche followed by an integration of its components into a harmonious, integrated whole. Participants were trained in self-acceptance, taking responsibility for their (working) lives, and trusting their 'inner wisdom'. In this way, meaning and purpose in life were (re)discovered, and participants' ability to choose behavior that is in line with their work-related goals and expectations was strengthened.

Finally, in the burnout literature, some empirical evidence on the effectiveness of *Organizational Development* (OD), i.e. a program of planned interventions that should improve the internal operation of an organization, can be found. For example, Golembiewski and Rountree (1991) described an OD program that was carried out in a chain of nursing homes to – amongst others – reduce burnout by releasing human potential for collaboration. In the five experimental homes, pairs of directors of nursing and chief executive officers received a 2 ½-day intensive training in team-building. After 1 year, the levels of burnout in the experimental pairs had dropped significantly compared to five matched pairs from other homes who didn't participate in the training.

So, although organizational interventions do seem to have great potential value for burnout intervention, more high-quality research to firmly establish their effectiveness is clearly needed. In addition, it is rather difficult to draw general conclusions about the effectiveness of specific burnout interventions based on the studies that were discussed in this and in the previous section. As these studies use different samples, procedures, time frames, measurement instruments and intervention methods, results are difficult to compare. In addition, some of these studies suffer from methodological inadequacies such as the lack of control groups and small numbers of participants (Schaufeli and Buunk, 2003). Perhaps the only conclusion that is (re)confirmed is that neither changing the workplace, nor changing the individual workers is enough; effective change occurs when both develop in an integrated fashion (cf. Maslach et al., 2001). A methodology to achieve this goal is offered by action research, which we will discuss in more detail in the following section.

Action Research

According to Halbesleben et al. (2006), perhaps the most significant limitation of organizational burnout intervention programs is that they tend to seek out universal solutions for organizational issues without taking into account the significant variety of stressors that may lead to burnout and the uniqueness of stressors that appear in any one organization. Moreover, some experts in the field of worksite stress management (e.g. Griffiths, 1999; Semmer, 2003) argue that organizational interventions designed to promote health and well-being can only be effective if they are based on workers' own experience and active participation. What is needed is a framework that does not include universal solutions for burnout, but one that helps determine the *specific* causes of burnout in a *specific* organization and allows organizational stakeholders to develop tailor-made interventions based on those organization-specific causes of burnout (Halbesleben et al., 2006). (*Participatory*) *action research,* i.e. an empirical and reflective process by which traditional research participants are engaged in a participative fashion to work towards a positive, practical outcome (Stringer, 1999), is based on this principle. It takes workers' (view of their) specific situation as a starting point and grants control over the design and the implementation of interventions that are part of the research to them as well. So, instead of treating participants as objects of intervention, in action research participants are the subjects of the change process thereby integrating theory and practice. Workers collaborate with expert researchers in identifying problems (e.g., job stressors) that are typical for their working situation and in developing, implementing, and evaluating plans to tackle them. In this way, the capability of teams or work groups to solve self-identified problems (Hughes, 2003) is increased as workers (re)gain job control.

Results of scientific studies evaluating the effects of action research approaches showed that these have been effective in e.g. decreasing depressive symptoms (Heany et al., 1993), registered absenteeism (Munz, Kohler and Greenberg, 2001; Van Gorp and Schaufeli, 1996), psychosomatic complaints (Van Gorp and Schaufeli, 1996), and work-related stress (Mikkelsen, Saksvik and Landsbergis, 2000), as well as in increasing work-unit performance (Munz et al., 2001). Moreover, already in 1986, this kind of approach was specifically recommended for burnout intervention by Golembiewski, Munzenrider and Stevenson, because it allows employees with a common history to solve problems specific to their own stressful environment. In a study by Halbesleben et al. (2006) among employees of the U.S. Federal Fire Service, the efficacy of this approach for reducing burnout was empirically demonstrated. In addition to giving a detailed description of the research process, this study evaluated the effectiveness of the action research intervention on burnout. Survey results indicated that employees were experiencing significantly less exhaustion and disengagement one year following the conclusion of the project compared to the situation prior to its implementation. The results of a Finnish study among female white-collar rehabilitation clients, showed that a new, participatory strategy was effective in reducing burnout, i.e. feelings of exhaustion and cynicism, during the 1-year rehabilitation period whereas the traditional strategy was not (Hätinen, Kinnunen, Pekkonen and Kalimo, 2007). Increased job control was identified as the mediator of change. Finally, another recent Finnish study provides some empirical evidence for the usefulness of this kind of approach to burnout intervention at the micro-level (i.e., the individual worker) as well. Salmela-Aro, Nataanen and Nurmi (2004) showed that two types of psychotherapeutic interventions were able to cause major changes in participants' so-called work-related personal projects (i.e., changes in project-related emotions and action tendencies and in project-related progress). In turn, over time, a reduction in negative emotions related to these personal projects was found to be related to a decrease in burnout levels.

In the final part of this chapter, we would like to present our own recent research on a participatory action research program, entitled Take Care!, that was implemented among oncology care providers working in general hospitals in the Netherlands (De Geus, Van Son, Le Blanc and Schaufeli, 2000; Le Blanc, Hox, Schaufeli, Taris and Peeters, 2007). Next to a description of the contents of the program, its effectiveness - in terms of changes in staff burnout levels – is evaluated. The chapter is concluded with some recommendations for future action (research).

Take Care!: A team-based burnout intervention program for oncology care providers.

Our burnout intervention program was especially geared to oncology care providers - i.e. nurses, physicians and radiotherapy assistants working in direct care of cancer patients - whose jobs can be considered quite stressful (Le Blanc et al., 2001; Le Blanc and Schaufeli, 2003). Because of the emotionally demanding nature of their jobs, oncology care providers can be expected to run a relatively high risk to deplete their (emotional) energy, and consequently to 'burn out'. The results of a preceding, nationwide questionnaire survey among members of five professional associations of Dutch oncology care providers ($n = 816$) indeed showed that they scored significantly higher on each of the two core burnout dimensions (emotional exhaustion and depersonalization) compared with norm-scores for Dutch health care providers. In addition, the quality of the working relationships with colleagues turned out to be of great importance for the well being of care providers in oncology (Le Blanc and Schaufeli, 2003). Therefore, we decided to focus our intervention on the *work-group, i.e. team,* level.

Participants

In total, 260 care providers working in 9 different oncology wards (teams) from 9 different general hospitals in the Netherlands were approached for participation in the intervention program. Participation in the program was voluntary, however, as the focus of the program was at the team level, as many staff members as possible were recruited. Participation rates across the staff of each of the 9 wards varied from 80 to 100 per cent (the number of participants per ward varied from 14 to 43 workers). Participants' mean age was 36 year, 72 per cent of them were females and on average they were working for almost 10 years in oncology. The control group consisted of a comparable sample of 404 care providers (working in 20 different oncology wards) who did not receive any training.

A Stepwise Approach

The intervention program Take Care! (De Geus et al., 2000; Le Blanc et al., 2007), was developed by researchers from Utrecht University in close collaboration with two experienced team counselors. In developing the program, the 'best practice' recommendations of Kompier and Cooper (1999) were used as a guideline. Before the program started, a detailed questionnaire survey on participants' (perceptions of their) working situation and well-being (Time 1 measurement) was performed, as one is poorly equipped to design a comprehensive intervention that targets occupation-specific stressors without an accurate assessment. To ensure lasting effects of the program, management support was acquired by means of extensive intake interviews, and a systematic and stepwise approach that was based on the principles of action research methodology (worker participation and control) was adopted.

The Take Care! program was designed following the six steps of a systematic intervention trajectory described by Janssen, Nijhuis, Lourijsen and Schaufeli (1996). As already mentioned, before an intervention program is started, attention should be paid to creating support within the organization. Even if an organization (i.e., the management) decided to participate in an intervention program, this does not automatically imply that employees have been consulted and that they are eager to participate. Actually, it is not unusual that employees have an aversion towards – yet another - intervention program! Therefore, the team counselors held extensive intake interviews with the management - e.g., head nurses, coordinators, and team leaders - of all wards (i.e., teams) where the Take Care! program was to be implemented. During these meetings, the protocol of the intervention was clarified, and potential effects of the intervention ('benefits') were discussed. The counselors also inquired after the ward management's reasons to participate in the intervention program, their main objectives, and their criteria for the successfulness of the intervention. Moreover, they gathered information on the structure and policies of the larger (i.e., hospital) organization. Finally, the ward management's perception of the working situation, including the main sources of job stress, was discussed. By means of this extensive intake procedure, the team counselors tried to increase the ward management's motivation for the implementation of organizational change processes. In addition, the team counselors performed a detailed review of documents (e.g., annual reports, policy memos, info-leaflets and newsletters) to get a clear picture of the 'status quo' in the participating hospitals.

Next, so-called kick-off meetings were organized for the entire teams of each of the 9 wards in which the program was to be implemented. During these meetings, the team counselors presented the protocol of the intervention program. In addition, a university researcher explained the design of the study that would be conducted in order to evaluate the short- and long-term effects of the Take Care! program on staff burnout levels. Staff was encouraged to ask questions. The main aim of these meetings was to increase staff's commitment to participate and to promote positive attitudes towards the program. In addition, these meetings should provide staff with a realistic picture of potential outcomes (effects) of the program.

For each ward, the information that was gathered during the intakes and the kick-off meetings was written down in a so-called take off-document, which was the first in a series of reports about the planning, progress and results of the program. Together, these reports formed a log-book on the intervention process, which was also used to keep all participants informed during the periods in between the training sessions. After the last training session, the team counselors wrote a final report with guidelines for the continuation of the change processes by the participating wards themselves.

The training program itself consisted of 6 monthly sessions of 3 hours each, and will be described in more detail in the following paragraph. The sessions were run for each of the 9 wards separately, so in total, the program consisted of 36 (9x6) sessions. The sessions were facilitated in several ways by the wards' management. Meeting rooms (outside the wards themselves) were booked and catering arrangements for the participants were made. Moreover, in between the training sessions, the topics that were discussed during the latest session and the plans and agreements that were made were put as items on the agenda of the work-meetings of the respective wards.

The Training Program

The framework for the training program was a classification scheme for the analysis of organizational problems that has been developed by one of the team counselors (De Geus and Brakel, 1996). This framework includes four categories of 'causal factors' that can be related to (the level of) staff well-being, i.e. external factors (i.e. factors outside the organization), organizational factors, job-related factors, and personal factors. In the Take Care! program, this framework was used to classify potential determinants of burnout and related occupational health problems, to map team functioning and relate it to the broader organizational context, and to structure and stimulate the exchange of information between team counselors and program participants.

The 6 training sessions were supervised by both team counselors. The first session formed a general introduction to the training program. It started with some education about (the working mechanisms of) job stress. Next, the results of the questionnaire survey dealing with participants' (perception of their) working situation were fed back by means of the survey feedback method that is known to be useful in driving action research projects (Nadler, 1977). The classification scheme was used to assist participants in structuring their ideas and feelings, by providing them with relevant topics for discussion and for their plans to reduce work stress. At the end of the first session, the major job stressors that were to be dealt with during the training period, were selected by the participants. The remaining sessions each consisted of an educational part and an action part.

During the *educational* part of the second session, attention was paid to ways in which groups/teams preserve 'health-impairing' ways of working together and how to break out of these ways. Participants had to write 'team recipes' to create unwanted, stressful situations. The idea behind this is that, by writing down, participants will gain insight into the way they themselves contribute to these 'health-impairing' practices. This, in turn, is likely keep them from continuing this type of counterproductive behavior in the future. The third session addressed the (usual) ways of communicating and giving feedback between team-members, and how to improve these. Next, team members were educated about different types of work-related social support, followed by a discussion on the availability of and the need for specific types of support within their own team. In the final part of this session, participants made a start with building a social support network within their team. In the fourth session, ways to create a 'healthy' balance between job-related 'investments' and 'outcomes' was central. During the fifth session, participants were educated about (the distinction between) change processes and transition processes. Whereas the first type of processes are 'objective' and directly observable, the second ones concern the psychological acceptance of changes. A potential problem in intervention trajectories is that these processes do not always run in parallel. In order to prevent stagnation or early termination of change processes, the team counselors offered some guidelines to recognize and deal with this problem. In the sixth and final session, attention was paid to the consolidation of the change processes that had been started during the past months, to the ways in which team members could continue to contribute to these as well as future processes, and to the role played by external factors (outside the organization).

During the *action* part of the sessions 2 to 6, participants formed so-called problem-solving teams that collectively designed, implemented, evaluated, and re-formulated plans of action to cope with the most important stressors in their work situation that were identified in session 1. In the sixth session, participants' own experiences of the past months and the current 'state of affairs' with respect to the tackling of job stressors were presented by each of the different problem-solving teams and discussed plenary. Based on (the outcomes of) these discussions, teams decided upon some measures for continuation and consolidation of changes upon leaving of the team counsellors. So, even though the general intervention method was similar across all wards, i.e. PAR, the specific contents of the action part could differ between wards.

Results

Directly after the training program ended (Time 2 measurement), as well as 6 months later (Time 3 measurement), all program participants were again asked to fill out the questionnaire on their working situation and well-being. Then, the participants' scores on all three measurements were compared with those of the control group members who also filled out the questionnaire at the same three times. There are no significant differences in either emotional exhaustion or depersonalization between the two groups at the Time 1 measurement (before the start of the training). However, both at the Time 2 and the Time 3 measurements, the level of emotional exhaustion is significantly lower in the training group than in the control group. At the Time 2 measurement, the level of depersonalization is also significantly lower in the training group than in the control group, but at the Time 3 measurement the difference between both groups has ceased to be significant. Closer inspection of the data reveals that burnout levels in the training group remain stable between Time 1 and Time 3, however, this is not the case in the control group. In the latter group, we see a rather sharp increase in burnout levels between the Time 1 and the Time 2 measurements, followed by a slight decrease between the Time 2 and the Time 3 measurements.

Next, some statistical analyses[9] were performed to see if changes in staff burnout levels are related to the key features of the intervention program (i.e., social support, control, and participation in decision making). Increases in social support and control between the Time 1 and the Time 3 measurements were significantly related to decreases in both burnout components, whereas an increase in participation in decision making between the Time 1 and the Time 3 measurements was related to a decrease in emotional exhaustion only. So, based on these findings, we conclude that the key features of our program are indeed significantly and meaningfully related to changes in oncology care providers' burnout levels.

In addition to the above, all members of the intervention wards who participated in the Time 2 measurement ($n = 231$) filled out some evaluative questions on the Take Care! program. Results showed that the participants were of opinion that the Take Care! training is of high quality, addresses topical issues in their working situation and makes (the tackling of) these issues a team's shared responsibility.

RECOMMENDATIONS FOR FUTURE ACTION (RESEARCH)

Our findings convincingly show that (even) a relatively brief, team-based intervention program can be effective in reducing burnout. Not only the stress-component of burnout (emotional exhaustion) decreased - as was the case in some previous studies - but also its motivational component (depersonalization). Given that Take Care! already had a stabilizing effect on burnout levels in the current sample - consisting of people who are (still) at work

---

[9] These analyses and the corresponding results are reported in more detail in Le Blanc et al. (2007)

despite of their stress complaints - one might expect much stronger effects, i.e. decreases in burnout levels, in samples that suffer severely from burnout. The results of this study do not only corroborate the importance of social support at work, but also underline the effectiveness of an action research approach to burnout intervention by tailoring the contents of the intervention program to the specific working situation of its participants.

Based on the high, voluntary participation rate in the training group as well as participants' positive evaluation of the program, we conclude that the action research methodology is appealing and relevant to health care providers. Of course, the usefulness of action research as a tool for burnout intervention is not restricted to workers in hospitals or health care institutions in general, but can be extended to all different kinds of organizations where people perform (some kind of) team-work and are willing to take 'collective responsibility' to optimize their working situation. Its significance might even be enhanced by e.g. adding so-called 'booster sessions' as a follow-up to the main part of an intervention program, or by expanding interventions to the organization (hospital) level instead of the unit (team) level.

Our study, and the ones by Halbesleben et al (2006) and Hätinen et al. (2007), have provided the first empirical evidence for the usefulness of an action research approach to burnout intervention. More, well-designed scientific studies in different samples are needed to further strengthen its empirical basis. In addition, like Hätinen et al. (2007), these studies could take a closer look at the psychological processes through which this kind of burnout interventions work.

REFERENCES

Ahola, K., Honkonen, T., Virtanen, M., Kivimäki, M., Isometsä, E., Aromaa, A. and Lönnqvist, J. (2007). Interventions in relation to occupational burnout: The population-based health 2000 study. *Journal of Occupational and Environmental Medicine, 49*, 943-952.

American Institute of Stress (2002). *Job stress.* New York: Author.

Berg, A., Welander-Hansson, U. and Hallberg, I.R. (1994). Nurses' creativity, tedium and burnout during 1 year of clinical supervision and implementation of individually planned nursing care: Comparisons between a ward for severely demented patients and a similar control ward. *Journal of Advanced Nursing, 20*, 742-749.

Brown, L. (1984). Mutual help staff-groups to manage work stress. *Social Work with Groups, 7*, 55-66.

Cartwright, S. and Cooper, C. (2005). Individually targeted interventions. In: J. Barling, E.K. Kelloway and M.R. Frone (Eds). *Handbook of work stress* (pp. 607-622). Thousand Oaks, CA: Sage.

Cooley, E. and Yovanoff, P. (1996). Supporting professionals-at-risk: evaluating interventions to reduce burnout and improve retention of special educators. *Exceptional Children, 62*, 336-355.

Corcoran, K.J. and Bryce, A.K. (1983). Intervention in the experience of burnout: Effects of skill development. *Journal of Social Service Research, 7*, 71-79.

Cordes, C.L. and Dougherty, T.W. (1993). A review and integration of research on job burnout. *Academy of Management Review, 18,* 621-656.

De Geus, A.C. and Brakel, F. (1996). *Preventie, diagnostiek en behandeling van werkgerelateerde psychische klachten: kwaliteitshandboek [Prevention, diagnosis and treatment of work-related psychological complaints].* Amsterdam: SBGO.

De Geus, A.C., Van Son, A.M., Le Blanc, P.M. and Schaufeli, W.B. (2000). *Take Care! Een teamgerichte interventie ter bevordering van welzijn op het werk [Take Care! A team-based burnout intervention program].* Houten: Bohn Stafleu Van Loghum.

Dollard, M.F., Dormann, C., Boyd, C.M., Winefield, H.R. and Winefield, A.H. (2003). Unique aspects of stress in human service work. *Australian Psychologist, 38,* 84-91.

Enzmann, D., Berief, P., Engelkamp, C. et al. (1992). *Burnout und Burnoutbewältigung. Entwicklung und Evaluation eines Burnoutworkshops* [Burnout and coping with burnout. Development and evaluation of a burnout workshop] (Projektbericht des Studienprojekts). Berlin: Technische Universität Berlin, Institut für Psychologie.

Freedy, J.R. and Hobfoll, S.E. (1994). Stress inoculation for reduction of burnout: A conservation of resources approach. *Anxiety, Stress and Coping, 6,* 311-325.

Golembiewski, R.W. and Boss, W. (1992). Phases of burnout in diagnosis and intervention: Individual level of analysis in organization development and change. In: W.A. Pasmore and R.W. Woodman (Eds.), *Research in organizational change and development* (Vol 6, pp. 115-152). Greenwich, CT: JAI.

Golembiewski, R.T. and Munzenrider, R.F. and Stevenson, J.G. (1986). *Stress in organizations.* New York: Praeger.

Golembiewski, R.T. and Rountree, B.H. (1991). Releasing human potential for collaboration: A social intervention targeting supervisory relationships and stress. *Public Administration Quarterly, 15,* 32-35.

Gorter, R.C., Eijkman, M.A.J. and Hoogstraten, J. (2001). A career counseling program for dentists: effects on burnout. *Patient Education and Counseling, 43,* 23-30.

Griffiths, A. (1999). Organisational interventions. Facing the limits of the natural science paradigm. *Scandinavian Journal on Work Environment and Health, 25,* 589-596.

Halbesleben, J.R.B. and Buckley, M.R. (2004). Burnout in organizational life. *Journal of Management, 30,* 859-879.

Halbesleben, J.R.B., Osburn, H.K. and Mumford, M.D. (2006). Action research as a burnout intervention: Reducing burnout in the federal fire service. *The Journal of Applied Behavioral Science, 42,* 244-266.

Hätinen, M., Kinnunen, U. Pekkonen, M. and Kalimo, R. (2007). Comparing two burnout interventions: Perceived job control mediates decreases in burnout. *International Journal of Stress Management, 14,* 227-248.

Higgins, N.C. (1986). Occupational stress and working women: The effectiveness of two stress reduction programs. *Journal of Vocational Behavior, 29,* 66-78.

Houtman, I.L.D. (2005). *Work-related stress* (EF05127). Dublin: European Foundation for the Improvement of Living and Working Conditions.

Heaney, C.A., Price, R.H. and Rafferty, J. (1995). Increasing coping resources at work: a field experiment to increase social support, improve work team functioning, and enhance employee mental health. *Journal of Organizational Behavior, 16,* 335-353.

Hughes, J. (2003). Commentary: Participatory action research leads to sustainable school and community improvement. *School Psychology Review, 32,* 1-6.

Jansen, P. (1996). *A differentiated practice and specialization in community nursing* (Doctoral dissertation, Maastricht University). Utrecht: NIVEL.

Janssen, P.P.M., Nijhuis, F.J.N., Lourijsen, E.C.P.M. and Schaufeli, W.B. (1996). *Gezonder werken, minder verzuim! Handleiding voor integrale gezondheidsbevordering op het werk [Healthier work, less absenteism! Manual for complete worksite health promotion].* Amsterdam: NIA.

Kompier, M. and Cooper, C. (1999). *Preventing stress, improving productivity.* London: Routledge.

Larson, D.G. (1986). Developing effective hospice staff support groups: Pilot test of an innovative program. *Hospice Journal, 2,* 41-55.

Le Blanc, P.M., Bakker, A.B., Peeters, M.C.W., Van Heesch, N.C.A. and Schaufeli, W.B. (2001). Emotional job demands and burnout among oncology care providers. *Anxiety, Stress, and Coping, 14,* 243-264.

Le Blanc, P.M., Hox, J.J., Schaufeli, W.B., Taris, T.W. and Peeters, M.C.W. (2007). Take Care! The evaluation of a team-based burnout intervention program for oncology care providers. *Journal of Applied Psychology, 92,* 213-227.

Le Blanc, P.M. and Schaufeli, W.B. (2003). Burnout among oncology care providers: Radiation assistants, physicians and nurses. In : M.F. Dollard, A.H. Winefeld and H.R. Winefield (Eds), *Occupational stress in the service professions* (pp. 143-168). London/New York: Taylor and Francis.

Lee, R.T. and Ashforth, B.E. (1996). A meta-analytic examination of the correlates of the three dimensions of job burnout. *Journal of Applied Psychology, 81,* 123-133.

Maslach, C. (1978). Job burnout: How people cope. *Public Welfare, 36,* 56-58.

Maslach, C. and Goldberg, J. (1998). Prevention of burnout: A new perspective. *Applied Preventative Psychology, 7,* 63-74.

Maslach, C., Leiter, M.P. and Schaufeli, W.B. (2001). Burnout. *Annual Review of Psychology 52,* 397-422.

McNiff, J. (2000). *Action research in organizations.* London: Routledge.

Meichenbaum, D.H. (1985). *Stress inoculation training.* New York: Pergamon Press.

Melchior, M.E.W., Philipsen, H., Huyer Abu-Saad, H., Halfens, R.J.G., Van de Berg, A. A. and Gassman, P. (1996). The effectiveness of primary nursing on burnout among psychiatric nurses in long-stay settings. *Journal of Advanced Nursing, 24,* 694-702.

Mikkelsen, A.,. Saksvik, P.Ø. and Landsbergis, P. (2000). The impact of a participatory organizational intervention on job stress in community health care institutions. *Work and Stress, 14,* 156-170.

Munz, D.C., Kohler, J.M. and Greenberg, C.I. (2001). Effectiveness of a comprehensive worksite stress management program: Combining organizational and individual interventions. *International Journal of Stress Management, 8,* 49-62.

Nadler, D.A. (1977). *Feedback and organization development: using data-based methods.* Reading, MA: Addison-Wesley.

Pines, A.M. and Aronson, E. (1983). Combatting burnout. *Children and Youth Services Review, 5,* 263-275.

Rabinowitz, S., Kusnir, T. and Ribak, J. (1996). Preventing burnout: Increasing professional self-efficacy in primary care nurses in a Balint group. *American Association of Occupational Health Nurses, 44,* 28-32.

Rowe, M. (2000). Skills training in the long-term management of stress and occupational burnout. *Current Psychology, 19*, 215-228.

Salmela-Aro, K., Nataanen, P. and Nurmi, J.E. (2004). The role of work-related personal projects during two burnout interventions: A longitudinal study. *Work and Stress, 18*, 208-230.

Schaufeli, W.B. (1995). The evaluation of a burnout workshop for community nurses. *Journal of Health and Human Services Administration, 18*, 11-31.

Schaufeli, W.B. (2003). Past performance and future perspectives of burnout research. *South African Journal of Industrial Psychology, 29*, 1-15.

Schaufeli, W.B. and Buunk, B.P. (2003). Burnout: An overview of 25 years of research and theorizing. In: M.J. Schabracq, J.A.M. Winnubst and C.L. Cooper (Eds.), *The Handbook of Work and Health Psychology (2nd Edition)*, pp. 383-425. Chichester: John Wiley and Sons.

Schaufeli, W.B. and Enzmann, D. (1998). *The burnout companion to study and practice: A critical analysis.* Wahington DC: Taylor and Francis.

Semmer, N. (2003). Job stress interventions and organization of work. In: J. Campbell Quick and L.E. Tetrick (Eds), *Handbook of Occupational Health Psychology* (pp. 325-353). Washington DC: American Psychological Association.

Stringer, F.T. (1999). *Action research* (2nd ed). Thousand Oaks: Sage. Te Brake, J.H.M., Gorter, R.C., Hoogstraten, J., Eijkman, M.A.J. (2001). Burnout intervention among Dutch dentists: Long-term effects. *European Journal of Oral Sciences, 109*, 380-387.

Van Dierendonck, D., Garssen, B. and Visser A. (2005). Burnout prevention through personal growth. *International Journal of Stress Management, 12*, 62-77.

Van Dierendonck, D., Schaufeli, W.B. and Buunk, B.P. (1996). The evaluation of an individual burnout intervention program: The role of inequity and social support. *Journal of Applied Psychology, 83*, 392-407.

Van Gorp, K. and Schaufeli, W.B. (1996). *Een gezonde geest in een gezond lichaam [A healthy mind in a healthy organization]*. Den Haag: VUGA.

Van Rhenen, W., Blonk, R.W.B., Van der Klink, J.J.L., Van Dijk, F.J.H. and Schaufeli, W.B. (2001). The effect of a cognitive and a physical stress-reducing programme on psychological complaints. *International Archives of Occupational and Environmental Health, 78*, 139-148.

West, D.J., Horan, J.J. and Games, P.A. (1984). Component analysis of occupational stress inoculation applied to registered nurses in an acute care setting. *Journal of Counseling Psychology, 31*, 208-218.

In: Handbook of Stress and Burnout in Health Care   ISBN 978-1-60456-500-3
Editor: Jonathon R. B. Halbesleben   © 2008 Nova Science Publishers, Inc.

Chapter 16

STRESS AND BURNOUT IN HEALTH CARE: WHERE DO WE GO FROM HERE?

Jonathon R. B. Halbesleben
University of Wisconsin-Eau Claire

This book had two primary objectives: to provide a summary of the state of stress and burnout research in health care and to suggest directions for future research. Each of the authors has presented some ideas for future research in their respective chapters. My goal in this chapter is to integrate and elaborate upon those ideas to set an agenda for future research concerning stress and burnout in health care contexts.

Interestingly, but perhaps not surprisingly, the main areas of need in the stress and burnout literature more broadly are highly consistent with the needs within the health care literature (Cordes and Dougherty, 1993; Halbesleben and Buckley, 2004; Maslach, Schaufeli, and Leiter, 2001; Shirom, 2003). Consistent themes emerge, including more development and testing of theory, more development of measurement tools, expansion of international and multidisciplinary research, and an increase in intervention research. A further theme is the need for more research on the conceptualization, measurement, and impact of engagement. While research on this topic has grown dramatically (cf., Schaufeli and Salanova, in press), so has interest from a practical side within health care in part due to an emphasis on workforce engagement as part of the Malcolm Baldridge National Quality Program in the United States. The convergence of interests from health care practitioners and researchers could lead to significant advances in the understanding of the role that engagement plays relative to burnout.

DEVELOPMENT AND TESTING OF THEORY

One could argue that there is always a need for further development, refinement, and testing of our theories. In the case of stress and burnout, this is particularly important as theories are newly developed (e.g., Laschinger and Leiter's Nusing Worklife Model) or extended beyond their original conceptualization (e.g., Gorgievski and Hobfoll's extension of Conservation of Resources theory into the realm of engagement). Additionally, researchers need to carefully consider how the theories that have been proposed intersect with the variables they are studying that are unique in health care environments, such as Shirom's research on work hours and workload or Geiger-Brown, Rogers, Trinkoff, and Selby's research concerning work schedules.

One important aspect of theory development and testing to consider as researchers move forward is the manner in which stress and burnout theories can predict health care-specific outcomes. For example, Halbesleben, Wakefield, Wakefield, and Cooper (in press) used Conservation of Resources theory to explain why burnout would be associated with error reporting behaviors (and safety behaviors more generally). As Neveu noted, there is relatively little work on burnout outcomes to begin with; as we move forward, tying those outcomes to theory and to health care-specific outcomes will increase in importance and potentially serve to increase the urgency for burnout research in health care.

MEASUREMENT

In their chapter on measurement, Demerouti and Bakker provided both answers and questions with regard to the Oldenburg Burnout Inventory (OLBI). On the one hand, they added to the mounting evidence that the OLBI is a valid measure for burnout that is occupation-free. On the other hand, they present initial evidence that the OLBI may be a valid tool for the measurement of engagement. As engagement has become a very hot topic in the literature (and in fact, appears multiple times in this volume), measurement strategies have become a very important issue. However, Demerouti and Bakker's work suggests a need to continue to thoughtfully consider the appropriate conceptualization of engagement and need for further validation of engagement measures both within and outside of health care.

Of course, further research is also needed to validate other measures of burnout and engagement that have been proposed beyond the OLBI and to understand the implications of each measure for the conceptualization of burnout. Examples include the Shirom-Melamed (Shirom and Melamed, 2006) measure of burnout, which focuses on and expands the exhaustion component of burnout, and the Copenhagen Burnout Inventory (Kristensen, Borritz, Villadsen, and Christensen, 2005) which expands the domain of burnout beyond work to include personal burnout, work-related burnout, and client-related burnout. These measures, along with the OLBI and commonly-employed Maslach Burnout Inventory have raised questions regarding the proper conceptualization of burnout (cf., Schaufeli and Taris, 2005) and suggest a need to revisit the base upon which we have built much of the burnout research.

One potentially important, but highly practical, issue with measurement of burnout is the development of shorter tools that can more quickly capture burnout for health care professionals. Such tools are needed not only because the complexity of health care demands quicker tools, but also in light of emerging day-level, within-person research on burnout and engagement that requires frequent measurement (cf., Sonnentag, 2005). The demands of such research on health care professionals may mean that researchers will need a more concise way of assessing stress and burnout. One option may be to move beyond self-report measures to other physiological or observational/behavioral measures (Semmer, Grebner, and Elfering, 2004; see also Westman and Bakker's chapter in this volume).

INTERNATIONAL AND MULTIDISCIPLINARY APPROACHES

A number of authors in the present volume (e.g., Breaux, Meurs, Zellars, and Perrewé) have suggested a need for expanded international research on stress and burnout. Glazer, in her chapter, has discussed at length the importance of cross-cultural issues and the need to expand that research. She hits on an absolutely critical area of need: "why, when, and how culture impacts stress." It has become common for researchers to collect data in two countries, compare the results, and conclude a cross-cultural difference. While certainly interesting, this does little to get at the crux of the cultural issue by helping to explain why culture had an impact. However, the burden of such research falls not just on empirical researchers but on theorists as well. Theories of stress and burnout have not fully accounted for the mechanisms by which culture should impact stress and, subsequently, burnout.

As a related issue, the call for multidisciplinary research has been voiced in a number of chapters as well. Elfering and Grebner eloquently highlighted the need for nursing and occupational health psychology researchers to come together to build on each others' strengths with regard to theoretical development and access to solid data. As I noted in the introduction, while my hope was to bring together a wide variety of perspectives in this volume, that does not necessarily mean they worked together to produce the chapters. While isolated multidisciplinary studies of stress or burnout in health care do exist (cf., Halbesleben et al., in press), they remain isolated. Such research is needed in order to resolve the situation described by Neveu where each discipline tells "their part of the story" such that we miss the full complexity of stress and burnout within health care. One solution may be the recent trend in funding for clearly multidisciplinary projects. Such funding has the promise of bringing together excellent researchers and developing more valid research that is more clearly translatable to the field.

INTERVENTION, EVALUATION, AND PREVENTION

I saved the most commonly suggested, and arguably the most pressing, need for future research for last: the need for intervention, evaluation, and prevention research. Most of the chapters made calls for intervention research (or more intervention research). As LeBlanc and Schaufeli point out in their chapter on intervention, a variety of studies exist to test intervention programs, including promising studies that utilize the action research approach. However, more research is needed both to further validate that approach and to examine the impact that the approach has on psychological processes that influence stress and burnout (in other words, answering the question of why the approach seems to work).

Moreover, some of the chapters included specific ideas for policies or programs that are in need of further evaluation for their potential role in reducing stress and burnout. As Cimiotti, Aiken, and Poghosyan note, legislation such as AB394 in California governing nurse-to-patient ratios may have the effect of lowering stress and burnout among nurses; however, such a claim has not been fully validated by research. Similarly, the notion of magnet status may also hold potential in reducing nursing burnout, specifically to the extent that it represents an excellent practice environment for nurses; again, this has not been tested through research. The point is that we may have some tools to reduce stress and burnout in place already but we will not know for certain until they are tested. Along these lines, Geiger-Brown, Rogers, Trinkoff, and Selby suggest that public knowledge of health care professional work schedules might improve patient safety, suggesting that better work schedules might result from public understanding of the demeaning schedules of health care workers. While the potential to improve safety exists, one might also argue that the potential to reduce stress also exists in such cases. Again, however, this is a potential public policy change that would need further evaluation if implemented.

Wheeler's chapter highlights the need and possibility for prevention research. He puts forth the intriguing possibility that organizations could develop human resource management systems that would prevent (or at least significantly reduce) stress for employees. While still in need of testing, his organization/systems perspective offers a unique take on burnout prevention and intervention and one that may hold promise, particularly for health care.

Summary and Concluding Remarks

I conclude the chapter and book on a note of optimism. It is unlikely that anyone can fully "fix" the problems of stress and burnout in health care. However, it is truly comforting knowing that a significant amount of research resources, as represented by the contributors to this book, are being dedicated and engaged in making working life better for those who seek to make our health better. I salute those working on this research and know that in due time their work will translate to real solutions for health care professionals worldwide. Without such hope of my own, I know that I would lose engagement in the topic and fall victim to my own burnout.

References

Cordes, C. and Dougherty, T. W. (1993). A review and an integration of research on job burnout. *Academy of Management Review, 18,* 621-656.

Halbesleben, J. R., B., and Buckley, M. R. (2004). Burnout in organizational life. *Journal of Management, 30,* 859-879.

Halbesleben, J. R. B., Wakefield, B. J., Wakefield, D. S., and Cooper, L. (in press). Nurse burnout and patient safety outcomes: Nurse safety perception vs. reporting behavior. *Western Journal of Nursing Research.*

Kristensen, T. S., Borritz, M., Villadsen, E., and Christensen, K. B. (2005). The Copenhagen Burnout Inventory: A new tool for the assessment of burnout. *Work and Stress, 19,* 192-207.

Maslach, C., Schaufeli, W. B., and Leiter, M. P. (2001). Job burnout. *Annual Review of Psychology, 52,* 397-422.

Schaufeli, W. B., and Salanova, M. (in press). Work engagement: An emerging psychological concept and its implications for organizations. In S. W. Gilliland, D. D. Steiner, and D. P. Skarlicki (Eds.), Research in social issues in management. Greenwich, CT: Information Age Publishers.

Schaufeli, W. B., and Taris, T. W. (2005). The conceptualization and measurement of burnout: Common ground and worlds apart. *Work and Stress, 19,* 256-262.

Semmer, N. K., Grebner, S., and Elfering, A. (2004). Beyond self-report: Using observational, physiological, and situation-based measures in research on occupational stress. In P. L. Perrewé and D. C. Ganster (Eds.). *Research in occupational stress and well-being: Emotional and physiological processes and positive intervention strategies* (vol. 3, pp. 205-263). Oxford: Elsevier.

Shirom, A. (2003). Job-related burnout: A review. In J. C. Quick and L. E. Tetrick (Eds.). *Handbook of occupational health psychology* (pp. 245-264). Washington, DC: American Psychological Association.

Shirom, A., and Melamed, S. (2006). A Comparison of the Construct Validity of Two Burnout Measures in Two Groups of Professionals. *International Journal of Stress Management, 13*(2), 176-200.

Sonnentag, S. (2005). Burnout research: Adding an off-work and day-level perspective. *Work and Stress, 19,* 271-275.

ABOUT THE AUTHORS

Linda H. Aiken, Ph.D., RN is the Claire M. Fagin Leadership Professor of Nursing, Professor of Sociology, and Director of the Center for Health Outcomes and Policy Research at the University of Pennsylvania. She is a prominent nurse researcher and an authority on nurse workforce issues in the US and globally.

Arnold B. Bakker (Ph.D., Groningen University) is full professor of Work and Organizational Psychology at Erasmus University Rotterdam, The Netherlands. His research interests include positive organizational psychology (e.g., flow, work engagement), burnout, and crossover of work-related emotions. His research has been published in the major journals in psychology and organizational behavior.

Denise M. Breaux is a Ph.D. student in Organizational Behavior and Human Resources Management at Florida State University. Her research interests include abusive supervision, job stress and burnout, workplace deviance, and accountability.

Jeannie P. Cimiotti, DNSc, RN is a Research Assistant Professor in the Center for Health Outcomes and Policy Research at the University of Pennsylvania School of Nursing. Her research interest is the patient care environment and outcomes of infants and children.

Evangelia Demerouti (Ph.D., Carl von Ossietzky University, Oldenburg) is an associate professor in the department of Social and Organizational Psychology at Utrecht University. Her research interests include burnout, work engagement, work-family interface, crossover, and job performance.

Achim Elfering (Ph.D., University of Frankfurt, Germany) is an Assistant Professor in the Department of Psychology at the University of Berne, Switzerland. His research interests include patient safety, occupational low back pain, and stress.

Jeanne M. Geiger Brown (Ph.D., University of Maryland) is an Assistant Professor in the Work and Health Research Center at the University of Maryland School of Nursing. Her research interests include the role of work schedules on sleep, neurocognitive functioning and safety and health outcomes in health care work environments.

Sharon Glazer (Ph.D., Central Michigan University) is an associate professor in the Department of Psychology at San Jose State University, CA. Her research interests include cross-cultural issues in organizational psychology, particularly occupational stress, value congruence, temporal orientation, organizational commitment, social support, communication, and structural alignment.

Marjan J. Gorgievski-Duijvesteijn (Ph.D., Utrecht University) is an assistant professor at the Department of Industrial and Organisational Psychology at the Erasmus University Rotterdam. Her research interests include burnout and engagement, the relationship between well-being and performance, and psychological aspects of entrepreneurship and small business ownership from a COR-theoretical perspective.

Simone I. Grebner (Ph.D., University of Berne, Switzerland) is an Assistant Professor in the Department of Psychology at the Central Michigan University. Her research interests include stress at work, subjective success, coping, physiological stress responses, stress-management, and patient safety.

Jonathon R. B. Halbesleben (Ph.D., University of Oklahoma) is an assistant professor in the Department of Management and Marketing at the University of Wisconsin-Eau Claire. His research interests include stress, burnout, the work-family interface, and health care management.

Stevan Hobfoll (Ph.D., University of South Florida) is currently Distinguished Professor of Psychology at Kent State University and Director of the Applied Psychology Center and the Summa-KSU Center for the Treatment and Study of Traumatic Stress. Formerly at Tel Aviv and Ben Gurion Universities, he has also been involved with the problem of stress in Israel. Dr. Hobfoll has authored and edited 11 books, including *Stress, Social Support, and Women; Traumatic Stress; The Ecology of Stress; and Stress, Culture, and Community*. In addition, he has authored numerous journal articles, book chapters, and technical reports, and has been a frequent workshop leader on stress, ranging from burnout to extreme stress situations. He maintains a practice as a clinical psychologist and organizational consultant.

Martyn C. Jones (Ph.D., University of St Andrews) is a Senior Lecturer at the School of Nursing and Midwifery at the University of Dundee, UK. His research interests include the link between stress and care provision in student and trained nurses, the work-family interface and real time data collection.

Heather K. Spence Laschinger (Ph.D., University of Ottawa, Ontario) is Distinguished University Professor and Associate Director Nursing Research at the University of Western Ontario, School of Nursing, Faculty of Health Sciences in London, Ontario. Her research interests include workplace empowerment in health care settings, burnout, and nurses' health and wellbeing.

Pascale M. Le Blanc (Ph.D., Utrecht University) is an assistant professor in Occupational Health Psychology in the Department of Social and Organizational Psychology at Utrecht University, The Netherlands. Her research interests include job stress and burnout (interventions), leadership and teamwork.

Michael P. Leiter (Ph.D., University of Oregon) is Canada Research Chair in Occupational Health and Wellness, is Professor of Psychology at Acadia University in Canada and Director of the Center for Organizational Research and Development that applies high quality research methods to human resource issues. He is actively involved in research and consulting on occupational issues in Canada, the USA, and Europe.

James A. Meurs is a Ph.D. candidate in Organizational Behavior and Human Resources Management at Florida State University. His research interests include occupational stress, personality, and organizational politics.

Jean-Pierre Neveu (Ph.D., University of Toulouse 1, France, is professor in Human Resources Management at the University Montesquieu in Bordeaux, France. He also conducts research in the LIRHE, a unit of the National Center for Scientific Research in Toulouse. His research interests include stress, burnout, commitment, organizational climate and service quality.

Nurit Nirel (M.A., Tel Aviv University) is senior research scientist in the Brookdale-Meyers Research Institute, Jerusalem, Israel. Her research interests include healthcare manpower and healthcare management.

Pamela L. Perrewé (Ph.D., University of Nebraska) is the Distinguished Research Professor and Jim Moran Professor of Management in the College of Business at Florida State University. Dr. Perrewé has focused her research in the areas of job stress, coping, organizational politics, emotion and personality.

Lusine Poghosyan, MPH, RN is a Ph.D. candidate at the University of Pennsylvania School of Nursing. Her research interest is job-related burnout in registered nurses, and she is currently validating the Maslach Burnout Inventory as a measure of burnout among registered nurses in eight countries.

Steven Pryjmachuk (Ph.D., University of Manchester) is a Senior Lecturer and Head of the Mental Health Division in the School of Nursing, Midwifery and Social Work at the University of Manchester, UK. His research interests include stress, children's mental health and the support and guidance of university students.

Valerie E. Rogers (doctoral student, University of Maryland School of Nursing) is a Nurse Practitioner whose research interests include sleep disturbance and its physiologic and neurocognitive effects on adults and children.

Wilmar B. Schaufeli (Ph.D.,Groningen University, The Netherlands) is full professor of Work and Organizational Psychology at Utrecht University, The Netherlands. His research area is occupational health psychology and more particularly job stress, job engagement, workaholism and burnout. For more details see www.schaufeli.com.

Victoria Selby (BSN, University of Maryland) is a graduate research assistant. She is interested in the impact of environmental stressors on the health and well being of individuals.

Arie Shirom (Ph.D., the University of Wisconsin-Madison) is professor (emeritus) in the Faculty of Management, Tel Aviv University, Israel. His research interests include vigor and burnout and their relationships with physical and mental health among employees.

Alison M. Trinkoff (ScD, Johns Hopkins) is a Professor in the Work and Health Research Center at the University of Maryland School of Nursing. Her research interests include health care work environments, patient outcomes and worker injuries.

Mina Westman (Ph.D.., Tel Aviv University) is a an Associate Professor and Chairperson of the Organizational Behavior Program, at the Faculty of Management, Tel Aviv University. Her primary research interests include job and family stress, work-family interchange, crossover in the family and the workplace, the effects of vacation on strain, and the impact of short business trips and expatriation on the individual, the family and the organization.

Amiram D. Vinokur (Ph.D., the University of Michigan-Ann Arbor) is senior research scientist at the Institute for Social Research, the University of Michigan – Ann Arbor. His research interests include stress and strain at work and SEM modeling.

Anthony R. Wheeler, SPHR (Ph.D., University of Oklahoma) is an assistant professor with the Schmidt Labor Research Center and College of Business Administration at the University of Rhode Island. His research interests include HRM effectiveness, multilevel issues in HRM, and person-environment fit.

Kelly L. Zellars (Ph.D., Florida State University) is an associate professor in the Department of Management at the University of North Carolina - Charlotte. Her research interests include job stress and burnout, justice in the workplace, and the work-family interface.

INDEX

F

G

H

M

P

Q

R

S

T

Y